MW00577423

BURN BOSTON BURN

'THE STORY OF THE LARGEST ARSON CASE IN THE HISTORY OF THE COUNTRY'

WAYNE M. MILLER

Copyright © 2019 by Wayne M. Miller

All rights reserved. No part of this book may be reproduced or transmitted in any form or by any means, electronic or mechanical, including photocopying, recording, or by any information storage and retrieval system, without permission in writing from the author.

Printed in the United States of America.

Cover design by Mike Clark Design

Subjects: Non-fiction, crime

Paperback ISBN-13: 978-1-7333403-0-4
E-book ISBN-13: 978-1-7333403-2-8
Hardback ISBN-13: 978-1-7333403-1-1

To all those who have been victims of fires,
To the firefighters who fight them, and
To the fire investigators who go the distance,
May you all have the strength to carry on.

CONTENTS

FOREWORD

Boston has been no stranger to fire. Since its earliest days, dating back to British North America, the port of Boston experienced frequent devastating fires. The abundance of wood led the fledgling town to construct buildings of wood and brick with wood. All would prove ample fodder for future conflagrations.

Being North America's closest port to Europe, Boston soon established itself as the most important of the new colonies. Trading was one of the major enterprises. This led to the construction of many densely packed wharves and warehouses, providing for an even greater fire hazard. Ship building and maritime trade were conducted exclusively with wooden vessels.

After several conflagrations swept the young town, its first fire engine was imported from England in 1678. This engine was strategically located in Dock Square with men assigned to tend the engine. The roots of the Boston Fire Department are traced to this first engine which has direct lineage to today's Engine Co. 7.

Not all fires in the new town were accidental. Arson, a most feared and heinous crime in any settlement, was not taken lightly. When the arsonist(s) were caught, they were dealt with severely. Throughout its history, Boston, like any other large city, has had its share of arson and arsonists. The reasons are readily known: revenge, profit, pyromania, spite, espionage, terrorism and psychotic disorders.

Major arson outbreaks occurred following World War I when large scale unemployment fueled a wave of anarchy and communist activism. A group known as the "Red Roosters" set numerous fires in Boston. During the years of the Great Depression, many businesses fell victim to the "torch" as enterprises failed. Arson was suspected in several major fires in Boston during World War II. In April of 1967, an arson epidemic in the North End threw that congested Italian neighborhood into a panic. Five fatalities resulted from the fires and vigilante groups patrolled the streets at night. No one was ever charged with the crimes and the fires ended as quickly as they started. During the mid-1970s an "arson for profit" ring operated in the Westland Avenue/Symphony Road area of Boston until brought to justice. Soaring gasoline prices in the late 1970s resulted in thousands of automobiles torched annually in Boston. Aggressive investigation and prosecution by the Boston Fire Investigation Unit brought the problem under control.

In the late 1970s a tax-limiting movement, Proposition 13, took root in California. Citizens worn out by an ever-increasing tax burden jumped aboard the referendum and similar petitions surfaced across the country. In 1980 Proposition 2½ was placed on the ballot in Massachusetts and was overwhelmingly approved by the voters. The measure limited the increase in property taxes to 2½ percent per year, thus saddling politicians with a new reality of stringent budgeting and accountability. In Boston Mayor Kevin H. White, in his twelfth year as mayor, flexed his political muscle and said he would show the voters budget cuts unlike any seen before. He would cut public safety and education. His arrogance was shown when he declared his "political operatives" as important as any fireman or cop.

Nineteen eighty-one began ominously for the Boston Fire Department. Three multiple alarm fires occurred on January 4th. January

7th was another cold winter day where the temperature barely got above freezing. Early that morning a 29-year-old-woman perished in a one alarm fire on Monson Street in Lower Mills. At 3:36 that morning a two-alarm fire swept through a three- decker at 1454 Tremont Street in Roxbury. Early that afternoon a baby girl died in a Mattapan fire. At 3:08 that afternoon, a fire was discovered in a four-story brownstone building at 16 Arlington Street in Boston's Back Bay. Heavy fire was showing and multiple alarms were sounded in rapid succession. As the interior attack on the fire continued, a partial collapse occurred trapping many Boston firefighters. Extraordinary efforts were put forward over the next several hours to rescue their comrades. In the end, Fire Lieutenant Paul M. Lentini and Fire Fighter James M. Gibbons, both on Engine 37, were fatally injured.

The next morning a nine-alarm fire swept through an apartment building at 307 Huntington Avenue, which resulted in one civilian fatality. Weary Boston firefighters were called out again that evening for another nine-alarm blaze in an apartment complex in Brighton. Another major fire broke out on January 9th at 10 Museum Road – a stone's throw from Engine 37's quarters.

The rash of fire activity had little impact on Boston City Hall. The planned closing of Boston fire companies scheduled for the following month would proceed.

On February 2, General Order No. 9 was issued, deactivating Engine Co. 25 and 43 and Ladder Co. 20. Engine 43 and Ladder 20 were two of the busiest companies in the city. Further cuts took place on April 10th when Engines 1, 12, 26, 34, 45, 50 and 54, Ladder 5, 8, 22, 30 and 31 and Rescue 2 were deactivated. On October 20, Engines 11, 36 and Ladder 13 were deactivated. Along with the company closing, hundreds of firefighters were laid off and fire officers were demoted. Retirement incentives led to a significant departure of senior officers and members of the department, a serious impact for the department that would be felt for years to come.

To keep minimal staffing on the remaining fire companies, the department had to hire overtime personnel on every shift. Fewer companies were fighting more fires and the members of the department were feeling the effects as injuries mounted.

The mayor made it clear that until a measure which would give the city a new source of revenue, the Tregor Bill, was passed there would be no rehiring of the laid-off firefighters. It had become a political issue with the fire and police departments being the pawns.

Nothing gave any indication of what would take place commencing in late 1981 and into 1982. The usual heavy fire load took a sharp upturn when simultaneous multiple alarm fires began occurring with alarming frequency. Without a specific pattern, serious fires began breaking out, one right after the other, in various parts of the city. Investigators were stymied; all angles were checked trying to find any indicators that could provide solid leads towards finding the perpetrators or predicting where they would strike next. The depleted Boston Fire Department was being exhausted, taxed to its limits and the city was near panic.

Special Agent Wayne Miller, an investigator for the Bureau of Alcohol, Tobacco and Firearms, was part of that team of investigators that ultimately solved the greatest arson ring in Boston's history. In penning *Burn Boston Burn*, he has documented those harrowing nights in the City of Boston when this group of individuals terrorized the city, but more importantly, the how and why the crimes were committed is covered in chilling detail.

By Paul A. Christian, Boston Fire Department Commissioner and Chief of the Department, November 9, 2001 – September 4, 2006

INTRODUCTION

THE ARSON CAPITAL OF THE NATION

Arson; the crime of maliciously and intentionally, or recklessly, starting a fire or causing an explosion. (NFPA 921, 2017 Edition) *Arson; the willful or malicious burning of property (such as a building) especially with criminal or fraudulent intent.* (Merriam-Webster)

This case had the ingredients of a movie thriller, but it was real life. Nobody could have imagined what was uncovered by an arson investigation that spanned almost three years, from 1982 to 1984. How could nine men conspire in, and collaborate to carry out, an insidious plot to burn so many buildings within the City of Boston and four surrounding counties? During one stretch in the summer of 1982, fires burned almost nightly, leading national news outlets to dub Boston the "arson capital of the nation."

Incredibly, most of the men involved were police officers and/or firefighters, as well as security personnel, who were sworn to serve and protect the public. Most of them had wanted to become professional firefighters. All of them were actually fire buffs, known informally as "sparks."

However, these men were a militant faction that splintered off from the legitimate hobbyists.

Some nights there were more multiple alarm fires in Boston than are now experienced in several months. Property damage was counted in the tens of millions in early 1980s dollars. Although there was no evidence that anyone died from any of these fires, a couple hundred firefighters plus some civilians were injured during the arson spree.

The following account provides the reader with viewpoints from the investigators, the prosecutors, the firefighters who fought the fires, the citizens who lived in fear, and the arsonists themselves—their thoughts, their actions, and their actual words. You will be amazed, shocked, and bewildered by their reprehensible individual and group motivations and gain insights into their chilling scheme to set a record number of fires that had everyone baffled and drew national media attention.

The main motivation of the arson ring members for setting so many fires in such a short period of time was an attempt to extort the City of Boston and Commonwealth of Massachusetts into changing the property tax-cutting initiative known as Proposition 2½, which had been passed by a sizable majority of the citizens of Massachusetts on the November 1980 ballot. Prop 2½ cut local tax revenues of over 350 Massachusetts towns and cities by some 450 million dollars, with little hope for Federal or state funds to make up the difference, forcing localities to cut public services and jobs.

Some of you may think that these guys were patriots rightfully exercising civil disobedience, with some of their idealistic actions actually resulting in successful government reversals. Indeed, they initially thought of themselves as a twisted modern-day version of Robin Hood and his gang of merry men; if enough fires were set, then all of the laid-off firefighters would be rehired and the closed firehouses would all be reopened. And they imagined that their actions would teach people a valuable lesson: that firefighters and police were essential assets of the community, not pawns to be sacrificed on a political game board. However, their warped plan took on many dimensions beyond their alleged initial motivation so that they ended up being mere common criminals.

Make no mistake about the offenders in this case; they were domestic political terrorists, long before the term became commonplace in the United States. They hurt many innocent people and destroyed lives and properties, at great cost to the rest of us. Their serial fire-setting became a tool to harass and intimidate firefighters and the fire investigators who were dedicated to tracking down those responsible for the fire epidemic. Finally, the arsonists had the arrogance of many common criminals; they enjoyed the cat-and-mouse game, viewing the relentless light show of blazing buildings as a perverse kind of nightly entertainment.

You will come to understand the difficulties we investigators faced while trying to solve this interminable series of arsons. The criminals had the upper hand for far too long, burning building after building. After all, arson is one of the most difficult crimes to solve and even tougher to successfully prosecute. Furthermore, this investigation involved over 250 arsons by experienced public servants who acted under the cover of darkness. Often, solving arson cases depends on lucky breaks. We eventually did get some remarkable breaks, but they were not all the result of luck. The breaks resulted from the hard work of lots of dedicated, vigilant people plus teamwork among numerous entities.

The following account is as accurate as can be 30 years after the fact. Some interpretation and extrapolation was necessary to fill in some of the blanks. This case was my life and the lives of numerous other investigators for three years. My recollections are scattered everywhere throughout this narrative, supported by Bureau of Alcohol, Tobacco and Firearms (ATF) diaries that we were required to keep daily; by the words reported by myself and others in the Boston ATF Arson Group; and by many other primary source notes, papers, news articles, tape recordings, and court documents such as warrants, indictments, and trial transcripts.

I was fortunate to have had the opportunity to confer with and pick the brains of several individuals who were also involved in various aspects of this case. Their insights rounded out this story. Without them, this chronicle would have been written from a far too narrow viewpoint.

One critical source—one that provided me with the deepest awareness and understanding of the conspirators themselves—was a treatise completed by convicted arsonist Gregg Bemis while he was incarcerated. This document was given to me by former Boston Fire Lt. Stephen McLaughlin, who received it from Bemis himself. It is far more than a daily diary of the who, what, when, and where of most every fire set by the conspirators. It is also a record of Gregg's thoughts and actual words; he explains why they did what they did. The Bemis log provided a direct line into the group, a path that gave me, and gives you the reader, the opportunity to know what they thought as well as what they did. Although I spent hundreds of hours in 1984 and 1985 debriefing Bemis and former Boston Police Officer Robert Groblewski, also a convicted arsonist, the Bemis journal added so much more to this record. The quotes of the arsonists coupled with the descriptions of the areas and the fires are from Bemis, verbatim. In writing this book, I have reconnected with Gregg, who has filled in additional blanks. More than 35 years removed from his crime, Bemis is largely remorseful about his arson history.

I had no intention of covering every fire that these guys set with the same detail that Bemis entailed in his dissertation. But in reading it closely, date by date, I ended up covering far more fires than I had planned, realizing that there were juicy tidbits about their behaviors and criminal actions that deserved to be documented.

Unfathomable is a good word to describe what occurred during the early 1980s in and around Boston. It is a story worth telling. You will find yourself shaking your head on several occasions because it is still hard to believe that their diabolical scheme could have gone on for so long. The successful culmination of this investigation occurred after a lengthy struggle to identify the arsonists responsible for this rampage and an even longer effort to collect sufficient evidence to bring this case to court.

The story of this arson case has previously been partially covered in numerous newspaper and magazine articles, not only in the Boston area, but throughout the United States and even in Europe. Various parts of this case also served as a basis for the novel Ring of Fire: A Rescue One Firefighting Mystery by the late George Hall. *LIFE Magazine* had a multi-page spread on this case by famed journalist, Chris Whipple in the April 1985 "We Are the World" issue. An excellent short chapter on the subject is included in Boston on Fire by Stephanie Schorow. The late Boston Fire Captain Richard Connelly also touched on this case in his Characters, Tales and Tragedies in the Boston Fire Department. Burn Boston Burn is as close to a complete accounting as possible of one of the most riveting and incredulous arson cases in United States history.

▲

Throughout this book, I utilized a triangle icon to separate sections within chapters. The choice was deliberate; it symbolizes what is known in fire science as the fire triangle, which represents the three components---heat, fuel, and an oxidizing agent, usually oxygen—essential for most fires to ignite and continue to burn in an uninhibited chain reaction. Removing any of these elements usually causes a fire to cease. Firefighters try to cool fire with water to take the heat component out of the equation. On the other hand, the arson ring members made fire by intentionally introducing heat, in the form of a lit cigarette and matches, to readily combustible fuels in the presence of the ambient air. The fire triangle icon is the perfect symbol to emphasize the yin and the yang, the contradictory and inseparable, seemingly opposing, yet complementary forces of the arsonist and the firefighter.

I ask of all the firefighter readers to please forgive any errors in terms or potential mistakes relative to any particular fire. As a non-firefighter myself, I tried through various sources to be as accurate as possible. At times, there was a difference between sources on some details.

For further information, photos, and details about the case that could not make it into the book, please be sure to check out my website, www.burnbostonburn.com.

CHAPTER ONE

THE BEGINNING OF THE END

As the flames leaped a hundred feet above the burning lumberyard, Boston Police Officer Robert "Bobby" Groblewski instantly regretted his actions on that wood pile. He had acted recklessly, waving his handgun in the air as if on a bucking bronco. Little did he know that those actions were the beginning of the unraveling of a monstrous conspiracy, though it would be another 14 months before he would feel the sting of arrest. But he did not regret setting the fire.

The fire he set that night, early Sunday morning, November 21, 1982, we termed "Gerrity II." Gerrity I had occurred barely a month earlier, but it had been contained to only one section of the lumberyard and millworks due to the skill and hard work of the firefighters.

By the time Gregg Bemis arrived at the trailer in Boston after work on Saturday, Donald "Donny" Stackpole, Joe Gorman, and Groblewski were waiting for him. He asked, "Well boys, what's the good word?"

"Nothing yet, but we have been doing some planning. We're going to get Gerrity Lumber again," replied Donny. Bemis thought that since the previous fire had been several weeks ago, any heat from the Boston Arson Squad had probably subsided, so he had no qualms about agreeing with the strategy.

They all climbed into Gregg's car to head for the Hyde Park section of Boston. Bobby proposed that Donny and Joe drop Gregg and him off at the beginning of the dead-end street near the railroad tracks. Two devices were assembled in the car before they exited. Bobby told Donny and Joe, "Okay, guys, give us about 15 minutes. Then drive past here every few minutes until we return."

Bobby and Gregg slipped out of the car, disappearing into the darkness. A slight fog created a milky haze over the area. Repeating their tracks of some five weeks earlier, they quickly covered the half-mile to the lumberyard fence and climbed over the fence at the same spot.

This time, though, they targeted a very large, tall, single-story brick building. The pair walked to the front of the structure, where they found the large overhead door wide open; only a screen of narrow strips of clear plastic hung down like a waterfall to help keep rain and birds out of the building.

Once inside, the boys were amazed to see huge stacks of plywood some 6 to 12 feet high. Bobby exclaimed, "Holy shit, this place will go like a volcano!" After checking out the layout further, the duo chose two separate areas to plant the two devices to maximize the effect. Once the devices were lit, the torches met at the front doorway to make their escape.

"Okay, Bobby, we have to haul ass if we want to get away before the whole place goes up." After running back to the pick-up point, they sat in the bushes until Joe and Donny scooped them up.

The boys headed to the DD's (Dunkin' Donuts) in Dedham Square to await the fire call. While crossing over the Sprague Street Bridge, they slowed down to see if the fire was visible yet. The building was emitting a slight glow, and a column of smoke was rising into the sky, but the light haze did a decent job of masking the early evidence of the fire.

As they sat with their coffee and donuts in the DD's parking lot, the call came in for the fire. The arsonists sped out of the parking lot. At that point, a massive red glow was visible in the sky, in spite of the now thickening fog. The view caused Gregg to step on the gas in anticipation of what lay ahead. From a half-mile away, flames were visible, soaring furiously into the sky. He yelled, "That fuckin' place is going like crazy!"

Meanwhile, WBZ cameraman and fire buff Nat Whittemore was hanging out with Ed "Eddie" Fowler at the Howard Johnson's parking lot near Boston Fire Headquarters. These guys had been close friends for many years. Ed was a professional photographer as well as a full-time fire investigator for the Cambridge Fire Department; their dual interests had cemented a natural friendship. Boston Fire Alarm transmitted Box 8223, mutual aid to Dedham for a fire at the Gerrity Lumber Yard on the southwest border of the Boston-Dedham town line. Nat and Ed squealed out of the parking lot, as did a dozen or so other buffs. Second and third alarms on Box 8223 soon followed as Dedham transmitted additional alarms on its system.

Back atop the Sprague Street Bridge, the arsonists gazed at flames blowing high above the lumberyard. A section of the building's roof had already collapsed. Engine 49 was just approaching the front gate of the lumberyard complex. The boys decided to drive around for a few more minutes until some spectators had a chance to arrive at the scene, so as not to call attention to themselves.

When Ed and Nat turned off River Street onto Whiting Avenue Extension, they saw enormous plumes of smoke and flames rising over the lumberyard. Once they had alighted from their vehicles, Ed made a keen observation. He spotted the vehicles belonging to the militant sparks with their car tracks through the wet grass. A big line, laid from a nearby hydrant but not yet charged, lay on top of the grass and over the cars' tracks, indicating to Ed that these guys, possibly the arsonists, had arrived at the scene very quickly, before the arrival of multiple alarm companies. Eddie pointed this out to Nat.

Within minutes, the entire area came to life with fire apparatus and onlookers. Because the fire was right on the City line, both Dedham and

Boston were striking additional alarms. Off-duty Boston Firefighter Ray Norton joined the arsonists at the fire scene. The radiant heat from the fire was so intense that the boys had to relocate, moving back away from the fire several times until finally finding a comfortable spot to sit down on a lumber pile.

Nat and Ed split up to reconnoiter the area to resolve the tire imprint question. Nat was first to hear a group of men hooting and hollering. They were rooting for the home team—not the firefighters, but the fire itself. Making his way around a stack of lumber, Nat spotted several loud, raucous men sitting on another woodpile sparking (watching) the fire.

Whittemore framed his shot, focused, and rolled his camera on the crew capturing the entire episode on videotape as one man among them, wearing a green military jacket, yelled, "Let's all pull our guns!" But only he pulled his handgun out from his waistband, momentarily training it in the direction of Nat. The man in possession of the gun was Boston Police Officer Robert Groblewski. As part of his ill-conceived moment of intimidation, Bobby then waved the weapon erratically in the air.

Nat later told me how he responded to Bobby's pulling his firearm. When Bobby's right arm went across his waist, Nat instantly recognized the "cross draw." He steadied himself for whatever was going to happen next. Nat had on his bulletproof vest and was carrying a piece himself. Standing beside another stack of lumber, he momentarily shut off his camera to put that pile between him and the perceived threat. Then, Nat turned it right back on as he gritted his teeth, thinking to himself, "Fuck them, if he fires I'll keep rolling, these bastards have to be put away." Mental pictures of injured firefighters at the Enlisted Men's Club Military Barracks fire in Southie flashed across his mind.

Nat held the camera steady, recording the entire scene as Groblewski lifted the handgun into the air over his head, waving it around in a circle and back and forth as if riding for his life on that bronco. Bobby's friends seemed to shrivel in embarrassment or fear. Nat was incensed by the behavior of this crew. He was determined to chronicle this scene, the very incident that initiated the beginning of the end for this crew of arsonists. It was captured on tape for all to view. It was to become of the utmost interest to investigators.

Donny advised Joe and Bobby that Whittemore was filming them. Bobby nonchalantly placed his firearm back into his holster. A couple of years later, we would learn that Bobby didn't take any pictures of the Gerrity II fire because he didn't have his camera with him that night. Maybe he should have had it with him; it might have kept his hands busier so he would not have pulled his gun out and waved it around.

When Eddie arrived next to Nat, he instantly recognized these militant sparks, a rowdy bunch that seemed intent on causing trouble. He had seen them at way too many fires. He had also seen them way too early at many of those fires. And, on top of those coincidences, he had noticed some of them earlier that evening at the buffs' parking lot, and now he remembered that they had left the lot sometime before the latest fire had been reported.

Ray Norton, the firefighter, felt mischievous; he started antagonizing any buffs who happened to pass by. When he spotted Fowler, he became more irate, mumbling, "Why doesn't that fuckin' asshole go back to fuckin' Cambridge?" Ray noticed Fowler talking to Nat Whittemore from Channel 4. He focused his ball-busting on them. Trying to get their attention, Ray kept running behind a large lumber pile and acting suspiciously. Bobby and Joe were getting a big kick out of the look on the faces of Fowler and Whittemore. They joined Norton in egging on the two men.

Getting the attention of a Dedham police officer, Ed requested that the officer investigate the man brandishing the gun. Fowler pointed the cop in the direction of Groblewski.

Gorman made a joking attempt to cover his face with his jacket to avoid the camera. Seconds after the filming started, the episode was over, but not before the Dedham cop approached the group and questioned them about the gun-waving incident. Bobby had a little talk with the officer, and after realizing that Bobby was a Boston cop, the Dedham officer was satisfied. The officer returned to notify Ed and Nat that the guy with the gun was a Boston officer and he had told him to put it away, end of story, much to the dismay of Ed and Nat.

Norton started up again, ranting and raving at Eddie Fowler for stirring up the shit. Ray was never at a loss for words when it came to imagining that people were not minding their own business. It's simply incredulous when you realize that Ray and the others believed that people like Ed Fowler and Nat Whittemore were not only minding their own business, they were trying to resolve the rash of arsons in and around the City. As is repeated daily for safety purposes today, these two men saw something and did something.

The fire destroyed one-third of the sprawling lumberyard, at the cost of millions in losses. Luckily on this night, there were no major firefighter injuries.

CHAPTER TWO

THE ARSON RING

"Mom, we're going out on a spree tonight." "Spree" was what Bemis and his cohorts called setting several fires in a single night. Gregg had always confided in his mom; now he was alone with her. Their location was darker than dark. It was quieter than the quietest of places. Gregg was at his mother's graveside that night, where he sometimes stopped before he tended to his other nocturnal activities. Some nights, in an eerie ritual, Gregg would set a fire in the cemetery to help calm himself.

Gregg had been close to his mother right up until her death from cancer a few years earlier. She was the person who took him to the local Maynard, Acton, and Stow, Massachusetts fire departments, the area where he grew up. These were small rural towns, distant suburbs of Boston. Old family photographs show Gregg with fire apparatus as a boy. Looking at those photographs now, in hindsight, with the look on his face, his wide eyes glazed in amazement, could make someone think that Gregg was destined to become a fire-setter. But that boyhood fascination alone didn't mean Gregg was destined to become a fire-setter. The reasons that led him to become an adult arsonist were complex, combining many aspects of his life up to the early 1980s.

Gregg M. Bemis was born in Concord, Massachusetts, in November 1960. The irony is immediately apparent with his birth being in Concord. In a sad parallel, Concord was the site of one of the first battles of the American Revolutionary War. Like the Minutemen a couple of centuries before, Gregg would become a militant participant in his own rebellion against the government.

Growing up in Maynard, Massachusetts, Gregg spent lots of time with his mother, and her death when he was 16 left a vast void in his life. Within a couple of years, his father remarried and informed Gregg that he was moving to Maine, leaving him to live on his own in the family homestead. His mother's death and his father's departure, along with other life circumstances, led him to become one of the most prolific arsonists in the history of the country.

Some life circumstances are out of an individual's control. For instance, a U.S. male born during the middle years of the twentieth century may or may not have been drafted into the military based solely on his birth date and year. Each person's path is partly destined by his time and location in history. For Bemis, that was certainly true.

Gregg had an ordinary childhood, just passing through his early years like many others who grew up in the rural old mill town of Maynard during the 1960s. But he was attracted to the fire service from the beginning. When he was about five years old, he developed friendships with other kids who shared the same interests. Gregg recalled that as strange as it may seem when kids at that tender age dreamed about their potential life careers, several of them ended up working in the fire service.

He liked everything about the profession: the apparatus—the trucks, the ladders, the gear—and especially the camaraderie of other firefighters and the people on the periphery of the business. By age 10, Gregg had received his first camera, a Kodak Instamatic, which provided the means for him to become an avid, even obsessive, junior photographer. He later bought newer, sophisticated cameras, eventually amassing over 8,000 photographs, mostly related to fires, firefighters, and fire equipment.

By age 14, Bemis and his buddies all had radio receivers so that they could listen to the fire activity all over their region. Their knowledge base relative to firefighting was as extensive as that of many professional firefighters.

On his sixteenth birthday, Gregg was appointed to the Acton Auxiliary Fire Department, in a town neighboring Maynard. Like many such local volunteer outfits, the purpose of the Auxiliary was to support the paid-on-call and full-time fire departments. The organization had its own station and, initially, one piece of apparatus, an old rescue truck. A second piece was subsequently acquired, a used vehicle converted to a brush firefighting truck. The Auxiliary responded to building fires in town and to other emergencies, as needed. The members refilled air packs at fire scenes, carried a generator for lighting scenes, and had other equipment for overhauling fire scenes, a process that entails opening void spaces such as ceilings and walls to search for any fire extension and salvage operations. The brush truck gave Bemis more active duties, like fighting numerous brush fires, over a three-year period.

In the spring of 1977, Gregg went "sparking" in Boston for the first time. It was a momentous occasion. One who goes sparking is known officially as a fire buff or a spark, or unofficially as a sparkie. Some tried-and-true fire buffs think the word *sparkie* is derogatory—among the general public, it carries a bad connotation, referring to a fire-setter rather than a hobbyist. Fire buffs, or sparks, with expertise in fire photographs, fire equipment, and fire history, make fire their hobby. The terms are often used for those who race to active fires to watch and photograph the blaze. Fires become their spectator sport. Some fire buffs like to observe the firefighters with all of their equipment, their apparatus, and the techniques they utilize to fight fires. Around the country, there are numerous legitimate clubs and organizations of fire fans—in the Boston area these include the

Boston Sparks Association, founded in 1938, and the Box 52 Association, established in 1912.

The tradition of sparks goes back a couple of hundred years. They came from all walks of life. One of the most famous Boston fire buffs was Boston Symphony Orchestra and Boston Pops maestro Arthur Fiedler, who sparked fires from the 1950s to the 1970s.[1] Another well-known Boston businessman and philanthropist, David Mugar (Executive Producer of the Boston Pops Fourth of July Fireworks and WHDH-TV Channel 7 executive, among many other activities), also sparked fires for years in Boston. Scores of firefighters are also sparks; they are the lucky ones who make their hobby into their career. Many other firefighters merely tolerate the rag-tag and sometimes peculiar group who often marry themselves to a particular firehouse, with their corresponding apparatus and their firefighters.

Throughout this book, the terms *fire buffs*, *sparks*, and *sparkies* are used nearly interchangeably, although the purists may cringe at that. However, my usage was based on the customary wording used by Gregg Bemis and the other participants in the arson ring during their streak of fires as well as by the prosecuting and defense attorneys throughout subsequent litigation.

That first night sparking in Boston, Gregg "caught" (meaning had the opportunity to be present and observe) several car fires, a garage fire, and a working fire. The term *working fire* is typically used for a structure fire or an outside fire with a considerable fire load that, according to the observations of the officer or senior firefighter upon arrival, will likely use all manpower and apparatus currently responding. It is a signal to the first responders that they will be engaged and that the fire will require some effort to extinguish.[2]

At a garage fire in the Mattapan neighborhood, Gregg was glad for the chance to watch Engine 52 and Ladder 29 for the first time. These had become his favorite Boston Fire companies via years of listening to them

---

1 Stephanie Schorow, Boston on Fire, Commonwealth Editions, 2006, pp. 197–198.

2 Wikipedia, http://en.wikipedia.org/wiki/Glossary_of_Firefighting, February 25, 2018

on his scanner. That same night, Bemis also caught fire blowing out of the upper floor of a multistory duplex. He had heard a box striking over his fire radio. *Striking* refers to the actual fire box number being sounded out—that is, the individual numbers assigned to the box counted out, indicating the physical location of the box. Gregg did not know the location of the box, so he had to refer to a printed directory to get that information. In the ensuing years, he would memorize the location of more boxes in Boston than most firefighters could.

"A fire alarm box, fire alarm call box, or pull box is a device used for notifying a fire department of a fire or other incident. Often installed on street corners and mounted on a utility pole, a dedicated post, or a building, a fire alarm box was the main means of summoning firefighters

When the box is activated by turning a knob or pulling a hook, a spring-loaded wheel turns, striking a pulsed electrical signal corresponding to the box's number. A receiver at the fire alarm office enunciates the pulses through flashing lights or tones, or via a pen recorder, and the box number is matched to a list of box locations." [3] In the 1980s Boston had hundreds of voice boxes. Any person reporting a fire could open the call box, pick up the receiver, and speak to a fire dispatcher.

The first telegraph fire alarm system was developed in Boston in 1852.[4] In 1855 John Gamewell purchased regional rights to market the fire alarm telegraph, eventually obtaining patents and full rights to the system in 1859. The fire alarm boxes played a key role in the Great Boston Fire of 1872, which destroyed over 700 buildings and killed 13 people. There were numerous reasons for the magnitude of destruction, but a major contributing factor was that the fire alarm boxes were locked at the time to thwart false alarms. Only police and store owners had a key for the boxes, and the stores were all closed for the night. The locked boxes caused a delayed response of about 20 minutes by the Boston Fire Department.[5]

3 Wikipedia, http://en.wikipedia.org/wiki/Fire_Alarm_Call_Box, February 25, 2018

4 Wikipedia, *Sweeney, Emily (January 27, 2008).* "No cause for alarm," *Boston Globe.*

5 Wikipedia, Boston Fire Historical Society-Hardware.

The Gamewell Fire Alarm Telegraph Co. was later formed in 1879 with Gamewell systems installed in 500 cities by 1890.[6]

So, with over 1,500 fire boxes in Boston, it is easy to see that Gregg must have had quite a knack for memorizing the box numbers and their locations. That same memory would be on display years later after his arrest.

On that first night in Boston, Gregg was totally impressed with the Boston firefighters who worked that structure fire and knocked it down within minutes without requesting a second alarm. In the communities where Bemis had experience, the firefighters would have needed far more manpower to contain a similar fire. The Boston "jakes" were obviously very professional and experienced.

The term *jake* has its origins with the Boston firefighters, later referring to other firefighters throughout New England. *Jake* is possibly derived from the term *J-Key*. As explained above, the first fire alarm boxes were based on the telegraph system. Inside each box, next to the automatic alarm mechanism that tripped when someone pulled the hook, there was a small telegraph tapper, called a telegraph key that firemen could use to convey messages to headquarters. They tapped out a signal using the telegraph key inside of the fire alarm box. The fact that a firefighter held the key to open the box, and that the key was shaped like the letter J, is likely the reason that firefighters, in general, were called jakes. It remains an affectionate and respectful term for a firefighter.[7]

In 1978 Gregg became a member of the Stow call department, in another town adjacent to Maynard. A paid-on-call, or call, firefighter is usually a resident of the area who has an interest in helping the town whenever a fire, accident, or other natural disaster strikes. The Fire Department depends upon the timely response of members of the paid-on-call department, who selflessly serve their community when the alarm sounds. Many towns utilize volunteer and/or call firefighters to supplement their

---

6 2018 Honeywell International, Inc.. website; About Us; Our Company-Our History (Gamewell FCI).

7 Rockland, MA Professional Firefighters' website, January 19, 2007.

full-time firefighters or in place of a full-time professional fire department. Gregg, as did many others, used the call position as an opportunity to gain experience that could prove vital when seeking full-time professional firefighting status.

From 1978 to 1980, Bemis held several firefighter positions. However, his heart was in the big city, Boston. Although he was extremely busy in the suburbs, he still found time to spark in Boston. The Boston Fire Department and its firefighters were the elite to Gregg. Even if he couldn't become one of them, he still wanted to follow the Boston guys and their activities. The magnetic pull of Boston led him to the hangouts of the Boston sparks, where he made numerous close friends. Sparking with friends in Boston gave Gregg a sense of belonging to a community. These friendships were to become fateful connections.

Thursday, February 18, 1982, was the night that changed the lives of so many—the arsonists, the firefighters, and the residents of Boston. It would also change the City itself. The City would be held hostage by domestic terrorists who would frighten and torment its citizens for the next two years.

Bemis and his tight-knit group of spark friends had planned this night for weeks. Gregg headed into town with Lenny Kendall. Born in 1962, Leonard A. Kendall, Jr., came from Acton, Massachusetts. He and Gregg hung in the same circles as teens. As sparks, both had a keen interest in fires and firefighting. Kendall had been an auxiliary firefighter in Acton until some sort of unidentified problem caused him to leave. Kendall had also been an apprentice firefighter with the Stow Fire Department. Lenny was a very young looking, lean and slight, clean-cut 20-year-old. He was rather quiet and mild-mannered. He became a member of this budding conspiracy only due to his close friendship to Bemis. If he had never met Gregg, Lenny Kendall might never have become a criminal.

That night, they were physically prepared to set fires, as they brought with them the components to make time-delayed incendiary devices. But they weren't quite mentally prepared to take that ultimate step to become full-fledged arsonists. Could they actually bring themselves to light a building on fire, or would their conscience prevent them from crossing that line? When the two arrived at the orange-roofed Howard Johnson Restaurant across from BFD Headquarters, the fire buff parking lot was practically empty, pretty unusual for that hour on a Thursday night. The meeting of the group had been prearranged, so Bemis knew that the others would be along soon.

But after a while, when nobody else had shown up, Lenny and Gregg took a ride. Before they drove two blocks, the fire radio started to strike Box 7161. By this time in his sparking career, Gregg's phenomenal knowledge of the box locations was right on the money, "Hey, that's West 1st and E Streets, let's take it," he said, referring to a location less than a mile away in South Boston.

Lenny had not spent many nights in Boston with his best friend and his crew of sparks, so he was raring to go and at least enjoy catching a couple fires; whether they set the fires themselves or there was some other cause for the fire made no difference to him.

The radio confirmed fire showing at that location. Gregg and Lenny arrived with the third due engine company, but they were disappointed that the fire had already been knocked down. "Hey Gregg, is that Bobby and Donny standing across the street?" asked Lenny, pointing toward two men.

"It sure is. Let's go see what they're up to," replied Bemis, starting across the street.

The group tried to converse, but the engine noise was deafening, so they walked around the corner onto a side street. Donny grinned like the Cheshire cat, "Hey, we don't need any of that time-delay shit. Look what one lousy match did to this old joint."

"Donny, did you and Bobby torch it?" Gregg asked in disbelief.

With a nasty, dastardly grin, Donny realized that he and Bobby had just broken virginal ground. "Yes, we did it. We saw a pile of trash and brush near the back of the building, so we just dropped a match in it and screwed." They had all recently settled on setting fires in vacant buildings to ensure getting publicity and a public outcry to support their protest. Bemis hadn't expected Donny and Bobby to set the first fire without him.

Donald Stackpole, a few years older than Bemis and Kendall, grew up south of Boston in a lower-middle-income household. Like the men he hung out with, Stackpole wanted to become a firefighter or even a police officer. He had several problems, though, that prohibited him from becoming a civil servant. Donny was rather short and overweight; he wasn't one for exercise and dieting. Thus, he couldn't pass the physical necessary to get on the job. He also didn't have a high school diploma or equivalency, which is a requirement almost everywhere to become a full-time professional firefighter in Massachusetts. Finally, Stackpole had a felony criminal record, having been arrested and convicted for theft. This alone disqualified him from applying to become a firefighter or police officer.

Stackpole took this slight to heart. He became one pissed-off individual when it came to firefighters in general and the Boston Fire Department in particular.

However, he enjoyed being a fire buff. He still had a deep interest in chasing and watching fires and hanging out with like-minded individuals. But he had no particular admiration or respect for firefighters. He loved watching firefighters work for their money, rather than just sitting around the firehouse. His was a vindictive mind that could care less if firefighters got laid off or were hurt. Injuries might even benefit his friends at some point. As will be seen in the coming chapters, Stackpole tended to carry his hobby a little bit further than other sparks. He suffered another slight when neither the Boston Sparks Association nor any fire buff's club would admit him into their social circle.

Stackpole sometimes drove a red Ford station wagon with a light bar on top, resembling a fire chief's car, complete with a Massachusetts license plate that read FD-2 and Boston Industrial Fire Department printed on the door. He also had his own fire truck with South Shore Fire Department emblazoned on the truck body. He was often observed dressed as a fire chief.

More than a few people thought Donny Stackpole was just plain nuts. Some stayed away from him because they didn't like him. Our investigation of Stackpole revealed a rough, mean individual who could be very shrewd when it counted.

When Gregg first met Stackpole, Donny drove truck for a living. He later ran a private security company, Metro Security, that gave him complete access to the back alleys of South Boston at all hours of the day and night. Eventually, due to a licensing issue, Metro Security became ETR Security. The security company quarters soon became the arsonists' headquarters.

Stackpole's close friend and recently anointed arsonist Robert Francis Groblewski, an adopted child, was the same age as Stackpole. His adoptive parents were a few years older than most parents. Early on in life, he knew he wanted to be in public safety. His first career choice was to be a firefighter, his second choice a police officer.

After high school, Groblewski did a stint in the U.S. Coast Guard. He felt that this branch of the armed services performed a needed public service. After the Coast Guard, Grobo (as he was nicknamed) sought to become a firefighter. He took the civil service exam for a Boston firefighter position a half dozen times. His high score on the tests was an excellent 102, including two additional points he received under the Veterans Preference Points program within the Massachusetts Civil Service system.

However, the stars and the times were not aligned in Groblewski's favor; a position for Bobby as a Boston firefighter was not available. He felt fortunate, though, when he got hired as a Boston Police Officer in the late 1970s. Even though he had that good job, he still had hopes of becoming a firefighter should the opportunity arise. In the meantime, he became a serious fire buff, spending many nights at Boston fires and eating dinner with firefighter friends at Ladder 15 in the Back Bay.

Bobby had lots of energy. People remember him as affable, often with a smile on his handsome face. With his dark hair, mustache, and tall and solidly lean build, he looked the part of a BPD officer with a good, well-paying, and respected job. He worked hard and played harder. Much of his play involved sparking fires several nights a week in Boston.

Now, as he stood outside this fire scene in Southie on a cold night, newly ordained arsonist Groblewski was amazed that, within minutes, the trash fire had spread to the rear of the building. The power of fire was just beginning to reveal itself to Bobby.

Gregg noticed that within the pile of trash were charred remains of several discarded vehicle tires, which had evidently been the fuel that caused the rapid fire spread. Unknown to him at the time, this seemingly harmless observation was later remembered and used by the group to further escalate or accelerate their group goals.

With the fire now under control, the boys headed back to HoJo's to discuss the new developments. Bemis chided Donny and Bobby, "Boy, you guys are stupid to take a chance of being seen like that. You should have at least used the device so nobody would see you." The device Gregg referred to was simply a matchbook with a cigarette woven through the matches. Depending on the positioning of the cigarette, the matches would flare some minutes later hopefully igniting other readily combustible secondary fuels.

Bobby's only reply was, "Oh, don't worry about it. Nobody saw us." Gregg continued to argue with them because, if anything went wrong, he felt they all would be in big trouble, and any stupid move could prove to be fatal. But Bobby asked, "Did you bring the stuff so we can try it out?"

Bemis replied affirmatively, retrieving the works from his trunk. Master arsonist-to-be Gregg Bemis had a surprise in store for the group. He told them that he had purchased a gallon of Coleman lantern fuel that would suit their purposes perfectly, as he had tested it numerous times to be certain that the fuel would not eat through the zip-lock plastic bag in his new, improved device. His testing was a textbook example of utilizing the scientific method without him even knowing it.

The new device was an updated version of the crude cigarette and matchbook device consisting of a brown paper lunch bag containing a pint or so of Coleman fuel (nicknamed by the group "la bomba juice") poured into a zip-lock plastic bag (also known as "el plastique"), topped with several loosely crumpled tissues. The lit cigarette laced through the matchbook was set atop the tissues at the last moment when placement of the device was imminent. The finished product was dubbed "la bomba," Anyone seen carrying the device from the car to the target location would appear to be merely carrying their lunch bag. It was discreet and inconspicuous. The components of the device were cheap and readily available at stores everywhere. Everyone agreed that this device would be used for now, unless something better could be devised.

The four men piled into Gregg's 1978 black "nerf" official police look-alike Chevy Impala. They rode through several neighborhoods looking for the perfect target on which to test the new device. Donny suggested, "Why not check out the Berry (referring to Roxbury)? That neighborhood is infested with abandoned buildings." For a couple of hours, they drove around, spotting scores of old, rundown dives, but for each target, someone in the group came up with an excuse not to burn that particular place. Perhaps they were still having second thoughts about taking this dangerous step. Finally, Grobo and Stackpole decided to call it a night.

After dropping those two off, Gregg and Lenny went on seeking the ideal site. As they say in real estate, location, location, location. Suddenly Bemis spotted what appeared to be *the* perfect target in the Roxbury Highlands section of the City, a rather poor black neighborhood where Malcolm X had lived years ago, now sparsely populated and plagued by abandoned buildings. "Hey, Lenny, look at that old joint behind those bushes." Lenny readily agreed it was perfect. What they didn't know at the time was the address of the building. The two young men could not have known on that cold night that two years later the structure at 4-10 Blanchard Street would become the first listed fire on a Federal indictment.

They drove around the block several times making sure it was safe for them to commit their deed. Parking in a dark spot, they assembled the newly designed incendiary device in the front seat of the car. Gregg had Lenny get into the driver's seat, directing him to drive up that narrow street with the headlights off so they could park next to the target building. Blanchard Street was extremely dark; there were no streetlights and no signs of life.

Gregg climbed out of the car, telling Lenny to wait until he returned. As he approached the building, thinking about what he was about to do, the chill running up and down his spine let him know exactly how scared he really was. This was the big step, finally. He was thinking, will I get away with it? Will I get caught and go to prison? Am I being a hero for all the firefighters and police? The eerie appearance of the darkened, vandalized old wood duplex reminded Gregg of a horror movie, which only increased his inner anxieties. All that was missing from the classic horror flick scenario was a thunderstorm.

Determined to complete his task, Gregg bit his lip as he entered the pitch black open doorway. Not having completely thought out the logistics of his first job, he had no flashlight with him. So Bemis placed the device against the wall on the stairway immediately inside the door. He noticed numerous holes in the old plaster walls exposing the wood lath beneath, which Gregg knew would assist the fire growth. Wood lath, a framework of thin, narrow stacked or latticed wood strips, separated by small gaps, was commonly used as backing for interior plaster walls and ceilings in buildings in the United States until the advent of sheetrock in the 1950s. When the plaster was stripped off during renovations or through neglect, the exposed lath was essentially kindling wood, a great fuel to readily ignite and accelerate a fire.

Gregg lit the cigarette, wove it into the matchbook, and placed it in the bag among the tissue. Then he ran like hell.

As he hopped into his car, his voice sounded an octave higher as he said, "Alright Lenny, let's get the hell out of here." He sighed in relief. They looped around the neighborhood, waiting for the fire to be reported over the radio. After 15 minutes, they saw smoke rising in the distance. Still no radio call. Even after another half hour, with flames now visible in the night sky, still no radio call. Just after 3:00 a.m., the call finally came for a building fire, a full 90 minutes after the device had been lit. Upon arrival, Ladder 4 reported heavy fire showing. A second alarm was ordered straight away.

When Gregg's '78 Chevy Impala returned to the scene, the duplex was fully enveloped in flames. Fire had broken through the roof, catching fire to a nearby utility pole. Live electrical wires burned off the pole, wildly arcing on the street. Lenny finally spoke: "Holy Jesus, I can't believe that nobody saw this fire sooner than they did." It was then they realized that the people in this part of the City had become so accustomed to the constant wail of sirens that they no longer paid any attention, or no longer cared. Bemis had been to this devastated, battle-scarred neighborhood several times in the past few months sparking numerous other fires.

Taking photos of the blazing fire, Bemis immortalized their first structure fire set with the new device. These photos would prove to the other guys how well the device had worked. The firefighters quickly darkened the fire down with several deck guns. Gregg said to Lenny, "Let's head home now; we did our share of work for the night. You know, Lenny, that place gave me the creeps when I went inside."

Lenny's only response: "Well, that whole area gave me the creeps." While driving home, they discussed their accomplishments, agreeing that the other group members would be pleased with the results. Their emotions had run the gamut that night—fright, excitement, pride. It was almost light out when they parted. It had been a long, fruitful night, one that they would not soon forget. You always remember your first.

▲

A couple days later, Donny phoned Gregg. Bemis informed him that he had used the incendiary device with great success. Donny couldn't wait to try it. They met Bobby and Joe Gorman around 10:00 p.m. at the usual parking lot. After Gregg filled in the boys about the Blanchard Street job, the others were jumping to see the burned-out building. They headed to Roxbury Highlands in Gregg's car. As they turned onto Blanchard, he proudly pointed and said, "There it is."

With a bright smile on his face, Donny exclaimed, "Holy shit, that place is gonzo, isn't it?" Bobby and Joe were equally impressed. Now they were all eager to try their hand with the device on another building to get a firsthand look at how it worked. After riding around for a short time, the quartet spotted an abandoned taxpayer on the corner of Harvard and Greenwood Streets in Dorchester.

A taxpayer in Boston dates back to the early 1900s. The term usually refers to a small one- or two-story building built to generate enough income to cover the owner's annual property tax assessed for owning a parcel of land. Typically, it is a commercial structure containing several storefronts characterized by a flat roof plus, unless these spaces have been partitioned over the years, a common cockloft and basement. These buildings can be particularly hazardous to firefighter safety when the fire spreads horizontally across either the cockloft or basement. The cockloft fire could drop onto firefighters or get a new influx of air and flash through the smoke layer, capturing firefighters unaware in seconds. A fire in the basement extending the length of the building could cause collapse under the firefighters. Boston and other older cities were full of taxpayers.

In this instance, the building had been boarded up after a previous fire, but the boys saw a small hole in a wall. Inside, they saw the bone-dry wood lath of a partition wall. Excitedly, they all jumped out of the car on Greenwood Street, which was absent of any sign of life. The device was lit and carefully placed within the wall. They took off, driving around the neighborhood. When they drove past the building again, fire was issuing from the opening, venting to the exterior. Unfortunately for the group, a cab driver spotted the fire and called it in. The arsonists were disappointed when the BFD quickly knocked down the fire, resulting in little damage.

They didn't set any other fires that night, but a week later the same quartet targeted the same building a second time. This time, they were more successful. A working fire was ordered on the box, essentially leveling the building. Perhaps most significantly, that night the co-conspirators all accepted the incendiary as the go-to device to be used from that night forward.

▲

It was somewhat natural that the group's members had banded together. They all had the same interests, the same career goals, the same hobbies, and, crucially, the same resentments. Most wanted to be Boston firefighters or if that lofty aspiration couldn't be attained, at least work as full-time firefighters on a decent department.

They loved spending their spare time chasing fires so that they could watch and photograph them. They especially enjoyed critiquing the actions of the firefighters. Sometimes the fire won; sometimes the firefighters won. If the firefighters lost the battle, was it because they had screwed up? This particular band of sparks would routinely demean the firefighters if they lost a building that the sparks felt, in their infinite wisdom, should have been saved. Conversely, they gave the firefighters credit when they did a good job.

The Boston fire buffs who chased fires would meet at three or four locations—the old HoJo's (Howard Johnson restaurant), the Mobil gas station across from the Doughboy Donuts in Edward Everett Square, or the

Dunkin' Donuts in Andrew Square, South Boston. This particular group parked their "tuna fleet" of vehicles and waited until a fire call sounded on their radios. Their vehicles looked like unmarked police cars, either Ford LTDs or Chevy Impalas, often black in color, always with a series of antennas, with at least one long whip antenna that was necessary to receive the low-band frequencies used by Boston FD and other cities. Thus, when they all parked in a row, backed in so that they were ready to head out at a moment's notice, they resembled an ocean-going fishing fleet with their long fishing rods pointing high into the air.

Virtually all of the "roving" sparks were white males between the ages of 18 and 45. Plenty of fire buffs of all ages rarely, if ever, spent their nights roaming the streets; they just liked to collect memorabilia, books, and photos and talk to others with similar interests. The age of the mem-bers of the roving faction had no upper limit. The lower age limit was usu-ally defined by the freedom afforded by being post-school age and having enough money and a vehicle to facilitate travel and leisure time.

From the late 1970s forward, these guys mingled and conversed at the parking lots while awaiting fire calls. This is how Bemis met and became friends with Robert Groblewski and Donald Stackpole, as well as Joe Gorman and Boston Firefighter Ray Norton. This was the core group of the arson conspiracy. Gregg brought in Lenny Kendall, his longtime friend.

Bemis and Lenny were the youngest of the clique, by a few years. Groblewski was already a Boston cop who wanted to be a firefighter. Stackpole's firefighter dreams had already been dashed, but he liked to hang out with the other wannabes. Bemis and Groblewski had taken the test to become a Boston firefighter, but they didn't have a chance due to affirmative action combined with budget cuts, an emotional blow that fueled their resentments.

These guys spent hundreds of hours together. They not only sparked together, they also ate together and spent time at each other's houses and each other's workplaces. Their bond grew stronger over the period 1979 to 1981.

As it does in every time and place, the circumstances of their lives that were matters of chance—their birth lottery, as we might say today—affected the paths they took and even the choices they made. Their birthplaces and birth years, the chronological sequencing of your birth, that is, the day of birth, played a role in many significant aspects and events of their lives.

Gregg and his cohorts grew up enthused with firefighting in the Boston area. More importantly, Bemis, as did many others, grew up as a white male in an age when many professions, including police and firefighters, diversified their workforces to include more women and minorities. Also significant to Gregg and the others was the tax-cutting measure passed in 1980 in Massachusetts known as Proposition $2^1/_2$. As would soon be experienced by Bemis, his friends, and hundreds of others, neither he nor anyone else would have much chance of getting hired as a firefighter or police officer for the foreseeable future.

That is, unless maybe this group of wannabe firefighters could think of some form of civil disobedience that could support their cause. After all, this was the home state of Henry David Thoreau, author of the famous 1849 treatise known as Civil Disobedience, which reasons that disobedience may be just in response to an unjust state. Civil disobedience is defined as a peaceful form of protest expressed by the refusal to obey certain laws or pay taxes. Sometimes, however, dissenters confuse or equate civil disobedience with anarchy. And anarchy is exactly the path that this rebellious group of young men decided to take to push their agenda. Their actions would be better defined as very uncivil disobedience.

4-10 Blanchard Street fire, the first building fire set with the incendiary device.

Personal Fire Pumper owned by Donald Stackpole (driver) with Boston Police Officer Robert F. Groblewski standing behind cab at Boston parade

(Photo courtesy of BFD {retired} Photographer William Noonan)

CHAPTER THREE

THE MAKINGS OF A CONSPIRACY 1980–1981

Fire is one of those worldly natural phenomena, like ocean waves or cloud patterns, that is as beautiful as it is vital; we stare at it for hours, fascinated, enchanted, and charmed, as if bewitched. We sit by the fireplace or campfire gazing at the dancing yellows, oranges, reds, and blues of the ever-moving flames. But, just like water and weather, fire has vast destructive power and wreaks havoc across the country every year. An unwanted or fugitive fire destroys real property, personal property, and mementos, as well as causes thousands of injuries and deaths each year in the United States. In the wrong hands, fire is usually disastrous in one way or another.

By 1981, Boston was only beginning to become the rehabilitated, world-class city that it is today. Mayor Kevin White had been in office for over a dozen years. He was leading the way for the revitalization of some of the City's dilapidated areas. The huge tourist magnet of Faneuil Hall Marketplace had been renovated, drawing locals and travelers by the thousands. The financial district and the rundown wharfs on the waterfront were attracting investors who would develop those areas with soaring multi-million-dollar properties. However, the residential neighborhoods, particularly Roxbury, Dorchester, Mattapan, and Jamaica Plain, if not outright blighted, attracted few investors or public renewal efforts. They needed some serious attention. That was not to come for another decade, or two.

The City was healing after a bitter and violent stretch in the mid-1970s relating to court-ordered school busing in an attempt to relieve segregation in the Boston school system. There was so much press coverage and public scrutiny that almost nobody noticed that fires were routinely occurring within the City. These fires centered in the Fenway neighborhood of Boston, an area that was very congested with old apartment buildings near the famous Symphony Hall. The Boston Fire Department was not making any progress on investigations of these fires. There was something rather sophisticated going on there.

A neighborhood group started to put it together and screamed loud enough to get the attention of First Security Services, a young Boston-based company that was hired by the insurance industry to look into a series of over 30 fires. Years later, I often conferred with Larry Curran and Dan Cronin, who were driving forces of the First Security investigation. They conducted a thorough paper chase into the fires and found a coordinated arson-for-profit ring involving the rapid turnover of the buildings with escalating prices for the rundown properties. The ring involved property owners, public officials, attorneys, insurance adjusters, and real estate agents.

The State Attorney General's Office conducted the public investigation. The combined effort, with First Security securing the cooperation from the "torch" who had set several of these fires, resulted in the arrest and conviction of the players. The hard work put into the analysis of those fires was to be the standard that the Federal Bureau of Alcohol, Tobacco and Firearms (ATF) wished to follow when the ATF jumped into the arson investigation business.

Fires and plenty of arsons were still ongoing within the City and surrounding counties, but there was little success in making arrests. At the time, neither state nor municipal agencies had put much effort into the investigation of arsons. Most fire departments, being small agencies of town governments, were lucky to have one semi-trained fire investigator capable of determining whether a fire was an intentional or an accidental event. Further, fire investigators had little or no training as criminal investigators, lacking the many skills that a police officer or a detective would have. By 1981, virtually none of the small towns had a team with both fire and police personnel assigned to investigate fires.

The cities usually had a Fire Prevention Bureau, but their members had to perform numerous duties, including inspections, putting on presentations to school classes, and conducting fire investigations. They rarely had the time, the money, or the skills necessary to conduct a thorough fire investigation. A typical successful case centered around a domestic dispute during which an angry boyfriend was witnessed pouring gasoline in a doorway of his girlfriend's place. These cases were relatively clear-cut and did not involve a complex investigation.

Even the Boston Arson Squad was pretty unsophisticated at the time. The name of the unit, Arson Squad, was itself a misnomer because not every fire that was investigated was arson; only years later was the name changed to the more accurate Fire Investigation Unit.

In the 1970s, the Squad largely consisted of firefighters who had been injured on the job while assigned to a fire company and could no longer handle the rigors of firefighting. Not yet ready to retire, such a firefighter would be assigned to the Arson Squad. Other members of the Squad were older guys who also could no longer fight fires. None of them particularly wanted to be a fire investigator. Worse yet, none of them had any training as an investigator when they came into the Squad. They were sent to a two-week school, and that was about it. This all started to change, albeit slowly, during the 1980s.

The Massachusetts State Fire Marshal's Office at that time, as it is now, was populated with Massachusetts State Troopers, mostly "road warriors" whose duties were mainly to patrol the highways and byways of Massachusetts. Investigations by the patrolling Troopers into serious criminal activities were usually limited until they became detectives or were assigned to county district attorney's offices. The Troopers mostly volunteered for the Fire Marshal's Office. In the late 1970s and into the early 1980s, their training usually consisted of two weeks at the National Fire Academy (NFA) and another two weeks at the MA State Fire Academy, whose training nearly duplicated that of the NFA. They often brought with them a rigid State Police paramilitary persona to their investigations that was, at times, both helpful and a hindrance to the case at hand. During the 1980s, the State Fire Marshal got serious about the fire investigation business. Leadership, training, and money, as well as the dedication of the Troopers themselves, forged the State Fire Marshal's Office into an investigative team to be reckoned with, which continues to this day.

How was ATF different from the state and local agencies? One, our badge said U.S., meaning that our jurisdiction was nationwide, not hindered by town, county, or state borders. ATF investigated any place in the United States. Funding, time, training, equipment, and experience were all accessible. Special Agents were trained criminal investigators, with those Special Agents assigned to Arson Groups able to focus full-time on fire investigations.

For example, I had already attended the National and State Fire Academy two-week courses in 1980. By 1982 I had also attended seminars and the ATF Arson-for-Profit school. I was still a "newbie," but over the next 20 years, I attended over 2,500 hours of classes, including college courses through the University of Maryland's Fire Science program. I had set or had participated in at least 30 training fires, exercises in which we set the fires to analyze them visually and with computer analysis. I also had the opportunity to teach over 70 investigation classes plus two semesters at Cape Cod Community College as an adjunct professor.

During my 20 years working fires with ATF, I participated in approximately 1,000 origin and cause investigations of fires and explosions. Up to that time, few people had the luxury of amassing those credentials. Local guys only got to see a handful of fires per year, unless they worked in a major city. Troopers in the State Fire Marshal's Office had the opportunity to investigate 50–100 fires a year, but, with rare exceptions, few Troopers stayed in the unit for enough years to amass experience in 1,000 fires.

During the years, I was often teamed with some of the best local and state investigators at the time. They taught me that, without the corpus delecti, a Latin term meaning the "body of [the] crime,"—that is, a solid determination that the fire was intentionally set—then the rest of an investigation was virtually a waste of time.[8]

Regarding this arson ring conspiracy, the period covering late 1980 and early 1981 was pivotal for the soon-to-be militant group of sparks. A major event transpired that affected every citizen of Massachusetts. Politics became the triggering factor for the revolutionary group to be formed, compelling them to take up arms against the establishment.

On a warm September 1980 morning, Gregg was restless after completing a midnight shift as Stow Police dispatcher, so he drove through thick, congested, everyday Boston morning traffic from Stow, northwest of Boston, to Donald Stackpole's house in Weymouth, about 12 miles south of Boston. After Gregg pounded on the door of the trailer, a sleepy-eyed Stackpole answered the door. "Donny, are you planning on going into Boston tonight? Do you want to take a ride for something to do?"

Donny replied that he was heading into Boston later, but as to going for a ride, "No, I'm going back to sleep for a little while. I need my beauty sleep, you know."

8 WEX LAW, Legal Information Institute, Cornell University.

"Well, in that case, Donny, I think you better hibernate for the whole winter!"

Grinning, Donny responded, "Fuck you, smart guy."

Gregg then left, taking a circuitous route along the beach on Quincy Shore Drive. He parked his car and quickly fell asleep in the warm vehicle, thinking that he had better take a nap because he probably would be up half the night sparking in Boston. When he awoke midafternoon, he again found himself in stop-and-go traffic on the Southeast Express Way, also known as the "distress way" since it seldom promotes express travel. He soon learned the reason for the delay. His fire radio announced that there was a car fire up ahead.

When Gregg finally worked his way past the burned skeleton of a vehicle, he continued into Southie to get one of his favorite roast beef sandwiches. While waiting for his sandwich, he noticed a headline in the *Boston Herald*: "Proposition 2½ to be placed on November ballot." Gregg, like thousands of others, thought that the tax-limiting proposal for real estate property and automobile excise tax sounded like a good idea. But, he also figured that the usual targets, the municipal employees, could be in big trouble. Everybody was talking about the pros and cons of the ballot initiative, but nobody could accurately predict what the initial and long-term consequences would be. Like Gregg, the masses generally felt that the measure would not make it onto the ballot. Now that it was announced that it was to be voted on in November, Gregg was stunned. Still, deep in his heart, Gregg felt that there was no way that this measure would ever pass.

After a long, hard-fought battle, the main advocates of the measure, Citizens for Limited Taxation, managed to get a referendum onto the Massachusetts ballot referred to as Proposition 2½. The tax-cutting plan referred to the 2.5 percent ceiling on total property taxes annually as well as the 2.5 percent limit on property tax increases. If passed, Proposition 2½ was to go into effect early in 1981.[9]

The people of Massachusetts felt that Proposition 2½ would lead to a more responsible and efficient government with more voter control. At the same time, the people also thought that public sector jobs would become riskier. Some feared the loss of their jobs or the decline in quality or quantity of public services. They feared that household services would be greatly affected.[10]

An inevitable result of Proposition 2½ was that local revenues would decline, which meant a real decline in other local tax rates and local spending ability. An exception to the law allowed for the taxpayers of each municipality to override the 2.5 percent cap to address specific needs of the community, thus giving the citizens of each locality direct control over their taxation. This override could be accomplished only by a majority vote within the municipality where it was proposed.

The chief provision of Proposition 2½ required every one of Massachusetts' cities and towns to cut their tax rate to 2.5 percent of the assessed real estate value in said community. The levy would be lowered in increments. It was expected that property taxes in the average Massachusetts district would be reduced by over 40 percent. Even more dramatic, the decrease in older cities like Boston could exceed 70 percent over time.

People both feared and cheered that Proposition 2½ would undeniably lower property taxes in many Massachusetts communities. But in a peculiar way, it would only enhance inequities. The older, poorer cities where the public services are most needed and most cash-strapped would feel the most pain. In the wealthier communities, where the value

---

9 Citizens for Limited Taxation and the Citizens Economic Research Foundation, "Celebrating Proposition 2 ½ after 30 Years," November 4, 2010.

10 Gist, J. R. (1988), FISCAL AUSTERITY, GRANT STRUCTURES AND LOCAL EXPENDITURE RESPONSE. Policy Studies Journal, 16: 687–712. doi:10.1111/j.1541-0072.1988.tb00679.x.

of property and housing are high, services would hardly be affected. The haves would suffer the least, as usual, while the poor would be hurt most.

It was only about 5:30 p.m. when Gregg pulled into the Howard Johnson's lot, still a couple hours before anyone else would show up. He decided to visit some of his firefighter buddies at Engine 17 and Ladder 7, the firehouse on Meetinghouse Hill. With its commanding view of Boston Harbor, the top of the hill was the highest point in Dorchester and home of the oldest public school in the United States, established in the 1600s. After a cup of coffee and some conversation, Gregg headed back to HoJo's. His departing words to his friends sounded like prophesy, "I'll see you at the big one."

About 8:00 p.m., Donny pulled into the lot. "Hey Skinny, it's about time you got here. You'll be late for your own funeral." "Skinny" was the ball-busting occasional nickname the guys gave the ample-sized Stackpole. Groblewski showed up a few minutes later. No fire calls had come in as of yet, so the trio rode around Boston for a while.

Gregg needed to talk to them about the Prop 2½ article, which irked him. When he did, Groblewski immediately got pissed: "Oh, that's just a crock of shit; it will never pass. Don't worry about it."

Gregg submitted, "Oh, I agree, Bobby, but what about the public? What are they thinking?" The discussion among the three of them got heated.

Donny, in his usual irritating fashion, interjected, "I don't know what you're getting all bent out of shape for anyway."

"Donny, you know exactly what will happen if it passes. There will be lots of layoffs."

"Oh, who cares? The cops and firemen are all a bunch of useless drunks anyway."

Further dejected and angered by his friend's comments, Gregg shouted back, "There you go, talking out of your ass again, Donny!" After arguing a while longer, they dropped the subject. Gregg felt that arguing with Stackpole was like trying to talk a hungry dog out of a meat truck.

A short while later, Boston Fire Alarm struck Box 1726: one beep, a pause followed by seven beeps, a pause followed by two beeps, and a pause followed by six beeps. This process was then repeated. Showing his knowledge of the box locations, Gregg said, "1726, that's Norfolk Ave. at Magazine Street," referring to a section of Roxbury. (I had been familiar with this area because as a rookie agent, my G-ride, my official government vehicle, had been stolen from behind my apartment building and found the next day on Magazine Street.)

Bemis and his spark buddies responded immediately to the scene, where they encountered the first due companies heavily engaged, working a well-involved fire in a two-story wood-frame warehouse with fire blowing out of several second-floor windows. A second alarm was quickly ordered. The jakes were laboring to knock down the heavy fire when Donny wisecracked, "Hey, look, those guys are earning their pay for a change." Bobby and Gregg looked at each other, just shaking their heads, but they didn't respond, knowing that to do so would only spark another argument. Stackpole often showed his disdain in this way for firefighters and the BFD in particular.

▲

Tuesday, November 4, 1980, was an exceptionally significant day in the life of Gregg Bemis. That day was Gregg's twentieth birthday. It was also Election Day on both the local and national level. Gregg had a huge dual birthday wish; he wished for the defeat of Ronald Reagan against incumbent President Jimmy Carter, and he wished for the defeat of Proposition 2½. Neither wish came true.

Proposition 2½ passed by a fairly wide margin. The fate of Boston and all other Massachusetts cities and towns would be greatly affected by the "yes" vote. However, at that moment, Bemis was trying to stay calm and not worry about the effects of Prop $2^1/_2$. He had no idea how much chaos would be wrought on the City of Boston and other communities over the next years.

On Wednesday, February 4, 1981, just three months after Prop 2½ passed, the first cutbacks were felt in Boston like a smack in the face. First came the deactivation of Engine 43 and Ladder 20, both on Mass. Ave. in Roxbury. Also, Engine 25 in downtown Boston was taken out of service. The loss of these companies was only the beginning of the closings and deactivations that would eventually affect every neighborhood of Boston. Bemis noted immediately when, a few days later, a fatal fire occurred only blocks away from the firehouse where Engine 43 and Ladder 20 had been deactivated. Gregg felt that the delayed response of the firefighters who came from a firehouse more distant to the fire was responsible for the fatality. To Gregg, this outcome was predictable, but he didn't think it would happen so quickly. It was this type of tragic event that would propel Gregg to his militant stance, his terroristic form of uncivil disobedience.

April 10, 1981, was a far worse day for the Fire Department and its firefighters and, mentally, for Gregg and his associates. The second wave of deactivations for the BFD occurred on this date: Engines 1, 12, 26, 34, 40, 50, and 54, plus Ladders 5, 8, 22, 30, and 31, were put out of service due to cutbacks related to the passage of Proposition 2½. Approximately 200 firefighters were laid off on this one fateful day, out of a total full-strength complement of nearly 1,500 uniformed personnel—over 13 percent of their workforce.

The uproar from the people of Boston was incredible. The cutbacks affected every neighborhood in a very scary way. The moms and dads were feeling extremely vulnerable, afraid for their families and their properties.

If you have ever seen a fire in Boston on a windy day, you would understand the fear.

My wife of 20-plus years experienced one of these nasty fires in East Boston, before we were married, when three triple-deckers burned within 30 minutes. She and her five-year-old son were in their apartment on the third floor in the second of the three buildings. Only when smoke came through the floorboards, did she realize there was a fire. Try to imagine that feeling of panic trying to traverse the darkened, smoke-clogged stairway to safety with a five-year-old in tow. Then, imagine standing there hugging your son while watching your home being consumed in front of your tear-filled eyes, with flames blowing sideways from building to building. Finally, imagine realizing that, yes, you and your son are safe, but everything you own is gone, including virtually every photo of your son before he was five. This may sound overly dramatic, but that is real life when the winds blow in Boston's congested neighborhoods.

The people of Boston have never been known to stand still when they felt wronged. Just check your history for the Revolutionary War-era activities by Bostonians like John Hancock and John and Samuel Adams and political protests such as the Boston Tea Party. The actions of the Bostonians in the spring of 1981 would have made the Minutemen proud. In Charlestown, the residents held the firehouse with Engine 50 hostage. They refused to allow the City to remove the apparatus from the otherwise vacant firehouse. In Readville, where Engine 49 was deactivated, the area citizens held the engine captive for over a year. A similar protest was ongoing in East Boston, where locals occupied the house of Engine 11. Human chain blockades were conducted in the to-and-from Sumner and Callahan Tunnels that connected Eastie and Logan Airport to the remainder of the City. Without adequate coverage within East Boston itself, companies were forced to travel over a mile through one of the tunnels, which were often blocked with traffic. That delayed response could certainly be the difference between life and death and a full-blown conflagration.

Bemis, as well as a large segment of the City population, blamed Mayor Kevin White for using the Police and Fire Departments as political pawns in an attempt to compel the state to provide additional funds to the City to compensate for lost tax revenue. The firefighter's union condemned their Commissioner with a "no confidence" vote and even proposed a strike despite a no-strike clause in their contract.

Morale was crashing. Racial tensions within the firehouses were strained to the limit when the U.S. District Court ordered that minority firefighters be rehired even though they had less seniority than their white colleagues. This order was due to affirmative action policies that bound the City to employ certain minimum levels of minority employees. Many of those black firefighters weren't very happy with the situation either. They realized that they didn't deserve the preferential treatment, but if they wanted a job with the BFD, they had no choice. Work was not fun for anyone amid the racial tension and manpower shortage. Nobody wanted to think about what more could happen on July 1, when Proposition 2½ took full effect. Though major cutbacks in the Police and Fire Departments had already occurred, rumors persisted that worse was to come. The outlook was bleak.

Gregg continued to visit the firehouses where some of his friends remained on the job. He was sickened by the despair that he witnessed in every face. He could see that their spirit had been broken. Dissension was growing daily among the ranks, as it seemed that nothing was being done by the Mayor or the Commissioner to remedy the situation. And Bemis felt the general populace wasn't going to do anything to resolve the problems either.

Boston Police Officer Robert Groblewski was laid off from Boston PD effective July 7, 1981. There were many others laid off on the same date. While he collected unemployment, ironically he worked for a small fire investigation company, getting paid under the table, until March 1982, when Weymouth Police offered him a patrolman's position. In July 1982,

Grobo was reinstated as a patrolman with Boston PD, but although he felt fortunate, the insecurities of the layoff had already done much to his psyche.

On Labor Day weekend in September 1981, Gregg headed to the Boston HoJo's lot. Besides meeting Grobo and Skinny there, Gregg spent time catching up with another buff, Joe Gorman.

Gorman, originally from Dorchester, was the same age as Groblewski and Stackpole. Gorman had had a childhood interest in becoming a firefighter: His father had been a fire buff who used to wake Joe in the middle of the night to head to local fires. When Joe moved from Dorchester, he became a high school classmate and close friend of Stackpole. The two sparked together during those years. Joe became involved with the arson ring conspiracy through his friendship with Donny, and because he enjoyed sparking fires. Stackpole introduced Joe to the others who became members of the arson ring.

As a young man, Joe became a rigger, basically an ironworker, at the Quincy Fore River Shipyard, which had its origins in the late 1800s. Over a century in operation, the shipyard built hundreds of ships for both private and military purposes.

Joe was somewhat of a misfit within the arsonists' group because he had applied to become a Mass State Trooper rather than following his earlier ambitions to become a firefighter. Neither dream ever came to fruition.

Later testimony would reveal that Gorman had been coerced by the group to participate in the conspiracy. He wasn't forced or threatened, but he was chided into going along. Despite being several inches over six feet, Joe was mild-mannered and a somewhat weaker member of the group. The other members told him that they could all be trusted and that nobody would talk. He totally believed this, until he learned otherwise. Gorman remained a fringe participant throughout the reign of the arson ring conspiracy, never becoming a dedicated, hardcore member.

As the sparks were catching up, their conversations were interrupted. "Attention Engine 17, Ladder 7, and Car 7, respond to a building fire at number 10 Holiday Street, reported people trapped in the building, striking Box 3332," sounded over their radios. The buffs tore out of the parking lot, not wasting a moment to speed toward the box. As the sparks neared the scene, District Chief Hurley in Car 7 called Fire Alarm, "Heavy fire showing, working fire." Gregg saw Engine 24 peel around the corner, nearly hitting him and his friends.

The sparks witnessed heavy fire blowing out of every opening on the first floor of the two-and-a-half-story dwelling. Occupants of the building were huddled in their bedclothes crying as they watched the inferno. Reportedly, two children were still missing in the building. Chief Hurley was trying to position the few firefighters he had at his disposal to gain access to the building for a rescue attempt.

With trees and power lines partially blocking the front of the structure, Ladder 7 had difficulty raising its 100-foot aerial into position. The shortage of manpower resulted in too few hands to raise a ground ladder to the upper floor while, at the same time, trying to slow the rapid spread of the fire. Chief Hurley quickly called for a second alarm. Then, astonishingly, the Chief turned to Gregg and his friend and yelled for them to help him raise a ground ladder to the second floor. Without hesitation, Gregg set his camera on the ground, and the two of them assisted the Chief in raising the heavy aluminum ladder to the second floor.

An Engine 52 jake, who responded with the second alarm, climbed the ladder, struggling with a hose line in one hand and an axe in the other. When he reached the second-floor window, he smashed out the glass with the axe. The room immediately transitioned to flashover; flames burst from the window to the exterior, nearly scorching the firefighter, knocking the jake back for a few moments until he could open the nozzle. He washed down the room for a few minutes to absorb the heat, which allowed him to climb into the room while the thick black smoke was still spewing from the window. Gregg witnessed the heroic actions of this firefighter and thought to himself, knowing the effects of such heavy smoke, flames, and high temperatures, that there was no way a child could still be alive in that space.

Ladder 7 finally managed to break some of the tree branches with their immense steel aerial, maneuvering the stick around the power lines to provide access to the roof. With the aid of the second alarm companies to complement the undermanned firefighters, the fire was quickly knocked down.

Bemis watched as two black body bags were carried out of the charred ruins. The victims' family members started screaming in a grievous tone, a sound unlike any he had ever heard before in his life. He felt their anguish. The victims were not yet teenagers. If the layoffs and firehouse closings continued, Gregg mused, there was no doubt in his mind that there would certainly be more senseless deaths like these. Gregg never forgot the looks on the faces of the distraught relatives as the steaming body bags were taken out the front door of what had been a short time before the family home. The remainder of the night passed quietly for Gregg and his friends. They said goodnight and went their separate ways, but their minds kept racing with the events of the night. Their anger and hatred began to transition from the smoldering stage to the incipient flicker of action. Their moment of action was approaching.

Another devastating event shook Bemis again a few weeks later. On Friday, the 13th of November, Bemis, Groblewski, and Stackpole had been in town for some fire action, but it had been so quiet that around midnight they decided to call it a night. Gregg had been westward bound on Soldiers Field Road when Box 5286 was struck. He knew it was a Brighton box nearby, so he pulled a U-turn and immediately saw a column of smoke in the distance. He heard Car 11 reporting heavy fire and smoke showing on Litchfield Street. As Gregg neared the scene, he heard, "Car 11 to Fire Alarm, get me Edison right away. We've got live power lines down on Ladder 14 and we can't use the aerial." Arriving at Litchfield, Gregg saw the massive electrical arcing and sparking. He parked and walked close to the fire. Only a couple of pieces of apparatus were on the scene.

Bemis approached the front of a two-story story dwelling as a firefighter dragged an unconscious victim out the front door. The firefighter was alone with nobody around to assist him, so Gregg ran over to help the jake perform CPR on the victim. They worked on the male to no avail; they couldn't get a heartbeat or a breath. As Gregg looked up, he realized that a second alarm had been called and that additional firefighters were bringing out a second victim. The firefighters managed to get a heartbeat on their patient and moved him into an ambulance for transport to the hospital, but he did not make it there alive. Both victims were males, forever in their forties.

Gregg felt sick as he walked away from the still body now being loaded into a vehicle for transport to the morgue. Shortly thereafter, he overheard an off-duty Boston firefighter say to some bystanders that if Engine 34 had not been closed, this never would have happened, obviously blaming the double fatality on the delayed and shorthanded response. Engine 34's house was only two blocks from the fire. As Gregg pulled away from the site, he turned onto Western Avenue and coincidentally saw Engine 34's firehouse boarded up, "FIREHOUSE CLOSED" painted in large lettering on the old wooden overhead door.

Bemis shook his head in disgust at the sight he would never forgive or forget, finding it hard to imagine that Mayor Kevin White could so callously allow this dangerous situation within the City. It seemed to Bemis that Boston was being run as the Mayor's kingdom; he was the king and the fire and police were his pawns. Even other high-ranking City officials made statements similar to this, providing some validity to Gregg's thinking. Within two months, Bemis had witnessed two fatal fires. He wondered how many more deaths and injuries, and how much severe property damage, the severe cutbacks would cause.

The assist that Gregg had given to the firefighter on this night, and the assist he gave the Chief to raise the ladder a few weeks before, was actually against the code of conduct of Gregg and the rebellious sparks. To help the firefighters in any way was to hurt their cause. If citizens lent a hand every time the firefighters were struggling, the full effect of the layoffs would not be recognized. Many believed that if the firefighters drowned in the crush demanded by the fires, then maybe something would be done by the citizens and politicians to remedy the brutal situation.

Gregg neared home still lamenting the pointless loss of life he had witnessed. It was at this moment that Gregg realized that it would take a lot more than carrying a picket sign in front of City Hall to reverse the injustices being played upon the residents of the City.

These highly personal interactions with the fires and fatalities were too much for Gregg to bear. He was a young and very impressionable, sensitive man. Combined with the trauma in his own life, including his mother's death and his father's neglect, these meaningless deaths that seemingly were the direct result of the cutbacks pushed Bemis to the very edge. The precipice was directly in front of him; he only needed one last thing to push him over the brink. That one thing ironically would be the support of his tight-knit group of sparks. In this case, that support became defined as a conspiracy.

▲

Conspiracy is a strange legal animal. The crime of conspiracy was created to address the inherent dangers posed to society when people band together to commit criminal acts. An individual often does not have the nerve or means to plan and execute the acts necessary for certain crimes, in this case, an arson spree in which 264 buildings are burned over two years. Also, a single person most likely could not have the time, energy, money, or experience to successfully commit such a series of crimes. A single person rarely commits a long series of crimes without accomplices or others' knowledge; there are of course notorious exceptions, such as serial arsonist fire investigator John Orr of California, serial murderer John Wayne Gacy, and innumerable serial rapists.

However, the danger of a conspiracy lurks when a person has a supporting cast who can reinforce one's cravings or grudges and ease one's fears or doubts. The crimes can rapidly multiply and escalate. Conspirators can conceive of more ideas to evade detection and succeed in carrying out the primary crime that is the aim of a conspiracy.

Conspiracy can be generally termed as a partnership in crime. Legally, a conspiracy exists when two or more persons join together and form an agreement to violate the law, and then act on that agreement.

Conspiracy law makes it possible for law enforcement to apprehend and charge conspirators as well as perpetrators of crimes and underlies the prosecution of conspirators, based on the theory of vicarious liability. Members of a conspiracy can become criminally responsible for the reasonably foreseeable actions or omissions of any co-conspirators committed during and in furtherance of the conspiracy. As an example, when a team of bank robbers recklessly brandish firearms during the robbery, the shooting of a police officer or civilian is a foreseeable consequence of the actions of the conspirators. All of the conspirators can be charged with the shooting even though they may not have directly participated in the act. Another principle of conspiracy law is that statements made by co-conspirators during and in furtherance of a conspiracy are not considered hearsay, so the statements can be used at trial against other conspirators.

The Federal crime of conspiracy requires that five conditions exist:

1. Two or more persons
2. intentionally
3. make an agreement
4. to violate Federal law or defraud the United States and subsequently

5. commit an overt act in furtherance of the agreement.

Based on these conditions, the crime of conspiracy is a specific-intent crime. The government must prove that two or more persons intentionally entered into an agreement to commit some criminal offense. An undercover officer and confidential informant would not count as one of the two or more conspirators because they wouldn't have the required criminal intent (condition 2) to commit the specific crime. Likewise, the overt act completed in furtherance of the agreement must occur after the agreement has been made (condition 4).

Significantly, the crime of conspiracy is separate and distinct from the substantive or underlying crime. Thus, a person can be charged and convicted for both the underlying crime and for the conspiracy to commit that crime. The fact that two or more persons agreed to commit a criminal offense is not, in itself, a conspiracy as defined by the law. Some overt act in furtherance of the agreement must be committed after the agreement has been made.

An overt act is an affirmative act performed by one or more of the co-conspirators. Done in furtherance of the agreement, the overt act establishes that the agreement has progressed from words into action. So instead of merely discussing a potential crime, the conspirators have actually taken a step toward making it a reality. The agreement is a prerequisite of the overt act. Once the overt act occurs, the Federal crime of conspiracy has been perfected as defined by Title 18 U.S.C. § 371.

The law also provides that an individual who joins a conspiracy after the initial agreement and overt act, while the conspiracy is ongoing, is legally a co-conspirator. Someone who joins a conspiracy at any time after it has been formed is still criminally responsible for being part of the conspiracy and is also responsible for any reasonably foreseeable criminal acts performed by any of the co-conspirators after and while the person is a member of the conspiracy. However, a person who joined the conspiracy late could not be held criminally responsible for criminal acts committed prior to his joining the conspiracy.

Another important facet of the law acknowledges that a person may withdraw from a conspiracy before its completion. Withdrawal from a conspiracy requires more than merely no longer participating in the scheme. In order to withdraw from a conspiracy, a co-conspirator is obligated to take two affirmative actions. First, the individual must perform an affirmative act that conflicts with the goals of the conspiracy. Unless the co-conspirator can establish quitting the conspiracy, participation in the conspiracy is presumed to continue. Second, the co-conspirator must take an affirmative act that reasonably conveys to a fellow co-conspirator or law enforcement, his withdrawal from the conspiracy. A defendant must prove an affirmative defense of withdrawal from a conspiracy.

This primer on the law of conspiracy clearly applies to the formation, and confirmation, of an agreement between two or more persons to violate Federal law by (i) setting a series of fires in and around the City of Boston and (ii) utilizing an incendiary device to set the fires. The overt acts committed in furtherance of the conspiracy in this case are numerous—as in hundreds of overt acts—and flagrant. As you'll see, some individuals joined the conspiracy late. There were also one or two co-conspirators who harbored some thoughts, but took no affirmative actions, to leave the conspiracy.

This case eventually involved nine individuals who joined in the conspiracy, a fairly large number of members in a not-for-profit scheme. The arson ring conspiracy lasted nearly two and a half years.

This conspiracy, it should be noted, differed in key ways from organized crime such as the Mafia, outlaw motorcycle gangs, or cartel-style drug rings. All of these conspiracies are huge, with dozens to hundreds of members. Their chief goal is to make money in one form or another. And these conspiracies can continue for decades.

Two weeks after the last fatal fire, Bemis met with Stackpole, Groblewski, and Gorman at the HoJo's lot. Gregg parked in a row with other identical black 1978 Chevy Impalas. Others drove Ford LTDs. Their vehicles exactly replicated unmarked police cruisers, all dressed up with blackwall police pursuit radial tires, sway bars, no chrome, and antennas placed in the right positions. Their "nerf" cruisers were so realistic looking that often the State Police and City cops mistook them for comrades in arms. Only Stackpole chose to be the oddball in the group; he drove a red '78 Ford LTD II station wagon.

With no fire action yet, the foursome cruised through the famous Combat Zone to check out the prostitutes and drove through Bay Village to harass gays, but they soon tired of this. Boston's Combat Zone was so nicknamed in the 1960s. This seedy adult entertainment area was a stretch of strip joints, peep shows, and X-rated movie theaters, complete with drugs and prostitution.

To make conversation, Gregg spoke up, "Hey, I caught a flick in Brighton a couple weeks ago. It was a two-bagger on Litchfield Street. Two people got killed."

"Where the hell is Litchfield Street?" Donny showed his lack of knowledge of the streets.

"It's right behind Engine 34's house," Gregg answered.

Bobby interjected, "Well, that's one that 34 didn't get to," referring to the deactivated Engine 34.

Annoyed, Gregg replied, "Yes, that's one of the reasons why the two victims didn't make it."

"Well, if that's what the City wants, so that's what the City gets," Bobby added sarcastically.

"They were so short-handed that I ended up helping them give CPR to one of the victims."

Busting balls, Donny retorted, "Oh, look at the little hero!"

"Fuck you too, Skinny!"

Bobby wondered, "I didn't read anything in the papers."

Bemis answered, "That's because there was just a tiny article. That asshole of a Mayor obviously doesn't want the people to know the adverse effects of his stupid plan to eliminate the Police and Fire Departments." Grobo nodded in agreement.

Stackpole added, "You guys are always getting upset about the cutbacks. Don't you understand that the people don't give a shit about the cops and firemen?" Gregg did not agree. He felt that the majority of people didn't think like that. Stackpole was the only one in the group who had supported the proposal. Donny thought that Prop 2½ would help him afford to build a house. And he hated the Boston police and firefighters, claiming that they were overpaid and underworked. Stackpole's favorite expression was that he would like to see them on their knees. Donny continued, "There's only one thing that will get those guys back and that is a lot of fires and shootings, and what not."

Dejectedly, Grobo said, "Yeah, and if that's the case, I'll never get rehired, not the way it's been so quiet lately." There was not a single fire that night. Slow nights made the men tired, so they called it a night. However, each and every one of them went home with the seed of rebellion firmly planted.

Early in December 1981, Bemis hadn't heard from the guys since their last discussion. Gregg and new Air Force recruit Lenny Kendall drove into the City. Lenny had joined the U.S. Air Force with the hopes of becoming a firefighter in the Air Force. He did achieve that goal. Ultimately, his goal was to use Veterans Preference Points and military firefighting experience to become a full-time civilian firefighter.

Arriving at HoJo's, they saw Bobby's and Joe's cars, but no Bobby or Joe. They found them at the Mobil station at Edward Everett Square in Donny's car. "Hey, follow us," Donny waved out his window. He proceeded to weave through several streets, turning up one, down another. Suddenly, Donny and Joe in the back seat on the driver's side held their hands out of the car windows, each with a brick in his hand. As Donny drove slowly past a parked car, they threw the bricks through the vehicle's windows.

Bemis, at the wheel of his car, turned toward Lenny: "These guys are nuts."

To which Lenny queried, "What are they trying to prove?"

Gregg wasn't sure, but he had a pretty good idea that their actions had something to do with the conversation they'd had the other night. "These guys are nuts if they think I'm going to ride behind them and let someone get my license plate," at which point Gregg headed back to the Mobil station.

Several minutes later, Donny pulled up next to Gregg, exclaiming, "Where did you disappear to? Hop in and we'll show you guys what we did." He had a devious look on his face. In Donny's car, they drove up and down the side streets of Roxbury pointing to all of the windows they had smashed.

"What are you guys trying to do, create your own crime wave?" Gregg asked, with the hint of a smile.

A peeved Groblewski responded, "Fuck it, if the motherfuckers want to lay off all the cops, then they'll just have to do so much paperwork that they can't handle it anymore!" Stackpole pulled up to a vacant lot. Grobo jumped out of the car and grabbed several more bricks. Before he got back into the vehicle, he ran toward a dumpster a few feet away.

Stackpole didn't know what Bobby was up to, but as soon as Grobo lit a match, Donny yelled, "Don't do that you fuckin' idiot!" Bobby extinguished the match.

When Bobby returned to the car, he said, "What the fuck are you so worried about?" It seemed that Donny was more reluctant to get caught with matches than he was with a carload of bricks. They continued to ride around taking turns throwing bricks out of Donny's car, laughing all the way. As the hour turned late, they quit for the night. They had vented their emotions in vandalism and destruction of property; they had committed their first acts of uncivil disobedience.

This brick-throwing continued for several nights with dozens of vehicles damaged per night, but it failed to gain any media attention. They progressed to using a BB gun. It was far easier and faster to shoot out windows than to gather and toss bricks; now they damaged 75 to 100 windows a night. But still no press coverage.

The guys considered their next step and decided to start lighting trash and dumpster fires. Stackpole was initially reluctant: "We can't just go running around lighting dumpsters on fire, people will see us."

"Don't worry about that, I know a perfect device, with no chance of getting seen or caught," said a confident Gregg. "I saw a training film on arson detection a few years ago and they showed a lot of crude devices that could be used as time delays for lighting fires."

"Well, what do we use?" the anticipation was obvious in Donny's voice.

"Simple. A matchbook with a lit cigarette placed between the match heads," explained Gregg. He proceeded to assemble a device and showed them how it worked. The onlookers were amazed and quite pleased by how simple and cheap it was.

This modest device was the first step in violating state and Federal laws relating to the making of an incendiary device. But at that point these guys couldn't have cared less about breaking the law; they had an agenda and, come hell or high water, they were going to follow through with their new objective.

The militant sparks drove to Store 24, where they purchased a box of book matches and a couple packs of cigarettes. Gregg shared a thought, "There is only one problem with fresh cigarettes. Sometimes they burn out if they are not dried out enough, so we'll have to let them sit on a heating vent for a while to dry them up." A short time later Gregg said, "We are now ready to go to work and test the device."

Stackpole suggested, "Let's go try those dumpsters in the Back Bay; the alleys are filled with them." He was referring to the neighborhood between the Boston Public Garden and Boston University near Fenway Park, the home of the Boston Red Sox. This area had neat rows of early 1900s-era stately brownstone (a popular sandstone building material that was actually reddish brown) buildings and row houses that stretched about one and a half miles. The Back Bay was some of the most expensive real estate in the City.

The fronts of Back Bay buildings all faced main thoroughfares, like Beacon Street and Commonwealth Avenue, while the rear of each block was a numbered Public Alley. Dumpsters were parked behind every building for the residents' trash deposits. The boys hoped that enough affluent residents awakened in the middle of the night by enough sirens would complain loudly enough to the Mayor's office that the media would have to cover the hysteria the boys had instigated.

They started in the alleyway between Boylston and Newbury Streets, an area with a commercial flair mixed with residential structures. As they drove, they tossed lit devices into one dumpster after another. By the time they reached the end of the alley behind Engine 33's firehouse on Boylston, they heard a fire radio announcement, "Attention Engine 7, Ladder 17, Car 4. Respond to a dumpster fire." Only a few minutes later, Engine 7 reported several dumpster fires, asking for additional companies.

The aspiring arsonists drove down one of the perpendicular cross streets where they saw at least five more dumpsters blazing away. Almost immediately, more apparatus poured into the area. Gregg thought it must have been obvious to the BFD that somebody was busting their balls. Donny declared, "This is pissa," as they listened to the confusion blaring from the radio.

They added to that mayhem by targeting another stretch of dumpsters a few blocks away from the previous fires. Back Street is nothing more than a glorified alley behind the high-rent Beacon Street addresses running along Storrow Drive and the Charles River. It was one-way heading inbound toward downtown. There were dumpsters on both sides of their vehicle as they drove, so Bobby tossed the devices from one side and Donny threw them from the other side, ending up near the Esplanade, from which Boston's famed July Fourth concert and fireworks emanate.

Gregg suggested, "I think the best place to watch would be from Memorial Drive." This roadway parallels Storrow Drive, but on the Cambridge side of the Charles. It was a magnificent viewing area as the newly lit dumpster fires raged on the opposite side of the river. The group was even more elated by the disorder crackling on the fire radio.

However, these harassment fires failed to create major media attention; dumpster fires were all too commonplace in the City. It became apparent to the players that it would take hundreds of dumpster fires to create any news coverage. In spite of that, they continued these same escapades for the next few weeks into the New Year, 1982.

On Thursday, January 14, 1982, the City of Boston deactivated three more companies, including Engine 49, Aerial Tower 2, and Rescue 2. The total number of deactivated companies now stood at 22. The loss of Rescue 2 was the greatest loss; it left only Rescue 1 active in the City.

Boston Rescue 2 was first organized in 1926. In Boston as in most cities, the Rescue Company is used for most working fires and multiple alarms as it is a highly trained multipurpose company. The Rescue performs ordinary tasks and very intricate operations. Often the workhorse of the Fire Department, the Rescue Company has six major duties to carry out at every working structure fire. These duties include:

1. The all-important search and rescue for trapped people;
2. Forcible entry to allow access to fight the fire;
3. Ventilation of fire, hot gases, and smoke levels to assist with fire control;
4. Control of the utilities such as electric, gas, and water that were active;
5. Salvage, including securing and protecting items within the loss; and
6. Overhaul, the process of searching for and eliminating any possible hidden heat or fire that may reignite.[11]

Rescue 2 had been located on Blue Hill Avenue with Engine 52 and Ladder 29 in Dorchester. This Rescue was considered by many to be the busiest unit in the City. Bemis and his crew knew several of the personnel from Rescue 2. He felt that they were his friends and considered them first-rate jakes. When the first cutbacks were made, R2 had been relocated to Columbus Avenue. To Gregg, visiting R2 was not the same in their new quarters. Ultimately, the loss of Rescue 2 had a profound effect on Gregg.

The conspirators met to discuss this latest round of deactivations. They all berated the City for its unforgivable actions, but they could not agree on an alternative strategy to focus the media on the main issue of the necessity of reversing the cutbacks. They all recognized that setting buildings on fire may be the only option left that would work, but the members of the group postponed this last-resort action; they were not quite ready to

11 Daniel T. Hinkle, FIRE ENGINEERING, Rescue and Squad Operations, 09/01/2005.

take this drastic measure. As the next few weeks went by with no positive changes, they continued to mull over the next step. Finally, in February, they decided that they would target buildings. They did set strict criteria, though; target only abandoned and condemned structures to minimize the possibility of any injuries. Time would tell if they abided by their self-prescribed guidelines.

CHAPTER FOUR

THE ARSONS AND INVESTIGATIVE EFFORTS BEGIN

In March 1982 ATF Headquarters selected the ATF Boston Division as a location to institute an Arson Task Force Group that would assist state and local arson investigators. This was the Federal government's response to the serious arson problem that haunted major urban areas such as Boston. Other task forces were formed in New York, Chicago, and Los Angeles.

I volunteered for the newly formed Arson Task Force Group, also more simply known as the Arson Group. The original members of the Boston Group were Special Agents Terry Barry, Bill Murphy, Dick Cain, John D'Angelo, John Spooner, and Larry Murray. ATF Group Supervisor Jack Dowd rounded out the group.

We were assigned space at the Batterymarch Building, a 14-story 1928 Art Deco office building occupying an entire block in Boston's business district. Ironically, the Arson Task Force Group was housed in the building that once served as headquarters for the National Fire Protection Association, the worldwide organization, established in 1896, devoted to eliminating death, injury, and property and economic loss due to fire, electrical, and related hazards. There were even horse-drawn pumpers in the giant picture windows on the main floor.

Now a little about me. I was conceived in Austria, where my mom grew up. Her high school years were spent in the middle of World War II. She was even in the Hitler Youth as a teenager, not by choice. She married my father, an American postwar soldier. My mom already had given birth to my sister in 1949. They came to the United States late in 1952. I was born in early 1953 at the United States Military Academy Hospital, West Point, New York. I swear the hospital staff taught me how to salute when I was in the crib. My father left six months later, not to be seen again by me until I was 42 years old.

I grew up in a strict household. My stubbornness came to me early in life. I was often reminded that when I was five I ran away from home, but was found sometime later curbside in front of the apartment. "I thought you were running away?" asked my mother. I replied as the obedient person I was to become, "You told me not to cross the street alone."

She married my stepdad when I was five. He was a Rhode Island Italian to the bone, very close to his family. His mom (the only grandmother I ever knew) lived in her house on her own until she was 101, and his two brothers also lived nearby. In 1958 we moved to Coventry, Rhode Island, the largest town in the state, a suburb of Providence.

Loving the outdoors, I grew up playing army in the woods or one of several sports, particularly organized baseball and hockey, when I wasn't doing chores. But those tasks didn't kill me and I learned a lot of skills from my folks that continue to help me to this day. All my siblings had these same responsibilities, including my older sister; my kid brother, born in 1957; and my kid sister, who was born a year later.

I always did well in school, partly because I had some smarts, but I worked hard, reading and studying all the time. I had a goal in mind. In the fifth grade, I wrote to then Rhode Island Congressman John Fogarty about seeking entrance into West Point. I told you I was brainwashed while in the crib. I pursued that dream until I ended up second alternate for the state in 1971 for acceptance into the Academy. The Vietnam War was still raging, as were the debates at home about the war. My draft number that year was something like 153, but the draft only chose men up to number 95 that year. I never went into the military.

By age 13, I started working two jobs every summer. During my senior year in high school, the town formed a task force to address rising drug issues, which back then were minimal compared with the opioid crisis of today. I was asked to represent the student body. I accepted. Being the only teen on the committee was a great experience, except for being labeled a "narc" by some of my classmates. The task force had nothing to do with providing any incriminating information on students; it was only trying to define the scope of the drug problem and suggest some solutions to alleviate it. I never had any thought of being any kind of informant, and no adult had ever asked me for such information. I never had a single thought of going into law enforcement, either, but maybe those who harassed me, accusing me of being a narc, had planted the seed that grew into my eventual career.

I began college in the engineering program at the University of Connecticut. Having always done well in high school math and science, I figured engineering was right up my slide rule. Man, was I wrong. I struggled that first semester. Was I just a big fish from a small school in a bigger pond?

By Christmas break, I was looking elsewhere. I no longer felt engineering was for me. Somehow Popeye Doyle in *The French Connection*, *Dirty Harry*, and later *Serpico* led me to the Criminal Justice program at Bryant College (now Bryant University). I wanted to work undercover, bust organized crime and drug rings, or root out corruption. I loved the CJ program from the beginning to the end. It was fun and exciting to me. It got my juices flowing. And I flourished in the program.

My life circumstances made me a generally decent guy with some passive-aggressive tendencies, traits that played into both my personal life and my investigative mannerisms. I don't think that I ever played the part of the "bad cop" during interviews or interrogations; it wasn't in me. I could never have fooled a bad guy, or myself. Maybe that *Dirty Harry* was right: "A man's gotta know his limits."

Another one of those life circumstances occurred when I took a Winter Session course at Bryant, a drug course taught by the head of the Rhode Island Division of Drug Control. I was into the topic immediately, raising my hand often, asking lots of questions. One day near the end of the course, the instructor asked me if I would like to do some undercover (or UC) work. I jumped at the opportunity.

I did no UC work at Bryant, but I worked at other locations around the state for a year and a half, plus full time the summer before my senior year. I had to make up all sorts of stories for my roommates in order to go out weekends for work. We had minimal success in making good drug cases. Nevertheless, the experience was priceless.

During my senior year, the school held a law enforcement career day. That's when I first heard of the Bureau of Alcohol, Tobacco and Firearms. I mean, who had? BATF was under the Treasury Department along with U.S. Customs, the Internal Revenue Service, and the Secret Service. It had officially only been a Bureau for three years, even though it can trace its origins to the 1790s when the U.S. government first taxed alcohol and tobacco.

So I took the Treasury exam, which makes one eligible for applying to any or all of the Treasury Department agencies. I passed with a score high enough to surpass the scores of many of the military veterans who received a Veterans Preference Program bonus of 10 points.

However, breaking into law enforcement as a career was difficult, to say the least. You just couldn't apply to a local police department (PD), the State Police, or some Federal agency and get hired. One, the agency had to be hiring. Two, you had to take the test for that particular level and, if you passed the test, pass the interview process and the physical. Finally, if you were hired, you had to pass the academy. And if you were good enough and a little lucky to get on the job, then you spent a probationary year in which you could get yourself fired for almost any shortcoming, no questions asked.

Upon graduation from Bryant at the top of my criminal justice class, I had no prospect for a job. It was a very stressful time.

I applied to my local Coventry Police Department, but I never would have been happy confined by the borders of the town. I also applied to the RI State Police, but my chances were slim to none to get hired. I also applied to ATF. I really wanted to work there. I felt it would be a good fit. However, it was all watch and wait and wait some more.

My RI Division of Drug Control contacts helped me get a summer job with the Dennis, Massachusetts, PD, on that glorious playground of Cape Cod. Hundreds of young people worked as cops for one of the dozen towns on the Cape. But my job was different. I worked not in uniform but undercover buying illicit drugs around town, only going to the police station twice all summer. I had a cover job for a while, but otherwise, I hit the beaches and the bars, all with the aim of locating drug dealers. Again, I only had modest success, but the experience was invaluable. It was a great summer; I worked very hard and played equally hard!

I still had no real job and no offers on the horizon. Next up for me was another chance for play combined with a pseudo-enforcement job, but this time in the private sector. It was a semi-break from real law enforcement work, but at least I had a job. I was hired to work in Vermont as night security for Killington Ski Resort, "The Beast of the East," the largest ski resort in the East. For 10-hour night shifts in freezing weather, my job was to check Killington's multi-properties to make sure nothing burned or was vandalized. And yes, it was a great winter, I *only* skied 60 days for free that season, not a bad gig.

Finally, exciting news came in April 1976. ATF called to schedule me for an interview for a Boston, Massachusetts, position. The Boston ATF Division, which covered all of New England, put 40 new Agents on in 1976. I was fortunate to be one of them. It took Boston ATF two more decades to put another 40 Agents on the job.

My first day on the job coincided with the first day of summer, June 21, 1976. I did a fair amount of UC work on the streets of Boston and elsewhere, worked on motorcycle gangs, became a member of the local Latin Kings chapter, and had a 46 machine gun case, as well as making some paper cases against felons with guns. But I knew after three or four years that I wanted more from my career.

So when the Federal government and ATF grew serious about working arson cases, and arson for profit cases, in particular, I got serious about my destiny.

A quick history of the Federal effort on arson and explosions is in order. The Organized Crime Control Act of 1970, Title XI, 18 U.S.C., made arson a Federal crime in a roundabout way. (The Organized Crime Control Act now is referred to as the Comprehensive Crime Control Act.) In particular, 18 U.S.C. § 844(i) outlawed malicious damage or destruction, or attempts to damage or destroy by explosive, of property used in interstate commerce or in any activity affecting interstate commerce.

ATF was the designated agency to work this crime. An interesting aspect of this law was that the property had to be damaged or destroyed by means of an *explosive*. What did that mean to the investigating Agents? Subsection (j) of 18 USC § 844 defines "explosives" as any chemical compound mixture, or device, the primary or common purpose of which is to function by explosion; the term includes, but is not limited to, dynamite and other high explosives, black powder, pellet powder, initiating explosives, detonators, safety fuses, squibs, detonating cord, igniter cord, and igniters.

At the time, investigators had to prove that an explosive or a bomb was used to damage or destroy the property. This was often difficult. From approximately the 1970s until 1982, an explosive may merely have been the utilization of gasoline, or a similar ignitable or flammable liquid, that when used in sufficient quantity in a defined room or compartment in the presence of an ignition source, whether inherent to the premises or introduced, such as an open flame, could explode. Of course, if an explosion did occur at the loss site, then we only had to determine the origin and how it occurred; that is, the cause. If no actual explosion had occurred, but we determined that a fuel such as gasoline had been used, then we had to perform calculations to prove the elements of the crime.

With cases being so difficult to perfect, prosecutions under this limiting statute were few and far between. Then something so simple but so significant occurred. In the early 1980s, the Federal government took a tougher stance on the war on crime. President Ronald Reagan and Congress called for tougher Federal solutions by federalizing crimes that were often thought of as local crimes that would normally be under state jurisdiction.

In October 1982, President Reagan signed into law the Anti-Arson Act of 1982, which amended the Federal criminal code to extend the coverage of offenses involving the use of explosives to include the use of fire. The change to the law, and the manner how arsons would be investigated by the Feds from that day forward, involved the addition of just two words—"of fire," This is the statute, 18 U.S.C. § 844(i) as it read after the change in the law:

Whoever maliciously damages or destroys, or attempts to damage or destroy, by means **of fire** [emphasis added] or an explosive, any building, vehicle, or other real or personal property used in interstate or foreign commerce or in any activity affecting interstate or foreign commerce …

Those two added words affected not only the Federal investigators, but also the efforts of state and local authorities. This gave the Feds the opportunity to easily assist state and local authorities, which often lacked the funds, the expertise, or the time to handle the more complex cases. Relative to the fire origin and cause, the where and how the fire occurred, we could now work a fire when an explosive had not been used.

One other critical phrase that differentiated Federal jurisdiction from the locals' abilities to make an arson case related to the commerce clause. That phrase refers to the fact that the burned property had to be used in, or affect, interstate or foreign commerce. The statute is rare because the character of the property, rather than the type of activity, activates Federal criminal jurisdiction.[12] That clause meant that Federal Agents generally could not investigate a fire and bring the case to Federal court unless the property or a business within that property was used in, or affected, interstate or foreign commerce.

Usually, this mandate was fairly easy to prove. Almost any business that bought or sold anything that crossed state lines qualified as affecting interstate commerce. Examples include restaurants that buy meat or eggs or Heinz Ketchup from out of state; a machine shop that purchased its metals from out of state, then sold the finished product in other states or countries; or a clothing store whose inventory included items made outside the jurisdiction. However, when a building burned, it no longer had the ability to affect interstate or foreign commerce because it was out of business. This is the gist of commerce clause within Federal jurisdiction. An example of a building that did not affect interstate or foreign commerce, as dictated by the courts, was a single-family house, even though most of the products used in the building of a house, or the electricity and gas used to power and heat the house, came through interstate commerce.

---

12 Thomas J. Egan, Urban Law Annual; Journal of Urban and Contemporary Law, Volume 48, The Jurisdiction Element of 18 U.S.C. § 844(i): A Federal Criminal Commerce Clause Statute, January 1995.

What did this all mean to me working in Boston? How did the Federal arson laws change my destiny? When ATF started the Arson Task Force Groups, I volunteered for the Boston Arson Group because the gun work and undercover cases were not satisfying me. With an arson investigation, there was always a puzzle to be solved. During any single investigation, besides working the fire scene itself, interviews of witnesses could include a homeless person, a cab driver, a business owner, insurance personnel, and bankers. I totally enjoyed trying to put all of the pieces together. I worked fire cases as a street agent from March 1982 until my retirement from ATF in 2001.

▲

Arsons occur for numerous reasons or motives. The main focus for ATF was on arson-for-profit cases, wherein property owners would intentionally burn their building to collect insurance money, get the insurance company to pay for planned renovations, or get out from under a debt, such as back taxes.

Sometimes the profit motive was related to removing a business competitor or burning older buildings to displace tenants so that a rental unit could be made into a condominium. Sometimes, entire tracts of older buildings were burned to make way for new development. All of these illegal acts became a business decision for business owners who had never committed a criminal act in their lives before. There are thousands of fairly new buildings in this country that you, as an everyday citizen, would never know had been built from insurance proceeds received after the previous building at that location had been intentionally burned.

Since many citizens aren't fond of insurance companies, arson-for-profit is often thought to be a "victimless crime," that is, arson of a building, wherein no injuries or deaths occur, doesn't hurt anybody but the insurance companies who have plenty of money. Well, don't be fooled, folks; of course, the insurance companies pass those losses onto you in terms of higher policy premiums.

There are several other motives for intentionally setting fires. Revenge fires are set as retaliation for real or perceived slights, drug deals gone bad, or domestic violence, or by someone aggrieved by some government or religious action. Fires are set to conceal other crimes such as theft, tax evasion, or murder, in an effort to get rid of the evidence by burning it. People set fires intentionally as very destructive acts of vandalism, the mischievous or malicious act that causes damage to property. Fires are set by thrill-seeking arsonists for excitement, recognition, attention, and sometimes for a feeling of power or sexual satisfaction. Extremist fire-setting is a form of civil unrest used to further political, social, or religious causes; terrorism is included in this category.

By 1982 Boston had already been burning for a decade, averaging between 900 and 1,000 "suspicious," "incendiary," "undetermined," and "vandalism" fires per year resulting in $16 million to $20 million in property damage, in 1982 dollars. Over 200 people had died with over 600 injuries in Boston over those 10 years. During that same time frame, only about nine percent of reported arsons resulted in arrests, with less than two percent ending with convictions.[13] These were some of the main reasons why Boston was chosen as a Task Force city.

As stated earlier, ATF primarily concentrated on working potential arson-for-profit cases. These cases could be complicated, costly, multi-jurisdictional investigations. Hence, these types of investigations were often beyond the means of the state and local authorities. Thanks to the Federal government, ATF had access to the necessary training, money, and nationwide coverage, just as the FBI has the ability to handle investigations that exceed state and local jurisdictions' capabilities.

However, ATF ended up working on arson investigations relating to fires set for every type of motive, not just arson-for-profit. It's just natural.

13 James P. Brady, "Why Boston Is Burning," *Boston Globe Magazine*, October 23, 1983, pp. 49–50.

We would never just show up and take control of an investigation; that was never our way. We often waited to be asked to assist by a jurisdiction in need. Other times we would call an agency immediately after a major event to offer our assistance.

Protection of one's jurisdiction and primary recognition always had to be respected. I soon realized that if I screwed anybody, my reputation was on the line. Sometimes, Headquarters or the front office, referring to the SAC, Special Agent in Charge, would tend to screw their own street Agents—in other words, throw us under the bus and put us in bad positions, such as when they went to the media without the locals being represented. We street guys had to work hard to overcome these missteps.

▲

The first-line supervisors in bureaucratic agencies such as ATF seemed to me to be the worst job in such agencies. They had to deal with the deficiencies, the personalities, and problems of the eight to 10 people they managed. They also had to stem the tide of crap that flowed downhill from the front office, as we referred to the Special Agent in Charge (SAC) and Assistant Special Agent in Charge (ASAC), and their associated administrators. To me, I never particularly wanted to move up; the extra pay couldn't entice me.

I found Supervisor Jack Dowd easy to get along with, as he was affable and a stand-up boss who had the backs of his Agents. Jack was a Middletown, Rhode Island, native. After high school graduation, he did active service in the Navy. Jack was talked into going to college instead of staying with the Navy.

After completing his degree at Providence College, Jack's interest in life was to serve the public in some way. A career in law enforcement beckoned. Just when he was about to become a Secret Service Agent, in 1969 he was offered a position with the Alcohol, Tobacco and Firearms Division of the Treasury Department. Jack felt that he could be a "true"

Federal investigator, one who follows leads, uses informants, and improvises to perfect criminal cases.

Dowd stood over six feet tall, but he seemed larger in stature, as he nearly filled a doorway. With a roundish face and a head of curly hair, people sometimes underestimated his talents, but he had a lot on the ball, becoming a Group Supervisor after only six years on the job. He held that position in Boston, until his retirement in 1999.

His first group in 1976 worked mainly illegal firearms cases since Boston was named one of the Concentrated Urban Enforcement (CUE) cities, wherein ATF worked with state and local authorities to help stem illegal gun dealing and possession. I was in that group when I worked on the streets, trying to buy illegal guns. I had gone to Bryant College with Jack's kid brother, Rick.

During 1982, Arson Group Supervisor Dowd met often with the heads of the State Fire Marshal's Office and with Boston Arson Squad Chief John "Jack" White. Living up to his name with a full head of white hair, Chief White was a tough, but fair, career Boston firefighter. He soon recognized that the fires were a problem both for the City and for him personally. Jack Dowd realized the same issues. If something wasn't resolved soon, the citizens of the City would revolt. The Mayor would feel the heat and, as the saying goes, crap rolls downhill. The heads of the investigation units would not only look bad, but they would most likely be re-assigned. Before that happens, the street guys—that is, the front-line investigators—would be pressured to make criminal cases, to arrest those responsible for the fires.

Generally, law enforcement agencies, which included the Boston Arson Squad, though technically part of the fire department, tended to protect their turf. It took work, but both Jacks hashed out a good, trusting relationship that bridged two somewhat competing organizations. Both bosses realized that they needed each other and each other's agency's resources.

Supervisor Dowd felt that Boston FD was really good at physically putting out fires, but its investigative end was somewhat lacking. It wasn't the Squad members' fault. It was an issue with the City. Fire investigation was often an afterthought; after all, money had to be spent to keep the brakes working on the trucks for the fire companies to do their job of protecting life and property. The main job was to fight fires. Investigations were not traditionally a fire department function. The police conducted investigations. The problem was, the police didn't know anything about fires.

During the early 1980s, fire origin and cause training of many local departments was somewhat deficient. Even though City fire investigators saw more fires than most, they were essentially trained by the older guys, who had little to no scientific background to apply to a fully competent origin and cause investigation. That's the way most fire scene work was in those days for most fire investigators, not just in Boston, but everywhere. Untested myths and theories about fire origin and cause analysis were passed down from generation to generation until the latter part of the 1980s. Boston, like so many other municipalities, just didn't focus its resources on its Arson Squad in the earlier years.

In spite of what he saw as deficiencies, every time Supervisor Dowd left the Boston Fire Department, he let them know that we were all the same, that nobody was any better than anyone else. We were all on the same level trying to do the same job. We ate at the same table. We all got dirty the same way digging fire scenes. We all learned from one another's different specialties and experiences. We were all after the same thing—to solve the arson problem and take care of the firefighters and the citizens of Boston.

Jack Dowd found Chief White to be a very professional, stand-up guy. As the fires progressed throughout 1982, Chief White was under increasing pressure, giving him constant heartburn. Chief White was also leery of ATF wanting to take over the entire investigation, and rightly so, without having direct knowledge of the workings of a Federal agency. Who hasn't watched TV shows where the Feds were complete A-holes who always took but never gave? Most of those shows were about the FBI. Chief White needed to be part of the entire investigation as the boss of his unit. The best way to reassure him would be to share everything that was happening, to keep the lines of communication open at all times.

Thanks to the abilities and attitudes of both men, White and Dowd, a relationship developed between the two groups that worked pretty well during the life of this investigation, with one exception—one major hiccup.

▲

Serial arson investigations are another unique animal. There are serial criminals at virtually every level of crime—serial robbers, serial rapists, serial murderers, and even serial bombers, among the more common miscreants. A serial crime is by definition repetitive, committed multiple times over a period of time, but that time could be defined as hours, days, weeks, or months, and infrequently the repetition of the crime could be spread over years. Although I have reviewed material on the serial nature of murderers or rapists in the fascinating but disturbing book Obsession by retired FBI profiler John Douglas and Mark Olshaker, my knowledge of the workings of those particular sets of criminals is limited. The following comments relating to those types of cases are mere simplifications intended for comparison with serial arson cases, where my experience is more extensive.

The habitual nature of the specific crime is completed with some sort of methodology and signature. For a rapist, multiple victims may be targeted in each case within a first-floor apartment where a window was open, or underwear may be taken from each victim as a trophy. For a murderer, victims may always be strangled or stabbed or always dumped or staged in a specific manner. A bomber's signature is usually the materials used and the methods of building the explosive device.

Almost all serial criminals establish some sort of pattern, sooner or later, depending on the smarts of the offender and the frequency of his acts. The patterns encompass the locations involved; the days and times the crimes are committed; the tools, materials, or arrangements surrounding the victim; and whether that victim is a person or building.

The serial criminal's motivations run the gamut. A serial rapist's motives, among others, often relate to power and control over the victim, the need to overcome inadequacies, abusive sexual satisfaction, or revenge for some real or perceived wrong in the past. The motive of a serial robber is fairly easy to establish—money, except when the robber feels that a certain financial institution has wronged the individual. In that instance, the thief may target numerous branches of the same bank. It is often more difficult to identify the motive of a serial murderer. Love, love triangles, falling out-of-love rather than divorce, money (greed), drugs, anger, and revenge are the more common motivations for premeditated murder. Random murders, killing for the sake of killing, are especially tough cases to investigate.

Establishing the motive of a serial murderer can be a most difficult task. When the first murder occurs and the suspect is not immediately identified, the investigators have to consider all possibilities, trying to narrow the motivation to assist in solving the crime. Then, when a second murder occurs, they have to go through the same process, although similarities to the previous murder may narrow the process. If the murders occur within the same jurisdiction, any similarities may be noted so that when another murder transpires, the investigators may realize they have a serial murderer on their hands. But if the murders happen in multiple jurisdictions spread over time, the motive of a serial murderer can be difficult to ascertain until the multiple acts are connected. Once the acts are associated, usually through the ritualistic nature of the crime and evidence, then the investigation can focus on possible perpetrators. The Boston Strangler case was a perfect example of this process.

So what makes the serial arson investigation and the serial arsonist different from other serial offenders? When the first fire happens, the responding investigators have to determine the origin (where the fire began) and the cause of the fire. Once the fire origin is defined, potential ignition sources within that area must be identified, examined, and, if possible, scientifically eliminated or confirmed as being the heat source responsible for the fire, leaving only one ignition scenario as the fire cause.

Fire cause is defined as identifying the competent ignition source and the first fuels ignited, plus the circumstances that brought the fuel and ignition source together. There are numerous accidental causes, such as unattended cooking, improper disposal of smoking material, and electrical or appliance failures. There are also a handful of natural fire causes, such as lightning or an earthquake's rupture of gas lines that ignites a structure.

When a fire occurs, a great deal of the evidence relating to the cause of the incident is often destroyed, depending on the size and intensity of the fire and the amount of destruction to the building. Destruction of evidence comes in many forms, including the fire itself, the water put on the fire by the firefighters, the collapse of the building or portions of the building, and the overhaul and clean-up after the fire. Extensive loss of evidence is not typical in cases of rape (if reported timely), murder (if the body is readily discovered), or bank robbery. The evidence in bombings, despite what offenders and the general public may think, is almost always found and identified as a result of a thorough scene examination, although the evidence does not look like it did in its original form and usually is in little pieces. Once the evidence in a bombing case is collected, the bomb and its components can often be traced.

In this particular arson case, with the Bemis-inspired incendiary device, one can see how difficult it would be to locate any evidence of the paper lunch bag, the tissue, the plastic baggie, the cigarette, or the matchbook. Each of these components would be unidentifiable after, and more likely substantially consumed by, a fire of any sizable magnitude. Since the

Coleman Lantern Fuel is not poured onto any surface within the building, it is not absorbed by any substrate, such as carpeting or wood flooring. Also, the liquid does not have the opportunity to seep into cracks or crevices where it may not be consumed by fire. When the plastic bag is compromised by the incipient fire within the lunch bag, the liquid vapors are quickly ignited, with a flash fire ensuing. Consumption may not be complete, but the investigators will have to be in the immediate point of origin in order to take a debris sample that can be laboratory tested in an attempt to identify the accelerant. Accelerant detection canines did not come into use until 1986.

Before an intentionally set fire can be identified as being one fire within a string of intentionally set fires, similar to in a serial murder case, an attempt to identify the motive for the fire must be undertaken. The ownership of a building or business must be checked out, as well as disgruntled employees or recently fired employees, competitors, enemies, financial situations, et cetera, et cetera; one can't rush to judgment. So many angles have to be examined to be able to identify a suspect.

If, and when, the scene evidence supports the conclusion that the fire was caused by an incendiary act, the investigators must then try to identify who is responsible for setting that fire. For fire #2 and fire #3 within a string of fires, the fire origin and cause must be identified each and every time. This differentiates arson from the other serial crimes; a rape and a bank robbery are rather easy to identify as such, as is a bombing. Usually, a death can be identified as a murder, often at the scene itself, or in the Medical Examiner's office.

If a series of fires can be related, then investigators could start to look into the fires as a serial crime. One or several motives may be theorized. Even when there is evidence to support a certain motivation behind the fire-setting, it still can be extremely difficult to identify one or more suspects. It is rare to find DNA (in 1982, impossible) or fingerprints at an arson scene, but these two key forms of physical evidence are often present at other types of crime scenes. Sometimes, tire tracks and footprints assist at fire scenes. These items can be preserved for comparison in the event that a suspect is identified, possibly providing a direct link to a suspect.

Should a suspect be ascertained, then an entirely new phase of the investigation begins. Several different investigative tactics must now be employed to establish the evidence necessary to perfect a case against the perpetrator(s). Surveillance, both physical and electronic, as well as tracking devices can be utilized, interviews can be conducted, and informants can be used.

In the following two years, we in the Boston Arson Task Force along with Boston Fire and the State Fire Marshals worked through the individual fire scenes and utilized numerous investigative steps to put this case together. It was a long, tiring, and arduous task. The investigators made some missteps along the way, as did the arsonists. This is understandable on both sides since we both had recently broken new ground. The arsonists were not experienced in the method and scale of crime that they were perpetrating. The investigators previously had not been involved in this type of investigation. Yes, we were all experienced investigators, but there still was a learning curve relating not only to arson investigations per se, but also to a serial arson investigation of this unique nature.

While we were forming our new group of investigators in the office, the crew of arsonists had no knowledge of our existence, nor did they care to know. Just two weeks after their first successful building fire, Bemis and Kendall met up with their cop friend, Groblewski, at HoJo's parking lot around 9:00 p.m. Gregg had enough supplies in the trunk of his car to keep them well-stocked should they choose to burn numerous targets. "Hey, Bobby, what's up?" asked Gregg. "I brought the stuff."

"Good, it looks like the only way we are going to get any action is with that stuff." Grobo was growing impatient with no fire activity. They looked for new targets in the Codman Square area of Dorchester, where long-time friend and spark associate Elliot Belin lived.

Elliot was an older small, mostly bald man with thick dark glasses whose appearance led one to think of a mole. Since he stayed out all hours of the night, the mole persona seemed to fit perfectly. Elliot had other distinctive qualities. He was basically the granddaddy of Boston fire information and the sparks during this generation. He knew fires, the fire companies, and the fire box locations, and he had unbridled access to Boston Fire Headquarters as a non-employee who did more for the administration than many of the paid staff. Elliot was a white man living in a predominately minority neighborhood, but he never complained of ever having any issues living there, and he never considered moving from the community. The area was a battle-scarred zone, infested with decrepit, empty dwellings.

The threesome noted suitable targets, but since they had to ensure that they could commit their deeds undiscovered, they waited until after midnight. Groblewski suggested, "Let's get one of the vacant triple-deckers across from Elliot's place. Let's park right over there and make a device," he added, pointing to an area between the buildings on Norfolk Street with easy access to the rear of the target building. Gregg knew that Grobo just wanted to bust Elliot's balls, so he didn't argue with him, although he knew there were better targets. After making the incendiary, Gregg and Bobby headed out while Lenny elected to remain in the car to stand guard.

Showing their knowledge of the terrain in and around Boston, they traversed an overhead walkway to the street on the opposite side of railroad tracks. There, they eyed two vacant duplex three-family buildings. The rear porches had been removed from both structures, which had been securely boarded up, but Bobby spotted a hole in the wall where they managed to finagle the device and ignite it. They returned to the car via the same pathway.

They drove around and passed by their target several times, but still there was no sign of fire. "Hey, Bobby, why don't we park on Ballou Avenue and walk over the footbridge? We should be able to see if it's going from there," Gregg proposed. He and Bobby exited the car, climbed the steep concrete stairs over the tracks, and made their way to the rear of the building. From this vantage point, they observed light smoke and saw that the hole was now enlarged and glowing. Gregg had another idea: "Alright, it's going, but we'll have to get another one going or Elliot will smell this one and report it."

"Okay," Bobby suggested, "let's go get that three-decker on Leston Street that we just looked at." This area was ripe with three-family dwellings that were so popular around 1900. Gregg readily agreed. Lenny did not say much. It was becoming obvious to the others that he was a little more scared than he wanted to show, perhaps realizing the criminal nature of their conspiracy. As they parked, Bobby asked, "Lenny, do you want to go in with us on this one or do you want to sit in the car so we won't have to lock it?"

"I'll stay in the car," he responded. Bobby just gave Gregg a look and shrugged.

"Okay, keep your head down, Lenny, so the natives don't see you." Bobby and Gregg both had on their heavy green Army jackets since it was one of those nasty cold early March nights.

As they walked down Leston, a group of several young black guys came out of a side street and spotted the two white guys. From about 50 feet away, one of them yelled, "Hey, you Honkies, what the fuck you doing in our neighborhood? You looking to get stabbed?"

Immediately realizing they were in a tight spot, and showing their devious versatility, Gregg opened his collar and acted as if he were talking into a jacket lapel-mounted microphone, "Bravo 326 to Operations ..." he said into his faux radio.

The young men turned and walked away, muttering, "Hey man, let's get out of here, it's the heat."

Bobby smiled at Gregg, "That was quick thinking." They continued on their quest, vigilant to avoid being seen. After hiding in the bushes for a few minutes, they tried the front entrance of the dilapidated house only to find that the front stairs and porch were too badly deteriorated to enter. They weaved through scattered debris in the yard, where they found a basement door wide open.

Using Bobby's flashlight to illuminate the pitch black basement, they instantly got excited when they saw the treasure trove of brush, wood, and trash piled nearly to the ceiling, a great secondary fuel for their purposes. "Holy shit, look at this," Bobby exclaimed. "Wow, this place will go up like a Roman candle! Let's put the device right here and get the fuck out of this place." Placing the device within the pile, they lit it, quickly departed, and returned to the car, where Lenny was still crouching in the back seat. "This place is going to take off," Bobby advised Lenny as they drove out of the neighborhood.

Upon heading back to the first fire set, they saw a slight haze in the night sky, a sign that the fire was cooking inside the building. They parked in an empty shopping plaza across from Engine 16's house on Gallivan Boulevard to await the action. After several more minutes with no call for either fire, they drove the few blocks to check on the Leston Street fire. As they came over a rise on Morton Street, a tall column of smoke was rising from the building. "It's going, look at all that smoke," Gregg said animatedly. "Good, let's go back to Engine 16's house and wait."

Another 15 minutes elapsed before Bemis saw a taxi race into the firehouse parking lot. "Bobby, look, that hack must be reporting the fire!" Sure enough, moments later, all of the lights came on in the firehouse and the overhead doors yawned open. Engine 16 and Car 8 roared out of the firehouse heading toward the fire. The boys traveled in the same direction, following at a safe distance. "Car 8 to Fire Alarm."

"Fire Alarm answering Car 8."

"Strike the box, we have heavy smoke showing on Leston Street."

Waiting a few minutes so as not to arouse suspicion, the arsonists pulled into the scene. Heavy smoke was pouring from the building, with flames blowing out the basement door that they had used just a short time before. Car 8 called for a second alarm. The boys took a few photos as the flames raced up the front of the structure. The photos would be among the earliest of their collection of photographic trophies that they would eventually amass. They waited for Elliot Belin, knowing he had not missed a single multiple alarm fire in the City unless he had car trouble, and even that didn't always stop him. Like clockwork, he showed up minutes later. As they talked to him, they were hoping that the fire they set earlier on Norfolk Terrace would come in, just to bust his balls in their little game. They might as well have extra fun while promoting their cause.

After what seemed like hours, they grew impatient and left to check on the Terrace again. Quite a bit of smoke was showing as the eastern sky lightened. Finally, the box struck for the Terrace. As apparatus converged on the fire, the guys parked their car and observed heavy fire blowing out the rear of the building.

Due to the congested area, second and third alarms were quickly transmitted. Norfolk Terrace was a tough place to stage apparatus as it was a very narrow and short street with only two houses on both sides and a tall fence at the end of the road by the railroad tracks. The fire was quickly knocked down, but the long-term burning within the structure had taken its toll on the building. It would have to be torn down.

As the sun came up, the guys headed back to HoJo's to drop Bobby at his car. He stated with satisfaction as he parted, "Well, that was a pretty good night if you ask me."

Gregg smiled at his friends. Lenny responded, "Yeah, I think we are getting the point across alright." Even though it was a long night, Lenny and Gregg decided to have breakfast at HoJo's to celebrate their successful fires before heading home.

Several days after their two-fire night, Thursday, March 11, Bemis, Grobo, and Stackpole agreed to meet in town. Gregg searched for Bobby, finding his car parked in front of the old three-story firehouse of Engine 24 and Ladder 23 in Grove Hall. Upstairs, Bobby was shooting the bull with a couple of jakes in the kitchen. After some more small talk, they headed out to look for Donny. As he exited, Grobo saluted his Boston buddies. "Take it easy, guys. We'll see you at the big one." He should have been a psychic.

They found Stackpole at HoJo's, who asked, "Hey, Gregg, where is Lenny?"

"He's leaving for boot camp in the morning, so we won't see him for a while," Gregg replied, referring to Kendall's entering the U.S. Air Force.

Bobby pushed them back to the present. "Gregg, did you bring the target list with you?"

"Yeah, I've got it right here." Gregg had been busy. They all would be busy shortly on this mission. This new progression in their program provided a neat list of vacant and abandoned structures that filled their needs without a lot of time wasted seeking out targets. Each member of the group, during their everyday travels, was tasked with tabulating a list of suitable objectives. Besides being empty, the targets had to be easily accessible, with escape routes. They had to be in certain areas so that they could spread the firefighters out and extend response times. Often, the buildings had the favored "gas shingles" as firefighters often referred to the old asphalt exterior siding.

"We have to make sure we do one near Engine 21's house. Mike Mullane just got elected as the union president and he said that things are going to be different now that he is president," Bobby explained referring to Boston Firefighters Local 718.

Donny wanted to know, "Yeah, so what does that have to do with us?"

"Because he is the Lieutenant on Engine 21 tonight and a good job in the area will give him that much more to piss and moan about," reasoned Grobo.

"Where did you find all this out, at Grove Hall?"

"Yeah, and that's not all. That former Fire Chief from New York City is supposed to be around for the next couple of weeks doing a City-funded survey on whether or not Boston has adequate fire protection and manpower since the layoffs."

Gregg commented, "Good, we'll show him how bad things really are."

After reviewing their target list, they chose a vacant three-decker on Brookford Street in Roxbury. Once parked near that location, the boys made an incendiary device in the car. All three made their way down the street into the front yard. This building was secured with windows and doors boarded over, but it was sided with gas shingles. They simply placed the lit device against the gas shingles on the old wooden rear porch and departed for their car. By the time they reached the car, a small glow was visible behind the building.

In order to establish an alibi, they rushed to the Mobil gas station in Edward Everett Square so that other sparks could see them there. Within minutes, Boston Fire Alarm transmitted the alert tone for the box at the fire location. Bemis and company approached Engine 21's house on Columbia Road. The Engine charged out of quarters en route to the fire. The boys fell in behind Engine 21 as it picked up speed. As they approached the scene, a shower of embers and flames flowed into the sky. The radio blared, "Engine 21 to Fire Alarm. Heavy fire showing, on orders of Lieutenant Mullane, strike a second alarm."

Gregg parked away from the fire to avoid getting trapped by the apparatus. After hopping out of the car, they witnessed the fully involved building, with fire spreading to a second occupied triple-decker via convection, radiation, and floating embers. The asphalt shingles provided enormous readily available fuel to the fire as the heat and flames moved upward, volatizing the shingles into a flaming sheet. When Car 7 pulled up, the Chief immediately called for a third alarm, with a fourth alarm soon following.

Groblewski got busy, snapping photo after photo (remember, they used film cameras in the early '80s) of the roaring fire. Donny was beside himself: "Look at that fucking thing go!" They all were amazed by the fire's quick growth. It was easily the largest fire in their short history of arson setting.

After a while, they departed from the scene and called it a night, quite satisfied with themselves. The former Chief from New York who they hoped would catch the fire was actually away for the weekend and missed it. But the fire did make the newspapers, much to the delight of the arsonists. Their plan was beginning to succeed.

Sometimes you win, sometimes you don't. On Monday, March 15, 1982, Bemis swapped a shift at Stow dispatch to have a night off. He agreed to meet Groblewski at HoJo's about 9:00 p.m., but when he arrived at the parking lot, Bobby was nowhere to be seen. As he waited, a box struck for a Back Bay address. Since it was an area not usually noted for fires, Gregg initially ignored it until Engine 33 reported smoke showing upon arrival. Gregg headed to the St. Botolph Street fire, where he thought Bobby would probably show up.

When he arrived, heavy smoke was showing from the top floor of the four-story apartment building, quickly followed by heavy fire. Four alarms were struck in short order. Grobo finally showed up at the scene.

Grobo asked, "You didn't do this one, did you?"

"No, but what do you think about giving them something else for good measure? If we were to set one now, there would still be a lot of companies tied up here," Gregg reasoned. He really wanted to keep the BFD busy to prove their point.

"Sounds good to me, let's go." They found an abandoned three-and-a-half-story dwelling in Roxbury. A device was placed on the rear porch, but this time the siding was wood, not the more combustible asphalt shingles.

After a few minutes they spotted ignition of the device, but it only burned for a short time before a passerby spotted it and pulled a fire box. The device failed to catch the building on fire. A little frustrated, and a lot disappointed, the boys figured that was enough for the night.

▲

Thursday, March 18, 1982, was destined to only have successes. On this night, Joe Gorman met with Stackpole, Grobo, and Bemis. With his boyish eagerness, Gregg loaded his camera with film anticipating a busy night of fire-setting.

When he arrived at the lot, Bemis was surprised to find them all waiting for him, even the ever-tardy Stackpole, who asked, "Hey, did you bring some of the juice?"

Proudly, Gregg responded, "Sure, I brought a whole gallon!" They aimed for Dorchester and chose a target from their list. According to Gregg, it was a "beauty"; an oversized three-story duplex on Thetford Street near Elliot's house. They were excited by the dilapidated condition of the building. They returned to the parking lot so that Donny and Joe could go in a separate car to be lookouts. The device was prepared in the HoJo's lot before returning to the target.

Bobby and Gregg gingerly crept through the bushes and debris in the yard, avoiding piles of broken glass so as not to make too much noise, as nearby houses were occupied. They were pleased when they found the rear door torn off, providing easy access. Just then a loose board loudly cracked as they heard two people entering the adjacent home. Gregg motioned for Bobby to freeze in place, but they had not been noticed.

Immediately finding a pile of trash and discarded lumber inside the doorway, they placed and lit the device. They hurried back to Gregg's car and away from the scene, not realizing that he had not turned on his headlights. Donny and Joe missed them as they went by. Within a few minutes, Fire Alarm transmitted, "On Box 3428, receiving calls for a building fire at number 87 Thetford Avenue. Okay Car 8?"

As Car 8 responded, Bobby and Gregg wondered how the fire had gotten going so fast that it had been reported. They questioned whether it was going to be a "good" fire or a "shit" fire.

Both firefighters and fire buffs have an unusual view of fires, not in insensitive terms, but just as a person who has an interest in the business of fires. A "good" fire is one that takes off, spreading within a structure with a great deal of visible flames. It also entails a certain amount of strenuous work by firefighters, often with good firefighting techniques used to control the raging blaze. On the other side of the coin is the "shit" fire, which never actually takes hold with little spread. These fires tend to be smoky, with little to no flames showing. Firefighters usually don't have to put forth much effort to subdue the fire, but they have to deal with the smoke and overhaul, checking for any hidden fire in void spaces such as the ceilings and walls. These two groups, sparks and firefighters, both appreciate a "good" fire. Victims of the fire do not.

Thetford Street was a good fire. Engine 16 observed heavy fire showing upon arrival and immediately called for a second alarm. When Gregg and Bobby pulled onto Thetford, they were awestruck to see flames lit up the entire street and shoot 60 feet above the roof. It was incredible how fast this fire had erupted into a full-blown inferno. Bemis started shooting pictures, having completely forgotten about the whereabouts of Donny and Joe. After a third alarm was struck, all of the boys caught up in front of the fire building. "Some look-outs you guys are," Gregg chuckled as he busted balls.

"We were just sitting there and all of a sudden I saw a reflection in my rear view mirror. When I turned to look, the whole place was going!" Joe exclaimed. They laughed and joked around for a bit as they watched the fire. They decided to leave because there were too many people around. As they walked down Thetford, Gregg spotted Boston Fire Lt. Steve McLaughlin walking toward the fire. Gregg knew McLaughlin from his visits to the guys on Rescue 2. When the Rescue was transferred, Steve had transferred to the Arson Squad. Now, he was also about to become a deputized member of the newly formed Federal ATF Arson Task Force Group. Nonchalantly, as if just two friends in passing, Gregg said, "Hi Steve, how's it going?"

The Lieutenant replied, "Not bad," as he headed to begin his investigation of the fire. If he only knew he was inches away from the culprits.

Once they maneuvered out of the now congested neighborhood, the arsonists immediately selected their next target. Grobo suggested, "How about that three-decker on Goodale Road?"

"That's perfect," Gregg responded. The group was still split between the two vehicles. Bemis parked in front of the building, where he and Groblewski brazenly manufactured the device. Gorman and Stackpole parked farther up the street in order to signal them with the car horn should anyone approach.

This building sat atop a steep embankment. After struggling up the hill, they again found that their luck was running, as there was an excellent fuel load in the form of trash and scrap wood just inside the rear door. They placed the device within the debris. Once back at the car, they all left the area to wait for the fire to be reported. From their vantage point, Gregg yelled, "Look. Look!" as flames leaped from the three-decker high on the hill.

Donny laughed, finding it hilarious that this fire was highly visible throughout the neighborhood, but had yet to be reported. More minutes passed before Box 3638 was struck. They were pleased that this fire would force a response from fire companies well outside the neighborhood. Sure enough, Ladder 1 showed up from the North End. The second alarm was struck. Another multiple alarm fire, just what the arsonists were hoping for.

As the boys again climbed the hill toward the fire, they saw a couple of other buffs dragging a feeder line to assist the shorthanded crews. Bobby yelled at them, "Hey, you bunch of fuckin' scabs, if you keep that shit up, they'll never rehire the laid-off jakes!" The fire buffs were clueless; they just shook their heads as if they didn't understand what he was talking about.

The rear of the three-decker was heavily involved, with fire showing from all floors. After again documenting their handiwork with photos, they headed home.

Only a few days after those "good" fires at Thetford Avenue and Goodale Road, the torches were at it once more. They were bolstered by the success of their technique. There were now signs that they were proving their point. The news media was reporting on the increase of fires within the City, but the press appeared to be stumped as to any motivation for the arsons.

All of the fires set by this crew thus far were in vacant buildings, which had none of the usual, inherent potential ignition sources. None of the buildings had power. There would have been no cooking and no heating. Therefore, once the Boston Arson Squad ruled out improper disposal of smoking material by someone trespassing in the building, they reasonably concluded that the fires were all intentionally set by a person or persons unknown.

The arsonists were in a position, due to their jobs, friendships, and hobby, to notice that there was increased activity around the Boston Arson

Squad at 920 Massachusetts Avenue, but it would not deter their fire-setting. With the marked increase in the number of incendiary fires and the corresponding escalation of scrutiny, the guys knew that they had to be extra cautious about arriving at any of "their" fires too soon. They felt a sense of ownership of the fires that they had set.

That last night of winter, Stackpole, Groblewski, and Bemis first chose a rickety three-decker with a hole through the roof in Dorchester, off main thoroughfare Blue Hill Avenue. Their plan this night was to target buildings on opposite sides of the City. With every window smashed out of the target, Donny remarked, "This ought to be good for two or three alarms." On the inside, the place was a battered mess, with the plaster torn off the walls. As Bemis placed the device within a wall cavity, a large rat jumped across the floor in front of them so unexpectedly that Donny nearly shit his pants.

Once they lit the device and left to cruise the neighborhood, it only took minutes for the flames to shoot from the windows on all three floors and the box to be transmitted sending out the first responders. Engine 52 arrived first, Car 8 next. At this point, the standard manpower on a company had been reduced from one officer with three to four firefighters down to the one officer with two firefighters. So the workload was markedly increased for each firefighter.

At this fire, the guys found it pitiful that the Lieutenant from Engine 16 and the District 8 Chief were operating a fire hose themselves. When Grobo saw this, he flipped his lid. He ranted and raged at the Chief for not calling for an additional alarm to get help for his men. After a few more minutes of Bobby's slurs, the Chief relented and called for a working fire. Although the additional hands helped, the fire was still too large for such a short-handed response. Eventually, after heavy destruction, the fire was knocked down.

Bobby griped as they left the scene. "Well, with Chiefs like that, we won't have any multiple alarms in the City."

"Let's go try something in the other end of the City," Donny suggested. From their list, they chose a building in Charlestown near Sullivan Square, only blocks from the Bunker Hill Monument and Breed's Hill, where a significant Revolutionary War battle had occurred over 200 years earlier. At that hour, it only took them 10 minutes to reach the area. Once they eyed the building, it was obviously a good target; it was a two-story, boarded up, vacant store.

"Boy, that looks ripe," Bobby stated.

"What about the jake on the patrol desk?" Bemis was concerned about the firefighter sitting on the desk at the firehouse for Engine 32 and Ladder 9 directly across the street from the target.

Showing his true colors again, Stackpole retorted, "Don't worry about him. He's probably asleep or drunk anyway." They parked in a spot that was blind to the firehouse, where they made the device. They all got out of the car, traipsed through trash, and placed the lit device in more trash at the open rear door.

Quickly leaving the area, they crossed the bridge to Boston's North End and parked behind the old Boston Garden, awaiting the fire call. After several minutes, when they were beginning to wonder why they hadn't heard anything on the radio, they saw two pieces of apparatus above them northbound on the highway bridge of Route 93. Swearing, they questioned what happened to Gregg's radio. Once they pulled out of the lot to drive toward the fire, in front of the Garden on Causeway Street, the radio started receiving again with report of a working fire.

Arriving at the fire, smoke puffed in and out through the cracks of the solidly boarded windows. Firefighters were making entry into the oxygen-starved building. A second alarm was transmitted. The gray smoke turned to a roiling black cloud. Then, flames appeared through the cracks where there had been smoke moments before. A third, then a fourth, alarm was transmitted as the building fire became a block-size job. It was quite some time before the companies put water directly on the fire, as they say, "the wet stuff on the red stuff." Once the fire self-vented through the roof, the firefighters finally made headway. Bemis and the boys called it a night and headed home.

CHAPTER FIVE

SPRING 1982

The winter of discontent became the spring of greater malfeasance for these newbie arsonists.

On Thursday, March 25, 1982, Bemis met Groblewski at the rear of the HoJo's parking lot. "The lot," as it was often referred to, was an ideal place for sparks to congregate, right next to Fire Headquarters between Mass Ave. and Southampton Street. A barrier guard rail ran down the middle of the lot to prevent drivers on Mass Ave. from using the parking lot as a shortcut to Southampton. Most of the fire buffs parked on one side of the barrier; the media parked on the other side. But the two sides were friendly and often fraternized.

On this night, the twosome reviewed the ever-growing updated list of targets. Boston, like many other cities in Massachusetts, had an overabundance of abandoned buildings. Without spending the money to properly secure them, it was impossible to keep these vacant structures buttoned up. Homeless people, vandals, gangs, drug users, and others bent on seeking shelter for whatever reason could access most of these neighborhood eyesores.

Another vacant three-story dwelling, this time on Fenelon Street in Dorchester, was the night's chosen objective. As was typically the case, the front of the building was secure, but, typically, the rear door was torn open. Leaving the lit device within open kitchen cabinets, they wandered the area, waiting for the fire, even whiffing the air. A trace of smoke was in the air, but no fire was ever reported. They departed and split for home, disappointed.

Or so it seemed. On Friday, after only a few hours sleep, Bemis visited his buddies at the Acton Auxiliary Fire Station. As soon as he walked in the door, one of the guys questioned him, "Hey, did you catch the big one in Boston last night?"

"What big one?"

"They had a four-bagger (four-alarm fire) in Dorchester around 4 a.m. this morning."

"That figures, I went home at 3 a.m.," Gregg replied. He was more than a little surprised that the fire had smoldered for several hours before it took off, but even more amazed that the fire had gone to four alarms. And he had missed it.

Bemis called Grobo about the fire. Bobby told him to come into Boston because Donny wanted to play. When Gregg met them, Donny was raring to go: "So, what are we going to get tonight? Let's get a few going tonight."

"Okay, here's the list. Take your pick." Gregg handed Donny the list for his perusal.

Bobby added, "Okay, Skinny, you pick 'em, we'll get 'em."

On the border of Roxbury and Jamaica Plain, they chose another vacant three-decker with their favored exterior siding, gas shingles. Bemis parked up on Parker Hill so that they could easily watch the house ignite. They all walked down the hill, stuffed the device in a hole on the outside wall so that the shingles could readily catch, and trekked back up the steep slope. This was especially difficult for Donny, who was not in shape for this type of terrain. Back at the car, they saw that the device had already ignited.

From that distance, the fire was readily visible, with the flames rapidly streaming up the siding toward the roof. Box 2384 beeped over the radio. They parked near the scene after arrival of the first due apparatus and heard a second alarm being ordered. One entire exterior elevation was blazing, totally engulfing the third floor. When the firefighters took control of the fire, the arsonists left to find another mark.

The second fire of the night was set at another empty triple-decker covered with gas shingles. It was on Bolton Street, not much more than an alleyway in South Boston. This time the front door was their means of access, having been previously smashed open. Stackpole set the device under the first-floor stairs. Upon returning to their car, they saw Engine 39 and Ladder 18 racing up the street. Although the fire had rapidly progressed, it had been called in too soon to develop into a multiple alarm situation. With the blaze readily controlled, the boys tired of the scene and sought another target.

If nothing else, the group's targets up to this point in time were predictable, but there were so many of these buildings throughout so much of the City that there was no way to forecast their likely next target.

In the 1990s, to help protect firefighters and others from the threat posed by the thousands of abandoned structures that had provided the feast for the voracious Boston arsonists of the 1980s, Massachusetts State Police Lieutenant Robert Corry of the Fire Marshal's Office (now retired) would be instrumental in assisting the City of Lawrence to establish an abandoned building program to better seal these vacant buildings from trespassers or raze them entirely. This program would become a model for countless other cities. With the same purpose, in the 2000s the International Association of Arson Investigators, through support from the United States Fire Administration, led by Project Manager Jon C. Jones and several others at the forefront of arson investigation and consulting, would develop the Abandoned Building Project. This venture provided an evaluation tool for communities to gauge the extent of, and respond to, their own abandoned building problem.[14]

That night, Roxbury Highlands became the next neighborhood to lose yet another vacant triple-decker. Dorr Street was eerily quiet and desolate—there were more vacant houses on the street than occupied dwellings. Donny stayed with the car as a lookout while Gregg and Bobby walked the few hundred feet to the objective. Once inside the building, they saw the decaying state of the structure, including large holes in the walls, the floors, and even the roof. The lack of a solid roof had allowed rain into the interior, causing a buildup of mold and mildew. "Boy, this place gives me the creeps," Gregg bemoaned as he attempted to find a dry spot in which to place the device.

"Yeah, I know. Let's just set it and get the fuck out of here," Bobby concurred.

Just as Gregg reached for a piece of scrap wood, a pack of wild dogs ran out the back door, only feet from him. The two men almost dropped from fright, but strangely enough, the dogs didn't bark at all, so no neighbors were alerted. After they set the device, they quietly headed back for the car. "Jesus Christ, the fucking place was filled with wild dogs. Scared the shit out of me," Bemis told Donny as they climbed into the car.

This fire took over 90 minutes to be reported. But by the time the boys arrived, the firefighters had already knocked down the fire. Since once again they were not having much luck, they headed home.

▲

For these fire setters, the only bloom April showers brought was more fires. Their activities would fully flower during April.

Friday, April 2, 1982, was their busiest night yet in their nascent reign of terror.

---

14 IAAI Field Manual, Evaluation of Vacant and Abandoned Properties

Shortly after 9:00 p.m., they targeted a large four-story brick structure (unlike their favored buildings to date) that wrapped around the intersection of Warren, Copeland, and Waverly Streets in Roxbury. Once they placed the lit device within the basement, instead of wandering around and waiting for the fire to come in as was their usual M.O., they immediately sought another target. Inadvertently, they got tied up when they ran into some friends. They were dismayed to hear the target reported too soon, as they were sure it would have been a multiple alarm blaze.

Having lost a lot of time already, the crew switched to Stackpole's car. In an area of factories and warehouses of many descriptions in South Boston, they chose an old one-story wood and tin-clad warehouse on Midway Street. It was full of pallets, a perfect fuel configuration often used in fire training sessions. The rear of the building had been built on wood pilings, like stilts. They placed a device in a woodpile there and immediately drove back to HoJo's to swap vehicles again in case Donny's car had been seen.

Watching the efforts of their work from the Summer Street Bridge, they could see fire start to develop. Ten minutes later, the building was producing copious amounts of heavy black smoke. Within another few minutes, Fire Alarm reported the fire. In short order, a second and a third alarm was ordered. Grobo and Bemis snapped numerous photos during firefighter operations before they left to stalk another victim.

The next building was a half-block-long, four-story abandoned brick structure with empty commercial storefronts on the first floor and residential apartments on the upper floors Green Street in Jamaica Plain across the City. There were two front doorways, both with the doors torn off; one led to the first floor, the other to the upper levels. On the first floor, the threesome found plenty of trash, but the walls were solid plaster, which would hamper fire growth. Checking the upper floors, they found tinderbox-dry walls in the stairways; they placed a device against one of those walls and departed.

After driving by the building and observing no fire, against their better judgment, they risked returning to the second floor, where they "re-seeded" the fire with another device. Again, they departed the building and the area.

They hit a large wooden abandoned three-decker on Washington Street in the Codman Square area. Although the building was boarded up tight, the three crawled under a sheet of plywood that covered a doorway to gain access to the basement, where they placed the device in a favorable spot among all sorts of combustibles. Crawling back under the plywood to escape the haunt, they drove around in anticipation of one or more fire calls coming in shortly.

Nearing dawn, it was too late to set another fire. After a half hour, the fire box was transmitted for the Washington Street fire, but that fire was quickly knocked down. As they drove toward Forest Hills to check out the JP fire, Gregg exclaimed as he saw a large plume of smoke rising in the distance, "Holy shit, it's going!"

But the closer they got to Green Street, the farther away the smoke appeared. Gregg declared, "Hey, that smoke isn't coming from Green Street." Just after he said it, the radio blared, "Engine 5 to Fire Alarm, urgent! Strike the box for Midway Street; we have fire showing!"

They all started to laugh when they heard that. "That's pretty good firefighting," Bobby chuckled, "The fuckin' place rekindles while the detail company is still going." A rekindle is a slap in the face to every firefighter. It means that some company was sloppy and didn't do its job.

"Yeah, and from the looks of all that smoke, it's going to go for a few alarms," Gregg said as they passed the Green Street building with nothing at all showing. As they turned toward Midway Street, a second alarm was struck, and before they arrived, a third alarm was ordered. At the site, the remains of the original structure were once again in flames, with the attached one-story building also fully involved. Fourth and fifth alarms were then ordered on the box. Donny was running around elated. The sun was rising. Again, they had breakfast to celebrate and calm down, then drove homeward bound.

On their nocturnal outings of April 23 and April 24, 1982, Bemis, Groblewski and Stackpole had big plans for a couple of hot nights. Bemis had enough supplies to light up the City. On the first night, it seemed that whenever they found a suitable target building, somebody was around to spoil their plans. Eventually, after a couple hours, they found a rundown two-and-a-half-story house hidden behind unkempt bushes. It had been torched before and wasn't very big, but they planted a device anyway and quickly left to find another place. The fire came across the radio, but it didn't amount to much, so they continued to their quest for another target. But this search ended up a bust. All agreed to try again that night.

About 10:30 p.m., they planted a device against the gas shingles of a single-story wood warehouse in Southie. But this fire was quickly discovered. The arsonists were miffed that the fire had been contained to a single alarm. However, they knew that they had to continue with their main objective or the cutbacks would surely get worse in the City in the coming months, when the full effect of Proposition 2½ was felt.

May 5, 1982, provided another night for Grobo and Bemis to have a little more fun. The new target, a vacant three-story brick, side-by-side duplex in Roxbury Highlands, was on such a quiet, dark street that they abandoned caution and pulled up directly in front of the building. Although the duplex was boarded up solid, they placed the device in a two-inch crack where the plywood didn't quite cover the front door. Gregg made sure the incendiary had ignited before heading out to await the anticipated action.

Fifteen minutes later, the call was transmitted. Slowly, the torches headed toward the fire. Engine 14 reported heavy fire upon arrival at the property, then called for a second alarm. Picking up the pace in Gregg's car, Bobby turned on the siren and alternating headlights in Gregg's mock cruiser. "You're a fuckin' nut," Gregg laughed. As they slid around a corner, a Boston Police cruiser was blocking the street.

"I don't fuckin' believe it," Gregg said incredulously since he had never seen a cop blocking traffic on a Roxbury street in such a quiet neighborhood in the middle of the night. In spite of this, out of bravado or recklessness, they parked right in front of the cop. When they left their vehicle, the cop just watched them, perhaps thinking that they were BFD Arson Squad members. Imagine, if maybe, the police officer had confronted these guys. Possibly with some proactive investigative work, the entire arson story yet to unfold over the next year could have been short-circuited.

They were astounded that the building was so swiftly fully involved, with flames leaping high through the roof. Bemis and Grobo sat on the front steps of another vacant structure across the street from the fire. Engine 14 put on an even better show than the fire itself. Using their deck gun to blast away, firefighters sent slate roof shingles, popular on nice houses built in this area over 100 years, flying in every direction and crashing to the ground. While viewing the action from their vantage point, Bobby asked Gregg, "Hey, do you think they would notice it if we drop a match in this one?" as he pointed at a hole in the wall of the building where they were sitting. Gregg laughed at the obvious joke. The buddies left the scene in a good mood with plans to meet around midnight on Friday.

▲

That Friday night's fog was Rudolph the Red-Nosed Reindeer dense; one could hardly see a few feet through the pea soup. They chose a three-story, wood-framed former dwelling on George Street in Roxbury. It was a target that the guys had wanted for a while, but they needed a nasty night like this one because there was always a lot of activity at an occupied house down the street.

The boys planted two devices in the structure, a half-hour apart, before a fire developed inside a first-floor window. After they cleared the neighborhood, the box was transmitted. Although Engine 14 reported heavy fire showing, only a working fire was ordered. After a few pictures were taken, with the fire knocked down, they called it a night.

The past couple of weeks were a strange stretch for the Boston arsonists. They were setting more fires but having less success, mostly achieving single-alarm fires when they were aiming for multiple alarm fires with good media coverage. Their goals were not being achieved. Thursday, May 13, into the 14th, was no different.

This night had a quartet of fire-setters—Gregg, Bobby, and Donny plus Joe Gorman. Donny asked Gregg, "Did you bring any of the stuff with you?"

"Well, I've got everything but the Coleman fuel. All the stores that carry it were closed by the time I got a chance to pick any up."

In his best Boston accent, Bobby quipped, "Oh, you're a pissa." The Coleman fuel was the crucial component of the device. Without the accelerant, all you had was lit paper.

With this chemical failure, they planned to hit a bunch of dumpsters in the Back Bay, the area where they first started their parade of fires several months earlier. They desired to make a dumpster fire night as spectacular as a dumpster fire could be.

After waiting a couple hours until the Back Bay crowds quieted down, they set a few on Providence Street, hit several more on Back Street, and then headed down the alleyway behind the brownstones on Boylston Street, which was crowded with dumpsters (and infested with rats). By the time they reached the end of the alleyway behind the firehouse of Engine 33, several blocks of dumpsters were lit up in unison. Even though the first dumpsters were being called in, in rapid succession they lit several more dumpsters in the alley behind ritzy Newbury Street. They then listened to and laughed at the chaos they heard on the radio. Absolute bedlam reigned when several extra companies were called in to assist, but nobody knew how to describe the location of the dumpster where they were fighting the fire.

One of the engines called Fire Alarm asking to have the box transmitted for a building fire on Newbury Street. Gregg and his pals looked at each other, wondering if one of their dumpster fires had ignited a building. Arriving on scene, they discovered that, in fact, the dumpster had caught the first floor of a clothing shop on fire. A working fire was ordered on the box. Knowing that this fire had created too great a risk for injuries since the upper floors were occupied residences, Gregg told the group, "Hey, we better cool it with any dumpsters too close to buildings from now on." They all agreed. Apparently, they did have some measure of restraint and conscience.

▲

On Friday, Bemis met with Stackpole and Groblewski at the Victoria's Diner on Massachusetts (Mass) Avenue, a preferred dining spot that has been family-owned and run at the same location since 1949. As they discussed target locations for the night, Donny came up with an unusual suggestion. "Why don't we try something on the old State Hospital grounds?"

In Massachusetts, the state hospital system had begun some 120 years before, housing psychiatric patients. In the 1970s, after horrific conditions and mistreatment of patients in state hospital facilities were brought to light, with insufficient funds available to make necessary improvements, the state hospitals were gradually shut down. Many of these properties were left to decay for years. Each hospital consisted of many buildings, mostly brick with multiple floors. With the large tracts of valuable land, the properties sat there, not sold off for decades.

Boston State Hospital, in the Dorchester and Mattapan sections of the City, had East and West sections divided by main thoroughfare Morton Street. The arsonists chose to target the East side because most of its structures appeared to be wide open.

After making a device, Gregg dropped Bobby and Donny off at the front door of a building known to them as the Skullery. While Gregg waited, the inside guys spent a great deal of time trying to find a suitable spot inside the creepy building in which to place the device. Finding an inadequate supply of readily available interior fuels, the boys located a tunnel between buildings that was lined with wood. They placed the device and finally appeared at the pre-arranged pick-up site. They explained the situation to Gregg, who didn't understand their description. However, he trusted them because they had both previously worked as Department of Mental Health (DMH) Police Officers at this location and knew the buildings inside and out.

A half hour later, they drove back to the building because no call had been reported for a fire. No evidence of fire was detected until they drove between the buildings where the tunnel was located. Gregg's headlights highlighted a slight smoky haze seeping from the tunnel. They planted a second device in the tunnel, and shortly after leaving the building, the DMH Police reported the fire. Engine 52 was the first company to arrive, quickly knocking down the fire.

The boys then tried to set another fire in the West section of buildings since the DMH Police were busy at the other scene. Stackpole dropped Bemis and Grobo off on the busy American Legion Highway.

The two torches did a "Frogger" routine, zigzagging like the video game through the traffic. They walked to rickety wood stairs attached to the rear of the three-story brick, institutional-looking structure, where they placed the incendiary. Running toward the highway, they tripped over chicken wire fencing from community gardens on the grounds which forced them to slow down to a walk. Lucky for them, Stackpole approached as they reached the road. Only minutes later, the fire was called in by a passing motorist, but again, the blaze was quickly brought under control.

The arsonists felt the night was more failure than success. Yes, they added two more obvious arson fires that BFD had to respond to, but they didn't achieve the level reserved for "good" fires, that is multiple alarm blazes that drew media attention.

Fires had become an addiction for Gregg Bemis, if not for some of his other cohorts. On Sunday, May 23, 1982, Bemis was working the evening shift at the Stow Police station, due to get off at midnight. He had no plans to head into Boston. However, while on his way home after work, a second alarm was transmitted for a building fire in the Mattapan section of the City. The pull of the fire was too great for Gregg to resist. It sounded like it would be a big one so he headed in, some 35 miles to the southeast. It wasn't long for a third and fourth alarm to be transmitted. Gregg quickened his pace. With virtually no traffic, he arrived in good time.

The fire had ravaged a large three-story occupied apartment building, but it was brought under control as he arrived. Gregg watched the firefighting operations for a while, then looked for Stackpole. He had not gotten his fix for the night.

Bemis found Donny at a doughnut shop in South Boston. After shooting the crap for a bit, they set fire to a vacant wood church right around the corner on Dorchester Street. Gregg was uneasy, as this was a very busy area and a cab stand was located on the street side of the church. The windows on the rear of the building were boarded up, so they just jumped out of the car and placed a device on a windowsill. They didn't get caught, but the busy area led to near-immediate discovery of the fire, which was easily extinguished. Another failure. Time to head home. Gregg never satisfied his yearning that night.

Four days later, Bemis had the night off. He found Bobby helping Donny clean out his pigpen of a car. "Hey, what are you doing? It hasn't been a year since Skinny cleaned his car the last time," Gregg said.

Bobby grinned and replied, "The trash was getting so deep in the back seat, you had a hard time looking out the rear window!"

"Hey, fuck you," Donny snapped, but they all roared with laughter. They always had fun busting Donny's balls.

Changing things up a bit, the arson team chose two different targets in Hyde Park, the southwest corner of the City near the Dedham/Milton town lines. Off Neponset Valley Parkway, they found a vacant commercial building with stacks of wood pallets piled 15 feet high on a rear loading dock. Bobby climbed onto the concrete platform of the loading dock next to railroad tracks, where he placed a device amid the stacks. They barely made it back to the car before flames erupted 20 feet into the air.

"Let's get something quick," proposed Stackpole, as they wanted to up the pressure on the Fire Department. A short distance away they placed another device, this time on a deeply recessed windowsill of an old warehouse. Just then, the box was transmitted for the first fire. Checking the progress of their fire, they saw flames roaring 50 feet above the building and spreading to an adjacent structure. Donny was the most amazed: "Holy, moly. Engine 48 is going to shit their pants when they see this one!"

As if on cue, Engine 48 careened into the site, calling for a working fire. Spectators soon filled the area, so many that the boys decided to vacate the area. They drove past the warehouse to check on their second fire of the night. Seeing only slight progression of the fire, they gave up for the night, planning to meet again about 10:00 the next night.

This Friday night was to be a little different from most of the previous outings. A new aspect of the conspiracy took shape, somewhat by accident.

Bemis arrived first at HoJo's. Right at 10:00, Groblewski drove in with Stackpole and associate fire buff Wayne Sanden, who had been missing in action for several weeks. Gregg stated to the others, "Hey guys, it looks like a perfect night," referring to the thick fog that enveloped the City, a frequent condition in Boston this time of year when cold ocean waters met warming May air.

Wayne Sanden, born in August 1955, had grown up in Boston. His father had been a police officer, but Sanden, like the others, had wanted to become a Boston firefighter instead. Again, since it was difficult to get his preferred job, Sanden had been hired as a police officer for the Boston Housing Authority (BHA). Showing proclivity for the job, Wayne was quickly promoted to the rank of lieutenant.

Sanden was of average weight and height, roughly five feet, 10 inches tall. He had limp, blond hair that contributed to the nickname, Blondie, given to him by his sparky friends. Sanden lived in Roslindale, a Boston neighborhood, with his wife and two small children. Given the time spent at his official job, the time he expended as a fire buff, and the time he would devote to his criminal activities going forward, one wondered when he had time to spend with his family.

In my dealings with Sanden, he showed a somewhat shuttered and reclusive personality. Although we talked often throughout much of 1983 and 1984, Wayne never fully opened up about his involvement with the arson conspiracy. He remained an enigma to his wife, family, friends, and myself from the beginning of our relationship to the end of the case.

Recalling a target that they had previously torched in March, the large duplex on Thetford Avenue, the co-conspirators agreed to hit it again. This was Sanden's first fire. Since there were four of them that night, Donny stayed in the car while the others crept through the fog, the trash, and the brush to the rear of the building. Because one side of the duplex had been nearly destroyed by their earlier fire, they set the device in the stairwell on the opposite half of the structure.

Back in the car, Sanden asked to be dropped off at home, saying he had to get up early in the morning. They then headed toward the fire as units were dispatched to the fire. The companies reported seeing an orange glow in the sky, but due to the fog they had trouble locating the actual fire. Once found, though, the District Chief ordered that a working fire be transmitted on the box. At the scene of the blazing fire, Bemis took several photos. Once the fire was knocked down, they were quickly on their way. In Roxbury, they targeted a large wastepaper company. The yard outside the building was full of large bundles of paper for recycling. However, they could not find access past the 20-foot-high fence that surrounded the property. But where there's a will, there's a way. Bobby suggested, "Hey, let's throw a road flare over the fence."

Gregg and Donny both agreed. Gregg popped his trunk and grabbed a flare. "Let me throw it," implored the least athletically inclined Stackpole. After a couple of unsuccessful tries, Bobby grabbed the flare, and with one toss the flare landed in a large stack of the scrap paper.

As they looked for more targets, while waiting for the fire to be reported, they spotted a car fire in the Orchard Park housing project. Donny suggested, "Let's call it in on the voice box," referring to the fire call boxes, which routed callers directly to Boston Fire Alarm, mounted all over the City in those days. (Remember, there were no cell phones in use yet.) He added, "At least it will tie up Engine 14 and Ladder 4 for a few minutes while the wastepaper plant gets going."

The arsonists were still setting several fires near the Engine 14 firehouse, trying to give their friends at the house some "good" action. It was becoming a trend.

Gregg pulled up to Box 1712. Bobby climbed out to call the fire in. When he picked up the phone, there was heavy static on the line making it extremely difficult for him to communicate with the Fire Alarm operator on the other end of the line. After Bobby finally got his message across, he grabbed the handset, yanking it, grumbling, "This fuckin' piece of shit!" The force of his initial wrench of the box pulled it halfway off the pedestal where it had been mounted. As Bobby started to climb into the car, Gregg urged him on, "Pull it again, Bobby." The next tug resulted in the box coming completely free from its mooring. Gregg jumped out of his car with wire cutters that he kept under his front seat and cut the connecting wires.

Bobby threw the box in the trunk of the car, saying, "Alright, let's get out of here before 14 and 4 get here," referring to the first due companies that would respond to the car fire. As they proceeded toward the wastepaper plant, the box for the fire was transmitted. Engine 37 reported fire showing upon their arrival. A working fire was ordered on the box. Arriving shortly after that, the boys saw that the fire had not extended to the building. Disappointed, they called it a night.

That firebox in the trunk of Gregg's car was just waiting to be discovered by investigators. The day that this box was located was one that this group of arsonists would surely regret.

As May turned to June, Bemis just got off duty at the Stow Police. He caught up with Stackpole at one of his security sites in Southie. As they checked targets in Dorchester and Roxbury, Donny suggested that they collect a couple more voice boxes. Gregg concurred, so they proceeded to yank on every voice box that they came across. Most of the boxes were fairly well secured on their pedestals, but they managed to grab a couple loose ones.

In a normal year, on average, there are one or two voice boxes that somehow go missing, which is usually defined as stolen. It is a felony to steal a fire box. If someone is found in possession of a fire box, they, too, have committed a felony, to wit, Possession or Receipt of Stolen Property, because the missing fire boxes—all property of the City of Boston—were presumed to have been stolen. The year 1982 would be abnormally rough on fire boxes; 14 boxes disappeared.

The first loose box they encountered on June 1, 1982, was Box 3396, located at an intersection in Dorchester. Bemis gave the handle a quick jerk, expecting a little resistance, but instead the box literally fell into his arms. He then snipped the three wires and dropped the box into his trunk, and they were off. Another trophy, another stolen box, and, in the future, another piece of physical evidence.

But on this night, the voice fire box served another function. The arsonists planned to set a fire in the area where the box had once stood as the means for a passerby who discovered a fire the ability to timely report the fire. Now, with the box missing, an eye-witness would have to search further for another box, thereby delaying the report. A delayed report meant a tardy response to the fire, providing a chance for the fire to grow two or three times greater in size than it would have been with the box in place.

Today, with cell phones ubiquitous, there is no longer a need for the voice fire boxes although the boxes routed you directly to Boston Fire Alarm. However, the cell phone 911 call usually is channeled through the State Police or the local police and then directed to the fire department. Thus, there is some built-in delay compared with the old voice box system.

In 1982 pay phones were few and far between in the residential neighborhoods that these arsonists frequented. Working pay phones were even harder to find, as they were regularly vandalized, often by yanking the receiver handset out, wire and all. And, another factor was in play. These fires were mostly set after midnight. The inhabitants of the area who would likely be sleeping would not take kindly to a knock on their door at such an ungodly hour. And that's a charitable statement. Plus, as has been mentioned previously, often these neighborhoods had more vacant structures than occupied dwellings.

With the box in the trunk of the car, they hit a vacant wood triple-decker adjacent to an equally empty three-story brick building on Dorr Street. This location provided a unique twist. Between the two structures was an impressive pile of discarded tires heaped against the wood siding and reaching all the way to the brick structure. The arsonists had not paid much attention to the value of tires up to this point. But it now became obvious to Bemis and Stackpole that utilizing tires as part of their device would provide a longer burning intense fire, an excellent way to accelerate the spread of the fire. And free tires were plentiful, discarded in many empty lots all over town.

"Hey, Skinny, let's put the device in one of those tires." Donny readily agreed, nodding his head as they crawled into the middle of the pile between the two darkened hulks. After setting the device, they headed for one of their favored high vantage points, Parker Hill. Bemis positioned his car in the direction of the impending fire. Since it was a beautiful clear night, they got out of the car to stretch.

"Look Donny, right over there." Gregg pointed to the first black mushroom cloud of smoke rising into the night sky over Roxbury Highlands.

"Look at all that smoke," exclaimed Donny with a smile. "The boys are going to have their hands full now!" As they watched, the smoke plume swelled. Engine 14 and Ladder 4 were dispatched to the scene. Upon arrival, Engine 14 reported heavy fire showing, ordering a second alarm.

From Parker Hill flames could be seen leaping through the smoke layer high over the City. Donny and Gregg raced down the hill toward the fire. Just as they parked near the scene, a third alarm was transmitted. The wood three-decker was fully involved with flames coming out of every opening and fire showing on the top floors of the adjacent brick building. Gregg furiously snapped away on his camera; this was a good fire to capture on film. The arsonists were pleased when they saw that the tires had rapidly accelerated the fire into a full-blown inferno.

After departing from the scene, they looked for additional voice boxes to steal They found Box 339 just up the street from the box that they had grabbed a couple hours earlier. Not finding any more loose boxes around Harvard Street, they checked for loose boxes in Roxbury Highlands. While firefighters worked the fire a couple blocks away, Bemis and Stackpole snatched Box 2261. Gregg said, “This ought to be a good souvenir.” Donny just laughed perversely.

June 3, 1982, was to be a really big night. This night categorically brought the Federal authorities into the picture. The crew finally set the first fire that we Feds could sink our teeth into.

Bemis gave up work for the night, arriving in Boston around 9:00. He found Donny with one of his security patrol employees. Because Donny did not want his guys to know that he was balls deep in a series of arsons, he ditched the kid and met up with Gregg at HoJo's.

Donny filled Gregg in on a large warehouse in South Boston that was right near his security patrol: “Bobby told me about it the other night and suggested we get it.” Gregg was eager to check it out, but they had to wait until the patrol employee they had dumped got off duty. So they targeted another building first in order to tie up some fire companies.

In Dorchester, they found a pair of wood three-deckers separated only by a sidewalk located on very busy Dorchester Avenue, known to the locals as Dot Ave. One of the two structures had gas-shingle siding all the way to ground level. They parked on a quiet side street, made a device, and walked down Dot Ave with lunch bag in hand. Disappearing between the buildings, they needed only a few seconds to place and set the device against the combustible shingles. With plenty of readily available fuel here, no additional accelerant was necessary. Carefully, checking to make sure nobody saw them, they exited the walkway onto the main thoroughfare and made their way to the car. "Let's get out of the area for a while," Gregg said as he pulled onto Dot Ave in a direction away from their targets.

Seconds later, Bemis spotted BFD photographer Billy Noonan in the BFD Photo Unit car (K7) coming toward them from the opposite direction. Gregg's mental antenna went up, sensing danger, but as they passed each other, he realized that Noonan had not noticed them.

Good thing; only moments later, the radio blared, "Attention Engine 21, Ladder 7, District 6 respond to a building fire at number 848 Dorchester Avenue, striking Box 7251." Within another few seconds, Billy Noonan radioed, "K7 (his call sign) to Fire Alarm, heavy fire showing on Dorchester Ave."

Boston Fire Photographer William F. Noonan had been an Army intelligence specialist in Vietnam. He had always had an interest in photography. Upon returning to civilian life, and getting laid off from his civilian job, Billy was hired by the Boston Fire Department. Initially, on Engine 3, he was asked to fill in for the Photo Unit when one of the other photographers was out. Billy never left the unit. For the next 30-plus years, Noonan took photos of more fires and other official events in and around Boston than almost any person ever. He was regularly on the streets of the City, highly recognizable with his round countenance, his navy blue FD shirt, a baseball cap on in reverse, and one or more cameras looped around his neck. He knew hundreds of people from the fire communities in and around Boston. And they all knew Bill Noonan.

After hearing the radio report from Noonan, Bemis headed back toward the fire. Engine 21 arrived on scene, instantly ordering a second alarm. Gregg parked near Doughboy Donuts and they hurried toward the fire site. Both triple-deckers were fully involved; a third and fourth alarm were transmitted in short order.

The torches were amazed at the ferocious growth of what would be known as the Spero fire. They realized that the close proximity of buildings in the congested neighborhood, along with the asphalt "gas" shingles, had caused a re-radiation effect; that is, the heat energy radiated back and forth between the buildings, resulting in rapid breakdown of the siding as the fire progressed. The flames followed the buoyancy of the upward-flowing fuel gases, burning into the interior of each floor through the windows and into the attic at the eaves, before finally burning through the roof. It took an amazingly short time for this fire to be off to the races.

A crowd of buffs convened on the scene. Bemis took his photos and conversed with several sparks. He was the incognito celebrity arsonist among the group. When the fire was darkened down, the torches left to check out the warehouse in Southie. After reconnaissance of the vast building, they realized that it spanned the entire block, some 200 to 300 feet long on one side by nearly 1,000 feet in length. If this one took off, they reckoned, it would prove to be their most massive effort to date.

Bemis parked in a deserted dark lot at the end of the target on Cypher Street. After making a device, they slipped into the darkness along railroad tracks that ran behind the warehouse. The boys continued past a long section of two-story concrete block construction until they came to a single-story that was mostly clad with corrugated tin. Fortunately for them, they found a patch of wood covered with thick tar paper. They knew that this would burn just like the gas shingles. They lit the device, then scrambled back over the railroad tracks to the car. Avoiding being in the vicinity when it ignited, they drove back toward the first fire.

A short time later, they perused the area trying to detect any smoke from the warehouse. Before they spotted anything, the call for the fire came over the radio. Engine 52, which was covering Engine 39's house since Engine 39 had responded to the Dot Ave fire, reported fire showing, but they didn't sound too excited. Approaching the scene, the boys observed minimal smoke above the building. "Shit, it didn't even have a chance to get going," said a dejected Stackpole. They figured they might as well spark the fire. So they parked and again walked down the railroad tracks.

They saw that Engine 52 had straddled the tracks and had knocked down the initial fire right where it had been ignited a short time ago. Something bothered Bemis, though. The firefighters had not made entry into the building from this rear side. This was usually an important function in order to check the interior for fire extension into the structure.

Gregg chatted with a pump operator he knew for a half hour, then said, "Hey, Skinny, look at this," pointing to thick black smoke pumping out from the interior. Donny's interest grew as he saw the pushing smoke.

Unbeknown to the torches, the building that they thought was vacant was actually the Spero Toy Company, an importer of cheap Chinese toys. Inside were thousands of cardboard boxes filled with plastic toys and stuffed animals, a combustible fuel load greater than they ever could have imagined. In fire analysis terms, the fuel load could provide hundreds of thousands of megawatts of energy in burning material.

The smoke plume became flame-filled with fire breaking through the roof shortly thereafter. Gregg and Donny initially took up a viewing position on a fire escape across the railroad tracks. However, the intensifying heat quickly forced them to retreat to a more comfortable spot.

The fire swiftly progressed to five alarms, bringing apparatus from all over the city. The blaze and the response were larger than any they had witnessed firsthand before. And it continued to propagate faster and faster. The companies finally had to cut their way through thick steel doors, but the fire had already spread past their location.

As the sun began to rise, so did the number of alarms, up to eight. Stackpole and Bemis headed over to a nearby Store 24 to buy some drinks and replenish Gregg's supply of film. As he walked by Engine 52, Gregg, with pure arrogance, asked the pump operator, "Hey, Paul, do you want anything to drink from the store?"

"Yeah, how about a bottle of grape juice," he yelled over the roar of the racing pump. In his car, Gregg dodged the snake pit of fire hoses strewn about the road. Once they retrieved their supplies, they re-positioned themselves at the building. The fire was still advancing, eating more of the structure as each minute passed. The firefighters and the water were not making much headway in extinguishing the inferno. This was purely a "surround and drown" operation, a defensive position for an out-of-control fire with no interior attack.

At last, Boston Fire Commissioner George Paul radioed, "C1 to Fire Alarm, strike a ninth alarm on the box." A nine-alarm order was the most manpower and equipment the City could muster without a special call for additional apparatus from adjoining cities, sort of a mutual aid response. Nine-alarm responses have rarely occurred in Boston during my adult life.

As Fire Alarm echoed the order over the radio, the jakes and the sparks in the crowd issued a loud cheer. To laymen, this cheer may have seemed odd; that ninth alarm call meant the fire was still winning the battle. But to the enthusiasts, the cheer was based on the jakes' strong resentment toward the Commissioner (C1), who, in their eyes, had failed to support the rank and file as the layoffs had swept through the Department. Snide remarks could be heard, as well as occasional slurs directed toward C1. The sparks had no doubt that the majority of jakes were fed up with the cutbacks and the political games that Mayor Kevin White and the Commissioner were playing with the BFD.

There was also no doubt that this fire was the biggest single fire that Boston had witnessed in years. The fire brought virtually every piece of apparatus in the City to battle the blaze. There were numerous out-of-town companies at the scene too, not to mention many other out-of-towners in the City to cover the now-empty firehouses.

By now, the sun was up. Bemis and Stackpole realized they were tired; it had been a long night and their adrenaline rush had subsided. As Gregg dropped Stackpole off at his car, Donny admonished him, "Hey, this is big time, so don't tell anybody that we did it." Gregg couldn't fully understand what he was getting at, but he agreed anyway as he headed home.

By that afternoon, the newspapers and television were reporting several stories on the massive fire, including injuries to a couple dozen firefighters. The arsonists had gotten media attention, but the news reports had not related this fire to the sharp uptick in fires within the City. Bemis heard rumors that ATF (the Federal Bureau of Alcohol, Tobacco and Firearms) was being called in to investigate the fire. To his knowledge, this was a first.

The arsonists were abuzz with additional rumors that the sprinklers within the building had been shut down before the fire. Something seemed suspicious. Had the building already been set up to burn? Had the arson boys inadvertently torched it before someone else did? They had even heard reports that there were multiple points of origin within the building and that traces of bomb fragments had been found at the scene. Despite Stackpole's warning to keep quiet about this fire, by the following night, Donny had already bragged about it to Groblewski and Joe Gorman. So much for secrecy.

▲

At least one rumor was true. ATF was responding to assist with the investigation. By morning, the newly formed Boston ATF Arson Task Force Group, or Arson Group for short, was a beehive of activity. This fire was a high-profile, enormous, occupied-business fire that had injured over 30 firefighters and had occurred within a business that affected interstate commerce. An investigation of a fire of this magnitude called for a larger response in terms of manpower, equipment, and money, all of which the Boston Fire Department was a little short of at this point. In other words, it was right up our alley.

ATF Arson Group Supervisor Jack Dowd was in close contact with both the BFD and also the front office, Special Agent in Charge Dan Hartnett (SAC), a strong proponent of the arson program. The SAC consulted with ATF Headquarters in Washington, DC to discuss the necessity for the National Response Team (NRT) call-out. Everything in ATF has to go through the chain of command, a process similar to that of the military and other civilian government agencies. Although the street agents, myself included, were working with the state and local fire investigators on a regular basis, the Spero fire called for the higher-ups to correspond.

The National Response Teams, of which there were four in the country, were formed in 1978 with the goal of assisting state and local efforts to work significant fire and explosion scenes. The teams consist of veteran agents with a variety of expert skills designed to push the investigation toward a successful conclusion. SAC Hartnett had been one of the originators of the NRT. He really wanted the Team in Boston for the first time.

There were prerequisites in order for the ATF NRT to respond to a fire or explosion. The jurisdiction that had the incident had to make a formal request, and there had to be loss of life, numerous injuries, and/or a high dollar loss. The Spero fire filled the bill, with both firefighter injuries and the large dollar loss. However, some jurisdictions liked to protect their own turf and investigate their own incident rather than welcoming an outside agency to nose about in their business. That was their prerogative; ATF didn't force anybody to accept the NRT services.

On this day, ATF offered NRT assistance along with the full effort afforded by the numerous Agents from the Arson Group. The head of the BFD Arson Unit, Chief Jack White, was the first person that Supervisor Dowd contacted. Chief White consulted with BFD Commissioner Paul, who in turn conferred with Boston Mayor Kevin White (no relation to Chief White). It is a wonder how anything gets done in government in a timely way. The City of Boston graciously accepted ATF's offer. A full team of Agents were on their way to assist the Boston Arson Squad and Boston Police to determine the origin and cause of the fire, including whether it was accidental or intentional, and, if the fire was determined to be arson, to try to determine who was responsible.

The logistics of bringing the NRT to town and of coordinating the efforts and roles of multiple agencies are daunting. Agents are tasked with picking up and chauffeuring NRT members who fly in from other cities due to the short notice and need to cover great distances in a short period. Hotel rooms in a suitable nearby location have to be reserved. Meetings with all involved have to be scheduled as soon as the boots are on the ground. Since the team members are due on site within 24 hours of the call-out, a lot has to be accomplished in a short time.

Also, on June 3, we had to make sure that the integrity of the scene was maintained by Boston Fire. This was not too difficult, since the hot spots required several companies to work the scene for another day or two. When I refer to securing the integrity of the scene in this instance, I am referring to maintaining custody of the property so that investigators can legally be onsite, not allowing any outsiders on the site without a significant reason, and making sure admitted outsiders are escorted at all times. By keeping the scene secured, any remaining evidence, in theory, will not be further disturbed and a legal chain of custody can be maintained.

There are few means to lawfully investigate these incidents. In many states, the Fire Chief or the State Fire Marshal has the duty to determine the origin and cause of a fire or explosion. When the Fire Department does not leave a fire scene due to normal duties and they maintain custody of the property, an investigation can legally be conducted as part of their mandated duties. Investigators can also obtain authorization from the property and/or business owner to conduct their investigation, as well as obtain either an administrative or criminal search warrant. When the initial scene inspection by public authorities is undertaken, in most cases it is unknown whether the fire cause is accidental or an intentional criminal act. Therefore, investigators have to treat everything they do as if they were, in fact, at a crime scene. It is also advisable for investigators, in the event that they uncover evidence of arson or other crime, to hit the pause button until a search warrant is obtained.

In 1982 the ATF NRTs utilized vetted origin and cause experts from outside agencies with various backgrounds as the designated expert to conduct the scene examinations. This was prior to ATF training Special Agents as Certified Fire Investigators (CFIs), a program begun in 1986. In this instance, ATF called upon David J. Icove, now Dr. David J. Icove. Since he is a good friend of mine, I will just refer to him as Dave. As of June 3, 1982, Dave was the Supervisor of the Knoxville, Tennessee, Police Department Arson Task Force, having previously been an investigator with the Tennessee and Ohio State Fire Marshal's Offices. At the time, Dave also had a Bachelor of Science degree in Fire Protection Engineering from the University of Maryland, one of the preeminent fire science programs in the country. Dave would go on to the FBI's Behavioral Science Unit, working on profiling serial arson and bombing cases. During his 40-year career in the field, he would take on various other fire investigative ventures and coauthor at least three of the principal, most authoritative books on fire and arson investigation with world-renowned fire scientist and investigator John D. DeHaan of California.

The Agent members of this NRT call-out all arrived at various times on Friday, June 4. Those Agents who were stationed within a reasonable driving distance from Boston drove their Government-owned vehicle (GOV) so that there would be extra vehicles available for investigative duties and to chauffeur other NRT members around town. Others whose assigned duty stations were farther from Boston flew into the City.

By the time everyone arrived in the City, it was Friday afternoon. As is customary when an NRT comes into a host community, the work started with a briefing, with representatives of both Boston Police and Fire present, from Chiefs to BFD Arson Squad investigators to BPD detectives, along with Boston ATF Agents, brass, and the NRT members. The Team was welcomed by the locals. They were briefed about the building and the fire details. Then, the NRT Supervisor and Team Leader discussed the logistics and Team assignments. Some Team members worked with the locals to conduct the scene inspection with origin and cause analysis. Others were assigned to document the scene with diagrams and photos. An ATF chemist was present to assist with taking debris samples for chemical analysis, as needed. Other Agents were teamed with BFD and BPD investigators to conduct interviews of witnesses, firefighters, building owners, business employees, and whoever else may be able to provide information that could be useful.

Late on Friday, all of the investigators, both local and Federal, visited the South Boston site to assess and familiarize ourselves with the situation and be ready to work early on Saturday. The true scene work would begin in the morning.

Saturday was a miserable day, weather-wise, in Boston for early June and for working a fire scene, mostly outside. I remember it well; it was just one of those days that stick in your mind forever. The temperature hovered in the upper 40s all day, and a chilling wind came in from Boston Harbor less than a quarter mile away. And it rained, poured some more, and rained on top of that. But since we worked in all sorts of conditions, we did our job.

People always express amazement at fire investigators' ability to figure out where and how a fire started, especially at a fire like this, with devastation covering acres. The totality of the damage can be overwhelming, but O & C (origin and cause) specialists are basically only concerned with the beginning of the fire and the manner of fire spread. I liken an extinguished fire to a movie that needs to be played in reverse to the opening scene. Except in rare circumstances, fires tend to start small at a precise location. Don't get me wrong; that precise location can be very difficult to identify at some fire scenes in spite of all the training and experience afforded to some investigators.

Eyewitnesses to the incipient, or early stages of a fire can be key resources for investigators. Often, a fire starts with no eyewitnesses. In other cases, a first eyewitness may not see the fire until much of a structure is involved in fire. When this occurs, investigators focus on that area of the building, if fire patterns and other factors point in that direction. In many other cases, when a person is present and discovers the fire in its early stage, again based on that information with other corroborating factors, the focus of the origin and cause analysis can be narrowed. Even when a person witnesses the early fire, there may be several potential ignition sources within that observed area. Each possible ignition scenario has to be fully examined in order to determine the true cause of the fire.

The Spero fire was witnessed fairly early, not counting the guys who set the fire, by a passerby who reported it. The experienced eyes of the first arriving firefighters provided information that was critical to the investigators. Both the citizen witness and the firefighters placed the fire on the rear wall along the railroad tracks some 75 to 100 feet from the south end of the warehouse. The firefighters saw the fire burning from ground level to the roof line some 10 to 20 feet across, at which point it progressed into the building.

I was assigned to work with Dave Icove and others to analyze the origin and cause of this incident. Armed with the interview information, we walked around the perimeter and inside the warehouse to further familiarize ourselves with the fire patterns, including an analysis of the fire progression patterns.

Much of the flat roof had collapsed. The contents of the building consisted of hundreds of pallets fully stacked with cardboard boxes containing toys, lots of plastics, and stuffed figures. Although the boxes themselves had all been damaged to varying degrees by water, smoke, and/or fire, much of the contents of the boxes survived. However, those contents were now trash that would soon occupy some landfill. The damage to these contents provided us with a pathway of fire patterns that led us back to the rear wall. Based on the foregoing, we concentrated our efforts at the rear wall where the firefighters first observed the fire.

This particular section was the only place where the wall had collapsed. About 20 horizontal feet of wall was lying flat, having fallen outward onto the ground. The remainder of several hundred feet of rear wall was still standing. With a great deal of manpower effort, we were able to lift the fallen wall in a single piece. And what a picture this section of wall presented to us.

There was a distinct burn pattern, narrow at the bottom, wider at the top. The exterior covering of tar paper had been consumed, with deep charring to the wood sheathing in what is referred to by fire investigators as a V-pattern. In simple terms, a V-pattern is formed when a fuel at the base of a vertical surface burns; the heat and flames spread upward on the surface, leaving behind physical burn patterns that can—but do not always—relate to the fire origin. The burn pattern fans out as the heat and flames extend upward and are blocked by something like an overhanging roofline, thus forming the V.

At the base of the V, we did not find an ignition source. There were no inherent potential ignition sources there, meaning there was nothing there prior to the fire that was supposed to be there such as an electrical source, cooking or heating equipment, or any other heat source. There was the base of the outside wall, period. There had not been any lightning or earthquakes in the area, so an act of God was ruled out.

Therefore, the ignition source had to be introduced to the area to cause this fire. There was no physical evidence to indicate that some homeless person had made this place a temporary shelter. When considering the possibility of improper disposal of smoking materials, we noted that there had been little to no dry vegetation along the exterior wall. It had been wet for most of the several days before the fire. Thus, merely dropping a cigarette in this precise area was an unlikely ignition scenario. This left only one final option; that is, that this fire was intentionally set by person or persons unknown. In other words, the cause of this fire was determined to be arson.

Where was the physical evidence of the device? Well, first of all, we did not know yet what device the arsonists had used. We tried to locate something on the ground that would give us some clue as to how the fire was set. Scraping the ground with definitely-not-high-tech tools like garden rakes, we carefully excavated any charred debris, but we didn't come up with anything. As described earlier, the ingredients of their incendiary device (paper bag, tissue, plastic baggie, matches) likely would all have been either consumed or charred to unrecognizability. Cooking the mixture with open flame in the range of 1,500 to 1,600 degrees Fahrenheit tends to change the combustibles into forms that are no longer identifiable.

That also goes for the cigarette. Most of it would have been quickly consumed, with possibly only fibrous filter remaining, but trying to find that filter after significant burning is very difficult, as hundreds of the charred pieces of wood look a lot like a burned filter. Add to the recipe several thousand gallons of water blasted at fairly high pressure, and any remains likely would have been displaced far beyond the point of origin.

That leaves the remains of the Coleman Camp (or Lantern) Fuel to be found. The arsonists used about one pint of fuel per baggie. Coleman fuel is a clear light hydrocarbon liquid with a distinct odor. The fuel is contained within the baggie until the fire inside the device perforates the plastic bag, volatizing the liquid and igniting the vapors. This treatise is not meant to be a detailed lesson on the physics and chemistry of fire, so when I tell you that solids like wood and liquids like gasoline do not burn in their normal state, please trust me; it is proven in fire science. Simply put, solids and liquids are broken down into simpler gases that burn. Most of the Coleman Fuel would have burned during this fire. And, again, the high pressure stream of water would have had a significant dispersal and dilution effect. This explanation may sound like excuses, but for these good reasons we did not find any residue of Coleman Fuel. Thus, we did not find any physical evidence of how the fire was initiated. Chalk one up for the arsonists, at least temporarily.

The report for the cause determination of this fire read that an open flame was intentionally introduced to the area by person(s) unknown, with the tar paper and wood being the first fuels ignited (after they were broken down to their simpler volatized component gases). The fire spread up the tar paper and plywood wall to the roofline. The fire spread into the structure due to a large opening at the top of the wall, approximately three feet square that housed a fan unit. It allowed the fire free access to the upper level of the interior, where firefighters had trouble fighting the fire.

Group Supervisor Jack Dowd brought SAC Dan Hartnett to the fire scene so that he could view the damage to the structure and get a look at the defined origin. Jack had been asking Hartnett for thigh-high waterproof boots, or waders, prior to this fire, but Hartnett just wanted to know how many in our group liked to fish. He also said no to the boots. But chance sometimes lends a hand. The SAC wore mid-calf fire boots, his suit pants tucked into the boots, as he walked along the railroad track behind the warehouse. Between the fire hoses and the days of rain, the ground was pocked with deep puddles of dirty water. The SAC slipped and lost his balance on the rails, landing feet-first in a puddle and soaking his nice suit pants to about mid-thigh. As he sat on a loading dock and emptied the water from his boots, Dan asked Jack, "Can you get those boots here by this afternoon?"

The interview teams and paper chase turned up no evidence or motive for anybody. Thus, this arson was without a known motivation or any identifiable suspect. Just to reiterate, this fire occurred in 1982. There was no Internet, no social media, where someone could brag, anonymously or not, about his illicit activities. There were none of the street view security cameras so common today. So, at this point, we were at a loss. This major fire would not soon be forgotten.

As an epilogue to the Spero Toy Company fire, the company folded shop in Massachusetts and moved to New Jersey. Three dozen jobs were lost along with the tax revenues and other benefits associated with an active business and property. Over thirty firefighters were injured. Luckily none of the injuries was life-threatening. But none of this, including the tens of thousands of dollars this fire cost the City and the Federal Government, concerned Donald Stackpole or Gregg Bemis or the other torches in the group of criminals. They viewed this fire only as a big trophy that supported their agenda.

LOUIS SPERO&C
WHOLESALE
TOY DISTRIBUTORS
Bill Noonan Fire Fotos

Bill Noonan Fire Fotos

Bill Noonan Fire Fotos

On a foggy, drizzly, rainy early Sunday morning, only three days after Spero Toy, Bemis was at it again, this time only with Wayne Sanden. Wayne may have been a sporadic participant thus far, but Gregg Bemis had been present at every fire up to this point. In fact, he would be the only member of this conspiracy to take part in virtually every arson committed by the group.

Gregg and Wayne welcomed the extra darkness afforded by the fog and rain as they slithered their way through back alleys. They checked out three side-by-side buildings near the corner of Clarendon Street and Warren Avenue in the South End, not to be confused with South Boston, for those of you not familiar with Boston. The buildings included a four-story abandoned brick structure, a large vacant brick church, and the former firehouse for Engine 22 and Ladder 13. Somehow, when you think of their deviousness and their reprehensible actions, the Dr. Seuss lyric, "You're a mean one, Mr. Grinch," comes to mind.

After searching for access to the church and the firehouse, but finding none, they gained entry into the multi-level brick structure via an open window at ground level. They set an incendiary amid combustible debris and quickly slipped through the maze away from the site. They rode around until the familiar odor of burning structure was detected.

But instead of sparking the fire, they set out to find another objective. In Roxbury, they spotted a large double three-decker, formerly housing six families, which looked ripe. It was located on a lot overgrown with weeds and bushes.

After crawling through the brush, Wayne found a windowless opening about eight feet above the ground. With a device in hand, Gregg boosted Wayne to the opening. Wayne placed the device on an upholstered couch just inside the window.

Back at the car, they heard the radio transmit a second alarm for the Clarendon Street fire. As they drove past the Roxbury location, they saw heavy fire already showing from that opening where the device had been placed. This fire went to three alarms, with fire venting from all of the windows on that level. The duo stayed at this scene, practicing their photography before heading home. With the Clarendon fire going to four alarms, they felt that they had already made it a successful night.

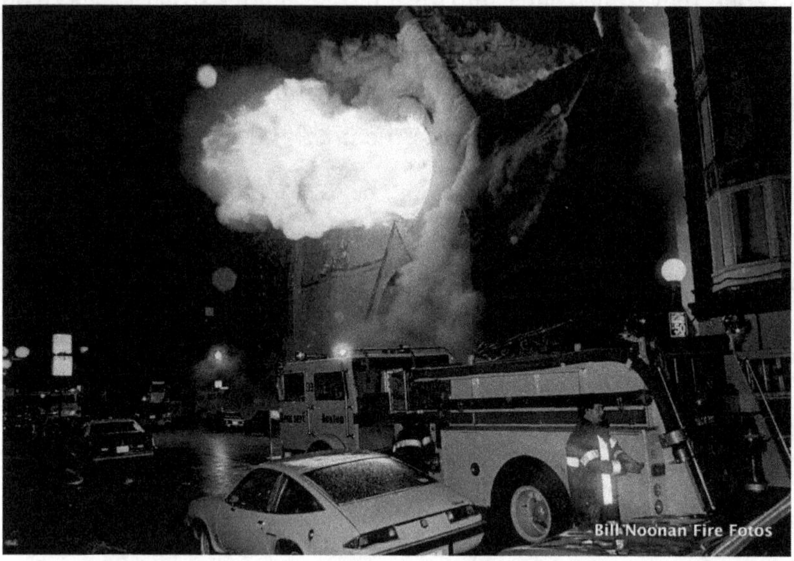

The Clarendon Street Church during and after the fire.

It is no accident that I haven't written about the personal life of any of the arson conspirators beyond their initial introductions. This is basically because their paid jobs and their "hobby" of setting and sparking fires left little time for anything else. They seemed to have scarcely enough time to get sufficient sleep to function. Wayne Sanden had a wife (and girlfriend) and children. Donny Stackpole also had a wife and dependents. Gregg Bemis had a couple of girlfriends during parts of this period, as did Robert Groblewski. I had no information about the love life of Lenny Kendall or Joe Gorman.

Except for Joe Gorman, there is no evidence that these guys did any kind of illegal drugs. Joe liked his coke on occasion. There is no evidence that these men partook of alcoholic beverages during their long nocturnal hours roaming the streets.

On June 7, 1982, Bemis, after work, went with Bobby to Dorchester, where they set fire to the first building they spotted, a vacant wood two-and-a-half duplex. Bemis was amazed that a building in such poor condition was still standing. Climbing through water-soaked bushes, as it was still foggy and showers were frequent during this miserable stretch of weather, they tried the basement first, but they couldn't find a decent place for a device. With no stairs left from the basement to the main floor, they hoisted themselves up to the first floor, which also was in terrible shape with water leaking from the open roof, making it a poor target to burn. Finding a semi-dry spot, they set a device anyway. Within 10 minutes after leaving the property, a call came over the radio for the fire. Engine 24 reported light smoke showing upon arrival. They knew then that it had to be a shit fire, so the two sought another target.

In Roxbury, they positioned a lit device directly in a dry area under overhanging porches against pink-colored gas shingles of an odd-shaped three-decker. Within five minutes, Box 2235 was transmitted over the fire radio. Engine 14 reported heavy fire showing at that location. A working fire was transmitted within seconds.

Simultaneously with the arrival of a Deputy Chief, Gregg and Bobby pulled up to the scene. Bobby knew the Deputy Chief fairly well. Brazenly and nonchalantly, he asked, "How are you doing, Chief?" They exchanged a few pleasantries as they walked toward the blazing structure. Another fire, another time when these guys had the audacity to act like they were buddies with those within the fire department while they were standing outside the fire they had just set. It seems that they still felt that they were heroes for setting all of these fires. With the fire quickly knocked down, they quit for the night.

With their big fire at Spero Toy a week behind them, as the weather finally started to heat up, the arsonists wanted to do the same. It was time to pick up the pace of their urban terrorist onslaught. Although Stackpole had warned Gregg to keep the Spero fire a secret, even from their co-conspirators, Donny felt confident enough to start crowing a little bit. He was so proud of the magnitude of the Spero inferno, so proud that it had achieved what he so desired, that is, bringing the fire department to its knees and making the firefighters earn their pay. He bragged to Bobby, Joe Gorman, and Wayne Sanden, who all praised Donny and Gregg for a job well done.

In keeping with their pattern of Thursday-Friday fires, Friday, June 11, 1982, was to be a busy, busy night. A full contingency of arsonists was on board. Bemis, Grobo, Sanden, and Stackpole all climbed into Gregg's arson-mobile. Gregg asked his posse, "Where do you want to check out tonight?"

Wayne suggested, "Let's check out Jamaica Plain. There hasn't been much activity over there for a while."

All were in agreement. As they started in the general direction of JP, Donny asked Gregg if he had listed any good targets there. Pulling out his list of potentials, Gregg named a few: "Let me see, there's Chestnut Ave., Brookside Ave., Germania Street, Bartlett Square."

"Hold it, Bartlett Square, isn't that the old warehouse next to the Southwest Corridor?" Donny inquired.

From the early 1960s into the 1980s, the Southwest Corridor was a controversial plan to continue Interstate 95 from Canton, Massachusetts, about 10 miles southwest of downtown Boston with a straight run into the City rather than taking the more circuitous crowded routes now in use. For various reasons, including lots of pressure from abutters to property where eminent domain was to take hundreds of properties, the idea was scrapped after millions already had been spent on partial bridges and roads to nowhere. An extension of the subway system eventually was constructed under a portion of the Southwest Corridor. Some green space was also built in those neighborhoods. In 1982 the area was still undergoing extensive construction, marked by street digging and partial road closures.

Gregg informed Donny, "Yes, that's the one. It looks ripe and there isn't a soul around." The Bartlett Square building was a combination two- and three-story brick warehouse that extended the entire block between Green and Williams Streets.

Donny was enthusiastic as he gazed at the abandoned tinderbox: "What are we waiting for? Let's find a spot to park and get busy."

They parked in a dark, quiet spot to make the device in the front seat of the car. After exiting the car, they walked to the rear of the huge building, where they found a smashed-out window. Wayne, then Donny and Gregg, crawled through the opening, careful to avoid shards of broken glass. Using the beam of Sanden's flashlight, they explored the first floor. Formerly office space, now it showed signs of extreme vandalism, with rubbish strewn throughout the area. Wasting no time in collecting scrap lumber and broken pallets, they stuffed a small closet with the debris, lighting a device at the base of the stack. They quickly departed.

Once back in the car, they drove around the block to make sure the device had "detonated." "Look, there's already smoke showing and I can see an orange glow," Donny called out with a tone of pride. They headed to HoJo's to drop off Sanden, who had to get to work as a BHA Police Officer. Just as they dropped him off, the box was transmitted for the fire. Next, Groblewski also called it a night, leaving just Bemis and Stackpole to carry on.

As they raced back toward JP, they grew more excited as the radio blared with activity, announcing calls for a building fire at the Bartlett Square old American Cellophane Company. The red-orange glow was now plainly visible high in the sky halfway across the City. "Engine 28 to Fire Alarm. Strike a second alarm and have all companies lay coming in." The second alarm was transmitted, with a third alarm following shortly. The fire was accelerating rapidly, doubling in size every minute. As the torches approached the scene, they saw to their joyous astonishment flames leaping a hundred feet into the midnight sky. A fourth alarm was transmitted as golf ball–size embers rained like meteorites from the intense blaze.

Donny, the least fire science savvy of the group, was astounded by the fire's swift growth to a fully involved structure fire. It had barely been 10 minutes since they had planted the device. Gregg snapped some photos before the companies had a chance to focus their deluge of water to tame the inferno.

Apparatus now converged from all over the City. It was like a parade without the marching bands. The Lieutenant on Ladder Company 29, Bob Winston, later District Fire Chief, recalled that, for whatever reason, since the Ladder was not on the cards, Fire Alarm dispatched the Ladder to this fire. Ladder 29 was an older spare piece at that time. When they arrived, the building was totally involved. There was not much for the L-29 crew to do. After a while, the Incident Commander sent them back to quarters.

With the ninth alarm, there were 21 engine companies, seven ladders, an aerial tower, and one rescue company at the scene. Low water pressure in the area further hampered extinguishment efforts, but after a while, sufficient water was obtained to loosen the grip of the blaze on the now blackened shell of a warehouse.

I have used the photograph of this fire, received from Bemis himself, as the cover for this book. It shows the four-story brick warehouse with flames spewing from every opening visible from Gregg's vantage point as he took the photo. I kept this photo on the wall next to my desk from 1985 until my retirement in 2001. Why? Because this particular nine-alarm fire was the only fire count in an indictment that we lost at trial. This photo was a reminder to me that if we could lose this count, I needed to work harder in order to perfect future criminal cases.

As incredible as this fire was, the night had just begun for the Boston firefighters. With the fire companies all still busy there, a building fire on Washington Street in Dorchester was reported. Ladder 29 neared quarters on Blue Hill Ave. when a box was struck for the fire. Lt. Winston looked toward the area of the box and observed a heavy column of smoke. He radioed Fire Alarm requesting that L-29 respond to the scene. That was immediately granted. They were one of the first companies to arrive at this fire. Heavy smoke was showing from what was the old YMCA building. Reporting to the Incident Commander (IC), L-29 was ordered to gain entry and find the seat of the fire. They did and found heavy fire in the center of the big structure moving laterally and vertically.

From the urgency in the voice of the first arriving company, Bemis realized that it was going to be another large blaze. Heavy smoke was reported showing. A working fire was ordered at 0056 minutes, that is, 12:56 a.m.

Stackpole was holding on tight as Bemis weaved through whatever shortcuts he could find to get across the City. A blanket of smoke covered the entire neighborhood. The strong scent of a structure fire filled their nostrils. A second alarm was transmitted on Box 3355. A third alarm was followed by a fourth, a fifth, and finally a sixth. This brick building had heavy black smoke pumping from every crack and orifice with a dangerous intensity. Moments later, the right mixture of air got to the superheated smoky gases. Instantaneously, the smoke burst into huge fireballs that rolled out from every opening.

Donny was on an all-time high, "Hey, this is great! A six-bagger to supplement our nine-bagger and we didn't even have to light it!"

"Yeah, that was pretty good timing; it saved us some work tonight," responded Gregg. He knew that the nine-alarm fire alone would tax the capabilities of the BFD to its limits in light of the cutbacks over the previous few months. Combined with the six-alarm blaze and what was yet to come from the two arsonists, this was destined to become one of the busiest nights in Boston Fire Department history.

Stackpole and Bemis left this fire for their next objective, a house in Hyde Park. A victim of a previous fire, the building was already in shambles, with holes in the roof and windows all smashed. Entering through the missing front door, they realized that they no longer had a flashlight, as Wayne had taken it with him when he left for work. Despite their limited vision, they lit and placed the device just inside the front door in a pile of trash, a perfect secondary fuel. They silently tracked back to the car unnoticed.

Not waiting for ignition, they elected to screw with the City by finding another site to light. "Hey, Donny, how about those used tire shops down from Engine 52's house on Blue Hill Ave?"

I had driven past those two shops often over my first six years on the job, thinking, Is there really that big a market for used car tires? But considering that the neighborhood was fairly poor, maybe there was.

Knowing most of Boston's companies were busy at one of the two earlier fire scenes, they first checked to see if anyone was covering the firehouse. No BFD apparatus were on the apron of the firehouse. As they drove past the tire shops, Gregg, at the wheel, motioned to Donny, "Look at all those old tires piled up against the buildings."

In response, Donny smiled and added, "Boy, this will really bring them to their knees now. Let's park on the side street and make two devices."

Gregg assisted Donny in assembling two incendiaries. The two businesses were one block apart. Each had a side street next to it that intersected Blue Hill Avenue. Gregg turned down one side street, with the building on his left. He opened his door to place one lit device within the pile of tires against the building. Looping the block, they came up to the next tire shop on the passenger side of the vehicle; this time Donny got out and placed the second device within the pile of tires against this building. They headed down Blue Hill Avenue. After only a couple of minutes, they noticed two nasty, black columns of smoke streaming into the sky and smelled the foul, nauseating by-products of burning rubber.

They parked where they could view their double-barreled action. Soon after the fire call had been transmitted, the avenue became congested with apparatus and firefighters battling the simultaneous fires merely a few hundred feet apart. Snickering, Donny said, "Look at all the oddball companies! I don't think there is a single Boston fire company there at all."

Gregg was in awe as the radio continued to blare out call after call on this most unusual of nights. Bemis began to realize that the fruits of their actions were being felt. He saw that the City was in deep trouble, unable to cope without the assistance of the deactivated companies.

His train of thought was disrupted by Donny: "Hey, let's find one more target just to put the icing on the cake."

"Okay, let's see what we can find. Hey, Skinny, how about those two burnt-out three-deckers on Sydney Street?"

When they cased those buildings, Donny exclaimed: "Look at all those gas shingles; it's perfect!" They immediately prepared a device. Very simply, they drove up to the front of one of the three-deckers, setting the device on the front steps against the asphalt shingles to ensure rapid spread of the fire. "Let's get out of here. I think the device is going to go off any second," Donny said with a twinge of urgency as Gregg peeled away from the curb.

Upon leaving the neighborhood, Stackpole asked Bemis to drop him at his car, saying, "I've seen enough fire for one night. Besides, I'll see it from the Expressway on the way home if it goes off."

After dropping Donny at HoJo's, Gregg followed him onto the Southeast Expressway southbound. Side by side as they passed by the area, he could see flames soaring above the vacant building. Donny blew his horn and gave Gregg a thumbs-up as they sped down the nearly deserted highway. At an off-ramp, Gregg turned off the highway to return to the fire. He heard Fire Alarm transmitting Box 1848, followed by, "Receiving calls for a building fire opposite 98 Sydney Street."

The fire was raging. Interestingly, the first BFD vehicle to arrive on scene was the BFD Chaplain, who had been heading to one of the other fires as the call came in. He radioed, "Car 17 to fire alarm. I am at Box 1848 and there is heavy fire showing from a vacant three-decker." Fire alarm responded that the companies were on the way to his location. Gregg parked a safe distance from the one-way, narrow Sydney Street so that he wouldn't get boxed in by the responding apparatus. Other spectators were showing up, but no firefighters had arrived yet.

The original building was a mass of flames, entirely engulfed, and the gas shingles on the exposure triple-decker were starting to melt. Bemis overheard a group of onlookers wondering why no apparatus had yet arrived. Seizing this opportunity, Gregg advised the people that there were several other fires in the City and that most of the apparatus were tied up elsewhere. The onlookers expressed shock at that news. One woman lamented, "I think it's a shame that they laid off all those firefighters and closed all those fire stations. It's no wonder the City is burning down." These words were music to Gregg's ears; his plan was working. Gregg secretly felt a sense of pride. In a weird, warped way, he felt that he was a hero.

It took another few minutes before Engine 56 arrived on scene, ordering a second alarm. Just as they laid their big line, the second three-decker burst into flames as the radiant heat from the first blazing building caused those volatile shingles to reach their critical ignition temperature.

A third alarm soon followed, bringing in apparatus from suburban cities and towns because the other companies were still busy at the other fires. Ladder 29 had just cleared the YMCA fire and was dispatched to the Savin Hill fire. No rest for the weary; this was their third multiple of the night.

Another box was transmitted for a fire in Jamaica Plain. The new fire interested Gregg. He started to leave the decaying fire for JP, but Engine 5 from the Town of Weymouth had boxed him in, much to his chagrin. He had no choice but to stay even though the JP fire had gone to three alarms.

As he walked back to the fire, Gregg heard a couple of Weymouth firefighters express amazement that they were fighting a fire in Boston. This was obviously a new experience for those guys. Most Weymouth jakes who desired big-time firefighting would give their left nut to work for the BFD. He heard one firefighter say to another, "Those Boston firefighters are all crazy; they're actually inside that building. They're nuts if they think I'm going inside that death trap! It looks like it's ready to collapse any second. Get me back to Weymouth quick." Bemis laughed to himself.

A half hour later, Gregg escaped from this fire scene to head to the now five-alarm fire in JP. He found a very large three-and-a-half-story wood-frame building that had housed a dentist's office and numerous apartments. At the base of the exterior char pattern was a large trash dumpster. A fire had obviously extended from the dumpster to the gas shingle siding. Bemis wondered if someone else had lit the dumpster on fire. As the sun was coming up, Bemis began his journey home after the long, adventurous night.

Longtime Boston area fire buff Dan O'Neill recalled this as one of the busiest nights ever for the BFD:

> It started around midnight with the nine alarms, the abandoned factory in JP. I was leaving the fire, talking

to Eddie Fowler, when Boston Fire Alarm struck a box for the former YMCA in Dorchester. I went to that six-alarm fire.

Leaving that fire, I responded to an outside fire at two neighboring tire shops on Blue Hill Ave. While we were standing around talking prior to heading home, we saw the K-7 car coming down the Blue Hill with Paul Finn hanging out the window pointing towards Mattapan Square. I believe Photographer Bill Noonan was driving. Quickly, Fire Alarm (FA) struck the box for a house on River Street. I believe the vacant building went to a second alarm, sparks friend John Campbell was the District Chief. I believe he only had one Boston company, an Engine from East Boston, at the fire. He had apparatus from Milton, Canton, etc.

When we were on River St., with the fire knocked down, FA struck a box for Sydney St. As they announced "Receiving calls" we jumped in our cars and headed to Dorchester. I was following the car of Stanley Forman {famous news photographer and spark} when he suddenly made a left turn at Blue Hill Ave. I thought he must have been told to go someplace other than Sydney St. I continued to Dorchester. What I learned later was that Stanley had Boston EMS on his scanner and they were reporting a fire at Hyde Square in JP.

As I was walking to the fire on Sydney Street, which was two adjacent triple-deckers, I heard Fire Alarm striking multiple alarms for the Cale Casio Building in JP. I also heard Monsignor Keating, the Boston Chaplain, tell fire alarm that he was leading Cambridge E 9 into the fire on Sydney St. I believe the rear porches fire went to three alarms while the Cale Casio fire went to five or more.

> I never responded to the fire in JP. I had to get some sleep as I had to head to a Boy Scout camp first thing in the morning.[15]

As WBZ Cameraman Nat Whittemore was taking in the Washington Street, Dorchester, fire, two out-of-town fire companies passed him, going the wrong way. Nat turned around and chased them until he caught up with the companies, blowing his air horn to get their attention. After pulling over, Nat informed them of their error, telling them to follow him as he was taking in the new job. They followed. Chief Campbell thanked Nat for his efforts.

The perspectives of Whittemore and O'Neill show how the other fire buffs, as well as the firefighters, were running from fire to fire all over Boston.

American Cellophane Building, Brookside Avenue, Jamaica Plain

15 Dan O'Neill in email dated 1/5/2019

Washington Street, former YMCA

Sydney Street

As if June 11 had not been an unusual night, June 12 and the early morning hours of June 13 were to be even stranger. On this night, the plot thickened.

First, a major fire occurred at approximately 6:15 p.m. in South Boston, the site of an ongoing business, Boston Plate Glass and Window Company. This site was only a few hundred yards from that monstrous Spero Toy inferno. This structure covered over 50,000 square feet. The roofing partially collapsed during the blaze. There was never any mention of this fire by Bemis in his journal. Also, this fire occurred early in the evening, contrary to the usual late-night prowls of the Boston arsonists.

Bemis had been scheduled to work the 4-to-12 shift in Stow, but he blew off work and headed into Boston, where he met up with Groblewski and Stackpole.

They took their plot to Roxbury Crossing, setting two buildings back-to-back. After making two devices, Donny dropped off both Gregg and Bobby. The two arsonists ran to a vacant two-and-a-half-story wood-frame house, where they quickly placed the device in trash inside the open rear door. They sprinted through vacant lots to the second target, a wood duplex three-decker on Centre Street. Behind the building, they wasted no time placing the second device in the basement, again in a trash pile. Bolting from the building, as they were a couple minutes behind schedule, they found Donny nearby.

The boys headed back to that ball field on Parker Hill to await the fires. Within minutes, smoke was showing from one of the structures. They saw Engine 42, red lights flashing, pulling out of their firehouse. E-42 reported smoke showing at Centre Street. A few minutes later, the radio blared, "Car 9 to Fire Alarm. We can see fire showing from another building just up the block. Strike the box for Centre and Cedar Streets."

The boys headed toward the action. Turning off Columbus Avenue, they saw that the second building was fully involved. The fire rapidly went to three alarms. Bobby and Gregg managed to take several good photos of the blaze before the rear porches collapsed.

"Hi, Ray, how's it going, pal?" Bobby inquired of off-duty veteran Boston Firefighter Ray Norton as he walked toward the group. Norton had been a friend of all the arsonists for some time. In the mid-1970s, at the Howard Johnson's parking lot next to Boston Fire Headquarters, Raymond J. Norton had introduced himself to a spark new to the area, Robert Groblewski. As Grobo was new to the city and did not know his way around, Norton routinely drove him while they sparked.

A nearly 40-year-old Boston firefighter, Norton was also the first person that Bemis had clicked with when he first came to spark in Boston. Norton was far older than most members of the buffs. He was old enough to be a father to Bemis. That may have been part of the reason that their friendship formed. Ray always seemed to form easy and close relationships with young males, and Gregg needed a father figure.

Norton was the youngest of four children in his Boston family. His father died of cancer when Ray was in elementary school. Around that same time, Ray exhibited behavioral issues, with problems evident at school. Briefly, he was professionally treated for emotional matters. Allegedly, during his adolescence, he had neurological problems for which he underwent electroencephalograms at Boston City Hospital to examine his brain activity, but he received no further treatment. Norton's behavioral problems persisted, causing him to have to repeat the fifth grade. Ray left school in the eighth grade to get a job as a dishwasher.

Ray grew into a large-headed, large-bodied man with somewhat oafish mannerisms and a lumbering gait. Due to his limitations, Norton continued working common laborer jobs into adulthood.

His hobby was always sparking fires; he was a fire buff from the time he was in elementary school. When Norton married in 1967, his firefighter father-in-law encouraged Ray to take the civil service exam for firefighters. He passed the test on his first try with a score of 77; a 70 was a passing grade. Despite his low score, Norton was hired by the Boston Fire Department, but he was never able to pass further tests for promotion. He and his wife had no children; the couple divorced in 1974.

Ray Norton loved being a ball buster. It was part of his antisocial personality traits. Many referred to him as "Crazy Ray." Some firefighters wondered how Norton ever became a Boston firefighter. Due to his brash, caustic character, a lot of coworkers thought he was not only a little odd but downright painful to be around. Besides his work and his friendships with teenage boys, his personal life was limited to his interests in fires and sparking with his crew of associates.

Norton often drove his personal vehicle to fire scenes, sporting a Massachusetts-issued license plate personalized with the unusual moniker ARSON. This plate would make most people conspicuous, but not Ray. Even when he was stopped by the police for a moving violation, the officer assumed that the ARSON plate meant Norton was "on his side," so to speak, as an arson investigator. He also had another vehicle with the personalized license plate LAD-5, a reference to the Ladder to which he had been assigned at some point.

Eventually, due to an injury, Ray was put on light duty as a watchman at BFD Headquarters on Southampton Street. To use a cliché, placing Norton in Headquarters was like putting the fox in the henhouse. Norton now had access to, and could keep an eye on, people and records relating to the eventual investigation into the 1982–1983 series of fires that his criminal associates were responsible for setting.

Responding to Grobo's salutation, Norton remarked, "I'm doing fine. There have been so many fires lately that it reminds me of the old days. It's great; whoever's doing this, we ought to take up a collection and give him some money for gas!" Bobby looked at Donny and Gregg. Bobby wanted to let Ray in on the plot. Walking away from Ray to discuss the situation, they all agreed to let Ray in on their plan.

"Hey Ray, come over here for a minute," Bobby called.

"Yeah, what's up?" No matter what Norton said, it always sounded a little on the gruff side. "What would you say if I told you that we've been lighting all these fires?" posed Bobby out of earshot of anybody but the small group of conspirators. He was taking a chance; Norton was not yet one of them.

Ray stood there for a minute mulling over what he had just been told. "You guys have been doing all this?" he asked with obvious skepticism.

The group's spokesperson, Bobby, explained with another query, "Well, have you got any better idea on how to force the City to rehire the laid-off cops and firemen?"

"No, I think it's great! But you guys are taking a big chance, aren't you?" Like many civil servants, Ray had a severe disdain for the tax-cutting measure Proposition 2½ as it threatened his livelihood. He feared for his job. He had even received notice that he was on the list to be laid off, although he never got the actual pink slip. As crazy as some thought he was, he was also one of the more cautious and shrewd members of the group.

They filled Ray in on a few of the basics, waiting to give him additional details at a more private location. "Hey, let's go get something else while they're still tied up here!" proposed Donny. The main players agreed, telling Ray to stick around if he wanted to catch another fire.

The torches located a vacant wood two-and-a-half-story duplex on Quincy Street off Blue Hill, still in Roxbury. With the front doors smashed in, access was no problem. Not hesitating for a minute, they pulled right up in front of the building. Donny, with a device in hand, ran to the front door, where he placed the incendiary.

Within minutes the fire was reported, giving them the feeling that the fire would be easily extinguished. But, to their disbelief, the first arriving engine reported heavy fire showing, instantly ordering a second alarm. The arsonists raced back to the scene, but the fire got knocked down quickly. The Boston Arson Squad showed up, so Bemis and the boys left for another section of the City.

In Charlestown, they hit a wood two-and-a-half-story duplex. It was easy, wide open. Bobby ran in and placed the device, and then they headed for another target. Near the USS *Constitution*, which was tied up at the Navy yard dock, was a vacant four-story brick warehouse surrounded by overgrown trees. Gregg waited in the car while Donny and Bobby crawled through the brush and planted their device. Within five minutes, they were back in the car.

Turning into City Square, smoke was visible rising from the Warren Street fire. Shortly thereafter, the box was transmitted for the fire. Engine 50 only had to travel a block or two to the fire. Because there was such heavy black smoke issuing from the structure, the engine crew realized that the fire was about to erupt, so they called for a second alarm.

When the torches arrived at the fire, Wayne Sanden, who was working security in Charlestown that night, was already there. One smile from the co-conspirators let Wayne know that his pals were the cause of the fire. Wayne was told there was a second fire brewing nearby. As the first fire had been all but extinguished, they wandered toward the other fire, which had not yet been reported, to check its progress. They saw a slight stream of smoke, but the fire was discovered and readily knocked down by a returning engine company.

To finish off the night, they targeted one more building. Back in Dorchester, they placed a device against gas shingles on the front porch. But the fire was quickly reported, virtually burning itself out before the companies arrived. Thus, after setting fire to six more structures that night, they called it a night.

A critique of the night yielded mixed reviews, with a couple of successes and a couple of busts. But now, the arsonists had a Boston firefighter on their side.

Early on Sunday morning, I received a telephone call at home from Group Supervisor Jack Dowd. He wanted me, and several other ATF Arson Group members, to meet him at the Wormwood Street Boston Plate Glass fire at 11:00 a.m. so that we could conduct some interviews and an origin and cause analysis at the scene.

I was the first investigator to arrive at the site, parking in a fairly large lot located on one side of the fire-ravaged structure. As I sat in my Government-issued Ford LTD, a black security company car pulled alongside my car. I looked over as a twenty-something, thin, dark-haired male stepped from the car and walked over to my driver's side door. He introduced himself by his first name only, Mark. He informed me that Boston Plate Glass was a client of the security company that he worked for. Although he wasn't on duty when the fire occurred, one of his coworkers had reported the fire and observed a man running from the building.

I explained that ATF would be conducting an investigation of the incident. Mark marveled at the two-way radio mounted on the center hub of my front seat. I never paid much attention to the equipment. Mark kiddingly asked if he could trade me something for the radio. We talked shop for a few minutes until other agents arrived.

I later learned that Mark's last name was Svendbye. Over two years later, Mark Svendbye would become the ninth person indicted for his part in the arson conspiracy.

The investigation of the fire revealed that it had been intentionally set, but we never identified the person who was seen running from the scene as the first smoke was observed. Additional inquiries eliminated any culpability on the part of anyone associated with the business. Again, this incident highlighted the challenges that we investigators faced every time a major fire occurred in a business during this period. After concluding that the cause of each incendiary act was arson, we had to follow through with a complete investigation as to the parties responsible for the arson. This took a lot of time and effort.

A couple of nights later, a momentous meeting was held at Norton's West Roxbury house. Besides Ray, present were most of the founding members of "Arson Anonymous," including Bemis, Groblewski, and Stackpole, plus Wayne Sanden. Before they discussed the entire plan with Ray to guarantee his support, with uncertainty about the crew's activities, Ray advised, "You guys are going to get caught if you're spreading gasoline all over the place."

Gregg corrected him: "No, Ray, we're using a time-delay device which leaves no trace behind." He further described the incendiary device, explaining the type of buildings that they were targeting. At this point, Ray Norton agreed with the scheme, officially became a co-conspirator. Ray was to be the lone full-time Boston firefighter involved in the conspiracy to burn down Boston. By 1982, when he joined the conspiracy, Norton had almost 10 years with the Boston Fire Department.

"Just do me one favor, guys. You better cover your tracks and don't target any occupied buildings," said Ray, several years older than all of the others and a little more cautious than the younger hotshots.

Bobby tried to assuage him: "Don't worry, Ray. We've got it all under control."

"Who knows about this anyway?" Ray inquired.

Again, Bobby replied, "Well, there's Gregg, Donny, Wayne, Lenny, Joe, and myself."

"Well, you better keep it that way. The more people that know, the more dangerous it gets." They talked some more, then, having no device components with them, headed home.

▲

The arsonists continued to ramp up the number of fires they were setting in June 1982. They had several "spree" nights on which the group set multiple fires in a single night.

The night of Thursday, June 17, into early Friday, June 18, was to be another spree night. Stackpole and Grobo walked up to the front steps of a three-decker in Jamaica Plain where they placed the device against the gas shingles of the vacant structure while Bemis waited at the wheel of his car. While they cruised the neighborhood, the radio squawked, "Attention Engine 42, Engine 28 and Car 9. Respond to a reported building fire at number 13 Armstrong Street."

Embers were visibly rising into the blackened night sky. A second alarm was ordered as the boys approached to spark the fire. Firefighters quickly darkened down the blaze, but the interior attack plus overhaul were going to take a while longer. "Hey, look who's here," Bobby said as he pointed to Engine 24. As the jakes came walking up the street, Bobby started joking with one of his friends from the engine company.

The jake, to remain unidentified, remarked, "Hey, Bobby, what's happening?"

"Same old shit." Really? As if setting fires was the same old shit. They hung around until the firefighter finished his job so Bobby could chew the fat with him. After the fire was extinguished, the jake came walking toward them from inside the blackened structure, when he made a wistful statement, "Hey, I wish we'd get more of these jobs on our group. The other groups have been catching all the jobs."

"Well, what can I say?" Bobby retorted with a smile on his face.

"Hey, Bobby, are you going to the Sparks Club picnic tonight?" asked the jake.

"Yeah, Gregg, Joe, and me are all going."

"Good, I'll be there too." The jake jumped back in the rig as it was leaving for quarters.

Bobby called out his familiar refrain, "See you at the big one!"

This was just another unbelievable example of the brazen arrogance of the arsonists, the militant sparks. Each one of them had friends within both the BFD and the Sparks Association. They felt comfortable enough to joke with their friends even as they set fires that caused injuries to other firefighters. With friends like Groblewski and his associates, who needed enemies? If only the firefighters knew that their offhand remarks were beefing up the egos of the torches and bolstering their hero self-image. That the jake wished for more fires on his shift meant only that these guys loved their jobs.

Time for another target. This time, back to Charlestown. "Hey, what about that old vacant three-story wood warehouse on Main near Sullivan Square?" Bobby asked.

"You mean the joint that's right next to the place we burned down a few months ago?" asked Donny, who added, "Boy, that will really bust the guys' balls in Engine 32's house."

They parked at the rear of the Bunker Hill housing projects, "Hey, Skinny, why don't you stay with the car so the project rats don't come and steal it while we're in the building?" Bobby directed. We used to kid around about Charlestown in those days that the white males who came from Charlestown grew up to be either armored car and bank robbers or cops and Federal agents. And a lot of those white males came from those projects.

With a freshly assembled device, Gregg and Bobby pulled a plywood cover off a window, climbed inside the basement level of the old wooden warehouse, and placed the lit device against an interior door before making their way back to the car.

The smell of burning wood was discernible all over Sullivan Square, but there were no visible signs of smoke, even though the arsonists knew where to look for smoke. After killing time for about an hour, the boys went back into the building to check on the fire's lack of progress.

Bobby and Gregg crawled back through the same window into the black darkness of the basement. The beam from Grobo's flashlight cut through thick smoke that filled their sinuses and burned their eyes. They found a small area with glowing embers, but no flames. "Give me the device and then head for the window," Gregg said to Bobby. As soon as he was sure that Grobo was back at the window, Gregg placed the device against the embers. The device exploded into flames. They hastily made record time back to the vehicle. It still took another 20 minutes before the box was transmitted for the fire.

Back to spark the fire, they saw a smoky situation with no flames. They tired of it right away and went back to HoJo's. "Hey, Gregg, what time do you want to meet at HoJo's tonight for the Sparks picnic?" Bobby asked.

"Oh, I'll be in around 5:00."

"Sounds good, it should be a good night."

Gregg asked Donny, "Hey, Skinny, aren't you going to go?"

"Fuck them Sparkies!" Gregg knew Donny wouldn't be interested, but he figured it was worth the try.

Groblewski was already in the parking lot when Bemis arrived. Bobby said, "Frankie and his brothers are supposed to be here shortly. His birthday is coming up so I brought him a present." Looking at Grobo inquisitively, Bobby opened his trunk and pointed to one of the voice fire alarm boxes that they had stolen. "He always wanted one of these." Frankie was another young fire buff; Gregg knew he would flip when he saw the box.

When Frankie arrived, Groblewski immediately opened his trunk again, presenting him with the fire box. Just as predicted, Frankie was elated. "Where did you ever get this?"

"You might say it was almost a steal," Bobby replied with a devilish grin. Frankie hid the fire box in his trunk.

The Sparks Club picnic was held at the Boston Fire Academy on Moon Island, a small island in Boston Harbor that is accessed via a narrow causeway from Quincy, south of the City. From the Fire Academy property, there is a picturesque view of the Boston skyline. There was quite a crowd at the picnic when the militant group of sparks arrived. It was a nice late spring night; the peacefulness of Boston Harbor was interrupted only by the steady flow of jets taking off and landing at Logan Airport just to the north.

Bemis and Groblewski saw many of their fellow fire buffs and firefighter friends. They ate with them while sharing a few laughs. One of the main topics of conversation from the sparks was whether the recently dubbed "Friday Firebug" would strike that night. Bobby and Gregg had all they could do to keep from grinning, knowing full well that they would try their damndest to fulfill the wildest dreams of the fire buffs once they left the picnic.

The reference to "The Friday Firebug" in mid-June was an early mention of the rash of building fires that had been occurring in Boston for the previous five months. The source of this moniker is unknown; most likely it was designated by the firefighters and sparks themselves. No one had seen a series of fires quite like this in Boston. The fires were occurring in multiples, often on Thursday nights into Friday mornings and on Friday nights. There was no particular reason for this group of arsonists to repeat their actions on those nights. It wasn't as if they were off from work on those days or went out to drink on those nights.

As often happens with serial criminals, a pattern develops. There are many types of patterns that can arise during repeated criminal activities. Sometimes the criminals are not aware that they are forming these patterns. However, investigators are trained to look for any suggestion of repetition that forms a pattern.

The Friday fires are an example of a temporal pattern; that is, these fires were often set on a certain day at a certain time of day. In this case, the fires were set under cover of darkness, obviously for the arsonists to evade detection. But, more specifically, most of these fires had been set after midnight and before 5:00 a.m.

Another pattern that was becoming apparent to investigators was that the targeted structures were mostly vacant three-deckers. The asphalt "gas" shingle siding was another pattern that we investigators had noticed, but this was inconsistent: A fair number of targeted buildings did not have those shingles. Remember, even Spero Toy had a rear wall made of wood covered with tar paper, basically asphalt covering. The problem for investigators was that there were hundreds of vacant gas shingle–covered buildings in Boston.

Other patterns were also emerging. First to be detected by the Boston Arson Squad was that fires were being set where voice fire boxes were missing, which could be a deliberate way to cause delays in notification. A learned arsonist knew that any delay was significant because just a couple of minutes made the difference between a minor fire and a serious blaze. To detect this pattern, one would have to be a firefighter or a fire buff, because one would have to correlate missing boxes to the arsons.

Another closely related pattern was that fires were set in locations that stretched the fire companies; that is, the normally first due companies were already occupied with a prior fire. Again, knowledge of fire department operations and company deployment would be paramount. Both firefighters and dedicated fire buffs, like Gregg Bemis, would have this unique understanding. The Boston Arson Squad also had this familiarity as they picked up on this pattern. ATF Agents and the general public would not have that specialized knowledge. This is exactly why task forces are formed with local and Federal investigators as members of the team.

One pattern that often becomes obvious after a few crimes are committed by a serial criminal, whether a murderer, a rapist, or an arsonist, is the location of the target. The first targets chosen by serial offenders are often in an area where they feel comfortable, such as an area where they grew up or where they now live or work. As a lawbreaker gets away with his (or more rarely, her) first offense or two, he or she tends to spread out to new locales as confidence is gained, leading the lawbreaker to become more brazen or reckless.

Investigators often placed pins in a map at the locations of the crimes associated with a serial offender. In many investigations, pins have a roughly circular configuration, with the first pin possibly representing the first crime within a series near the center and subsequent crimes spreading out from the center. A trained criminal profiler starts looking for the perpetrator near the center of the pattern.

However, the pattern analysis during this investigation only revealed that the fires associated with this arson wave had been set in nearly every neighborhood within Boston. Most of the fires occurred outside of downtown Boston, but that was because Roxbury, Dorchester, Jamaica Plain, Mattapan, Charlestown, and South Boston in the early 1980s were the poorer neighborhoods with more vacant structures available as targets.

In hindsight, think of the composition of the conspirators involved in this case. Most were not Boston residents, so they wouldn't start committing their series of crimes where they are most comfortable. Several of them worked in the City, but they had access to the entire City. As sparks, they knew all of Boston. So their first targets were not representative indicators of where they lived or worked. Additionally, they made lists of potential targets during their travels around the City. Their efforts, knowledge, and access all made it much more difficult for investigators to determine where they might hit next.

With all of that being said, by mid-June 1982, a few of the fires had occurred within occupied commercial businesses in South Boston. This was an escalation in their crimes, which would dictate some of our efforts in the near future.

Another aspect of the nickname "Friday Firebug" is that it was relished by the arsonists. It gave them an identity in the media and among the general public without revealing their actual identities. It gave them a renewed impetus, as if they needed it. It added to their arrogance and confidence. It cemented, in their minds, their image of themselves as popular heroes.

The bad guys fed on the news coverage. They were encouraged by it. The Friday Firebug loved the attention, the celebrity, the notoriety. The press and the public fed their frenzy.

The celebrities involved in this case were reinvigorated by the picnic talk from their "peers." Just basking in the others' curiosity and interest in the arson spree became a siren call to those militant sparkies to set even more fires in Boston.

One can hardly blame the firefighters who were pawns in the political game related to Proposition $2^1/_2$. In total, 10 engine companies and six ladder companies were permanently deactivated as a result of Prop $2^1/_2$. With so many of their coworkers laid off, they were putting their lives on the line each and every time they responded to a call. Their job was to fight fires and save lives and properties. They were Boston Firefighters; they were jakes. They wanted to fight fires, not sit around the firehouse.

And who could blame the fire buffs? It was their hobby and interest to observe fire and firefighting operations. Taking photos of fires, firefighters, and apparatus was no different than avid birders taking prized photographs of birds in the wild. To collect memorabilia was no different than antiquing. They had a legitimate club and a genuine pastime.

So, buoyed by the camaraderie at the Sparks picnic, Robert Groblewski, the Boston Police Officer and wannabe firefighter, along with Gregg Bemis, the Stow Police dispatcher, call firefighter, and wannabe big-time firefighter, headed out to light some fires for their fellow buffs. Gregg suggested, "Why don't we get that pile of tires behind the Motorola shop near the Keystone Building?"

The Keystone Building was a large, highly recognizable landmark former office and manufacturing building, later converted to apartments, that sits beside the Neponset River and the Southeast Expressway. This location, only four miles from the picnic, allowed easy access to the HoJo's parking lot. After walking through brush past a couple of old sheds, the boys placed one device each in two separate piles of tires. They rapidly headed back toward the car as both devices ignited prematurely. Upon reaching their vehicle, they raced up the x-way to HoJo's.

The box was transmitted for the fire as they pulled into the lot. Bobby hollered to friend Frankie and others, "Hey, Frankie, you guys hop in the back seat." After they climbed in, they sped back southbound down the Expressway. The traffic was moving too slowly for their liking, so Bobby suggested that Gregg turn on his alternating headlights and siren. After all, they were first responders, public personnel. They never stopped to think that their use of lights and siren was an abuse of power. I guess that was an extremely minor concern compared with setting fires.

A couple of miles down the highway, Bemis heard another siren and noticed another set of wig-wag alternating headlights behind him. "Shit, it's the fucken' Metro cops!" Gregg fumed. The Metropolitan District Commission (MDC), now defunct, had its own police department. The Southeast Expressway was part of its jurisdiction. Gregg edged his mock cruiser out of the high- speed lane into the center lane when the car sped up beside him. It wasn't the Mets at all; it was Joe Gorman just laughing at Gregg as he passed by. So Gregg stepped on the gas, pulled back into the high-speed lane behind Joe, and followed him the rest of the way to the fire.

Engine 20 was first to arrive on scene. Two separate, distinct columns of black smoke were visible above the scene. While viewing the fire, their jake friend from the fire the previous night and from the Sparks picnic showed up to spark the fire. "Hey, Bobby, it looks like it's going to be one of those nights," the jake mused. It recently became recognized that every time tires were involved in the fire setting, it was a pretty fair assumption that "Mr. Flare" was involved in some way. This was another new nickname. Gregg loved this one. He was very proud to be the primary arsonist responsible for this unprecedented major rash of fires. He identified as Mr. Flare although the press, firefighters, and fire buffs didn't yet know the nickname. Mr. Flare would play a larger role over the next few months, and even later.

Grobo pulled Bemis aside: "Hey, why don't we fill [the jake)] in about what we're doing?"

"I don't know if that is a good idea. Too many people already know about it now. Just remember what Ray said the other night." After a few minutes of mulling it over, they tabled the idea for now.

When the fire was knocked down, the larger-than-usual crew headed back to HoJo's. There was no activity over the radio for over an hour, so Frankie and the other guests headed home. Their departure was fine with Bobby and Gregg because they couldn't set any more fires while they were around. Just as they and Joe were planning the next hit, Donny arrived at the lot. "Hey Skinny, you're just in time," Bobby said.

"Good, I'm ready for some excitement anyway," Donny replied as he climbed into the back seat of Gregg's car. They targeted a vacant duplex triple-decker across from the house for Engine 41 and Ladder 14 in Brighton. Donny said, "This place looks ripe."

Gregg was not so sure. "Yeah, but the guy on patrol at 41's house will spot it too quick."

"Well, let's go find something that will tie them up until it has a chance to get going," Donny recommended. Within minutes, they found a warehouse sided with gas shingles. Making two devices, they placed one against the building, saving the other device for the duplex. As soon as they were sure that the device ignited, they headed for the previous building.

Three of them walked in the shadows staying out of view of the firehouse. Entering an open doorway to the target, they heard the unmistakable roar of apparatus diesel engines as they pulled out of their house, apparently heading to the warehouse fire. The device was planted in the basement within stacked boxes underneath the stairs.

The companies from the firehouse had not returned as they exited the building. Once back at the vehicle, they headed to fire number one. Although it had been knocked down already, the firefighters again would be tied up with overhaul, since the fire had gotten into the partitions.

Twenty minutes later, the box came in for the duplex fire. As the boys headed in that direction, the first arriving company reported heavy smoke showing, the indicator that the fire was going good within the interior, but was oxygen starved. By the time the arsonists arrived, the building had lit up, nearly fully involved. A second and then a third alarm was transmitted within minutes. This was one of those spree nights.

Since it was only 3:30 a.m., still early by their standards, they kept going, but this time all the way across the City to East Boston. In Eastie, they found an old mill complex in the Orient Heights section. But they wanted another target to complement this one. It was becoming their newest modus operandi.

An old gas station on Saratoga Street filled the bill because there was a large pile of old lobster traps (I'll bet you thought the draw was a pile of tires) and an old wooden boat against the rear wall of the gas station.

Again, they made two devices, hitting the factory first. Back at the gas station, they placed the device within the stacked lobster traps.

With the double fires set in two different neighborhoods, it was obvious to the Boston Arson Squad that something had been going on that night. When the arsonists checked out their fires, much to their dismay, both fires had been contained to single alarms. The torches finally gave up for the night.

CHAPTER SIX

EARLY SUMMER 1982

June 21, 1982, the first day of summer, was my sixth anniversary as an ATF Special Agent. Even with successes in previous cases, especially an investigation involving three arrests and the recovery of 46 stolen U.S. Armed Forces M16-A1 rifles plus a million dollars' worth of stolen goods, in my mind, I was still learning the job. I learned every day from colleagues from ATF, and from the state and local people that I associated with on a routine basis.

This arson case was still five months away from beginning to unravel for the conspirators. During the first three months of the fledgling ATF Arson Group's existence, we had been running from commercial fire to commercial fire, any fire that affected interstate commerce. With most of the fires set by this band of arsonists being in abandoned houses, they did not fall under Federal jurisdiction, so we did not investigate those fires per se.

However, with the major uptick in the number of fires, it had been determined that most of the blazes were incendiary fires. The possibility of accidental fires occurring within so many abandoned buildings was close to nil, especially when viewed in conjunction with the timing of the multiple fires during a single night. Because of this inference, a meeting was held with the Boston Arson Squad and the ATF Arson Group to discuss how to handle an investigation that began to focus on the possibility of one or more persons setting these fires in connection with the City-wide cutbacks.

As of this date, all of the fires had been set in Boston. Therefore, no other agencies, including the State Fire Marshal's Office, were involved in the meeting. As with many other major cities throughout the United States, the city fire departments often investigated the fires within their jurisdiction without assistance from the State Fire Marshal. In Boston, State Trooper Kevin McMahon was the sole State investigator who spent a great deal of time in the City. Trooper (later Lieutenant) McMahon had an ulterior motive to hang in Boston. He, too, was a fire buff; he loved the action in the City, and he had a penchant for firefighting operations and for the apparatus. However, he didn't start riding with us and BFD for another year.

Since many of the fires had occurred on Thursday night/early Friday morning, it was decided that we would conduct overnight surveillances in the South Boston industrial area where several of the recent fires had been set. The surveillances commenced about 11:00 p.m. and ended at sunrise, which was approximately 5:00 a.m. this time of year in Boston.

These surveillances entailed the use of dozens of investigators from ATF, Boston Fire, and Boston Police. Some were in vehicles, both stationary and mobile roaming units, with a mix of investigators in each vehicle. Their mission was to spot suspicious activity in the area, watch for vehicles cruising the neighborhood, and, if warranted, stop and identify the occupants of the vehicles. The law officers inquired of the occupants their reason for being in the area since this industrial area had virtually no residential dwellings. The surveillances covered an area roughly one-half mile by one-half mile. Some of the roads were used as a cut-through from downtown to the Southie residential streets.

To support the vehicular units, we utilized investigators on the rooftops of some of the warehouses around D and E Streets. The spotters on the roofs were armed with radios to maintain contact with the vehicles and with binoculars to identify any vehicles by make, model, color, and, if possible, license number for the mobile units.

These surveillances were conducted for a couple of days each week for several weeks of summer, with no results of any consequence. Dozens of vehicles were stopped. Maybe some b & e's (breaking and entering, burglaries) were prevented. A few lovers were disturbed and hustled on their way with coitus interruptus, probably averting a few unexpected or unwanted pregnancies. But no investigative leads were developed; an effort put forth to no avail. However, no fires occurred in this particular zone while the surveillances were ongoing. It made us wonder whether our operations were compromised; that is, if word of our plans had been leaked to the arsonists.

During one of the all-night surveillances, Group Supervisor Jack Dowd received a phone call from Special Agent Tim Ready, a true Boston Irishman. Tim was in Cambridge at a Democratic social gathering. He repeatedly implored Jack to come visit him there. Tim explained that a very important member of Congress and the Democratic Party was present and wanted to meet with Jack to talk about the arson problem in Boston. That politician was Thomas "Tip" O'Neill, the 47th Speaker of the House of Representatives, serving in that position for the third longest tenure (and longest continuous tenure) in U.S. history. Congressman O'Neill was a beloved, tough, old-style powerful politician.

Professional liaison was an important aspect of the job description for every agent, including agents in management positions. To form relationships with state and local police plus fire personnel, as well as politicians, was an extremely important mission of criminal enforcement. One would never know when those relationships would contribute to the success of a criminal case. The state and local people were closer to the streets and to the people who lived on those streets. Sources of information were developed through those people. Without the state and local help, ATF, and other Federal agencies would be at best less effective and at worst helpless. Partnerships are the backbone of successful intelligence gathering.

Without close interactions with politicians, their support would often wane, budgets would diminish, and an agency could cease to exist. For instance, when Ronald Reagan ran for president in 1980, he promised supporters of gun rights to do away with ATF. We needed sensible politicians who realized that Federal enforcement of firearms laws was necessary, not to take firearms away from law-abiding citizens but to go after criminals who violate the Federal laws. The business of fighting the crime of arson was a different animal. Again, ATF needed political support so that we could assist state and local agencies with cases that were beyond their capabilities, whether it was with expertise, manpower, or equipment.

Jack Dowd realized the importance of having the opportunity to meet with Tip O'Neill. After hemming and hawing about whether or not to excuse himself from the surveillance team, he headed over the short distance to Cambridge just for a quickie visit. Speaker O'Neill was genuinely interested in what was happening with the arson epidemic in Boston. He asked Jack very pointed questions. Dowd, without telling specific particulars of the investigation, explained to the Congressman in sufficient detail about the problems gathering evidence to prove arson, the motives behind the fires, and identifying the people responsible for the fires. Speaker O'Neill was impressed with the apparent dedication and efforts being put forth, not only by the ATF Agents, but by all the investigators who were working tirelessly to solve the fire problem. The Speaker indicated that he would do whatever he could to support those efforts.

When Jack returned to those dedicated, but very tired and hungry, investigators, he brought with him a smorgasbord of leftovers donated from the function, thank you very much. That was a good place to start with that promise to support the troops.

As explained to the Speaker, we had to resolve another vital aspect of the investigation that would be key to identifying potential suspects by name; that is, pinpointing the motive for the arsons. Often, when a motive could be clarified, a list of viable suspects could be formulated. All of the investigators were asked to provide any thoughts they had as to possible motives behind the fires. Most of the usual motivations were discussed but readily discarded, as there was no information to support them.

There were all sorts of theories for the incredible rash of fires that were plaguing Boston. Professionals like James P. Brady, sociologist, criminologist, and director of the Boston Arson Strike Force, offered theories that related to banking and insurance industry practices that made it easy for the criminal-minded property owners to sell their property to the insurance companies.

David Scondras, community activist, and Arson Strike Force member Michael Moore pointed to rising property values in some districts while other areas had severely decreasing building values. This dichotomy allowed the unscrupulous to take advantage of the economics in sophisticated arson-for-profit schemes. These concerned parties pointed to patterns where fires were set in apartments to force tenants out so that the buildings could be converted to condominiums. On the opposite end, where building prices collapsed, buildings were being burned to clear the land, which was becoming more valuable for redevelopment.[16]

Boston Fire Commissioner George Paul had his own ideas. He didn't think that the City had a serious arson problem; rather, he suggested that the media had latched onto some fires and blown up the story. (That sounds familiar: fake news.) He often repeated that "bored juveniles, idle during summer vacation" were mainly to blame for the fires, even though the arson rampage continued during the fall. Paul and City Fire Marshal John White also opined that vandalism as an act of protest or ethnic groups coming into the City showing their disapproval and those looking for welfare payments could be the motives behind the fires. At that time,

16 James P. Brady, "Why Boston Is Burning," Boston Globe Magazine, October 23, 1983, pp. 54–64.

Commissioner Paul admitted that the Boston Fire Department had never conducted a major arson-for-profit investigation.[17]

Those closest to the streets, the investigators in the Boston Arson Squad, including Henry Hickey, Robert Shaw, Rick Splaine, and others, expended a lot of time and effort exploring their theories. Since most of the fires occurred in abandoned properties that were uninsured, they discounted an arson-for-profit motive. The Squad eliminated revenge as a motive because, they wondered, revenge for what? However, some of the patterns supported the theory that maybe somebody had an axe to grind against the fire department, whether they wanted to get on the job or were disciplined while on the job. Relative to the arson spree, Shaw stated in 1982, "There is only one group of people you're hurting, and that's the firefighters."[18] Although the BFD Arson Investigators couldn't quite put their finger on the real defined motive, their theories later proved to be right in the ballpark.

The Boston fire investigators naturally struggled to believe that any laid-off Boston firefighters or union members could be involved in setting this rash of fires. Who could blame the BFD arson investigators for balking, considering that one or more of their own could be responsible for setting these fires? How could one of their own do this with so many firefighter injuries piling up? Could someone who has been laid off be that pissed? We were sure some could be extremely angry, but setting multiple fires was beyond most expected anger levels. It would be so embarrassing to the Boston Fire Department if some of their own were caught setting these fires.

We also considered that the board-up companies, which are hired to secure burned properties, usually by covering at least the first-floor windows and doors, could be setting the fires to gain more business. This would be a for-profit motive, but not a prime suspect. In Boston, the same two companies usually raced to every fire in order to attempt to win the

17 Ibid, pp. 51–52.
18 Art Jahnke, Who's Burning Boston?" Boston Magazine, December 1982

job. These guys were often well versed in the firefighting protocols and operations that could spread the fire companies thin around the City. Some were even active fire buffs.

Boston Fire provided a list of 20 to 25 persons of interest at this time, people who had piqued their interest in one way or another. Some of the usual suspects, that is, past accused or convicted arsonists, were checked out, but none of them were quite capable of pulling off this epidemic of fires. Some of the sparks' names were on the list, including Donald Stackpole and Wayne Sanden. We at ATF had no knowledge of these two guys at that time, but we all started to whittle down the list. We had no specific information or concrete evidence that any individual from the list was actually responsible for these fires. After some investigation, several names from the list were eliminated; other names were then added.

For now, talking with as many people as possible—people with knowledge of fires and people with knowledge of the ongoing firefighter budget issues—was one of the tracks that we followed. Interviewing people is an investigative technique that can yield significant results; in fact, eliciting information from any available source can make or break a case. Some people fail to realize the importance of interviewing as an investigative technique, but there are complete training classes and entire courses on interviewing techniques to be employed in many settings, not just the familiar police interrogation room setting of television and film dramas. However, many new investigators who may understand the value of interviewing people don't understand that it can take years to become an effective interviewer.

An investigator also has to find someone worth speaking to and listening to, because listening is a huge part of interviewing. As an example, during this period, I had the pleasure of working with Cambridge FD Fire Investigator Edward Fowler. Eddie was also a professional United Press International photographer. For decades he photographed Boston sporting events and other occasions, but his love was fires. He worked them, photographed them, and investigated them. It seemed to us at ATF that Eddie Fowler often saw the ghosts of arsonists in every shadow around the corner of every burning building. Initially, before we really got to know Eddie, we rolled our eyes at some far-fetched connection he tried to make between a fire and a suspected arsonist. But every investigation should have an Eddie Fowler because sometimes he was right on the money.

Eddie spoke about several of the guys who were, in fact, responsible for these fires. He often saw them at fires, but beyond that, it was their attitudes and actions at the fire scenes that not only irritated Eddie but gave him a bad feeling about their true intentions. The only problem with his information was that we didn't exactly know what to do with his suspicions.

So, for now, the surveillances continued and we set out to interview as many people as possible.

▲

Once again, Gregg Bemis skipped his shift at Stow. He called in sick so that he could go to his side job, that is, as a fire-setter. This was June 22, 1982, a Tuesday, a day not in keeping with the pattern of Thursday-Friday fires. Bemis and Groblewski found Wayne Sanden working at one of the BHA housing projects in the South End. Sanden was easily persuaded to join his pals when his shift ended at midnight.

As soon as Sanden arrived, they hit their first objective, a wood three-decker with gas shingle siding located on Blue Hill Avenue, only a few hundred feet from the firehouse for Engine 52 and Ladder 29. Wayne had reservations about the choice, which faced the busy street: "It looks good, but I think it will get called in too quickly."

Gregg overruled him: "Don't worry about it. By the time they get a call, those gas shingles will be going like hell." So, once there was a break in the traffic, the boys pulled right up to the front of the building, where Bobby jumped out and placed the device in the front door alcove. They drove south on Blue Hill, parking several blocks away from where they could still view the target.

Within several minutes, the arsonists lit up when they saw the building blazing away with flames rising into the night sky. In another few minutes, two apparatus, 52 and 29, raced out of the firehouse. The fire grew so rapidly that the guys thought for sure the firefighters would call for a second alarm, but they did not, limiting it to a disappointing single alarm. Groblewski was so pissed by this: "Those stupid assholes are fucking themselves while we're out here trying to help them!" Every one of the co-conspirators had no doubt that the more multiple alarms City suffered, the more pressure the Mayor would be under to reopen the closed firehouses and rehire laid-off firefighters.

Armed with renewed focus to wake up the City, the torches chose three more triple-deckers, all in Dorchester. But all three fires were basically failures, so they gave up for the night. Groblewski suggested, "Why don't you guys meet me here on Thursday night at about 9 p.m. and we'll go out again?" The others concurred; they all knew they needed to keep the heat on.

On Thursday night, when Bemis pulled into HoJo's, he found Stackpole already waiting with Grobo and Sanden. The first fire of the night was set in South Boston, at an empty two-and-a-half-story wood-frame house that was highly visible from their hangout at the HoJo's lot. Excited by tonight's possibilities, Bobby offered, "I'm going to give Ray a call and tell him to keep his radio on tonight."

Once inside the building, Donny and Gregg found the walls of the house stripped to bare wood studs, a great fuel load once an accelerant was set in the right place. Back in the car, they returned to HoJo's, where a spark friend approached them to talk. The arsonists tried to keep their friend distracted so he wouldn't see the smoke that was already showing across the Expressway. Finally, the box was transmitted over the radio, which prompted them all to look toward Andrew Square in Southie. The fire was raging.

Sanden left for working a midnight shift at the BHA. The others ditched their spark friend so he wouldn't get suspicious of their activities. Even though heavy fire had been reported by the first due company, the group headed for another target at the opposite side of Boston. Their goal was the Roberts VFW Post in West Roxbury, which had been previously damaged by a lightning strike a few months earlier. Bemis dropped off Stackpole and Grobo, who placed a device in a big hole in an outside wall.

Their next target was a second attempt to get a house on Norfolk Terrace, Elliot Belin's neighborhood. So as not to get caught by Elliot, they had Donny stay with the car on a dark side street while Gregg and Bobby ran across the footbridge over railroad tracks to the Terrace. After planting the device inside the structure, they quickly left the area to find another target without waiting to check their work.

Donny suggested a building on Fifield Street, right around the corner from Engine 17's house on historic Meetinghouse Hill. According to Wikipedia, Meetinghouse Hill is the site of the First Parish Church, established in 1631, and the Mather School, established in 1639, the oldest public elementary school in North America. Now, the Hill was about to be the site of one of the arsons committed by perhaps the most notorious gang of arsonists in modern U.S. history.

As Bemis steered for the target, the box struck for the VFW Post. "Beautiful, I didn't think it was going to go," Donny beamed. Just a cou-ple of minutes later, a second alarm was transmitted for the fire. Moments later, the call came in for Norfolk Terrace. As they reached Fifield Street, a third alarm came in for the Post.

Bobby said, "That must be going pretty good!" That third alarm tempted them to return to that fire, but they didn't want to waste precious time and they were already at their newest target. The first arriving company at Norfolk Terrace reported only light smoke, so it sounded like a shit fire. Pulling up to the front of the vacant three-decker with pinkish gas shingles, Bobby stepped out of the vehicle, placed the device on the ground up against the lowest course of shingles, and hopped right back into the car.

This was definitely a spree night for this crew. As the fourth, fifth, and sixth alarms were transmitted for the Roberts Post, they located another place to burn, just to keep the BFD jumping. The boys were pissed that they missed the six-alarm fire, but at the same time, the arson addiction pushed them to set another and another.

As Engine 17 pulled out of their station, the company reported heavy fire showing at the Fifield Street house. A working fire was transmitted. For the moment, they took a fire-setting break to steal more voice fire alarm boxes. At one corner, Gregg swerved to the side of the road, Bobby grabbed the handle of Box 3428, and with one quick tug, the box fell into his hands. He cut the wires and threw the box into the trunk, and they departed from the scene.

Sarcastically, Donny remarked, "That was like taking candy from a baby." Driving through Dorchester, they stopped at each voice box, trying the hard tug method with each one. Some boxes surrendered easily; others proved much tougher, and some did not giving way at all. After absconding with Box 3332, they got back to fire-setting.

Up next, they lit more gas shingles on the front elevation of a wood three-story house on Park Street. Then, the arsonists ventured over to Quincy Street (where I once ate pasta in a cockroach-infested house while working undercover buying guns a few years earlier), where they hit another vacant two-and-a-half-story house with gas shingles near Engine 17's house. Here Bobby and Donny put the device against the shingles on the front porch. Gregg advised the torches as they returned to the car that Park Street was already reported. "Let's go and check it out," Bobby said.

Donny dissented, "No, we should get something else going while they are tied up." Gregg agreed, but Grobo was getting pissed; they had torched several buildings without sparking any of them. After some heated discussion, they sparked the Quincy Street fire, where heavy fire was showing.

Leaving that scene, they drove about a half mile to Rossetter Street. With device in hand, they crept through dense bushes, entered the open front door, set the device within a large pile of trash, and then left the scene. Just for the hell of it, they stole one more voice box, number 1795 at about 4:00 a.m. "Well, we had a pretty good night, don't you think?" Gregg pronounced to the others.

Bobby still moaned, "Yeah, too bad we had to miss the Roberts Post though." That day happened to be Robert Groblewski's twenty-sixth birthday. Apparently, the arsonists attempted to set as many fires as physically possible to celebrate Grobo's birthday. Maybe the fires represented giant candles on his cake.

Dawn was breaking over Boston's eastern sky, so they quit for the night.

As Bemis pulled into his driveway after his long ride home, he heard the box for Rossetter Street transmitted. With a satisfied sigh of relief, he was happy that the last device had ignited; the group members had been trying to be extra careful not to leave any un-ignited devices lying around where they could be found by ATF or the Boston Arson Squad.

During the day on June 25, 1982, I was busy and mentally torn. My second daughter was born midmorning in Boston. That's where I was physically as a happy dad, but I couldn't help feeling uneasy because there were eight structure fires in the City during the night. Something was definitely going on with these fires. It was eating away at me. Something had to be done—soon.

Officially, I took the day off to spend time with my wife and two daughters, my firstborn being only 14 months old. However, while they all rested and napped, I made several phone calls to get some information. I spoke with Lt. Stephen McLaughlin, the Boston FD Arson Unit investigator who had been assigned to the ATF Arson Group. Stevie was in the unique position of knowing what the Boston Arson Squad had uncovered as well as what was happening in the ATF Arson Group. He advised me that at least five of the overnight blazes had been determined to be incendiary fires—that is, intentionally set.

Boston Fire Lt. Stephen McLaughlin was the only non-ATF investigator to be assigned to the group. He is the only person ever to have a business card stamped with the symbols and telephone numbers of both the Boston Fire Department and the ATF. McLaughlin, who had volunteered for the ATF assignment, was given a desk in our group and use of a government vehicle. He was deputized so that he could carry a firearm and assist with all aspects of our daily duties. He was also privy to grand jury information.

Steve was raised in that Irish enclave of 1940s and 1950s South Boston. After years in the Navy, McLaughlin took the Civil Service test for Boston Fire. After all, it was in his blood; his father and his uncles were firefighters. He entered on duty in October 1965. It took only seven years for him to become Lt. McLaughlin.

In one of those touches of irony that popped up during this case, as Firefighter McLaughlin, he was assigned to the firehouse on Blue Hill Avenue, Engine 52, Ladder 29, and Rescue 2. One of the busiest firehouses in the City, it was the firehouse adopted as a home away from home by young fire buff Gregg Bemis. He became friendly with several of the firefighters in the house. One of McLaughlin's insights about Bemis was that when he was around, they usually only had one or two calls per night, whereas when Gregg didn't show up at the firehouse, there were often more than a half dozen runs per night.

On that day off, I also spoke with numerous ATF Arson Group members. Between Lt. McLaughlin and the others, I learned that, although no person was identified as a suspect for any of these fires, the temporal and location patterns relating to these fires, in conjunction with those of the previous fires, solidified the notion that someone with knowledge of the BFD movements was setting these fires. But who, none of us had a clue. The immediate plan was to continue with those all-night surveillances.

Other fire buffs out on the streets were speculating about the identity of the arsonist. In particular, Nat Whittemore and Ed Fowler were naturally forming their own opinions; they were knowledgeable professionals, they had spent a lot of time during the previous few months chasing the Boston fires, and they knew most buffs who were also out nightly. Every jake knew the sparks, at least by face, if not by name.

Nat, a WBZ-Channel 4 news cameraman for some 20 years at the time, was an "honorary investigator" to us. If it wasn't for Nat out there chasing fires (Nat was a lucky man, getting paid for one of his hobbies as a fire buff), we wouldn't know the background and actions of some of this crew during the fire spree. Also, Nat would soon be "Nat-on-the-spot" for the event that led investigators to begin cracking the shell on the arson ring. Eddie had spent so many hours on the street as a photographer, fire buff, and investigator that he came to know the bad players long before they were known to us at ATF. Forming relationships with men like Whittemore and Fowler became the epitome of the teamwork that resulted in successful criminal prosecutions.

Although Nat and Ed had no hard facts that would hold up in any court of law, they had an itch when it came to some of their fellow sparks. A few of the sparks, especially Ray Norton and his friends, irritated Whittemore and Fowler. One of Norton's friends, Donald Stackpole, was not a member of the Boston Sparks Association, as the Club did not want him. Many people did not care for Stackpole and his gruff, nasty demeanor. Firefighters thought both Norton and Stackpole were real oddballs. But, beyond their character flaws, Stackpole's actions at fires, with his associates, caught the eyes and ears of sleuths, Fowler and Whittemore.

The Stackpole group was too often at fire scenes a little too early and having a little too much fun. They always seemed to be rooting boisterously for the fire to be the winner which was understandable from their point of view, since they were wishing that the multiple alarm fires might eventually result in the fire department cutbacks being rescinded, but not from fire-fighters' point of view). For the moment, Whittemore and Fowler mainly kept their suspicions to themselves, but they kept their eyes and ears open.

Bemis met with Sanden and Stackpole on Sunday night, June 27, 1982, another new night of the week, throwing off the pattern in an effort to defy any surveillance efforts. On Centre Street in Roxbury Highlands, Wayne and Gregg climbed onto the triple-decker rear porch. Both guys crashed through the rotted floorboards that gave way under their weight. But, unhurt, they managed to place a lit device among wood debris piled in a first-floor corner built-in shelf.

I doubt that Sanden and Bemis knew a lot about fire science, but their instincts were good; such a corner configuration would provide an added impetus for fire growth due to what is termed air entrainment. The length of the incipient flames would extend more rapidly to the ceiling than from a fire in the center of the room. The importance of this is that the fire would rapidly spread laterally across the ceiling, filling the room with combustible gases and smoke particulates. Within a short timeframe, the radiant heat energy would volatize more combustibles, heating the room to untenable levels. Then, bang! The transition to the flashover stage, where virtually everything within the room alights with ferocious flames nearly simultaneously. Suddenly, within moments, the fire in a room becomes a room on fire. Temperatures within a room escalate from the mid-hundreds to the 1,800-degree range. Flames erupt from the room to the structure's exterior and into other rooms within the building. With suitable air and fuel, the result is a roaring, massive fire.

This is exactly what was witnessed by the arsonists shortly after they positioned themselves to view the building. Once the glow of fire from the interior gained momentum, there was no stopping it. Fire shot through the roof as the box was transmitted over the radio. Within minutes, the structure was fully involved, a predictable consequence in keeping with fire science. A five- alarm fire resulted, a big success fire from the arsonists' point of view. On to another target.

In Roxbury, the boys found another wood three-decker sided with gas shingles. I sure didn't know, and I'm not sure if many other people did, that there were so many similar buildings in Boston that made such a fine fuel package. But these guys seemed to find them all. With device in hand, Donny stepped from the car's rear door and placed the package on the front porch. They checked on the Centre Street fire, which was now under control. Box 215 transmitted for the Roxbury fire, but that fire was easily knocked down.

They then made their second attack on the closed State Hospital buildings, like the first time in the East Group of structures. Donny stood guard with the car. In one three-story brick building, the other two found that all of the floors and stairs on all levels were concrete.

"Fuck, this place will never go!" wailed Gregg as they checked out the third floor. Then, he stated, "Hey, there must be some kind of a cockloft in the roof."

"Well, let's go up the stairs to the roof and see," countered Wayne. Sure enough, there was a hole chopped right in the middle of the roof. Gregg pointed his flashlight down into the hole, revealing a massive attic built entirely of wood. A slight problem arose; some other material besides their incendiary device was needed as a growth fuel to ignite the large structural timbers. Wayne came up with the solution: "Hey, how about this tar paper?" They pulled shreds of readily combustible tar paper from the roof and threw them through the opening. Wayne lowered Gregg into the cockloft, where he arranged the tar paper into a kindling pile into which he nestled the device. As fast as he could, he climbed out of the cockloft. These guys were innovative and were not easily thwarted in their efforts to set a good fire.

They scampered back to the car before the fire became visible to passersby. Smoke was already rising from the roof, but the fire was reported too quickly and held to a single alarm. Dismayed, Stackpole groaned, "This night has been a real dudzo," seeming to forget all about the earlier five-alarm job.

To appease Stackpole, they decided to "get" a couple more voice boxes. In Gregg's treatise, not once does he use the word "steal" when stealing the boxes. It seems to be an interesting way to minimize their culpability for their actions.

After wrestling with several boxes with no success, they finally absconded with Box 2287 after a single tug. A vehicle was heading toward them just as they cut the wires. To avoid a close call, Donny tossed the box in the back seat as Gregg floored the gas pedal. They laughed for a while about the theft and split for home.

As June 1982 came to a close, we at ATF and the investigators with the BFD Arson Squad were still no closer to identifying a suspect or group of suspects responsible for the arsons. We were still running from fire to fire, continuing to look at each fire as a distinct and separate incident. We had to use due diligence following an investigative protocol of interviewing owners, occupants, tenants, and other potential witnesses.

We also had numerous conversations with the Arson Squad, and, admittedly, we wondered at times whether some at Boston FD might not really want to stop the fires if the fires were helping publicize Fire Department issues.

There was another concern that we had to consider. Were our surveillance plans compromised? Was there a leak within the BFD, whether intentional or inadvertent? Bemis and company had many friends in the Department whom they could rub up against in casual conversation, all the while surreptitiously pumping them for information. Their source(s) of information may have innocently supplied the torches with investigative plans, completely unaware that their friends were master arsonists.

As of June 30, 1982, Mr. Flare and the Friday Night Firebug(s) had set at least another 50 structure fires in June, making their total since the beginning of their campaign 80 blazes. The City had taken notice. The citizens of Boston were also aware that there was a fire problem with sirens wailing so often; many people were becoming afraid to sleep at night.

On June 30, 1982, a significant event occurred to assist with the layoffs. Governor Edward J. King signed a financial measure to help Boston manage the Prop 2 $^1/_2$ tax squeeze. This should have pleased Bemis and his arsonist friends since the measure guaranteed the rehiring of nearly 300 laid-off police officers and firefighters. Nevertheless, the workforce still was about 400 members below 1980 levels in each department, and the firehouses still would not reopen. Thus, Mr. Flare felt he had a lot more to accomplish. He couldn't stop now. Besides, this was getting to be lots of fun.

CHAPTER SEVEN

SUMMER 1982

Four days later, Bemis found Sanden on patrol at a South End housing project. When Sanden went off duty, they stopped at Norton's house to let him know their plans for the night.

After filling in their friend, they chose a previously fire-damaged three-decker in Dorchester. The building stairs between the first and second floors were already burned out, and the roof above the stairs had collapsed. A lit device was placed against the exposed wood lath. When trying to leave the building, they were seriously delayed due to a taxi dropping somebody off in full view of their planned escape route. Worried that the device would ignite while they were still at the building, they both raced to the car once the coast was clear. Gregg turned up the first street he came to. It was a dead end. He instantly realized he had screwed up. He backed out of the street right away. The glow of fire was showing in the front hall. Gregg yelled, "Shit, it went already!" Then, he rapidly but quietly drove out of sight. Not knowing if anybody had seen them, the duo elected not to spark the fire, but cruised a nearby parallel street.

"Holy shit, look!" yelled Wayne, pointing across a vacant lot. Heavy fire was showing from the top two floors. Simultaneously, the radio tapped out Box 3536.

Gregg recommended, "Hey, let's get out of here and get our next target." A second alarm was struck for the fire minutes later. Gregg placed a device against gas shingles at the second building, still in Dorchester, only five minutes from the inferno they just set. They bolted for a third location.

A short distance away, target three was a previously fire-damaged mansion on Geneva Avenue. Access was easy. Inside, with numerous boards as additional fuel to accelerate the fire, they placed the device in the front stairwell walls within the wood lath. Over Wayne's portable radio came word that heavy fire was showing at the previous building. A second alarm was ordered.

Back at the car, Bemis pointed toward a cloud of smoke and glowing red embers visible from the second fire. "Car 7 to Fire Alarm. Strike a third alarm on Box 3336, this building is fully involved. We're going to deck guns." They immediately looked for another target, but, not finding anything suitable, they checked out the multi-alarm fire.

At the scene, the arsonists saw that the bulk of the fire had been knocked down, but some spark friends were there, including Elliot Belin. While speaking to their friends, the radio transmission came for Box 1798 with fire showing on Geneva Avenue. All the sparks raced toward the new fire. Gregg quickly found a parking spot. The fire was raging on the upper floor, with intense flames shooting through the roof. Second and third alarms were struck, but once the apparatus arrived and set up, the firefighters quickly knocked down the fire. Quitting for the night, Gregg dropped Sanden at his house, asking, "Hey, are you going to go with us to Providence on the third and fourth?"

"You bet I am."

"Okay, I'll call you tomorrow and let you know where and when we're all going to meet." Back in the 1970s and early 1980s, the capital city of Rhode Island, Providence, had an intense, sordid episode of arson fires over the two-day period of July 3 and July 4. This 36-hour stretch was legendary; the Fourth of July arsons in Providence were known nationwide.

Serious fire buffs often made the short trip from the Boston area down Route 95 to Providence.

On Saturday, July 3, 1982, six members of the Boston arson conspiracy—Bemis, Groblewski, Stackpole, Sanden, Gorman, and Norton—met at HoJo's and headed to Providence to spark some fires there. To their way of thinking, sparking in Providence was a little vacation from their nearly full-time job of being arsonists because they could just enjoy the night watching fires without having to "work." The first night proved to be busy, but not crazy busy, so they left for home early. As luck would have it, several fires occurred after they left. On the night of the Fourth, they returned to the Ocean State capital, caught a few more fires. and went home fairly satisfied, without setting any of their own fires.

▲

A couple of days had passed since Providence. The boys were anxious to get back to work—Bemis's words, not mine. As I wrote in the last section, the arsonists considered what they were doing as a job, and "vacation" was over. On July 7, Bemis met Grobo at HoJo's while waiting for Sanden to get off duty at midnight. Gregg suggested, "Hey, Bobby, let's hit Hyde Park again. We have to get them to reopen Engine 49." They still felt that they were the crusaders who would force the City to change, to rehire those laid-off firefighters and re-open the firehouses.

When Sanden arrived, Bobby filled him in. "Wayne, we're going to try and get a building on Vaughn Avenue first and then we're going to stir things up around 49's firehouse."

Grobo dropped off the other two. Gregg and Wayne squeezed through a hole in one fence along the MBTA tracks at the rear of the building. Avoiding the electrified third rail when crossing the tracks, they scaled the fence on the other side of the tracks. The four-story brick warehouse was totally secured. But this was not to be a setback; they were resourceful.

They placed the device against the rear wall of a wooden storage building belonging to a lumberyard.

Once Grobo picked them up at the preset meeting spot, they rode around waiting for the fire to take off. Smoke permeated the air. Rather than wait for the FD response, Wayne proposed, "Hey, since we're getting lumberyards, why don't we get one of the buildings at Morrell in Hyde Park?" The others enthusiastically agreed.

Once in Hyde Park, they first set a device against gas shingles at a single-story structure at Baker Asphalt Company, which was located closer to the firehouse than the lumberyard. Before they even reached the lumberyard, a smoke column was rising in the sky. It only took a minute for the asphalt company fire to be reported—another shit fire.

As Gregg dropped Wayne and Bobby off at a footbridge that crossed over the railroad tracks to Morrell Lumber, he pointed toward another rundown warehouse on a dead-end street over the other side of the tracks. The boys made a second device to take with them just in case the building proved to be a suitable objective. At Morrell Lumber they placed a device in some loose wood against a storage shed. They also placed a device at the warehouse at the end of the street. The first thing Sanden said as he hopped back into the car was, "This should be real good. They'll have to re-open Engine 49 after this."

By the time the boys had repositioned their vehicle near Cleary Square, the box had been struck for Morrell Lumber, so they drove in that direction. Engine 48 reported heavy fire showing upon arrival. When the arsonists arrived, the storage shed was fully involved, but the firefighters stopped the fire so that it did not spread to adjacent structures.

After leaving Morrell, they grew anxious waiting for the third building fire to be reported. Driving back to that location, they saw the structure still burning, but apparently, nobody else had seen it. One of the fire companies at the lumberyard fire called Fire Alarm asking if there were any other fires in progress in the area. Fire Alarm informed them that nothing had been reported. The company recommended that somebody check the area as they could see smoke from some other fire than the one they were mopping up. After a brief search, one of the companies located the fire, ordering the box to be transmitted. Once again, the fire was quickly suppressed, confined to a single alarm partially thanks to a sprinkler system inside the building.

With daybreak due shortly, they set one more fire for the night. The tired arsonists placed a device in a small opening in the plywood-covered window of a large vacant three-decker in Dorchester. Instead of waiting for the fire, the part-time thieves nabbed fire voice Box 3364 with one tug from its pedestal. Bobby snipped the wires and quipped, "Well, that's another one of these fucken' things that we don't have to worry about anymore."

"Yeah, they ought to hang the motherfucker who invented these fucken' things in the first place," Gregg added.

As they were about to split up for the night, the box was transmitted for the Dorchester fire. Shortly afterward, Engine 18 reported heavy smoke showing ordering a second alarm. With that, Gregg joked, "Well, at least we got one multiple alarm fire tonight."

On Friday, Bemis called Sanden to see if he wanted to go out and play after he got off work. Sanden told him to meet him at his house. Sanden was just pulling into his driveway as Bemis arrived. "Did you bring all the stuff?" asked Wayne.

"Sure, all we need is a box of matches and we're all set to go."

Once Wayne changed out of his uniform, the duo headed for some mischief. "Hey, I drove past the Wheatland Ave. fire the other morning after you dropped me off. The place was going good," Wayne advised.

"Yeah, well it's too bad the joints in Hyde Park didn't go any better," moaned Gregg.

"I don't know, maybe it did some good after all. That many fires in Hyde Park in one night will surely get the residents on Mayor White's ass about opening Engine 49 back up." Bemis had to agree since the residents of Hyde Park were already furious with the City for closing Engine 49 in the first place.

After buying a box of matches, they set a large two-and-a-half-story abandoned schoolhouse on fire. Back at the car, well hidden by thick fog, they saw a glow of fire from their position. The torches left the area for another target down Blue Hill Avenue, where they placed another device between metal grates and plywood that covered the windows of a four-story brick storefront. Wayne expressed skepticism that the device in this configuration would catch the building on fire, but Gregg had a wait-and-see attitude.

Just then Engine 24 reported fire showing at the schoolhouse. Passing by the site, the boys saw heavy fire blowing out of several second-floor windows. A working fire was transmitted. If this fire had been in a different area of the City, it would have called for a third alarm, but the fire companies in this area were highly skilled and experienced, and they handled the fire on their own with no problem.

Rather than hang around to spark the fire, Bemis and Sanden checked the progress of their second fire. As they approached the front of the building, the call for this fire was transmitted over the radio. Being at the scene of an arson fire before the fire companies arrived would not be good, so Gregg took evasive action to escape from the area, but not before they glimpsed heavy fire pumping from the window where they had placed the device. Again, the fire was held to a single alarm. The boys had had enough for this night.

On July 10, 1982, Bemis met Stackpole in town. The temperature finally rose to typical Boston July temperatures, toasty and humid. After midnight, they headed to Norton's house to inform him that they planned to torch a couple of joints.

In Roxbury, the twosome chose a vacant two-and-a-half-story duplex with gas shingle siding. Two identical porches ran the length of the front with the gas shingles all the way down the walls to the porch floors. Bemis said, "Hey, Skinny, that looks good."

"Yeah, we can drive right up, put the device on the front porch and screw," responded Skinny. After driving around the block and manufacturing a device, Gregg shut off his headlights and coasted to the front of the building in stealth mode. Donny climbed out of the car, strode the few steps onto the front porch, placed the device, and slid silently back into the car. Within a few minutes, they heard, "Attention Engine 14 and Ladder 4, respond to a reported building fire at about number 20 Circuit Street. We're striking Box 2147."

"Okay, Skinny, let's go," Gregg lit up as he headed for the fire.

Before they arrived, the radio blared, "Engine 14 to Fire Alarm, heavy fire showing on Circuit Street."

As Bemis and Stackpole pulled up to the scene, they spotted Boston Police Officer Robert Groblewski with a BPD wagon parked right near the building. What a picture that would have made; two arsonists walking up toward the arsonist police officer in uniform with the backdrop of a roaring structure fire. Gregg called out to his friend, "Hey, Bobby, what's up?"

"Nothing's up with me, but it looks like you guys have been busy," Bobby said with a smile, knowing that his buddies had obviously caused this fire. A working fire was transmitted on the box. The trio talked until Officer Groblewski got a call and had to leave.

Norton showed up at the fire moments later. After 10 minutes, the fire was knocked down, so they headed for another target. "Where should I head next?" asked off-duty Boston Firefighter Ray Norton.

Gregg replied, "I don't know yet. Why don't you hang around HoJo's for a while?"

A vacant triple-decker with gas shingles in Charlestown beckoned to them; they needed no coaxing to hit it. Since the building was buttoned up tight, they just placed the device against the shingles. "Okay, Skinny, where do you want to park to watch this thing?"

"Well, let's drive up Rutherford Avenue and make sure it's going first. If it is, then we can watch it from the lower deck of Route 93." Stackpole referred to the double-decker highway bridge that ran north-south elevated high above Charlestown offering a bird's eye view of the fire building. Approaching the target, they saw that the device had already ignited, so they made for the ramp to Route 93 southbound. As they pulled even to the building on the highway, heavy fire was showing and the column of smoke was rising even higher than their elevated position, about 100 feet above the fire building. "Pull up onto the median strip," suggested Donny.

It wasn't exactly the best place to park—traffic would normally speed by—but at this early hour, there were few cars, most of which stopped to gawk at the fire. They were surprised that the fire had not yet been reported. From the guardrail, they could hear several cars down on the streets below blowing their horns. Then, the sirens began echoing from the distance. With the first apparatus at the scene, three alarms were struck as the fire spread to a couple of exposure structures.

A crowd had congregated to watch the fire with them from the highway. Satisfied with their achievement, Bemis and Stackpole proceeded home.

▲

Another Thursday night–Friday morning was at hand; it was July 15, 1982. It had been a few days since the last fires, but things were still pretty hot. Since it was the night of the week that was becoming infamous, the

Boston Arson Squad and ATF were running with a full complement on the streets, expecting another busy night.

With plenty of supplies on hand, Bemis met Grobo and Sanden about 8:00 in South Boston. Too risky to set fires this early in the evening, they rode around the City updating their list with new targets and deleting some from their inventory. Still too early, they visited Norton at his house to discuss potential targets. Ray opened the conversation with a line of unexpected news, "Well, you guys must have gotten your point across last week in Hyde Park."

"Why do you say that?" queried Gregg.

"Well, the word is that Engine 49 is going to re-open on July 21st." Gregg and Bobby looked at each other, and then, like a couple of kids who just heard they are going to Disneyland, they ecstatically jumped up and down. They believed that their efforts had been justified, their objective achieved. Uncivil disobedience at its best, in their minds.

Bemis beamed, "That's fuckin' fantastic!" But not satisfied that their point was being made with the public and the politicians, they thought of additional ways to increase the publicity over the issue at hand. Gregg offered a momentous suggestion, "Hey, do you guys think it would be a good idea to send a letter to one of those TV stations explaining the motive behind all of this?"

"Why not? Maybe they'll snap as to why all the fires are occurring," Bobby mused.

Ray, the elder of the group, cautioned, "You guys better make sure that you don't leave any fingerprints for them to find."

"Okay, what do we want to say?" Gregg asked for suggestions. The discussion went around Ray's living room. They decided to emphasize the need for the closed firehouses and police stations to be reopened. Gregg took the point on this project: "Okay, I'll get to work on it and I'll show it to you before it's sent."

It was getting late, so the conversation got back to burning buildings. "Hey, Wayne, how about American Cellophane?" asked Grobo. "Did they take the attack dogs out of there yet?"

"Yeah, they did," Wayne replied.

"Are you sure? I don't want any dogs getting killed," Ray implored. (Never mind that a firefighter or some other person could be killed. Priorities can get skewed for a cause.) They decided to skip that target for the night anyway. They left Norton to get to work. This was to be a night of re-burns; that is, setting fire to buildings they had torched previously.

Setting Quincy Street first to divert some apparatus, Gregg stayed hidden in the dark with the car while Bobby and Sanden planted a device on an open windowsill in the rear of the building. Upon returning to the car, the arsonists immediately drove to Brookford Street, where the same pair carried a device toward the pair of fire-damaged triple-deckers. "Where did you put the device?" Bemis questioned after they got in the car.

"This time it should go like hell," Wayne believed.

"It's between the two three-deckers, next to the gas shingles," Bobby offered. Where else would they have put it but next to the gas shingles?

Hoping that Quincy Street would come in first, they were disappointed when the radio reported, "Attention Engine 21 and Ladder 4. Respond to a reported building fire at number 42 Brookford Street. We're striking box 1764." The torches headed in that direction.

Wayne speculated, "Boy that was awful quick. I hope it had enough time to get going."

"Don't worry, if it's gas shingles they'll have their hands full," Bobby said, trying to relieve Wayne's doubts. At the scene, a huge shower of embers lit the sky.

"Engine 21 to Fire Alarm. Heavy fire showing, report a working fire," blared over the radio. Groblewski and Bemis took photos of the blaze, souvenirs of their crime so that they could relive and fantasize about their past misdeeds.

Car 7, the District Chief ordered a third alarm, followed shortly by a fourth. Ray Norton appeared from the crowd of onlookers with a smile on his face. "Good job, boys!"

Bobby shot back, "Yeah, well just stick around for a while. This is just the beginning." From the apparatus radio, the call came in for Quincy Street, but that fire amounted to nothing, whereas the fire in front of them was now at seven alarms. Not only did the inferno encompass both side-by-side triple-deckers, but it also ignited the adjacent two-and-a-half-story wood-frame. There was no further spread of the fire, but the flames and the master streams had quite a duel with each other.

It was time for their relentless attack to continue. Bobby suggested an old house behind thick brush and trees on Paul Gore Terrace in Jamaica Plain, which he knew would be hard to find, possibly causing a significant delay in discovering and reporting the fire. Wayne and Bobby again took their turn setting the device within the ripe target.

Back in the car, Bemis proposed setting a fire at a two-and-a-half-story wood-frame house nearby on Centre Street. This time all three of the co-conspirators planted the device in a secluded rear corner of the building, then left to hit another building.

This was another barrage night, hitting multiple targets in a short period to put pressure on the fire department. Around the corner from Brookside Avenue, Gregg drove up to the front steps of a dilapidated triple-decker covered with gas shingles. Bobby climbed out, placed the device by the front door, and jumped back into the car.

As they pulled away, the box was transmitted for the Centre Street fire. The first arriving fire company reported fire showing. The sparkie-arsonists sparked the fire. Soon the box was transmitted for the Brookside Ave. neighborhood. Gregg, Wayne, and Bobby all smiled at each other as a mob of sparks at Centre Street headed for their cars, a reflection of their pride that Mr. Flare was out and going strong. Solely by the number of buffs that were around, there was a sense in the air that something special was materializing.

Bemis and company found the Brookside fire already a ball of flames. A second alarm was promptly ordered. The area suddenly swarmed with fire buffs. Several spark friends came over to them. The gist of all conversations was the subject of Mr. Flare and how busy the fire business was. One of the buffs stated that he had smelled smoke while en route to this fire. Groblewski assured him, "It's probably from this fire," while smiling over at Bemis. To them, it was obvious that the smoke detected by their friend was actually from Paul Gore Terrace, which still had not been reported. Finally, as Brookside was darkened down, one of the apparatus loudspeakers blasted over the diesel engine roar a report of the fire on Paul Gore.

Like a Charlie Chaplin fire drill scene, the fire buffs ran to their vehicles and raced toward the new fire scene. Although the boys arrived first at the scene, what better alibi could they have than to have been seen by a crowd of fire buffs at the last fire? The building was fully involved from the ground to the roof. The sirens were approaching, but they didn't arrive on scene for another couple minutes. Ladder 17 arrived first. Parking on the Terrace was a feat. The truck took the entire street. Ladder 17 called for a second alarm. Bobby knew the Lieutenant on 17. They greeted each other. Moments later, the Lieutenant ordered a third alarm. Bobby yelled, "Hey, Lieutenant, strike a fourth, strike a fourth!"

His friend the Lieutenant looked back at Bobby, smiled, and said, "Have Fire Alarm strike a fourth alarm!" The crowd was pretty rowdy by this time, cheering as the fourth alarm was ordered.

Bobby and Wayne climbed onto the roof of Ladder 17's tractor for a better view. A well-known spark/photographer was standing in front of the ladder truck. Bobby called out to him to take their picture. The photographer turned, focused on Grobo, and snapped a few photos. Tonight was a party, and the arsonists were playing the part of celebrities at the party; no one knew that they were also the hosts.

The conspirators spoke with their photographer friend for a while. He said to the arsonists, laughing, "I'd like to see how much gasoline this guy buys before a night of fires like this."

Bobby retorted, "I don't know, but it sure looks like he knows what he's doing."

Their friend continued to laugh, "I'll bet he's got a pick-up truck with a 55-gallon drum in the back. He gets his paycheck and heads for the gas station!" After the fire was darkened down, they all left for the night, but not before making plans to again meet at Norton's house later that day.

▲

Mid-afternoon, Groblewski and Bemis arrived at Norton's small Cape Cod-style house in West Roxbury. Bobby asked, "Hey, Ray, is there anything around here to get?"

"The only thing I can think of right now is that wooden stone crusher up the street at West Roxbury Crushed Stone."

Bobby and Gregg checked the property while it was still light out. Just a quarter mile down Grove Street, Gregg was about to drive past the entrance to the Crushed Stone yard when Bobby instructed, "Drive right into the yard."

Gregg hesitated, "The place is still open right now."

Showing his brazen cowboy style, Bobby explained, "They'll just think we're a couple of detectives checking the area out."

That was, in fact, the primary purpose of driving around in their unmarked black Ford and Chevy sedans, their "nerf cruisers." They wanted to fool the public into thinking that the cops were driving around their neighborhood keeping them safe. Nobody would pick them out as a gang of serial arsonists.

Gregg didn't argue with Bobby. He headed into the front entrance. After driving around the massive granite quarry, they decided that the wooden tower housing the stone crusher was the best target. This was an unusual gray four-story structure with the ground level on stilts so that trucks could drive through the lower level and get filled with crushed stone. The building looked likely to burn easily.

Satisfied, they returned to Norton's house. Ray was glad to hear that his friends decided to burn the place he suggested. This was far different than Ray's earlier attitude when he would mimic Sergeant Schultz from the *Hogan's Heroes* TV comedy: "I see nothing! I hear nothing! I know nothing!"

To kill some time, Bemis and Grobo cruised the City, updating their target list while it was daylight, then returned to Norton's to watch some TV. About 11:00 p.m., Bobby said, "Okay, it's late enough to get busy now."

Ray asked, "Where do you want to make the device?"

"Why don't you open your garage door and I'll bring the stuff into the basement where nobody will see us?" Gregg proposed to Ray.

With their freshly made lunch bag device in hand, Bobby and Gregg walked down Grove Street toward the quarry. When they were sure that no cars were approaching, the arsonists ran into the darkness of the yard. They double-checked the property for a more suitable target, but stuck with their original plan. Inside the stone crusher, they climbed iron cross bars to the second level of the building, where they planted the device on a two-foot-wide rubber conveyor belt that ran the entire width of the building.

Quickly they climbed down, then traveled through the woods instead of walking the road, until they were directly across from Ray's house. Ray was waiting for them at his front door, "Well, is it going?"

Bobby replied, "It should be going by now." Looking out Ray's living room window, they spied a flicker through the trees. From a second-floor bedroom window, the view was better, but trees still obscured the fire.

Within minutes, the call was transmitted for the fire. As the boys headed for the front door, Engine 55 and Car 10 raced past the house.

"Let's check it out," Ray suggested. Bobby and Gregg went over in Gregg's car, but Ray drove his car so as to not to be closely associated with the other two. The fire was held to a single alarm.

Back at Ray's house, Bobby said, "Ray, I think we'll head to Brighton to check out a few places. We should be able to get that joint on Islington Street across from Engine 41's house again, and I think I know of another joint near Engine 51's house in Oak Square."

A couple of significant events had already occurred this night. Ray Norton was no longer a passive co-conspirator. Norton planned with Bemis and Groblewski to set West Roxbury Crushed Stone on fire, providing his house as the location to manufacture the incendiary device. This target met another important condition of a conspiracy subject to Federal jurisdiction: It was an active, ongoing business that affected interstate commerce. However, the Chief who signed the fire report would rule that this fire was accidental due to an electrical failure. This type of finding on the fire incident report played havoc with the criminal prosecutions to follow.

On the Brighton-Newton line, there was a vacant two-story barn on a steeply graded hill off Washington Street. Parking on a dark side street, they walked with a device to the barn. An open door led to the basement level of the barn, where they placed the device in wood debris. Then they headed for the car.

Just as Bemis unlocked the door, a woman came out of her house next to their parking place. "Gee, you know this is a real bad spot to park your car." Before they had a chance to respond, she heard the radios in the car. "Oh, I didn't realize that this was a police car," she said with a smile. The boys didn't want to stick around and chat, since the device had probably already gone off. The fire could be visible at any moment. Nevertheless, she commenced explaining the problem with the parking spot, "You know, every time somebody parks on this corner, a drunk driver hits it when they go by." They sympathized with her, but without further hesitation, they departed from the neighborhood.

"Hey, Bobby, let's get Islington Street now so that by the time this one comes in, we will have that one ready to go." Once they got to their objective, they found the building boarded up after the previous fire, so they placed the device near the entrance where the gas shingles could catch.

The barn fire still had not been reported, so they rode by the building. While they waited for visible smoke, they made another device. This time they didn't park on the same street where that friendly woman might see them again. Once inside the same rear door, they encountered a smoky, smoldering fire. Piling up more boards, they set another device and immediately left the area.

As they departed, the fire on Islington was reported. They sparked that fire for a moment, but it was held to a single alarm so they checked the progress of the barn fire. From the rear of the barn fire was showing. Forgoing sparking this fire, they left Brighton before the arson squad arrived.

The boys set two other fires that night, a large row of five-story vacant brick building on East Berkeley Street in the South End and a Southie duplex, but neither amounted to much. It was now about 4:30 a.m., too late to target another building. Instead, they added some voice boxes to their collection. Detouring off Blue Hill Avenue, they nabbed loose Box 2151. By the time they could find a second loose box, the Boston Fire Alarm crew arrived at the location where 2151 had been. When the wires are cut, a signal is automatically received at Fire Alarm. A crew instantly responded to the locale to repair the situation. The next box to be relieved from its post was Box 3625. As they were preparing to leave town, Bobby tugged on one more box, but it wouldn't budge. "This fuckin' piece of shit," Bobby snarled as he cut the handset off the box. "There, that will fix them," he added as he climbed back into the car.

Over the radio came the transmission, "Fire Alarm to S12. They just robbed 3625."

"S12 to Fire Alarm. I have that message."

"Maybe if you move a little faster, you'll catch up to them," retorted Fire Alarm.

"If I'm lucky, they'll take them all," countered S12.

Gregg and Bobby looked at each other, laughing at the entertaining conversation. Gregg dropped Grobo at his car and pointed his car toward home.

▲

On Tuesday, July 20, 1982, Bemis met Sanden at the Cathedral Housing Project in the South End, where Sanden was working. Bemis had something to show Wayne: "Hey, I brought a Xerox copy of the letter I made for the TV stations."

"Let me see it." Wayne scrutinized the 8 1/2-by-11-inch sheet of paper with cut-out letters of different sizes and colors that had been clipped from several newspapers and magazines. The letter read as follows:

> **"I'm Mr. Flare. You know me as the Friday Firebug.**
>
> **I will continue till deactivated police and fire equipment is brought back. If abandoned buildings are torn down, occupied buildings will be targeted."**

"It sounds good," approved Wayne.

"Now, the only question is which TV station do we send it to?"

"Well, Channel 4 has been covering this whole thing the most, so why not send it to them?" That was the station where cameraman Nat Whittemore worked. Sanden asked, "What did the other guys think about it?"

"Bobby and Donny thought it was alright, but Ray hasn't seen it. It would be a good time to send it since they're supposed to open Engine 49's house back up tomorrow. Maybe we can push them to re-open a couple more with the media stirring things up," responded Bemis optimistically.

After midnight, they decided on three objectives. The first was a large abandoned brick church. In the rear of the church basement level, Gregg placed the device at the base of a broken splintered door. "That is not going to work," Wayne said over and over.

Gregg countered as they headed for the car, "Sure it will. Have a little confidence." A few minutes later, they drove past the building, where they could see a small fire showing in the doorway. Gregg added, "Okay, let's head over to our second target." Wayne persisted that the fire would not go anywhere.

Just blocks from the church fire was the same five-story abandoned brick building at the corner of East Berkeley Street that Bemis and

Groblewski had hit four nights earlier. Their previous attempt had been a shit fire; tonight Bemis led Sanden through the same open door that he had used a few days before. It still had the strong odor of smoke from the aborted fire. Bemis placed a new device in a pile of wood. As he did, Sanden's portable radio announced the church fire. "I still don't think that it's going that good," Wayne repeated.

Almost immediately, the radio blared, "On Box 1526, receiving calls for a church fire at about 7 Montgomery Street. Okay, Car 4?" Car 4 responded.

"It sounds like it's going pretty good to me," Gregg mocked Wayne. Gregg was first out of the opening into the night. "Holy shit, look at this," Gregg was incredulous at the golf ball–size embers flying through the air all over the neighborhood. Wayne's jaw dropped when he saw the sky lit up like a Christmas tree. "It won't go, huh?" Gregg teased.

Upon reaching their vehicle, Car 4 called for a second and minutes later a third alarm on the box. They sped toward the fire, parked, and walked to the scene. Bemis took several photos, but they left before the Arson Squad showed up. This turned into a large-scale inferno, going to nine alarms. Sanden recommended, "Why don't we get our last target now while all the companies are tied up?" Bemis agreed. And the East Berkeley Street fire had not even been reported yet.

Their next target was the brick warehouse on Brookside Avenue in Jamaica Plain. It was the opposite end of the same building that they had lit up to the tune of nine alarms on June 11. There was plenty of building left to possibly get another nine alarms. This was the same structure that had the attack dogs in it until just recently.

They parked, traversed fields, found a hole in a chain link fence, and entered the building through a punched-out wood panel on a large overhead door. The arsonists placed the lit device in a pallet and trash pile. Since they parked some distance away, they humped back to Gregg's car as fast as their legs could carry them.

A short while later they observed a column of black smoke pumping from the building with an orange glow ensuing. Box 255 was transmitted within minutes. As they approached the fire, heavy fire was visible. A second alarm was ordered. Fire buffs left the church fire and began to mass at the new scene.

Norton arrived at the fire with a smile on his face. Gregg just winked at him. The three talked as the fire progressed to a third and a fourth alarm. In a booming voice, Ray appealed obnoxiously to anyone and everyone within the sound of his voice, "Why isn't this scab striking the alarms a little faster?" referring to the Deputy Chief who had caught this fire. It was the same Chief who was in charge of Brookside I. The present fire became known to us as Brookside II.

Gregg agreed, "Yeah, this would have been nine alarms if any other Deputy was here." As they watched the fire consume several hundred feet of the structure, Ladder 10 in front of the building had such little water pressure that the squirting water coming from the ladder pipe couldn't even reach the building. The radiant heat energy became so intense that the paint on the side of the ladder truck burned off and the lights on the truck roof melted beyond recognition. "Come on you scab, strike a couple more alarms," Gregg yelled in disgust as they watched what they considered to be fire follies. After about an hour, when the building was already a total loss, the Deputy finally struck a seventh alarm.

"Hey, what else are you going to get?" Ray inquired. Bemis told Ray about the East Berkeley fire, which still had not been reported. In two vehicles, they took a ride past the target. A little smoke was seeping from the building. Thinking the fire would turn out to be nothing, they called it a night.

Later that day, Engine 49 was placed back in service. This act ended the battle between the Readville (Hyde Park) residents against Mayor Kevin White. Gregg was extremely angry with the Mayor. To Gregg, the Mayor was playing this up like he had saved the entire City by reopening Engine

49. In fact, more than 20 fire companies in other parts of the City were still closed. He felt that until some of those companies were reopened, Boston would remain undermanned and under-equipped for a major fire. Bemis fumed that Mayor White was using this reopening ceremony to placate the citizens of the City, to maximize the publicity while, at the same time, downplaying the rash of fires that were plaguing the City.

The Mr. Flare letter disappeared into a file drawer; not a single word of it was reported on the news.

Brookside II, American Cellophane

The arsonists set fire to three buildings during the wee hours of Tuesday, July 27. Who sets fires on a Tuesday morning? Well, this group of arsonists did. Obviously, random attacks made their actions harder to predict. But there was another motivation for mixing things up: This group couldn't help themselves from acting on their passion and pursuing their mission. When I refer to these guys as not being able to control themselves, I don't mean to imply that they were pyromaniacs, although a psychiatrist could possibly have diagnosed their actions as mania. The main difference between these arsonists and a person driven by an uncontrollable urge to set fires is that Bemis and company believed, at least during their first few months of fire-setting, that their actions had a higher purpose. They also planned their fires meticulously; they were organized arsonists, not disorganized like a true pyromaniac might be.

Bemis teamed with Sanden and Grobo to set their first fire of the night in a South Boston brick duplex triple-decker. There was a tremendous amount of dumped debris and garbage in the back yard that all three had to maneuver over and around. The basement had as much or more crap in it. Placing a device in combustibles near a breach in the wall that divided the duplex, they hoped that both sides of the building would get going simultaneously. Minutes later, heavy plumes of smoke billowed from the building. Shortly after, Box 7315 was transmitted for the fire. A second alarm was ordered upon arrival of the District Chief, but the arsonists had already moved on to set their second fire.

A change in the design of their device was about to occur: the intentional addition of an old tire in which to place the device. The arsonists no doubt believed this improved the power of their incendiary device, but they failed to consider that the additional component made it possible for investigators to locate remnants of steel belts from the tires at the point of origin. At fire scenes, once we identified an area of origin, the steel belts were a dead giveaway as to the point of origin. The discovery of this physical evidence also helped to firmly identify the incendiary cause. Another plus for us sleuths was that when we started seeing the tire remains over and over—that is, once we recognized the signature—we knew that the same person or persons, as yet unidentified, were responsible for all of those fires.

When the arsonists placed this new, improved device against wood debris, wood shingles, or their favorite asphalt shingles, those combustibles quickly ignited, causing more rapid spread of the fire. That is what happened at 42–52 Blue Hill Avenue that night. Stopping at a vacant lot with numerous discarded tires, the boys threw two into the car and proceeded to an empty three-story brick building with attached wooden rear porches. The area behind this structure was completely dark. Bemis couldn't help thinking that it was a perfect neighborhood for a murder. There would be no witnesses. And there were hundreds of overgrown vacant lots in which to dump a body. It was also a great area for arsonists to ply their trade.

Wayne stayed with the car. Bobby and Gregg grabbed one of the tires and headed for the rear porches, where they placed the tire against a wood door under the porch. They then placed the lit device inside the tire before they bailed from the area. No sooner had they parked at a good vantage point than they saw flames hurtling up the rear porches. With the additional heat energy provided by the tire, the rear of the building swiftly became fully involved with flames.

The radio silence broke as the call came over the air. Upon arrival, Engine 14 ordered a second alarm. The boys returned to spark the fire, shooting several photos. With the fire still spreading rapidly, a third alarm was transmitted. When the first deck gun was put into operation at the rear of the building, the porches came crashing down, flames and embers spewing in every direction. As the firefighters took control, the torches headed for their last target of the night.

Back in Southie, Bobby and Wayne set the device with the tire under the rear loading dock of a five-story brick warehouse on Congress Street. Again, they took up a position to watch the fire's progress. Black smoke began rising from the building with flames following. However, the group decided not to spark this fire, instead calling it a night. The fire was contained to a single alarm.

That was Mr. Flare's last fire for July. The July count of Boston fires that had some suspicious aspect stood at 99, at least 28 of which were set by Bemis, Groblewski, and their band of merry arsonists.

On Thursday, August 5, 1982, ATF Arson Group and Boston Arson Squad investigators held a meeting to discuss the fires happening around the Jamaica Plain neighborhood of Boston. Representatives of the Boston PD and the Suffolk County District Attorney's Office were also present. At the time, JP was somewhat of a rough area, with a large number of triple-decker homes mixed in among single-family residences, apartment buildings, and businesses of all types. It was, and still is, one of the most cosmopolitan and diverse Boston neighborhoods, home to people of dozens of nationalities, religions, and lifestyles.

There had been a rash of Thursday night/Friday night fires in the area. The City had already encountered numerous other Friday morning fires on June 11, June 25, July 2, and July 16. We investigators were now officially running around like a flock of chickens with our heads chopped off, running from fire to fire, trying not only to determine the origin and cause of each fire, but also to figure out who was responsible for those fires deemed to be arsons.

There was something slightly different about some of the Friday JP fires. Although they were set on the exterior of the buildings in the early morning hours like most of the fires in the past few months, they just didn't have the same feel of fires set elsewhere around the city. These fires didn't have the oomph that other fires had, but they were especially dangerous. The most important difference was that these fires were set to occupied residences, with a total disregard for potentially sleeping occupants. People in this area were scared. Some had trouble sleeping. Others slept with one eye open.

We planned a surveillance that night using numerous vehicles. Each vehicle had two occupants, one Federal agent and one Boston Fire investigator or Boston Police officer. That way, the local guys who knew the area best could get us around easier if the shit hit the fan. We all parked on and near Centre Street, which was the main drag through the entire length of JP. Centre Street is always busy, teeming with cars and buses and the people who ate, drank, shopped, and lived there. Every block had feeder streets, either heading up from Centre toward the mini-highway of the Jamaicaway or down toward a roughly parallel main drag, Washington Street, that extended the entire length of Boston.

The side streets were densely lined with the residences. There were hundreds of two-family and three-family homes. Most were built 50 to 100 years earlier. Some were decrepit looking, but their bones were structurally sound; they just needed some TLC. Others were stately homes with magnificent architectural detail. This neighborhood was ripe for the gentrification of the area that would occur from the late 1980s to the 2000s. A feature that was common to many of these homes was stacked porches, one per floor.

Just after 1:00 a.m., which coincided with the closing of the bars in the area, a fire was reported by one of the roving teams. It was a small outside fire, in the area of a wood porch of an occupied dwelling. Just down the street minutes later, a second fire was discovered. This fire, too, was in an occupied residence. Other surveillance teams were scurrying into this section of the neighborhood. Again, minutes later, a third fire in an occupied house was encountered by one of the teams. However, this time, the investigators detected a white male dashing from behind a house. The individual was immediately apprehended. Based on an investigation on the spot, with an interview of the person of interest and some physical evidence, Michael McDonald was arrested for arson relating to these three fires.

McDonald was only 22 years old. He lived right down the street from where the fires were being set. He was acting alone. McDonald only had a minor misdemeanor arrest record that included an arrest for arson of a building. In a way, the McDonald arrest was significant because it showed progress by being proactive rather than purely reactive. However, McDonald's fires, although they were dangerous because of the occupied status of the buildings, were minor in terms of damages in the overall scheme of the arsons that afflicted Boston.

We investigators never believed McDonald was solely responsible for the dozens of arsons that the City was suffering every month. A couple weeks later, I interviewed him at Bridgewater Correctional Institute, also known as the Old Colony Correctional Center, a high-tech medium-security facility that also housed Bridgewater State Hospital with its Massachusetts Alcohol and Substance Abuse Center. I didn't get much out of the kid. His brain was mush. Even though he had been drying out for about 10 days before I confronted him, his eyes and face were blank. There wasn't much left upstairs. I got no insight into the fires by him.

We independently learned that McDonald had a menial job in which he was paid weekly on Thursdays. He hit the local tavern on Centre Street most Thursday nights and sometimes on Friday until his money ran out. At closing time, he would drift aimlessly out of the place, walking down the side streets on his way home. He would then get an urge to set fires. Thursday night also happened to be when the residents dumped their trash outside for Friday pick-up. He would grab some paper trash, place it under the edge of a wooden porch or stuff it under the bottom edge of wood shingles, then simply light the trash and be on his way. He became a serial arsonist in a matter of weeks. These fires with this particular pattern stopped upon his arrest, but the rest of the City continued burning. The bosses from all involved agencies were excited by the arrest and were hoping that it was the solution to the arson problem. Not even close. Michael McDonald, the poor kid (I have always been a softy) was released to a halfway house a couple years later, where he committed suicide.

By late July and early August 1982, the *New York Times* and the United Press International, the international news agency, had picked up on the scourge of fires in beleaguered Boston and printed articles such as the following:

> **"Another Rash of 'Friday Firebug' Blazes Hits Boston"**
>
> **By ED LION Aug. 6, 1982 (UPI Archives.com)**
>
> BOSTON ---The fifth rash of 'Friday firebug' blazes in 9 weeks hit Boston early Friday, leaving 11 people homeless. One fireman suffered a minor injury in the latest series of fires, most of them in vacant buildings that caused about $200,000 damage.
>
> Federal agents on special arson patrol arrested a man believed responsible for a series of blazes and charged him with arson in a minor apartment fire, fire officials said.
>
> Firefighters coping with the lingering effects of drastic budget cuts raced across the city from fire to fire in the pre-dawn hours, calling on help from 15 surrounding communities. Three of the fires were termed suspicious.
>
> Other outbreaks of Friday morning fires were reported June 11, June 25, July 2, and July 16. 'We were really being overloaded—it was hectic,' said a harried Fire Department dispatcher. Firefighters have expressed fear privately that 'Friday firebugs' are intent on running the department ragged on Friday mornings. But Fire Department spokesman Ken Bruynell said, 'We really don't know—I think the timing is a combination of coincidence and people probably setting them. The fires are not setting themselves.'
>
> Boston fire officials have called in agents from the Federal Bureau of Alcohol, Tobacco and Firearms to investigate the fires and a special arson watch program

was instituted. There were 99 suspicious fires in the city in July alone.

Firemen battled for three hours to control an eight-alarm fire that raged inside a vacant building in Boston's South End, injuring one firefighter. The cause of that blaze was undetermined.

A blaze of undetermined origin broke out in a vacant three-story home in Jamaica Plain and another broke out in a store-apartment building and an adjacent home in Dorchester, leaving 11 people homeless.

Three blocks away from the Dorchester fire, a vacant three-story building caught fire in a two-alarm blaze. Its cause was undetermined. In addition fire officials reported minor, suspicious fires in a five-story vacant commercial building in Roxbury and an apartment building in Jamaica Plain.

Federal ATF agents charged a man identified as Michael McDonald with arson for the Jamaica Plain fire. Fire officials said he was believed responsible for a series of recent fires in Jamaica Plains.

"Boston Officials Arrest 2 in Crackdown on Arson"

(UPI / New York Times 1982)

Police and fire officials, trying to stem one of the worst outbreaks of arson in Boston's history, arrested two suspects today and issued warrants for six others.

John V. Ostiguy, 51 years old, and Robert J. Stanley, 18, were the second and third people arrested since the rash of suspicious fires began in June.

There have been no deaths or serious injuries in any of the fires. The Fire Department's arson squad investigated 176 fires in June and July, with damages estimated at $4.7 million. Fire officials said many of the fires may have been caused by either "firebugs" or insurance arsonists.

> Five suspicious fires broke out Tuesday night, the 18th time this summer that four or more suspicious fires erupted in one night.

The national TV media also got into the act. There were only three major networks in 1982: ABC, CBS, and NBC. Camera crews from those networks rode with our surveillance teams on Thursday and Friday nights. Boston was being reported as the arson capital of the country. The City wasn't fond of the negative press. However, ATF was getting more press than usual. It was good coverage, but everybody knew that some arrests that stopped the barrage of fires would make a welcome splash in the media. Although some minor arrests were being made, the rash of fires continued. We really did not have a viable suspect yet.

The heat was on all of us, no pun intended. Boston ATF was being scrutinized by the higher-ups at Headquarters in DC. Congress actually started to demand some action. Briefings were being held every week at the highest levels, with the crap rolling downhill, landing eventually on us street Agents. Something had to break and break soon.

▲

As we investigators were conducting our surveillance in Jamaica Plain and making the McDonald arrest, the gang of arson terrorists was at it big time. We made our puny arrest while Boston was blazing elsewhere.

Bemis and Sanden first hit a massive eight-story vacant brick building in the South End. With the front of the structure totally secured, they approached the building from the rear with a device in hand. They encountered a sizable obstacle; the rear of the eight-story building had a single-story section with no doors or windows, meaning no access. But these guys were not to be deterred.

The usually skeptical Wayne suggested, "Hey, how about climbing one of those trees and jumping on the roof?" Gregg thought that was too risky, but he agreed because the target was too good to pass up. Wayne climbed the tree first. Gregg passed the device up to him, and then he scaled up the tree. Both of them leaped onto the flat roof of the one-story section.

An open window on the second level of the eight-story section was an open invitation to them. With flashlight in hand, Wayne scanned inside the window, highlighting the trash-strewn floor and stacks of boards standing upright, leaning against a wall. Upon entering, Bemis told Sanden, "Watch your step," as he noticed the flooring was both buckled in places and had some holes in it. The ceiling plaster had completely failed, exposing the wood lath and the structural wood of the floor above them. The device was placed at the base of the vertically oriented boards. Carefully, a longer fuse for the device was prepared by placing the lit end of the cigarette farther from the matchbook. This delayed ignition provided more time for their getaway onto the roof, down the tree, and safely back to the car before the fire started. Even with the planned delay, light smoke was already seeping from the building by the time they settled into their vehicle.

While they waited for the fire to develop, Bemis and Sanden sought their second target, a vacant three-decker in Roxbury Highlands. Halfway to the rear of the target, they picked up a discarded tire from a vacant lot strewn with trash. At the rear of the building, the only open windows were on the second and third levels; the ground level was buttoned up tight. "Do you want to climb up to the first floor?" Wayne asked as he pointed toward the rickety rear porches.

Gregg had had enough climbing for one night, "No way, it looks like those fuckin' old things are ready to collapse any minute." The device was set against one of the boarded-up windows under the porch. Departing the area, they found Grobo at HoJo's. The fire in the South End had gone to a sixth alarm. They were anxious to spark it.

The Roxbury Highlands fire came in, but it was held to a single alarm. They all headed back out in Gregg's car for the new objective, which Sanden had scouted at work. It was directly across the street from one of the BHA Housing Projects.

Another large structure, the five-story building had wide open access to the basement from the rear. It was empty except for one of the most ideal fuel loads to be found, whether it's in a fire testing laboratory or in an abandoned basement: A floor-to-ceiling stack of wood pallets provided an airy mass of readily combustible kindling wood. The device was planted within the pallets. Again, by the time they drove away from the scene, traces of smoke were discernible.

While they were en route to the fourth target of the night, the South End fire went to eight alarms. The boys knew that lots of apparatus would be tied up at that scene, so the FD would be strapped when the additional fires came in. They hit a vacant three-decker on French Terrace in Roxbury. They pulled over in a dark spot; Bobby ran up to the rear of the building and placed a device on a windowsill, and they were off. By this time, the five-story structure with all the pallets was reported.

After not finding another suitable place to burn, they called it a night. By the time Bemis was halfway home, his radio broke silence striking Box 2366, which he knew to be for the French Terrace fire. He was quite surprised when the radio blared, "K7 to Fire Alarm, heavy fire showing." Bemis was too far away to turn around. He was not surprised to hear that it was K7 calling for the working fire because BFD Photographer Billy Noonan had been catching quite a few fires before any apparatus arrived on scene. As the fire went to four alarms, Gregg arrived home for the night.

These August 6, 1982, fires were eventually listed on a 1984 Federal indictment as fire numbers 101, 102, 103, and 104.

French Terrace

The arsonists were eating up the press coverage, referred to by their assigned nickname, "the Friday Firebug." Thursday night, August 13, 1982, they headed out again. Bemis met with Groblewski, Sanden, and Stackpole in South Boston.

Since their first target for the night was close to Boston Fire Headquarters, Donny suggested, "Let's drive past the Arson Squad's building first and see if there is any activity." As they rode past the Arson Squad's door, they could see numerous vehicles parked there. The torches instantly knew they had to be especially cautious because the Arson Squad would be out in full force.

After grabbing a few junk tires, they stopped in front of the first building, a two-story wood garage at the corner of Hampden and Howard Streets. With Gregg driving, Donny passed a tire to Bobby, who lit a device, stuck it inside the tire, and placed it against the side of the building.

Another binge night; they proceeded straightaway to a vacant building on Devon Street, off of Blue Hill Avenue in Roxbury. A lit device within a tire was placed against a boarded-up doorway.

The previous fire had not yet been reported. It should have taken off by then; something must have gone wrong. They returned to the site, thinking that they could not afford to let the Arson Squad find the tire and the device components. Bemis slowly drove past the building. The tire was sitting in the spot where they had left it, but not a wisp of fire was visible. "It looks like the fuckin' thing went out," grumbled the always less than effervescent Stackpole.

Taking off from the dud fire toward their next target, the radio announced, "K4 to Fire Alarm. Strike the box for a fire on Devon Street." K4, the Arson Squad, discovered the fire. The arsonists' suspicion that their counterparts would be out and about in heavy concentration was correct. The bad guys had intentionally gone back to the Friday morning pattern. Their reasoning was to screw with the Arson Squad and ATF, as they knew that we were now actively involved. Another factor for them was strategic. By concentrating on the same night of the week, later on, they could catch the investigators off guard by striking on odd nights.

The third choice for the night was an empty triple-decker on Ballou Avenue in Dorchester, again moments away from the main thoroughfare, Blue Hill Avenue. Bobby and Gregg had forgotten to bring a flashlight, but fortunately, there was no need for one; the rear door was wide open. Gregg placed a device at the base of a huge pile of two-by-fours.

Back in the car, the quartet learned that the Roxbury fire had gone to a working fire. They drove a little farther south, crossing over Blue Hill Avenue to their fourth target, a vacant three-decker. This time Donny and Bobby set the tire and device inside the doorway of the graffiti-riddled structure.

While the arsonists were still inside that target, the order came over the radio to strike the box for their third fire of the night. Gregg's personal antenna was up. He said to Wayne, "Holy shit, they weren't far behind us!"

"Yeah, we better get the fuck out of this area," replied Wayne.

As the two torches returned to the car, they informed the other two that they had managed to plant the device.

But Gregg was a little edgy: "Never mind about that, the Arson Squad found the last fire already."

"Well, let's get out of here," Donny interjected. Meanwhile, K4, the call sign for the Arson Squad, was giving details to Fire Alarm about the progress of the fire and their belief that the culprits must have left the scene just before they arrived.

Gregg thought aloud, "That sounded like Steve McLaughlin's voice in K4, didn't it?"

"Who gives a fuck who it was?" countered a testy Grobo. "Let's get out of the area before the whole Arson Squad shows up!" Gregg pulled off of busy Blue Hill Avenue after spotting several BFD vehicles.

Another of their fires had gone to a working fire, but their first one still had not been reported. Bobby was being cautious about that fire: "We aren't going back there anyway. There's too much heat back there."

Bemis tried to placate the group's fears, including his own. "Well, as long as the device is out of sight, we shouldn't have to worry about it." The Arson Squad was blanketing the Blue Hill Avenue area, finding that last fire only minutes after it was set.

"Hey, since those nitwits are all playing cat-and-mouse back there, why don't we find something in the South End?" Donny proposed. That was typical Stackpole, through and through. He not only had no respect for the Arson Squad or law enforcement in general, he actually had a disdain, even hatred, for them all. This night was exactly as he described it. The cat-and-mouse game was on full tilt, with the arsonists tormenting and playing with the public authorities, while managing to stay a couple steps ahead of them, up to this point anyway.

From their list, they targeted a large row of vacant five-story brick apartments on Columbus Avenue. This was a busy area. Bobby and Gregg headed for the rear of the building with bag device in hand, but sans tire. Since the exterior was brick, they had to gain entry to the building, so this time the lack of a flashlight posed a problem.

The structure was tightly secured except for a small crawlspace that led into the basement. "Hey, light a match and make sure there isn't anything in there before we go in," Bobby said. Just because they were focused on their mission didn't mean they were willing to enter a basement full of nasty creatures like rats.

Gregg lit a newspaper with a match and held it inside the opening. The light revealed a musty, cluttered basement full of cobwebs. The duo crawled through the tight opening. They lit another newspaper, then an actual campfire, so they could see what they were about to do. Bobby recommended, "Hey, I'm not going to come back down here if this doesn't go, so why don't you just light the bag of the device on fire and we'll screw." Gregg agreed, so he made sure the device and additional fuels were ready. He told Bobby to start crawling out of the building. After lighting the brown paper lunch bag, he too made his way out of the opening with Grobo's help. They raced back to the car to make their getaway.

It didn't take long for the box to be transmitted for the fire. It went to two alarms as the fire spread through the walls and blew out of the roof. Since this was one of the largest fires of the night, they sparked the fire, took several photos, and headed home. To them, it was a satisfying night. Not all of their fires were good fires, but they managed to get the apparatus running around and they did screw with the Boston Arson Squad.

August 17, 1982, was a Tuesday. Donny said to Gregg with a smile, “Well, the Arson Squad will never suspect that we’re going to hit tonight.” Gregg agreed, knowing that things were getting too hot on Fridays. A change in their pattern was now necessary. The boys discussed patterns further that night. The arsonists decided to strike more randomly to avoid any cycle or pattern whatsoever. Their high stakes game continued.

That night they drew up a new list of targets, striking properties that they had already burned or that were no longer attractive targets. This would be another busy early morning for Groblewski, Bemis, and Stackpole, and Ray Norton would add a little spice to the activities.

While Donny and Bobby were doing the first deed of the night in a Dorchester duplex, Bemis sat in his car watching a group of rats fighting over discarded garbage in the vacant lot across from the target. The whole area now comprised vacant lots that were being used as dumping grounds for trash and garbage. Periodically, as conditions there deteriorated, the City had to bring in bulldozers to clear the lots. As the two torches scurried around the corner of the target building, the rats did the same in the opposite direction. “Okay, let’s head for the next one,” Bobby said.

Blocks down the street from Codman Square, the same dynamic duo, Donny and Bobby, placed a device between two garages at the rear of a wood triple-decker. No sooner had they pulled away from that property than the box came in for the first fire. Instead of sticking around, they hit a five-story brick apartment building in Roxbury Highlands, directly opposite the first building they had lit six months earlier. The Dorchester fire had now become a working fire.

Gregg took his turn with Bobby. Entering an open bulkhead door, they saw that the stairway leading to the basement was so full of dirt and rocks that they would have to crawl on their bellies to make their way into the basement. Once inside the damp basement, a cold breeze swept over them. Bemis got a chill as they continued down a dark, cobwebbed hallway, "Hey, Bobby, make sure you don't lean on any of those beams or the whole place might cave in on top of us." Some jobs are more hazardous than others.

After stacking scrap wood under the stairs and placing a lit incendiary, they made their way out of the bulkhead. Donny informed them that the last fire had already gone to three alarms. "Well, this one will go for more than that," Gregg informed Donny as they departed.

The boys were going big this night; their next target was another five-story apartment building. Bobby and Gregg placed their lit device in a bathroom against exposed wood lath kindling. They checked on the progress of the first five-story fire. Finding a large column of smoke coming from the structure, they knew it would be reported shortly.

Once the box was transmitted, the trio of torches headed for the fire. The first arriving company reported heavy smoke showing. To their mild surprise, Ray Norton showed up at the fire. "Hey guys, it looks like another one of those nights!" he beamed.

Bemis smiled back at him and motioned for Ray to move away from the diesel engines so that he could talk to him above the din, "Stick around, Ray. We've got a big one brewing not far from here."

"You mean there's another one going right now?" Bemis just shook his head in affirmation. The fire in front of them went to a working fire. About 30 minutes expired; the other five-story fire had not yet been reported. Gregg was wondering whether it was going to go at all. He walked down the block and peered in the direction of the other building. He saw a large cloud of smoke billowing into the sky. Quickly, he strode back to the others to advise them that the other place was going like hell.

Before Bemis even finished his sentence, the box was transmitted over the apparatus loudspeaker: 1-2, 1-2, 1-2-3-4-5, 1-2. "That's it," bellowed Gregg as they listened for the subsequent report.

"On Box 2252, receiving calls for a building fire in John Elliot Square." The torches ran for their cars, as did the other buffs massed in the lot. As soon as they turned toward the fire, smoke and flames were clearly visible on the hill ahead of them.

"Holy shit, I guess the place is going!" Grobo exclaimed. The fire spread so rapidly throughout the upper floors of the old brick structure that it took only minutes for the fire to rage to six alarms.

Norton spied one of his old adversaries, whom he had not seen in a couple years. Typically, as I learned from my dealings with him and conversations that I had with others who knew him, Ray immediately started harassing the guy. "Hey, Hollowhead, why don't you go back to Weston where you belong?" Ray jeered as he passed the member of the Boston Sparks Club. At first, the guy tried his best to ignore Ray, but after Ray kept up his abuse, the spark assailed back, "Hey, Norton, you're a fucking nut!"

"Yeah, I know. Just remember that so if I kill you, they won't be able to do anything about it," growled Norton. This summed up Norton's abrasive personality. The rest of the group just laughed, knowing that Ray was such a ballbuster.

Apparatus were still pouring into the area to match the six-alarm callout. The battlefield was being set up: men with water versus an unrelenting fire.

Bobby was taking photos of the operations. Norton took an opportunity to have his photo taken. Ray positioned himself beside Engine 7. He pulled out a Bic lighter, lit it up, and held it high in the air. Grobo made sure that the roaring fire was behind Norton and snapped a few shots. Ray laughed as he looked right at the man nicknamed Hollowhead, who could only shake his head in response.

Once the firefighters got the upper hand, the arsonists went directly to set another building, wanting to keep the pressure on the BFD. On Circuit Street, they targeted the same two-and-a-half-story duplex that Bemis and Stackpole had hit a month earlier. The previous fire had successfully destroyed the right side of the duplex. Tonight, the left half of the building was vulnerable. With a newly manufactured incendiary device, Bobby jumped out of the car in front of the structure, placed the device against the gas shingles on the front porch, and ran back to the car.

Trying to set another fire before Circuit Street was discovered, they traveled only a few blocks to a vacant four-story duplex on Blue Hill Avenue, where Bobby and Donny slid a device onto the front porch.

Just as they left the neighborhood, Box 2148 was transmitted for Circuit Street. The torches and a gaggle of less toxic fire buffs converged on the fire scene. The building was fully involved. A second alarm was immediately ordered. Ray showed up again. He was advised that another place was cooking nearby. Ray just smiled, his face reflecting the glow of the blaze.

The boys were disappointed to hear that there was only a small fire on the porches at the Blue Hill Ave. duplex. So they set another empty three-story house on fire in Dorchester. This fire was also quickly reported and held to a single alarm. Since it was close to 5:00 a.m., they gave up for the night. Seven fires in a single night was accomplishment enough.

▲

One of the interesting aspects of conducting this investigation, and of the job generally, was the quirky things we learned about people we met and sometimes considered persons of interest.

On August 21, 1982, at 2:50 a.m., a fire was reported at 394 Atlantic Avenue in downtown Boston, an old commercial building in what is today a high-rent district. That particular building was occupied by a business run by Paul Fireman—yes, his real name, but just a peculiar coincidence—who in 1979 had acquired the North American sales rights to Reebok, one of the most popular athletic shoe companies in the United States. Mr. Fireman later purchased the entire British-based parent company and helped build Reebok into a shoe and apparel empire. Since he was the owner of the building that burned and he planned to move his business from that location to larger quarters, Mr. Fireman was one of those persons of interest for a very short time. However, all information and evidence quickly exonerated him from having any other connection with the fire, aside from being a victim. Neither the fire scene evidence nor any other information helped us to identify any suspects for this arson at the time.

Bemis and Stackpole had already set two fires that night. Both ended up being shit fires. Both were in East Boston, an area they had not targeted for a while. It seemed that the arsonists were not the most knowledgeable fire setters. Too many of their incendiaries were placed, without a tire, against what turned out to be highly visible front and side elevations where they were readily discovered. Because of their hastiness or lack of expertise, both of the Eastie fires were contained within minutes.

To avoid detection by the Arson Squad, the duo traveled through the Sumner Tunnel back downtown to continue their onslaught. Now, Mr. Flare and his sidekick were onto the two-story wooden warehouse on the Atlantic Avenue waterfront, the building owned by Paul Fireman. The structure was situated behind the eight-story brick building directly on Atlantic Avenue. The only access to the two-story warehouse was via a small tunnel that had been built under the main structure. After parking near Rowe's Wharf and walking to their target with the lunch bag device in hand, Bemis and Stackpole saw that a truck had parked inside the narrow tunnel, virtually blocking access. "Boy, they'll have fun trying to get past this truck," Donny chuckled as they made their way past the truck into the darkened passageway.

Gregg figured that the decaying building would likely burn to the ground before the firefighters could even get water on it. The warehouse was merely a shell. It had been built atop large wood pilings embedded in the murky water of the Fort Point Channel, a waterway that separates South Boston from downtown and feeds into Boston Harbor. In less than a year from the date of this fire, the Fort Point Channel would play a significant part in this case.

Gregg and Donny piled wood pallets that had been scattered all over the place against the building. After placing the device within the pile, they slipped back to the car. Meandering back toward the fire building, they saw a shower of embers pumping into the sky. Gregg shouted, "I don't fuckin' believe it!"

"That shows you how unconscious these stupid motherfuckers are," complained Donny. They couldn't believe how this fire could be going so well in this busy area without anybody reporting it. At 2:50 a.m. the box transmitted for the fire. The arsonists avoided the fire to dodge the Arson Squad.

At a vacant three-decker in Dorchester, they placed a device against gas shingles on the front porch. They traveled south to their last target for the night. About halfway to their objective, the fire they had just set was called in. Upon arrival, Engine 21 reported heavy fire showing ordering a second alarm. The boys continued onward rather than spark that fire.

This duplex was boarded up solid. They grabbed a tire from a junk pile outside a gas station and pulled up to the building. Stackpole placed a lit device with a tire against one of the front doors of the duplex. After the box was transmitted for the fire, they both turned onto the Southeast Expressway southbound. A second alarm was ordered at that time. As the boys raced each other down the highway, they saw a lot of smoke so they both continued for their beds. They could sleep soundly with visions of the night's five fires dancing in their heads.

By late August, Bemis had a new diversion and a new dilemma. The diversion was a young lady, an ex-girlfriend of his who had just been hired at the Stow Police Station to work the midnight shift as a dispatcher. A few years earlier, Gregg had had a real crush on her, but after things didn't work out, they lost touch. Now she had come to work at the same place where Gregg worked, and a new relationship sparked. He hoped that spark would turn into a flame, and indeed their relationship steadily progressed over the next several weeks. The dilemma arose from the gnawing feeling that he was getting tired and somewhat scared of participating in setting fires. With this female in his life, Gregg considered quitting the conspiracy. Gregg would have done anything for her, especially during this new stage of their courtship. There was only one glitch; she disliked the City of Boston.

On Monday, Groblewski called Bemis asking him to meet him in town. After debating with himself for a few moments, Gregg agreed to join Bobby, who said that he already had a few buildings lined up for the night. Gregg was thinking about his female friend, but he wasn't ready to mention her to Bobby or the rest of the gang yet.

In rapid order, they hit three targets, a brick duplex triple-decker, an old school, and a vacant wood three-decker. The duo did the brick duplex first by placing a device within a stack of wood in the basement. Immediately, they headed to the old school. Scooping up an old tire in the trashed playground, they placed the device with tire against a boarded doorway, then ran like hell to the car before the device erupted. As soon as they settled in the car, the first cloud of black smoke rose from the old schoolhouse. The box was struck for the first fire.

The third target was set with a device in a pile of lumber under the rear porch. A second alarm was struck for the first fire, plus the box was transmitted for the school fire. The last fire was readily contained as was the school fire, so they headed home.

As of Saturday, August 29, 1982, the Boston Arson Squad and ATF were no closer to solving the mystery of the Boston arsons. And Gregg Bemis was no closer to bailing out of the arson conspiracy. The lure of his friends, the fires, and the object of the conspiracy—that is, set enough fires to have all of the laid-off firefighters rehired and all of the closed firehouses reopened—was too great for Gregg to quit at this time.

After both men completed their shifts, Gregg met Wayne Sanden at his house. Two buildings in Brighton were chosen as targets because this village had not been hit in a while. First, a vacant four-story brick apartment building was set with a device planted in wood pallets stacked against a boarded-up doorway. Bemis drove them to the opposite side of the Massachusetts Turnpike, where they had a perfect vantage point to watch the fire when it took off. And it did. As soon as they parked, the orange, red, and yellow flames were lapping 20 feet into the night air. Wayne suggested, "Hey, why don't we go and call Ray so he can come and spark it?"

Gregg found a phone booth located directly across the street from Engine 41 and Ladder 14's firehouse. He dialed Norton's number. Ray answered. "Hey, Ray, it's Gregg. It's time to get up for work." That was a code that the co-conspirators had worked out in case investigators were tapping the phones. Fear of getting caught was affecting their actions and their paranoia was growing.

Both parties heard the radio report the fire. "Okay, I'm on my way," Ray said.

Gregg hung up the phone. The apparatus roared out of their house. A working fire was then transmitted for the fire.

The boys' second target for the night was a partially vacant three-story brick commercial structure. Wayne and Gregg rolled a couple of tires through a field toward the building, placing them against a wood door with the lit device. The first flicker of flames was already visible as they reached the car. However, the fire was promptly discovered. BFD held it to a small fire.

It was about this time that these guys were getting a little too sloppy. They were getting a little too cocky, too. Despite Bemis's previous insistence that the device they used would be unidentifiable by investigators, using tires as an addition to the device meant that now, in any fire that was discovered shortly after the fire was set and easily contained, the tire remnants and their steel belts were readily recognized at the origin of the fires. With the highly defined origin and the physical evidence of the tire remains, the cause determinations became far easier for the investigators. Furthermore, the detection of the tires at smaller fires encouraged the investigators to look for more tires at the suspected origin of future large fires. The tire connection became another piece in the investigation puzzle. For some reason, Gregg and the others never seemed to be concerned about the possible discovery of the tires and how the tires could contribute to the downfall of Mr. Flare and his cohorts. However, the remainder of the actual Coleman Fuel device was still elusive.

As the two arsonists split up for the night, Gregg broke the news to Wayne about his girlfriend. Wayne laughed at the thought of Gregg messing around with girls. It didn't take long for the remainder of the gang to find out that Bemis had a new love interest.

▲

The following Monday, Groblewski called Bemis. After he busted Gregg's balls about being "married," Bemis acquiesced to Grobo's request that he come into the City. Bemis was conflicted— he didn't really want to go into Boston, but he knew that it would be difficult for his gang to accept that he didn't want to be involved with the conspiracy anymore.

Meeting the boys at Norton's house, Bemis asked, "Well, Ray, did you make it out to Brighton the other night?"

"You fucking guys woke me up for that shit. That building was the same building that I fucked up my back when I was working on Ladder 11. Then, to top it all off, you didn't even finish the fucking place off." Gregg hadn't known that it was the building where Ray had gotten hurt.

On to a different topic, Groblewski cut in, "Hey, Gregg, I hear that you're pussy whipped."

Bemis smiled back, "Fuck you, asshole." The digs continued for a few more minutes before they got down to more burning issues.

"Hey, Gregg," Bobby interjected, "Ray told me about a couple more buildings in Brighton that we can get." Although Ray Norton may not have been directly involved with setting any fires, his suggestion of targets for his friends got him deeper into the conspiracy. Their strategy for the night was to set their first fire in Roxbury so that the Arson Squad would head in that direction. Bobby instructed Ray to give them a head start before he headed out.

Bobby and Gregg headed toward the rear of a ripe vacant three-decker through an overgrown lot, disturbing a dog that started loudly barking. Quickly they changed direction to the other side of the property. Pulling a loose board off a basement window, they crawled inside, then planted the device on the stairway to the second floor. They found an open doorway to the exterior, but their egress was blocked by the yapping canine, so they climbed out a window.

They maneuvered through the overrun lot. Just as the duo reached the car, Gregg reached into his pocket for the car keys, but they were gone. "Shit, Bobby, I can't find my fuckin' keys!" Of course, the car was locked. It was the middle of the night in a rough neighborhood. And his car, like most in those days, was locked by pushing down the door lock button. There was no remote locking mechanism in those days.

"Oh, that's just pissa," Grobo moaned.

At first, Bemis feared the keys had dropped out of his pocket while he climbed in or out of the basement window, but then he looked through the car window. Sure enough, they were in the ignition. "Bobby, go back and try to put the device out while I find something to get this door open." Bobby shook his head in disbelief as he took off running toward the fire building.

Bemis searched around the ground among the trash for a wire or something that he could use to unlock the car. But he couldn't find anything. To make matters worse, Bobby came sprinting back from the building warning Gregg that the device had already ignited and he couldn't put it out.

Instead of totally panicking, Gregg said, "Well, there's only one other thing to do and that's smash the fuckin' window." He pulled out his Smith & Wesson .357 Magnum revolver and gave one of the vent windows a firm blow. Glass shattered and sprayed all over the car seat, but at least they could escape before anyone saw them.

"That was a real bright move," Bobby said dryly.

"Oh, fuck you." Gregg knew that was a close call due to a dumb mistake. He wasn't worried about the window because he could just head to a junkyard the next day to get a replacement.

Since they were now behind schedule, they headed straight for Brighton. At a vacant two-story, wood-framed house, Bobby and Gregg walked right onto the front porch, where the device was again placed against gas shingle siding. They headed directly to the next building.

The car key fire had just gone to a third alarm. At a vacant stucco three-story apartment building with Spanish-style terracotta roofing tiles, they hurriedly placed a tire with a device against a wood door since the structure was too tightly secured to get inside.

Engine 41 had reported fire showing at Brighton fire number one. The torches checked it out, but it was already knocked down. Then, the stucco building fire was reported. They turned right around returning to spark it. A fair amount of smoke was showing, but that smoke had been mostly generated by the tire. The fire was quickly brought under control. The building did not burn at all. The evidence of arson was right at the doorway.

Several sparks had converged on this fire, including Ray, who walked toward them as soon as he spotted them. "Hey, that was a good flick in Roxbury, but that other one sucked."

"Yeah, well this one didn't get going too good either," Bobby quipped. They decided to get one more building in another part of the City, advising Ray to stick around Jamaica Plain.

Jamaica Pond is an idyllic oasis within JP, acres and acres of fields and lush woods in a densely populated section of the City. This park was a link in the Emerald Necklace, a series of almost a dozen green spaces designed by famed landscape architect Frederick Law Olmstead in the last quarter of the 1800s. Buildings on the Pond included a boathouse and an Outdoor Theater that had been used by a city-sponsored community arts program.

This vacant two-and-a-half-story brick building had been partially burned a few years earlier. Since it was located at the end of a long drive, the boys figured that it probably would be fully involved before anybody spotted it. They parked on an access road, made a device, and climbed an embankment to the building. The building was well secured, so they placed a couple of tires with the lit device against a doorway.

Rather than stick around, they headed toward Ray's house. Before they were halfway there, the box was transmitted for the fire. "Who the hell could have seen the fire this quickly?" Gregg asked. Since the fire was contained to a single alarm, they headed home.

Mr. Flare and his entourage tallied at least 34 more arsons for the month of August.

▲

Bemis had a night off from work. Instead of committing crimes in Boston with his friends, Gregg took his girlfriend out for the night. Between their work schedules at the Stow dispatch and Gregg's other hobby, it's a wonder that he had any time for a girlfriend.

The couple cruised around for a while. Then, Gregg asked her if she would like to take a ride into Boston. When she agreed, Gregg drove her to some of his hangouts, showing her what a romantic guy he was. Of course, he took her to the HoJo's parking lot. Groblewski, Stackpole, and Gorman were there. As he entered the lot, his buddies started giving him funny stares. Gregg just laughed; he knew that the guys were only busting his balls.

As he introduced his girl to his friends, Bobby joked, "I wonder if Mr. Flare is going to strike tonight."

Donny added, "I doubt it. He's probably on vacation with his wife or something." Gregg knew that this went right over his girlfriend's head, but their not-so-subtle digs were aggravating. The couple then went to get something to eat and rode around some more before heading home. Over the next few weeks, the couple spent a great deal of time together, even driving into Boston a couple more times. Then, just as he was beginning to think that he had broken away from the conspiracy, things between Gregg and his girl went downhill.

▲

September 1982 brought big changes to the arsonists' activities and the locations for their choices of targets. With investigators blanketing Boston, flocking to every fire of suspicious nature, the crew decided that it was time to spread their wings to other towns outside Boston. The gang felt that setting fires outside the City would still be related to Proposition 2½ in two ways. The feint of moving some fires outside the City would loosen up Boston by confusing the investigators, so that the arsonists could continue their mission in the City. Also, multiple fires in smaller cities and towns, where Prop 2½ also triggered cutbacks, could possibly lead some of those municipalities to bring back laid-off firefighters and closed fire companies.

On Friday, September 10, Gregg had his head under the hood of his car when he heard a car pull into his driveway. Looking up, he saw something unexpected: Donny exiting his car. Bemis asked, "Hey Skinny, what's going on?"

"Oh, I was just out fucking around so I thought I'd take a ride out to see what you were up to," replied Donny, as if the ride from Boston to Gregg's house was a Sunday stroll, when in fact it was at least 25 miles in dense traffic. The two discussed new areas to target outside Boston, planning something for later that night.

Donny, Gregg, and Grobo congregated at Ray's house after dark. After discussing this new strategy, they targeted a couple buildings in Quincy first, a few miles to the south of Boston, plus set something in the congested little city of Chelsea, just north of Boston. This plan was very doable, especially after midnight, as long as there was no highway construction.

Leaving Ray behind, they headed for Quincy, known as The City of Presidents, the birthplace of two presidents, John Adams and his son, John Quincy Adams (previously part of Braintree, MA). Donny had previously found a vacant two-story brick warehouse there, their first building for the night. After making the device while driving around the location, Donny dropped the other two at the building, which was obscured by overgrown bushes. In the rear of the structure, the device was placed within discarded wood crates and pallets against a large wood loading dock door. They reunited with Stackpole, then headed to the second objective in Quincy.

Only a few blocks away, Donny dropped the same guys at a vacant wood church. All was quiet in the neighborhood, too quiet for Gregg's taste because when they climbed over a four-foot-high chain link fence, the rattling noise seemed to echo more loudly than it might have in a noisier neighborhood. They slid the device into a tight space between a window and a sheet of plywood covering it.

When they climbed back over the fence, Donny was nowhere to be seen. They kept walking since they didn't want to be too close when the device ignited. A couple of minutes later, they spotted Norton's car pass by at the end of the street, but he apparently didn't see them as he drove by. He didn't even slow down or hesitate. "Where the fuck is Skinny?" asked an annoyed Grobo, who was getting a little fidgety outside his comfort zone for the first time.

Bemis shook his head, "Who the fuck knows?" Just as Gregg responded, several sirens wailed in the distance.

Bobby cried out, "Shit, that's all we need is the fuckin' place to go while we're walking around the neighborhood!" Moments later, Stackpole raced up to them. "Hey, you fat motherfucker, where the fuck have you been?" hissed the pissed-off Groblewski.

"Oh, I got tied up in traffic because the cops blocked some streets for the fire on Penn Street."

"Well, is the fire on Penn Street going?" Bemis asked.

"Yes, but it's just smoke, no fire showing," Donny replied.

The torches waited for the church fire to be reported. Within minutes, the box was transmitted. They drove near the scene, but stayed out of sight. Norton found them shortly thereafter. A second alarm was transmitted for the fire. After a few minutes of sparking, they headed for Chelsea on the other side of Boston.

Arriving about 3:00 a.m. in Chelsea, the smallest city in Massachusetts in size and one of the most densely populated, the trio looked for a good target. They strategically placed a device against a vacant three-story warehouse covered with gas shingles. The guys went directly to the opposite side of Chelsea, passing into the next city of Everett.

The target, an oversized single-story wood shed that ran several hundred feet long, looked like it would blow over in a good windstorm. As Bemis and Stackpole climbed out of the car, the other Chelsea fire was reported. Finding tires lying all over the place, they piled several against the old shed with a lit incendiary. As Grobo picked them up, he informed the boys that the other fire had gone to two alarms. "That's perfect. There won't be anyone to come to this fire," commented Donny.

The arsonists hit a third target, a four-story wood warehouse with gas shingles on Revere Beach Parkway. The building was just blocks away from the last set, so it only took moments to get there. Once again, the lit device was placed against the siding. Awaiting discovery of the fires, a large column of smoke and fire was already issuing into the night sky.

Because the second fire was right on the Chelsea-Everett line, both cities struck a box for the fire at the scrapyard shed. Within minutes, the fire went to four alarms. The boys sparked the fire. Bobby and Gregg took several photos of the blaze. Donny just watched. Norton showed up, greeting them with a smile when he saw the extent of the raging inferno. "Hey, this ought to really fuck up the Feds and the Arson Squad," Ray stated with a grin. The others advised Ray that another fire had been set a few blocks away. They waited anxiously for the box to be transmitted, but when it was reported, it was held to a working fire. That was it for the night. With the new territory being explored, it was definitely an interesting night.

This last fire had an unusual connection to another one to be set by this crew on June 19, 1983, near the Dedham/Boston line. That structure fit the pattern of so many of the arsonists' previous fires. The building was an old, decaying multi-story former mill. It was tucked a hundred yards back from the road, down a dirt drive. The trees and bushes were overgrown all around the property.

The fire wreaked havoc on the place; it would have burned to the ground if a security patrol had not discovered it early. As part of the investigation into the fire, I accompanied a Massachusetts State Trooper from the State Fire Marshal's Office to interview the property owner. The interview took place in a building adjacent to the fire. The Trooper conducted most of the interview. He was an imposingly authoritative figure, standing over six feet tall, in his thirties and in excellent physical condition. Picture him standing over the property owner, who was sitting in a worn office chair. This gentleman was an old, mostly bald, bespectacled Jewish businessman in his mid-seventies who was very slightly built, probably under five feet eight inches and less than 160 pounds. He happened to be the owner of not only the Dedham property, but also the building on the Chelsea/Everett line.

Because this gentleman owned two properties that were separated by 20 miles, both victims of arson, there was naturally suspicion that the motive for these fires was arson-for-profit. This was one of those difficulties for investigators during the rash of arsons. Investigators have a hard time believing in coincidences. As both buildings were in disrepair and underutilized, it was reasonable to consider that the owner may have used the string of arsons as cover to burn his own buildings; that is, sell them to the insurance company the assumption being that the fires were part of the epidemic of fires. It was even possible that nobody would connect the two fires since they were 20 miles apart in different counties. Now, we certainly didn't believe that this somewhat frail man had lit the fires himself, but who knows whom he could have used to physically light the fires.

So, here we were, the three of us in the owner's office. The Trooper was aggressive by nature. He started pressuring the subject, soon escalating to fully berating and verbally abusing the poor old guy, accusing him of lying to us. The Trooper's barrage would have been impressive under other circumstances, but struck me as a little unnecessary here, since we had no information that this man was involved with the two arsons other than owning the two properties. Although the man cowered under the fusillade, he never faltered. He was just an innocent businessman who owned several properties, two of which, coincidentally, Mr. Flare and his accomplices had burned.

On Tuesday, September 14, 1982, as summer was coming to an end, so did Gregg's summer romance. He and his girlfriend were no longer a couple, and he was feeling down. A night out with the gang would get his mind off the breakup.

Stackpole and Groblewski were already at Ray's house when Bemis arrived. The discussion centered on the dramatic increase in the number of arson patrols in Boston. All agreed that the only way to safely target buildings in Boston and to avoid detection was to set only one fire per night in the City. If they wanted to set more than one fire on any night, they would have to do so outside the City. Everyone agreed with the strategy, then planned the night's activities. Sanden joined the other conspirators at Ray's and rode with Gregg and Donny. Unusually, on this night had Bobby as a passenger in Ray's car.

Boston Police Officer Groblewski had found the first target while he was on patrol; it was a huge pile of tires at a company in Hyde Park. Wayne and Donny walked across railroad tracks toward the business. Gregg watched from his car. Donny boosted Wayne over a chain link fence. Wayne placed the device within a 15-foot-high pile of tires, and both men returned to the car. The two cars of arsonists rode around until they saw smoke rising from the fire. They parked on a hill a safe distance away, and all five guys watched the blaze until the box came in. Immediately Ray and Grobo wanted to spark the fire, but Donny told them, "Hey Ray, we're going to head for Canton now." Ray and Grobo said they would be along shortly.

With Donny providing directions, Bemis drove south along Route 138 over the old Route 128 (now officially Interstate Route 93) bearing right onto Washington Street, which continues through the small downtown area of Canton. Their target, a large decades-old barn, was on their right just a short way down Washington. "That looks ripe, Donny, but is it vacant?" Gregg asked.

"As far as I know, it is." In a nearby church parking lot, they made the device. Donny dropped Wayne and Gregg by the side of the road. The twosome climbed through a wooden post fence. They walked a hundred yards over a rough field to one end of the barn. The occupied farmhouse was another hundred feet away.

The boys checked the barn to make sure there were no animals inside. Just as Gregg was ready to plant the device against a rotten door, he noticed something out of the corner of his eye. "Hey, Wayne, is that a tire I see sitting over there?"

"It sure is," he replied, walking over and picking it up.

"Well, if I didn't know better, I'd say somebody had this planned for us ahead of time," wisecracked Bemis, callously unconcerned about the damage and problems that he was about to cause. Wayne smiled while handing him the tire. Gregg placed it against the door with the lit incendiary inside. As they ran, stumbling, across the dark field, suddenly a horse that had been standing in the field got spooked and started neighing and running. They didn't know who was more scared, them or the horse, but it was too late to run back to stop the device from igniting.

Donny scooped them up after they crawled through the fence. He told the others that he wanted to go home; he was just too tired. Gregg and Wayne weren't pleased, but they drove him home anyway at speeds of up to 90 miles per hour. It only took about 10 minutes to drop Donny off and turn around to head back to Canton.

About two miles from the highway exit to Canton, the fire was transmitted over the radio. Gregg pushed his car a little harder. They could see an orange glow through the hazy dark sky. Just then, the radio squawked, "Engine 1 to Engine 2, lay two feeder lines, it's going to the moon!" The arsonists snickered at the choice of words. I happened to know the Lieutenant on Engine 1 who screeched those words. He later admitted to me that he was a little excited, as the fire was one of the biggest he had ever seen.

Parking in the church parking lot, they walked toward the property. Norton and Grobo joined them. A big crowd of spectators gathered. More and more apparatus arrived at the scene. The barn was now burning end to end, over 150 feet in length. It was also burning top to bottom. The inferno caused the roof to crash in, shooting additional flames well into the sky. After a while, the gang left for home.

This fire had several interesting wrinkles. First, why did Stackpole choose this location to burn? Was it just because it looked like a good target? The answer is no. Stackpole had a mean, vindictive streak. The owner of the barn had had an antique fire truck parked in front of the barn for years. Stackpole had approached the owner about buying the truck, but the owner had sold it elsewhere. So Stackpole decided to burn the barn.

Second, the owner of the barn and occupant of the house nearby was Tobe Deutschmann, an elderly son of German immigrants. Tobe had become a wealthy industrialist who was an expert in avionics, radar, and electronics. After World War I, the Navy veteran started a successful electronics company. He was a co-founder of Radio Shack. Tobe was an extremely enterprising, interesting man.

Finally, Mr. Deutschmann was not using the barn for animals. He stored all sorts of old equipment in the building. Had there not been a fire, it would have been a picker's paradise. However, the fire revealed the nasty side of some of the contents. The old electronics included transformers that released carcinogenic PCBs and other toxic compounds that contaminated the air and ground. The neighborhood had to be evacuated overnight and checked for air quality purposes. Several Canton firefighters ended up with health issues. And a feisty old gentleman suffered greatly due to the loss of his property. None of these consequences ever seemed to bother the gang of arsonists.

Another day brought another fire and another twist. On Friday night, a meeting was held again at Ray's house, the center of operations as of late. When Gregg arrived, Stackpole and Groblewski were already there. Gregg was surprised when he saw Bobby wearing his Boston Police uniform: "Hey, are you working or what?"

"No, but I have to go in at midnight, so I wore my uniform," replied the arsonist police officer. They discussed the fire at the Canton barn. The news media had covered the fire in great detail, including reporting the presence of the PCBs. The group members proclaimed that they had better be more careful with their choices and their actions.

Getting down to business, they chose to burn a two-story brick building behind the Dedham Mall, just west of the Boston line. The building was formerly a commercial laundry service warehouse, but now trees had completely swallowed the structure. Around 11:00 p.m., Bobby, Donny, and Gregg traveled the half mile or so from Norton's house to the target, after a brief stop to pick up a couple of old tires from a garage. Gregg dropped Donny and the corrupt Boston Police Officer at the building, where they carried the tires with a device into the bushes.

They returned to Norton's to await the fire, which didn't take long. It was a good set, as it quickly went to four alarms. It was nearly midnight, so Officer Groblewski left for work. The rest of the gang sparked the blaze from the mall parking lot. However, there were too many people around for the group's comfort, so they didn't target any other buildings for the night.

▲

For their last night out during the summer of 1982, Bemis met Stackpole in Southie. Since the investigative heat was too intense in the City, they planned to get something outside Boston. They mulled over a few choices before settling on Lowell, Massachusetts. It would be their first foray in that direction and in that city.

Lowell, the fourth-largest city in Massachusetts with a population of over 110,000, is located approximately 30 miles north of Boston. Established in the 1820s, Lowell became the cradle of the American Industrial Revolution due to the expansive textile mills that were built along the Merrimack River. Many of the mill workers were newly arrived immigrants. By 1982, the City was in a state of flux; the textile industry had largely left Lowell, and the now-rundown mill buildings were starting to be renovated and repurposed. In the following decades, Lowell's population would remain multiethnic and multicultural.

Although Bemis and Stackpole had no particular building in mind as they embarked on their drive to Lowell, they felt sure they could find a few vacant mill buildings there. There was only one problem that they tangled with during the ride; they were pondering how they would let the arson investigators know that any fires in Lowell were related to the string of fires in Boston, with the same agenda. "Why don't we call them on the phone?" Donny suggested, referring to the public authorities.

Gregg agreed to make the call as long as it was made to the business phone line that most likely would not be a recorded line. Arriving in the City, Bemis remembered a vacant factory from a fire that he had assisted with fighting a few years earlier. That fire had been so huge that mutual aid had been required from surrounding municipalities. A large section of the building was still standing, as the original building was about 1,000 feet long. With any luck, it could go for at least four or five alarms.

After checking out the building, Donny made another suggestion: find another place to set first so that the fire companies would be tied up when the mill came in. Their next selection was equally impressive in size. It was a vacant five-story brick complex that stretched another 1,000 feet along Jackson Street. There was a canal on the other side of the mill. Hundreds of windows were smashed out of the building. "Holy, fucking moly," exclaimed Stackpole when he observed the vastness of the property.

The street alongside the property was dark and deserted. Gregg was also astounded: "This place will burn for a week!" After finding a couple of tires nearby and making a device, they sought a good spot to plant the incendiary. Bemis turned off his headlights and parked, and they both climbed out of the car. The device with a tire was placed against an old wooden doorway that had been partially broken open. As they climbed back into the car, Gregg stated, "Now, as long as the sprinklers are off, this place should really go."

Back at their other objective, halfway down the length of the building, they set another device with a tire under an old wood stairway that looked like it would burst into flames just being in too much sunlight. Just then, the box was transmitted for the Jackson Street fire.

Finding a pay phone in a different section of the City, Bemis called information and asked for the business number for the Lowell Fire Department. Over the radio, the arsonists learned that the first fire was already contained—apparently, the building still had a working sprinkler system. Gregg wrote the phone number down and then dialed the number. After a ring or two, a voice answered, "Lowell Fire Department."

In his best attempt at a disguised voice, Gregg said, "The Boston arsonist is in town so you better pull your boots up." At that, he hung up.

Within seconds, the radio broke silence, "KCF-947 to Car 3." No response. Once again, "KCF-947 to Car 3."

Donny chuckled at the obvious urgency in the dispatcher's voice. "He sounds like he's shitting his pants!" There had been no response from Car 3 as numerous calls were reported for the second fire.

"KCF-947 to Car 3, I've got several calls on this one and can you call me by phone as soon as possible?" The arsonists could see the flames from quite a distance. Engine 11 reported heavy fire showing as they pulled out of quarters. Within minutes, six alarms were struck for the blaze. Apparatus came in from all over. This is exactly what Donny and Gregg had hoped. They parked a safe distance from the scene, walking the rest of the way to spark and revel in their achievement. After an hour and a half, the fire was brought under control, so the boys went home for the night.

By the end of summer 1982, only slightly over six months into their arson barrage, Mr. Flare, the Boston arsonist, the Friday Firebug, and his associates had set over 140 structure arson fires, with at least 130 of those occurring within the City of Boston. Nobody could ever recall such an onslaught of fires. The dollar amount of damages was escalating, but due to the vacant and abandoned nature of most of the targeted buildings, the costs were not as high as could be imagined for 140 building fires. The large number of fires had stretched the limited budget of the City. Over 100 firefighters had also been injured. Of course, these injuries created an even greater financial burden on the City in many ways. The cost in human terms of the injured bodies and minds would be tolled for years.

We investigators knew all this. However, we were mostly focused on the task at hand, which was still trying to find out who was responsible for this domestic terrorism offensive. Besides gathering evidence from the fire scenes and conducting nocturnal surveillances, we had been busy gathering information. Lists of persons of interest were being tabulated. Each person was then evaluated. But by the date of the autumnal equinox, there were still no clearly identified suspects.

CHAPTER EIGHT

EARLY FALL 1982

By the fall of 1982, this arson business had become just a big, hilarious game to the criminal team of players. At times they seemed like they could have cared less about Proposition 2½ and the laid-off firefighters. In fact, enough money had been found in Boston City coffers and other municipalities to rehire many of the laid-off firefighters, and some of the closed stations and apparatus had been placed back in service. Now, the arson ring players were simply out of control (as if they weren't already).

Now they just wanted to fuck with the investigators. With over 140 separate arsons by this time, they had succeeded with getting away with their deeds easily up to this point. It was truly a "cat and mouse" game to them. The mice were prolific; their offspring, the fires, were their babies. They were laughing at us and savoring every minute as heroes to the cause. The media played up the fires so often, it gave them swollen heads.

Knowing that Boston was so "hot," what was the smart thing for a bunch of arsonists to do? They broke their temporal and location patterns, choosing other towns and cities where they had never ventured before. They had already hit Quincy, Canton, Chelsea, and Lowell, but in the coming weeks, their string of multiple fires in one night within one municipality would trump their previous activities.

For instance, in the early morning hours of September 22, 1982, Bemis set three fires in rapid succession in the City of Lawrence, another struggling former mill city about 30 miles north of Boston with a largely Hispanic population. Within 10 years, Lawrence was to become the new arson capital of Massachusetts. During an 18-month period, the multi-agency task force that we were part of in Lawrence in the early 1990s made over 120 arrests for arson. But back in 1982, Lawrence was fairly quiet when it came to fires.

On this night, Bemis and Groblewski discussed hitting Lawrence, although they didn't know their way around the city or any suitable buildings to burn there. They called Ray Norton to fill him in on the details, advising him that the fires would start after 1:00 a.m. when they found some targets.

Norton enlisted another spark to go with him to Lawrence. The fire fan was incredulous that Ray wanted to go all the way to Lawrence instead of staying in the City, where most of the fires were happening. This spark didn't know that Norton had insider information about the fires. He just looked at Ray and said, "You want to go sparking in fucking Lawrence?" Nobody went sparking in Lawrence.

Gregg and Bobby found a stretch on South Broadway, the main north-south road that ran through Lawrence, where there were numerous vacant buildings. They also searched for and found several tires at a gas station that would be used at three separate sets. Across from the station, Gregg eyed a pay phone. "Hey, Bobby, look. There's a good place to call the fire department after we set the devices."

Three devices were manufactured at a boat ramp next to the Merrimack River, which bisects South Lawrence from the rest of the city. Their rapid fire-setting plan was about to go bang, bang, bang, or in this case, burn, burn, burn.

Traveling down an alleyway behind the Broadway addresses, they first hit a three-story wood-frame building with first floor storefronts and residential apartments on the upper two floors. The exterior siding was gas shingles. Gregg pulled right up to the building. Grobo stepped out of the car, placed the tire against the shingles, and lit the incendiary within the tire well. By the time he jumped back into the car, less than a minute had transpired.

A couple blocks farther south along the alley, they repeated the procedure. The building was similar to the first. The last building, just seconds away from fire building two, was a wood warehouse connected to several other structures. Of course, it too was covered with gas shingles. Bemis pulled up next to the building. Grobo placed the tire with a device against the side of the structure. All three devices were planted within five minutes.

They raced back to the gas station to call the Lawrence FD. Gregg pulled up to the phone. Bobby called information for the business number for the department, again thinking it most likely would not be a recorded line. Bobby dialed the number. When the dispatcher answered, Bobby said in a disguised voice, "Hey, you better pull up your boots because the Boston arsonist is in town." He smiled as he hung up the phone.

Back to South Broadway after the first fire was reported, the boys saw an engine pull out of the firehouse. There was a building burning to their left, another to their right, and one right in front of them. The fires actually were all reported to the Lawrence Fire Department within a minute's time, all recorded at 3:16 a.m.

Bobby snickered as he pictured the officer on the engine not being able to make up his mind which way to turn. The arsonists were extra cautious; they knew the police would be combing the area within minutes. As they approached the fires, they spotted Ray drive by. "Hey, who's that with Ray?" Bobby fumed.

"It looks like his sparkie friend."

"Oh, that's just pissa! All we need is for him to go flapping his mouth and we're all screwed."

Bemis proposed, "Well, why don't we get out of here and he won't see us." Gregg suggested going back to Lowell to set something because they were going to miss sparking these fires. Bobby agreed because he wanted to see the buildings that Donny and Gregg had burned a few days earlier. These guys put more miles on their vehicles in six months than most people put on in a year and a half. Good thing the cars weren't leased.

About 3:45 a.m., the duo arrived in Lowell. Gregg showed Bobby the other fire sites, one of which was now just a pile of rubble, at which Grobo commented, "Good stop, huh?"

After driving around to find a new target that didn't have a police cruiser near it, they found a two-and-a-half-story former mansion. Bobby placed the incendiary just inside a doorway in a trash pile. The mansion fire was reported quickly, so the arsonists bolted from the city and headed home before any cops spotted them.

Early Friday, September 24, 1982, Sanden met with Bemis at HoJo's. Both guys were leery about setting a fire in Boston with the Arson Squad running around. This didn't stop them, however, from looking for someplace to burn. They parked on a side street, made a device, and crawled through a hole in a chain link fence that protected an abandoned two-story wood shed near the Broadway MBTA Station in Southie. They traversed numerous train tracks that paralleled the Fort Point Channel. After checking for people in the area, they crept under the Broadway Bridge to reach the target.

The building had been a control tower for the train yard in years past. It was now abandoned, wide open to the arsonists. After climbing inside the structure, they placed the device, but since several trains were still running in the vicinity, they left a longer fuse with the cigarette so that they could safely get back to the car.

Driving over the Broadway Bridge, they saw that ignition had occurred. They decided to ride through the Combat Zone. As they approached Chinatown, a car ran a red light and crashed into another vehicle that had the green light. Citizens Wayne Sanden and Gregg Bemis, who both had emergency medical training, jumped into action to check for any injuries. Luckily, nobody was hurt, but the woman who drove through the light appeared to be seriously drunk. She made several attempts to flee the scene, but they confiscated her keys. Wayne called 911 from a nearby pay phone.

Meanwhile, a plume of smoke appeared in the distance, clearly visible from their vantage point at the vehicular accident. Five minutes later, the box was transmitted for the fire. Gregg moaned, "Oh, that's just great! The fuckin' fire is in and we're stuck with a drunk broad." They couldn't just leave her for fear that she would leave the scene.

A police cruiser finally pulled up and took control of the situation. As they were getting back into Gregg's car, one of the Boston cops informed them, "There's a big fire by the Broadway Bridge."

Bemis just smiled at Wayne, saying, "If he only knew." They went toward the fire, but the area was blocked off. A second alarm was transmitted due to problems for the firefighters forced to access the fire from the surrounding streets and over the railroad tracks. The two torches put away their matches for the night.

▲

Early Sunday, Bemis met with Sanden in Boston. Wayne asked, "Well, what do you want to get tonight?"

"I don't know if it's a good idea to get anything right now," Gregg said, concerned about being caught by the Arson Squad. But once again, they threw caution to the wind and decided to hit just one building.

In the Parker Hill area, they carefully positioned a device under an open window against gas shingles of a three-story house. Minutes later, they saw a wall of flames through the trees surrounding the property. "Holy shit, let's get the hell out of here," yelled Bemis. They bailed out of the area for fear of detection and went home.

Their actions seem to be a reflection of an addiction. The addicted party tries to talk himself out of reoffending, but the compulsion is too great. The offender commits the deed, but then, immediately, the miscreant tries to hide his actions, becomes cautious, even repentant, and vows not to do it again. But the cycle continues unless something intervenes. How long would these arsonists actually keep up with their felonious activities?

October 1982 was to be the third most prolific month in terms of the number of fires set by Mr. Flare and his band of merry men—29 arsons in Boston and six more outside Boston in two other counties, Middlesex and Norfolk. Yes, they were all very merry, even giddy about their accomplishments.

When they first started setting their fires, their thinking was, if we set enough fires and produce a great uproar from the local citizenry, the firefighters will all be rehired. Thus, they felt they were doing a public service to firefighters, to the police, and to the public.

If they cared at all about firefighters, though, this month of October could have fooled anyone. Maybe it would have been easier to believe that they thought, if we hurt enough firefighters, then our friends could be hired.

Still, by this time, there was no evidence pointing to any member of the arson ring for any fire. The only thing they could be charged with was acting like an ass in the nighttime. More and more local investigators were getting suspicious about the group's actions, particularly Ray Norton, Donald Stackpole, and even Boston Police Officer Robert Groblewski.

One of those investigators, Rick Splaine of the Boston Arson Squad, had told some of his colleagues of his suspicions that a Boston cop may be involved with setting these fires. One reason for his suspicions was that the arsonist was setting fires in one area of the City, engaging available fire apparatus, then setting a second fire in another section and finally setting a third fire to cause havoc with the fire department. Splaine looked askew at these guys as that they rode around in their "nerf" wannabe cruisers with the whip antennas. Splaine also noticed that the same sparks were too often the first ones at a fire scene, sometimes arriving at the same time as the first apparatus.

Investigator Splaine did not know Bobby Groblewski by name yet, but he would within the weeks to come. However, he was familiar with Norton and Stackpole. He knew Norton since he was also a Boston firefighter, now assigned to Fire Headquarters on light duty. Splaine found Norton to be odd and irritating, besides being one of the fire buffs who hung with a militant group of sparks who hooted and hollered at fires. Norton even rode around in a car with an ARSON license plate.

Investigator Splaine also had no love for Stackpole, who not only hung out with Norton, but rode around in a red car and his own fire truck, acting like a fire chief. He felt that Stackpole was a Charles Manson type who led of a pack of people committing grievous crimes, in this case arson, not murder. Some of Splaine's associates started conducting surveillances on Stackpole's security company trailer location in South Boston. The investigators didn't always try to hide that they were out there, making their presence obvious just to see what Stackpole and his friends would do. In response, Stackpole and company would park across the street from the Arson Squad, blow their horns, and heckle the Arson Squad members.

Still, the fires continued relentlessly, and the serial arsonists stayed several steps ahead of the investigative efforts.

On October 2, 1982, Bemis and his comrades for the night, Groblewski and oft-absent Joe Gorman, came up with an unusually nasty plan for their night's undertakings. Grobo informed them, "I've got a good place all picked out. It's that old military barracks on E Street."

Bemis knew exactly what building Grobo was talking about. This old military barracks was a Quonset hut–style structure, one of thousands of half circular buildings that were constructed during the World War II era. This entire section of South Boston had been both an Army and a Navy installation for decades, even prior to WWII. This old military barracks in the industrial section of Southie was the only one of its kind remaining in the area. It was a short distance from that major Spero Toy Company inferno.

Grobo knew something else very significant to their plan. The Boston Police Bomb Squad's office was immediately adjacent to their target. After discussing the predicament, they came up with the brilliant idea to call 911 to report a bomb scare in a building downtown, which would tie them up for a while.

They made a device, then found a pay phone at the corner of Summer and C Streets. Bemis made the call. Disguising his voice, he reported a bomb at Mass Eye and Ear, part of the Massachusetts General Hospital complex, blocks away from the Boston Garden. Immediately, the trio returned to E Street to make sure that the Bomb Squad had left their quarters. They had.

Joe dropped Gregg and Bobby off on F Street. The two climbed through a hole in a fence that led to a large field behind the abandoned barracks. There were several broken windows that afforded access into the building.

However, there was another problem, although somewhat smaller than the presence of the Bomb Squad. The windows were exceptionally high above the ground. Gregg found a window with some sort of vent under it. "Hey, Bobby, let me give you a lift onto that vent and you can climb in the window." Grobo agreed and Bemis lifted him up onto the unit.

Bobby crawled into the window. Gregg handed up the device and waited outside. Grobo returned to the window: "Hey, I can't find anything in here to burn, but there's a set of shelves on a wall over here. Should I put the device on one of the shelves?"

"Yeah, go ahead and try it." After Bobby placed the device, Gregg helped him to the ground. Running for the hole in the fence on the opposite side of the field, the duo encountered one more complication. While the arsonists were doing their business at the barracks, a pair of lovers had parked directly beside the hole in the fence that they had come through only minutes earlier. Gregg spotted the car early enough so that the couple probably hadn't seen them. They headed farther down the fence line, out of sight of the vehicle.

Looking back at the building, they saw fire shining in the window. Gregg exclaimed, "Holy shit, the fucking thing went off already!" As they reached a place to climb over the fence, they heard the lovers start their car and speed off. It was quite obvious that the paramours had seen the fire, but the arsonists could not be sure that the couple had not seen them.

Bobby leaped onto the chain link fence and climbed over it. As luck would have it that night, Bobby caught his green Army-style jacket on the fence, tearing it badly. "Fuck, the jacket is only a week old," griped Grobo. Once Gregg successfully made it over the fence, Joe drove up. They checked the progress of the fire. It was still burning, but appeared to be little more than a shelf fire.

Within minutes, Engine 39 and Ladder 18 responded to the scene. "Shit, the fucking thing isn't even going yet," Bobby protested. It looked like the fire was getting smaller rather than larger. The sirens were drawing closer. To the disbelief of the torches, suddenly the fire erupted in intensity just as the apparatus pulled up the E Street side.

Things didn't go well for the firefighters from the beginning. The chain link fence and gate had to be cut before they could set up to get water on the fire. After that delay, Engine 39's pump initially wouldn't operate.

These impediments contributed to the fire spread, but the criminal onlookers were still surprised by the rapid fire growth they were witnessing. Flames now blew out the top floor windows of the two-story structure. A second alarm was transmitted. A third alarm followed immediately.

After another 10 minutes, the fire began to shrink, so the arsonists headed out for another target. Minutes later, they heard a fourth alarm transmitted, with the Deputy Chief calling for a couple ambulances. The trio heard bits and pieces about a wall collapse, but they were already near their objective in Hyde Park, so they didn't turn around. When a fifth alarm was conveyed, the arsonists wondered what was going on back at the barracks. The radio traffic was vague and unclear.

At the barracks, numerous firefighters from the truck companies had laddered the roof and begun cutting holes to vent the fire. Suddenly, without warning, the roof buckled and collapsed, tossing the firefighters down into the blazing interior of the structure. Other firefighters raced into the building with complete disregard for their own safety. With a concerted effort, they managed to drag all of the fallen firefighters to safety. All told, 22 firefighters were injured, some with serious burns, others with broken legs and backs. Much of the rescue was caught by WBZ News Cameraman Nat Whittemore, who had been running ragged all over the area shooting video of several dozen fires over the past few months. But none had ended as ugly as this one.

While all hell was breaking loose at the fire scene, the men responsible for that mayhem had reached a one-story wood-frame factory that they had hit several months earlier. After placing a device by the rear loading dock door, they headed home, unaware of what had occurred at the military barracks. Not until they were all home did the box come in for the Hyde Park fire. It only amounted to a shit fire. The apparent ease with which they went to bed without knowing what horrible havoc they had wrought at the barracks would make many readers think these guys didn't even give a crap.

The next day Bemis read the newspapers. He had hoped he would never read such shocking news. But it was implausible that he, and his cohorts, couldn't foresee that hurting firefighters was an inevitable consequence of their callous actions.

That morning, back at WBZ TV, Nat Whittemore was so troubled by what he had witnessed at the barracks fire that he reached out to veteran news reporter Shelby Scott. He filled her in on the history of the plague of fires, the patterns, and on the disastrous fire of the previous night. Nat enlisted Shelby to become his "partner" as the primary reporter covering the injured firefighters, their families, and their long difficult road that lay ahead.

Allegedly, the arson ring members had all discussed trying to avoid hurting anyone during their fire-setting orgy. How they had not thought this through before their purported worst fears came to fruition is incredible, even as I write this more than 35 years later.

On the night following the disastrous blaze, the gang of arsonists, including BHA Police Officer Wayne Sanden, Boston Police Officer Robert Groblewski, Stow Public Safety Dispatcher Gregg Bemis, Boston Firefighter Ray Norton, and security company owner Donald Stackpole, gathered in South Boston in the same neighborhood as the fire. The discussion centered on avoiding any more "mishaps" (Bemis's word from his treatise) like the one that happened earlier that morning.

Ruthlessly, Stackpole ranted, "There were too many guys on that roof anyway. With all that weight, the fuckin' place could have collapsed without a fire." He added that the firefighters were the ones who screwed up; their injuries were the result of their own careless actions.

The others agreed that there were numerous firefighters on the roof, but they couldn't agree with Stackpole's excuses and abrasive attitude. Norton railed against Donny, "That's no reason to just say fuck them!" The others all agreed with Ray.

By and large, the arsonists had gone to great lengths to target abandoned buildings to avoid injuries to civilians. The vacant structures typically kept firefighters outside so that they didn't risk life or limb trying to save an abandoned property. Their aim to prevent injuries had not been enough. A couple members of the group, including Bemis, were having second thoughts about continuing with the conspiracy.

However, with their protest movement starting to work, peer pressure within the alliance was too great for weaker members to back out now. This is a primary reason for conspiracy laws. If any of the members were solely on their own, acting as a single individual, the fires may never have started, or at a minimum, when the firefighters got hurt, an individual may have quit setting fires.

The thrill of the fire-setting and the cat-and-mouse game with authorities had now become the primary driving force behind their continued arson spree. Wait until you see what the arson ring did during the rest of the month of October.

Lt. Steve McLaughlin expressed it simply after the E Street military barracks fire: "We wanted these guys real bad." When that roof collapsed, Manny Gregorio, an 18-year veteran, broke his back, an injury that left him with permanent disabilities, unable to work for a year. Donald LaPorte broke a leg and a vertebra in his back. Firefighter Raymond Martin was so seriously injured that it took 17 months of rehabilitation before he could even be assigned to light duty.

▲

The arsonists waited a couple of days to convene again; none of them were in the mood to target any buildings after the barracks disaster. It was only by the grace of God that the serial arsonists weren't facing murder charges. As it stood now, if and when they were ever arrested for the arsons, the penalties for their fire-setting offenses automatically increased when firefighters were injured due to the intentional setting of the fire.

Just three days after the barracks fiasco, Bemis, Groblewski, and Stackpole resumed their assault on the City. When Bemis greeted his pals, Bobby stated, "Well, what should we hit tonight?" The nonchalance in his demeanor gave no hint of regret for the firefighter injuries the other night. There was no hesitation about committing more arsons.

Only Bemis remained ambivalent. On the one hand, he came into Boston with all of the necessary supplies in his trunk necessary to set more fires. Does that sound like a guy who wants out of the arson conspiracy? But he told the guys that he was still unsure if he was ready "to get back to work." These were Gregg's words. After only minutes of coaxing from his peers, Bemis caved and planned more fires with Bobby and Donny.

"You know that we have to be very careful because the Arson Squad will be out in full force after the fire at the military barracks the other night," Stackpole cautioned. He was more worried about getting caught and being arrested than about injuring or killing firefighters.

Their first target was a vacant five-story brick warehouse off Northern Avenue, again in the industrial area of South Boston. Apparently, for reasons unknown, the arsonists did not think that firefighters could get injured at this type of building. Gregg and Bobby walked down a dark rat-infested alleyway. Pushing a couple of tires against wood siding, Bemis placed a lit device inside one of the tires. As they jumped back in the car, the first glow was coming from the alley. The fire spread rapidly. When the fire was reported, the torches headed to their next goal.

Donny and Grobo set this one in the same South End building on East Berkeley Street that they had tried previously, but it had never taken off. This one didn't either; it was held to a single alarm. The earlier fire of the night was also readily extinguished.

Donny suggested a building he had found while working security in the area. After going through a tunnel and a maze of alleys, they climbed a web of fire escapes and placed an incendiary against a covered window on an upper floor. This fire went to a working fire due to the difficulty for firefighters to reach the fire. The boys couldn't spark this fire as it could not be seen from the street. So they headed to the next building on their never-ending list of potential targets.

Driving south of the downtown area, they lit an empty wood-frame, three-story structure afire on Freeport Street in Dorchester. After placing the device against exterior gas shingles, they drove onto the Southeast Expressway to watch the fire's development. Flames rapidly lapped up the side of the structure, but being another outside fire it was quickly reported and easily contained.

The E Street military barracks fire certainly did not slow their arson attack on their first night back after causing so many injuries. They continued to a wood two-story building, where the device was set among the trash-strewn interior of the house.

And they continued without hesitation to their next target within the old Baker Chocolate Factory complex in the Lower Mills section of Dorchester, where they set a device against wood loading dock doors. The loading dock was against railroad tracks. With water on two other sides of the warehouse, they felt that the fire would really take off because limited access to the location would delay the firefighters. The location was so obstructed that they couldn't even observe the fire from any vantage point. But somehow the fire was discovered and extinguished easily.

Five fires were set in Boston by this arson gang during this nocturnal outing. The firefighter injuries didn't slow them down at all, nor did the fear of getting caught. They rapidly moved from target to target, which made it nearly impossible to catch them in the act. After all, they had an endless supply of vacant buildings over a wide territory, but the investigators had limited resources. Successfully eluding the authorities again and again further emboldened the members of the arson ring. Five more morsels for the mice; nothing but futility for the cat.

Early Saturday, October 9, 1982, Sanden and Bemis met in South Boston. The two fire-setters hit a wide-open abandoned three-decker in Dorchester first. The interior was full of trash, furniture, and lath that had been pulled off the walls and ceilings. The fuel and ventilation were perfect for rapid fire growth. There were even holes through the wall, providing an easy path for spread to the other half of the duplex. All that was needed was an ignition source. The arsonists supplied a lit incendiary device onto an overturned couch and exited the building en route to a second location.

Heavy fog enveloped their next target, a vacant two-and-a-half-story house located a half mile from the first fire. A device was quickly planted against an interior lath wall and they headed back toward the first building.

Passing near the building, they saw a raging fire. The first arriving fire company reported heavy fire ordering a second alarm. The duo returned to their last location. There, the blaze was already through the roof, with flames shooting from second-floor windows. This fire went to a third alarm. The first fire went to four alarms. With these two good fires, Wayne and Gregg left before the arson squad spotted them.

Bemis and Sanden set one more fire, a Bolton Street three-decker that they had set before. The fire was set in the basement. Upon arrival, Engine 39 ordered a second alarm as heavy fire was showing. For them, the three fires that night were successful. Their fires were more fruitful that night due to learning from past failures. The main reason for the multiple alarms was that the fires had all been set inside the structures, providing a longer delay in discovery and a better fuel package for the fires to develop faster.

Bemis was working his shift at the Stow Police Station on Sunday, October 10, 1982. He was surprised when Stackpole and Groblewski showed up at the lobby of the station. Gregg smiled, "Well, look what the cat dragged in." He let them into the dispatch area so they could talk business. They planned the night's felonies right inside the police station. Too bad there were no security cameras with audio present in the station. The plan was to meet back in Southie when Bemis finished his shift.

The arsonists drove to Jamaica Plain where they set an interior fire within the trash-covered first floor of a two-and-a-half-story duplex former dwelling. Instead of waiting for the fire, the trio headed to Roxbury to target a pair of gas shingle-covered three-deckers that were only separated by a narrow walkway. After driving past the buildings a couple times, they pulled over to manufacture a device and pick up a tire.

Near the targets, Grobo said, "Pull over for a minute. I have to take a piss." Bemis pulled to the curb and turned off his headlights. While Grobo was relieving himself, a Boston Police cruiser turned the corner onto the street and approached them. Bobby saw it and ducked to hide behind the car, urination interruptus. The cruiser advanced slowly. When it was beside Gregg's car, the two cops just nodded to the two arsonists in the car, then drove on. When the cruiser passed, Donny and Gregg let out a collective sigh of relief as Bobby jumped back into the vehicle. They wondered why the cops didn't stop to talk with them. Perhaps the officers would rather ignore suspicious activity than to have to fill out reports. Another, more obvious reason was that the Bemis "nerf" cruiser looked like a detective's unmarked car, so maybe the officers didn't even think that it could be someone other than cops. After all, what other white person in his right mind would be parked on a dark street in the predominantly black Roxbury neighborhood after midnight?

Gregg asked Bobby, "Why the fuck did you hide?"

"Just in case I knew any of them."

"Well, do you think we ought to do this job now?" Bemis queried the other two.

Both agreed to continue with the plan. What balls! Gregg pulled up to the dark rear side of the buildings. Donny and Bobby placed the tire with incendiary device against one of the buildings on the narrow walkway. The torches went to check on the first fire. Heavy smoke was showing from the windows. Not wanting to be seen when the fire was called in, they found an observation point where they could view the second fire. Pulling into position, the box was transmitted for the JP fire.

From the car, the sparks saw the first flicker of flames licking up the siding of the two Roxbury buildings. The fire developed with great intensity due to the gas shingles arranged as vertically oriented fuel, plus the re-radiation of the heat volatizing the fuels faster. In addition to the readily combustible fuel and the configuration of the fuel, the air entrainment from the front and back of the buildings fed the flame growth.

Engine 42 arrived to the JP fire. A working fire was ordered. As Engine 22 was also responding to that working fire, the flames of the Roxbury fire were spotted by the firefighters. They ordered the box to be transmitted. Within minutes, second and third alarms were transmitted for the triple-deckers. That fire had jumped to another pair of structures. It was now safe for the boys to actively spark the fire, as several other fire enthusiasts had arrived on scene. By the time they reached the front of the blazing inferno, a fourth alarm was ordered.

"Hey, look who's tillering on Ladder 23," Gregg said as he pointed to Groblewski's apartment roommate. The tiller is a rear-steering position, the back of a tiller trailer that steers independently of the front half of the fire truck. The tillerman steers the back end of the truck. Bobby smiled and took some photos. Norton arrived shortly thereafter.

He said to the other guys, "I figured this was some of your work when it came in right after Heath Street."

"Yeah, but this isn't the last one," Donny remarked. After telling Ray where the next fire was to be set, they continued to spark the now seven alarm job. Since it was getting late, the arsonists headed toward their next fire-to-be before the other sparks started leaving.

The target was a large four-story brick former commercial structure on the busy corner of Massachusetts and Columbus Avenues. The front and side facing the busy thoroughfares were secured tightly. Bobby and

Gregg made their way through alleys toward the rear of the building, hoping to find access. It was so dark that they needed to use Bobby's flashlight. While scanning the pathway, Bemis spotted a person lying in a pile of cardboard boxes. Just then, the individual moved. He was a homeless drunk who had decided to nap in the normally quiet alley. The encounter reminded them that they had to be vigilant about setting fires where drunks could be sleeping.

"Hey, you," Bobby yelled, acting the cop, "have you been making noise around here?" He directed the beam of his light into the guy's eyes.

"No, I ain't made no noise," quivered the man.

"Well, we got a report of somebody making noise back here, so you better pick up your stuff and find someplace else to sleep," Officer Groblewski advised. With that, the drunk grabbed his jacket and stumbled through the litter-strewn alley toward Columbus Avenue. Once he was gone, the remaining twosome found an opening into the basement of their target.

They checked the entire cobweb-laced basement for any other sleeping people. Finding it empty, the arsonists placed a lit device on wood shelves that lined one of the walls. Donny picked them up on Mass Ave.

While driving around looking for any signs of fire, Bemis observed a cab driver who appeared to be looking for the source of smoke that was wafting into the area. There was a passenger in the taxi's front seat, one of the well-known spark photographers. Donny remarked, "Oh, look, the good sparkie is doing his public service."

Trying not to be spotted, they quickly drove away from the building. Then, Box 221 was transmitted for the fire. A few minutes later, they parked across the street from the fire. Norton pulled in behind them. They all crossed the street to the fire.

The same photographer saw Grobo and immediately started talking to him. "Hey, Bobby, I reported this one," beamed the spark.

Bobby didn't reply, but the ill-tempered Norton got more irate than usual and barked, "Some people ought to mind their own fuckin' business." Gregg and Donny knew Ray was pissed off because he wanted another multiple alarm fire.

When the jakes cut their way into the front door, smoke pumped from the opening. A necessary consequence of firefighter's goal of "getting the wet stuff onto the red stuff" in a multi-story building with smoke showing from a lower level was opening the structure to gain entry. This was usually a controlled process. The conundrum occurs because the fresh air supply feeds the fire growth, sometimes violently. For safety, other openings are often made to the roof and upper floors as vents for the smoke and volatile hot gases.

In this case, the smoke grew thicker and more energetic. This signified that the smoke layer could flash with flames momentarily. The buffs gathered to view the show, but the Mr. Flare crew walked around to the rear of the building to see what was going on there.

One fire company was breaking out a rear doorway from the inside. The doorway was about five feet above the outside ground level. The steel stairs that normally ran from the ground to the door were all missing except for the top landing outside the doorway. Smoke was pumping from the basement-level doorway, where the device had been set a short time before.

A couple of jakes carried a line out the now opened first-floor doorway with the intent to attack the fire through the basement opening. The billowing smoke obscured the firefighters' view on the landing. One of the jakes stumbled and fell off the stoop, tumbling into the trash piled at the base of the missing stairs. Awkwardly, with all of the gear and equipment, the firefighter regained his footing and headed to the basement opening.

Norton just shook his head, commenting in his usual nasty fashion, "Fuckin' spook can't even stand on his own two feet." Norton had always been prejudiced against black firefighters; he believed that they were not qualified for the job. He, like many other people, was even more upset when a Federal judge ordered all minorities to be rehired after they had been laid off during the Proposition 2½ cutbacks, regardless of their lower seniority status. It wasn't this guy's fault that he had been rehired, but he was now the object of racist wrath.

Once the hose line was opened onto the basement area, the fire was soon brought under control. The arsonists went back to their cars, where they sat and talked. Ray was still griping about the guy who pulled the box for the fire. The night was beginning to wane. The boys were too.

▲

On Tuesday night, Bemis and Grobo planned a blitzkrieg style of spree burning. The two torches revved up their activities, with six fires set in four different areas of Boston. So much for setting only one fire per night in Boston to avoid detection from the Arson Squad! And they ventured out on an off night to foil investigative efforts.

In Charlestown, they hit a vacant four-story brick warehouse. After placing a device under a loading dock, they went to their next target, a three-story wood-frame with gas shingles a half-mile from the previous building. Parking behind the former house, they placed the incendiary against the shingles.

Immediately, they hit a South Boston two-story tin-clad warehouse that was a client of Stackpole's security company. Bobby had suggested torching it to draw heat away from Stackpole. Their thinking was that it wouldn't make any sense to burn a building owned by a customer.

Accessing the building via a second floor window, Gregg boosted Bobby onto a tall stack of wood pallets, where a device was placed in the window frame. Once again, they immediately pushed toward the next building. Meanwhile, the two fires in Charlestown had been reported, but each one had been easily contained.

A two-story brick garage-style warehouse in the South End was next on their list. They forced their way into the building to set a device. Once back in the car, the radio blared instructions for Engine 2 to charge their line. "Hey, Bobby, they must have struck the box for the fire in Southie."

Checking it out, they spotted Norton. Ray came over smiling, stating, "You're crazy." Bobby told him that another fire in the South End was brewing. Moments later, a working fire was ordered on the box for that fire.

Restless for more action, Ray asked, "Hey, what are you going to get next?" Bobby told him that an adjacent pair of two-story wood-frame structures were on deck. Ray responded, "Fine, I'll see you there." The two arsonists departed for their objective.

At the new site, a device was planted between the two buildings against gas shingles. The two took up a position to view the buildings. Within minutes, the fire flared up the walls of both buildings. The box was transmitted quickly for the fire. First arriving apparatus ordered a second alarm. However, the short-term, large fire was readily knocked down before the fire had a chance to spread to the interiors of the buildings.

They headed toward their last set for the night in Roxbury. Bobby set a tire and device inside the open front hallway of a vacant triple-decker. He and Gregg rode around to await report of the fire. To their surprise, the fire was reported by Boston Fire Photographer Billy Noonan. If he had come by just minutes earlier, he could easily have caught the arsonists in the act, but they lucked out again. A second alarm was ordered. A busy night, indeed.

▲

On October 14, 1982, Bemis met up with Grobo and Wayne Sanden in South Boston. Sanden advised the other two that he had seen the Arson Squad out in full force. "What, do they still think Mr. Flare is striking on Thursday nights?' quipped Gregg. Bobby and Wayne snickered.

Discussing strategy, Bobby said, "I think we may be able to get one more good night in the City, but after that we're going to have to start targeting outside the City."

The others agreed, but Wayne asked, "Well, does that mean we can't do anything tonight?" They decided to set one fire in the City because the Arson Squad would not be able to catch up with them if they stuck to one fire. They chose to set a fire at the Boston State Hospital since they hadn't been there in several months.

In Mattapan, they quickly made it into one of the many buildings and set a device. They hung around until the fire was called in, but it was a dud. But they stuck to the plan and quit before midnight, very early for them, saving their energy for another big night out on the town.

That big night was early Sunday, October 17, 1982. The arsonists felt safer on this night; they figured Sunday broke the pattern and many of the investigators weren't working. This night, Bemis, Groblewski, Stackpole, and Joe Gorman were the ones "working,"

Just after midnight, they set one fire in the basement of a three-story brick building on Essex Street in the Chinatown section of Boston. By 1:00 a.m., they had set another fire downtown, this time a four-story brick warehouse on Broad Street, very close to our ATF Batterymarch Street office. Then Joe had to meet someone, so they dropped him at his car.

It was unusual for them to set fires downtown for a couple reasons. The heavy concentration of bars and restaurants downtown meant more people were likely to be out and about at all hours. Also, there were very few abandoned or vacant structures in the area. Those that were vacant often were well secured brick buildings with no access. However, by setting a couple fires downtown, the Arson Squad would be drawn away from the usual areas such as Dorchester and Roxbury, leaving a void that the arsonists hoped to take advantage of.

While waiting for the fires to be reported, the remaining trio set an exterior fire to a single-story wood-frame warehouse on the very narrow Necco Court. Gregg parked in the parking lot of the Channel Nightclub. The Channel, as it was known, ended up becoming the centerpiece of a 2018 Federal trial. Head mobster Frank "The Cadillac" Salemme, who was alleged to have a hidden interest in the club, was convicted for the murder of Steve DiSarro, the owner of record, murdered so that he couldn't testify against Salemme.

Now, finding the warehouse completely buttoned up, Bobby and Gregg walked along the rear of the structure directly above the Fort Point Channel. The device was subsequently placed against asphalt siding.

The two previous downtown fires were easily contained. Also, to their disappointment, Necco Court was discovered quickly and knocked down in minutes.

They headed for Roxbury because downtown was now buzzing with fire buffs and the Arson Squad. In quick succession, they used a couple of tires with a device to light up a beautiful old two-and-a-half-story wood mansion, then placed a device against the gas-shingled siding of a triple-decker. After setting the second fire, the first one was reported, again held to a single alarm.

Donny had enough for one night, so they headed toward Southie to drop him off. Before the boys got there, the radio broke silence with, "K7 to Fire Alarm. Strike the box for a fire on Howard Avenue."

"There goes fuckin' Noonan again," groaned Bobby in disgust, and then added, "We'll just have to get something else." Grobo came up with a new target. "Hey, how about Gerrity Lumber in Readville?" Gregg agreed. Readville is a village within the Hyde Park neighborhood.

Gerrity Lumber was a large family-run active lumberyard and millworks operation. The company had been formed in 1875. The family had 16 locations; Readville was the only Massachusetts yard.

The lumberyard was on a dead end known as Whiting Avenue Extension. It sat on the Boston/Dedham line. After parking on a side street, Gregg and Bobby traversed numerous railroad tracks that ran along the multiple building complex. They climbed over a chain link fence to access the yard. There was a wide open, tall brick structure with a two-story wood addition at the rear of the building. One side was open for loading purposes. The addition was filled with huge stacks of bundled cedar shingles on pallets. Bobby placed one device in the brick section of the structure. Gregg placed a second device among the shingles in the addition. The duo hustled the substantial distance back to the car. Embers were already floating on convective currents into the night sky by the time they drove away.

Bobby suggested that Gregg pull over at a pay phone so that he could call Ray since he lived near the now rapidly growing fire. While Bobby was on the phone, the fire was reported. They headed back to Whiting Avenue. Ray pulled in right behind them. The trio walked closer to the fire.

The blaze quickly went to four alarms, with both Boston and Dedham Fire Departments responding to the location. Sparks amassed at the roaring inferno. Ray was in an exceptionally cheerful mood. He asked Grobo to take his picture posing against a Dedham engine company with the fire also modeling in the background. After enjoying the show for a while, they departed for home as it was nearly 5:00 a.m.

That Sunday morning, ATF Arson Group Supervisor Jack Dowd telephoned me at home. He advised me of the fire at Gerrity Lumber and requested that I meet him there about 10:00. Putting aside any plans I had with my wife and two young daughters, I made the 15-mile drive easily with the light Sunday traffic. At the scene, Jack and I conferred with Dedham Fire Deputy Chief Dave Chisholm, an easygoing and capable person. Dave and I became good friends for years to come. The Chief walked us through the charred scene. Both the brick section and the wood addition with the shingles were severely damaged with collapse to both areas. He informed us that upon arrival of his crew, there were two large, but separate and distinct, fires, one in each section of the structure.

We interviewed the lumberyard manager, covering many topics, including when the last person was in the building and what potential ignition sources were in the area. When the interview was completed, we examined the scene in detail. On the basis of several factors, we concluded that the fire had been intentionally set by person(s) unknown in two locations. Although the actual ignition source was not firmly identified, the competent heat source had to be introduced to the area, as there were two separate and distinct fires with no potential ignition sources near either origin.

With several other fires in Boston the same night also being determined to have been intentionally set, the Gerrity fire seemed to be part of the long string of blazes. We didn't know that the Mr. Flare ring so liked the ease with which the lumberyard produced a large blaze that they would soon hit it again.

▲

Tuesday night/Wednesday morning was becoming the new favorite night for the arsonists to ply their trade. In breaking their old pattern of being the Friday Firebug, they were now creating a new pattern. But nobody ever tagged them with the nickname "Wednesday Firebug"; it didn't have the same panache.

Bemis met Grobo at HoJo's. Bobby was sitting in his car. He directed Gregg, "Grab all the supplies and put them in my trunk." It was extremely unusual for Bobby to drive on fire nights. Gregg didn't argue. Once in the car, Bobby told him the plan, "Ray wants us to meet him. He told me about some place on Route 1 that we can target."

They met Ray, who was working his part-time job at a liquor distributor. Ray provided details about the target building, then gave Bobby and Gregg a head start to scout the objective.

The boys were not very familiar with Route 1 south of Boston, but they easily found the building that Ray suggested. However, parking was a problem. So the pair continued down the roadway to explore the area. Then, right before their eyes appeared a delicious target. The building was the vacant, vandalized former Weber Duck Inn 1810 House, a century-old two-story inn. It was less than one-quarter mile north of the Foxboro State Police Barracks, but that never slowed down the team of Groblewski and Bemis.

After parking on a side street, they walked across the four lanes of Route 1 to the other side of the intersection. Traversing overgrown weeds and bushes to the rear of the building, they found an open window. Gregg hoisted himself in, followed by the passing of the device, and then Bobby climbed in the window. The interior of the place had been completely wrecked; smashed tables and chairs covered the floor. The device was placed within a pile of the debris against a lath wall. They scampered back to the car, again in a rush to beat ignition of the incendiary.

Just as Bobby put his car in gear and proceeded toward the traffic light at the intersection, the light turned red. Impatient with the fire building directly in front of them, Grobo ran the light by turning left, onto Route 1 south. Gregg spotted a glow inside the old inn as they turned. Unfortunately for them, at the same time, a Massachusetts State Police cruiser came over the rise in the road, seeing them run the light. On the semi-bright side, they were visibly out of sight of the structure when the Trooper activated his blue lights to pull them over.

"May I see your license and registration, please?" requested the Trooper as he stood at the driver's door with his flashlight trained on Bobby. Grobo opened his wallet wide so that his Boston Police badge was plainly visible. "Hey, you a cop?" inquired the Trooper. Bobby replied in the affirmative. The two law officers talked for a bit, then the Trooper said, "Okay, gentlemen, have a good night." Both arsonists sighed with relief. They quickly pulled back onto the highway and sped north toward Boston. There was no way that they were going to spark this fire. They called it a night, not willing to push their luck any further that night. Again, they had escaped detection. This was a close call. The fires would continue because these guys were cool, calm, and collected in the face of adversity.

Where did their nerves of steel come from? Dictionary.com defines *sociopath* as a person with a psychopathic personality whose behavior is antisocial, often criminal, and who lacks a sense of moral responsibility or social conscience. That moniker seems appropriate in this instance.

▲

The next night, the arson ring members struck again. Their actions were getting more bizarre, if that was possible. Bemis called Norton to see if he had made it to the Foxboro fire. He was very careful not to say anything specific in case the phones were being monitored by investigators. Their paranoia was growing, but at this point they were giving the investigators too much credit.

Bemis met Sanden and Groblewski at Norton's house. Discussion focused on the fact that the Arson Squad was keeping a closer watch on them. They planned to target more buildings outside the City to throw the Arson Squad off again. Their source inside the Boston Fire Department, Ray Norton, warned, "I would stay outside the City completely if I were you. They've got more guys working the Arson Squad lately than I've ever seen."

"Well, do you think they'll be watching West Roxbury?" asked Grobo.

Ray shook his head, replying, "There's nothing in West Roxbury for them to watch." They advised Ray that they had checked out a property that he had mentioned to them a few weeks earlier. Their reconnaissance showed that the building was prime for burning. Ray agreed that it would be safe to target the place.

Sanden suggested, "Well, why don't we get something outside of the City first? I think I know where there is another building in Canton." All four of them took a ride to a donut shop in Andrew Square. While sitting in the parking lot, Ray alerted his friends, "Hey, see that car going by? That belongs to the Arson Squad."

Bobby asked, "Are you sure?"

"Sure I am. I see it parked at headquarters all the time." The car drove by again minutes later. Ray was in a ball-busting mood, brought on by the attention from the Arson Squad. He walked over to a trash barrel, grabbed a discarded newspaper, and rolled it into a tube.

"What the fuck are you up to now?" inquired Gregg.

"Just watch when those assholes go by again," he answered. That statement alone shows which side Ray Norton was on. Why would he refer to the Arson Squad members in such derogatory terms when they were merely trying to do their job and catch an arsonist or two or three or four?

Like clockwork, the car drove by again. Psycho Ray lit the newspaper on fire. He waved the blazing torch back and forth toward the passing Arson Squad car. His actions certainly drew the attention of the investigators; they ended up driving through the intersection another 50 times.

About 10:00 p.m., a box came in for a building fire in Jamaica Plain. The boys and other fire buffs screeched out of the parking lot with emergency lights on, their personal sirens blaring. Right in front of them was the Arson Squad car. The first arriving apparatus reported heavy fire showing, immediately ordering a second alarm. Within minutes, a third and a fourth alarm were struck.

The arson ring boys arrived in record time at the fire scene, but they didn't care since they hadn't set this fire and the Arson Squad members were their alibi witnesses. The vacant four-story brick structure was fully involved. Actually, it had been one of their targets that they had hit several months earlier, but they never got it going.

Ray with a smile on his face said, “Boy, did we have a perfect alibi or what?”

Bemis smiled back, “Maybe they’ll leave us alone for a while now.”

Ray continued to bust balls at this point. When he saw the same guys from the Arson Squad at the fire scene who had been in Southie, he yelled, “Why don’t you guys watch for some arsonists instead of busting our balls all the time?” The Arson Squad members just smiled and walked away.

It was getting late. The crew stopped by Ray’s house to rearrange the car situation. Ray was to wait a half hour before he headed for Canton. Wayne and Bobby rode with Gregg to check out the building that Wayne had proposed hitting. They found the building, but it was occupied, so they passed on it.

The trio looked for another target. Just as they were about to give up, Gregg spotted a building down a quiet side street. As soon as they turned onto Walnut Street, Bobby remarked, “That’s beautiful.” The building appeared to be a vacant three-story wood-frame warehouse covered with gas shingles. The ancient structure stood no more than five feet from the road. After a few passes past the building, Gregg dropped Bobby and Wayne in a darkened area down the street. The two arsonists placed a tire with a device right against the front gas-shingled wall. Just after they lit the device, a car drove past them without taking any notice of two men on this quiet side street in the middle of the night. The torches turned to hide their faces. Moments later, Gregg picked them up.

“Okay, I’m going to stop at that gas station because I’m getting low on gas,” said Gregg. It happened to be the same gas station that I used regularly for gas, oil changes, and other maintenance, as I lived less than a mile away. I drove by that building nearly every day without paying much attention to it.

While at the gas pump, Bobby came up with an inspired idea: call the Canton Fire Department to give them a message. Gregg followed him to the pay phone several feet away from the gas pump. Bobby dialed the business line. The dispatcher answered, "Canton Fire Department."

Grobo, disguising his voice, said, "Hey, remember that fire you had a few weeks ago?"

"Yeah," the dispatcher replied, whose voice gave the impression of wondering where this call was going.

Bobby continued, "The one where Engine 1 said, 'Lay two lines. It's going to the moon.'?"

"Yeah?" questioned the dispatcher.

"Well, you better pull up your boots because you're going for another trip!" Bobby said, then hung up the phone. They snickered a little while climbing back into the car.

Seconds later, the fire was reported. As the boys approached Walnut Street, heavy fire was reported while a second alarm was ordered. When the arsonist-sparks arrived, the front face of the building was fully involved from ground to roof with reddish orange flames. The guys sparked the fire until other fire buffs from Boston showed up at the scene.

It was now after midnight, so they headed to that West Roxbury target. Gregg dropped Wayne and Bobby in front of the overgrown shrubs that partially hid the vacant two-story house. After circling the block, the torches appeared from the darkness and climbed into the car. Bobby informed Gregg, "We put the device under a couch that was lying against the outside back doorway."

While they cruised the streets, the box was transmitted for the fire. The radio reported, "Engine 30 to Fire Alarm. Heavy fire showing on Temple Street."

"Well, it sounds like it's going pretty good," Wayne said. As they arrived on scene, a second alarm was transmitted. They observed heavy fire showing in the rear of the building, with smoke obscuring the front of the house.

Norton joined his pals minutes later. "Well boys, it looks like the Arson Squad was in the wrong place tonight," Ray wisecracked.

Just then, Wayne reached into his pocket and pulled out a box of kitchen matches. "Hey, look at this," a smiling Wayne said while holding out his hand for perusal. The brand name was Three Torches Brand. It absolutely matched the situation. When the other guys looked at the brand name, they started laughing out loud.

By now the fire had broken through the roof. A third alarm had been ordered. "Hey, look who's coming?" Ray motioned to one of the Arson Squad inspectors walking toward them.

When the inspector came within hearing range, Bobby jibed in a ball-buster manner, "Hey, has anybody got a spare tire?" The arson investigator almost snapped his neck swiveling his head to see who was speaking. Bobby and Ray just stood there smiling at him. After taking a few more photos, the crew headed home.

Did Ray's lighting the newspaper on fire and waving it in front of the Arson Squad sound like an arson co-conspirator being more careful because of the added heat that they were garnering? Does the phone call to the Canton FD sound like increased vigilance to insure not being discovered? How about Groblewski's mocking and teasing the Arson Squad inspector? Was that an action of a smart careful criminal who was also a cop? It was interesting that Bobby mentioned a spare tire in front of the investigator. Nobody on the street was aware that tires were being used as part of the fire sets. That sounded like insider information.

These serial arsonists were now officially out of control. Their actions were becoming more and more reckless. As the arson ring success continued without detection, their cockiness translated into more irresponsible behavior, even by their standards. They had recently discussed being more careful, but in practice, they were doing the opposite.

When I referred above to the Walnut Street, Canton, building, I said that it appeared to be vacant. Well, it wasn't exactly vacant.

The day after the fire, I conducted an origin and cause investigation at that location. As part of that analysis, interviews were conducted. I learned of the call that was made to the Canton FD alluding to the barn fire and announcing that a second fire was on tap for the night. This appeared to connect the two fires and point toward an incendiary act as the cause. Yet the fire scene examination had to be conducted in order to verify the actual fire cause. The origin had to be determined first. Then, the ignition source, the first fuel ignited, and the circumstances that brought those two factors together had to be identified.

The scene examination could not have been any easier. The front face of the building against the road was completely charred from the ground to the roof with almost all of the gas shingles burned away. The building was about 100 years old, so under the shingles were wood planks rather than plywood. The planks were charred from bottom to top. Some of the fire had carried into the building, but the burn patterns indicated that the fire was initially an exterior fire that had spread to the interior, mostly via the windows on the upper two floors.

The exterior fire pattern on the wood planking formed a V-pattern. At ground level was the narrow base of the V. The pattern widened to the entire width of the elevation at roof level. This was significant. In this case, the V-pattern pointed down to the point of origin. At the base of that V-pattern, I found the remains of the steel belts from a vehicle tire. Samples were taken of the soil and sent to the ATF Laboratory in Maryland. Within a week, the results of the sample analyses came back negative for any residue of a combustible liquid. However, this did not deter me from finding that this fire was incendiary, having been set with an open flame or delayed ignition device by person or persons unknown. All of the information and data collected led to the conclusion that this fire was arson, a malicious act of intentional burning.

But what about the issue of the building being vacant? This is where this case got even more interesting than it already was. The occupancy issue, in this case, highlighted the problems that fire investigators faced when trying to find those responsible for setting each and every fire during this arson streak. Sure, this fire had a phone call that appeared to connect it to the previous Canton fire set by this group. But was this fire related to the string of fires or was it related to the sole occupant of the third floor?

The Canton Fire investigator, the State Fire Marshal, and I all saw something at this fire scene that seemed out of place. A half dozen telephone lines were going into the third floor. After checking further, it was determined that the third floor had been leased to a well-known bookmaker/loan shark from an adjacent town. Could the fire have any connection to that "business"? Could it have been a competition issue? Or could it have to do with a client who had a problem?

It so happened that I was very tight with the nearby Walpole Police Department. One of the Walpole Detectives had a relationship with the bookie. The Detective arranged a meeting between the bookie and me. Within a couple days, the three of us gathered in the living room of the Walpole cop.

I was more than a bit naïve about the whole bookmaking and loansharking business. After a few niceties, I let the bookmaker know that I couldn't care less about the trade that he was conducting. I had no jurisdiction over any of his business transactions. I only cared about who set the fire. I asked the bookie if he knew anything, anything at all, about the cause of the fire. He convinced me that there was no reason, to his knowledge, that the fire was connected to him in any way. He said that the location was perfect for him; it was close to his home and low key. He had had no recent issues with anyone, plus the fire wouldn't have helped anybody get out from under any debt. The detective informed me that he knew the guy fairly well and that he believed his story. My thinking, therefore, was that the fire was linked to the long string of arsons.

On Thursday, October 21, 1982, Gregg met with Grobo and Donny in Southie. "I hear you guys had a pretty good night last night," Donny said with a grin.

"We sure did," Gregg replied. The arson ring members loved to gloat about their good fires.

But not for too long. To them, there was always more that needed to be done. After discussing that the City was not safe for them, they decided to cross the Charles River to Cambridge. Grobo suggested, "Well, why don't we go find Wayne. He would know where all the vacant buildings in Cambridge are."

In the early 1980s, Cambridge had very little open land left; there were buildings everywhere, with lots of commercial structures and densely populated residential areas. Like Boston, there were many old vacant buildings in Cambridge in need of renovation or being torn down. Or even burned down, according to some parties.

Wayne was found working at one of the housing projects. They told him they planned to attack Cambridge, and he agreed to meet them after his shift. After midnight, the four arsonists prowled around the city of two of the world's great universities, Harvard University and the Massachusetts Institute of Technology. Their first target was an old four-story wood warehouse with gas shingle siding very near MIT. Today, thanks to urban redevelopment, the area that they targeted that night was part of one of the greatest technology centers of the world. What the torches didn't know about their target was that it housed extremely expensive equipment belonging to the Polaroid Corporation, maker of the famous Polaroid instant film, cameras, and other electronics.

“Well, this place looks good to me, but what can we do about the firehouse around the corner?” Donny asked.

”Well, we can call in a phony still [alarm] to get them out of the area,” Wayne proposed. It was a devious new tactic for the arson ring. First, they made a device, which they placed against the gas shingle siding. Then, they drove to a payphone near the firehouse and called the Cambridge Fire Department. Wayne told the dispatcher that there was a building fire on River Street near Memorial Drive. Momentarily, the Central Square firehouse emptied. This gave their fire a chance to develop. Minutes later, the box was transmitted. Then a second alarm was ordered for the fire.

They chose not to spark the fire. The radio then broke the silence, “Cambridge to Boston over Metro Fire,” came from the Cambridge Fire Dispatch. When Boston answered, Cambridge requested, “Yes, Boston, could you notify your arson squad that things are starting to heat up over here.”

“Boston has that message.” The arsonists knew that they had to get out of the area immediately, but not before nonchalantly stopping on Cambridge Street for coffee and cookies. It seemed that nothing fazed these guys.

▲

Early Monday morning was another off-pattern time for these guys to set their fires. They chose to hit the Chelsea area because it wasn’t Boston and they hadn’t been there for a while. One of the fires ended up being in Everett, on the line with Chelsea. This was another rapid multiple fire night.

Bobby, Donny, and Gregg chose a few suitable objectives in the area. On opposite sides of the same alleyway, there was a demolition company with several wood sheds and piles of junk cars. They prepared two devices, placing one by the sheds on the left side of the alley and the other against a shed on the right side of the alley. They raced onto Revere Beach Parkway, where they observed rapid development of the fires, both of which became quite visible in the night sky. The fires were both officially reported as two separate addresses at 2:33 a.m. and went to several alarms.

Instead of sparking these fires, they drove to another section of the city and set a wood warehouse afire using a tire with a device under the floor because the building was on stilts. This was the one actually in Everett. This fire was reported at 2:41 a.m., only nine minutes after the previous two fires. It went to two alarms.

Choosing again not to spark this fire, they headed for a three-story wood warehouse on the Chelsea River by the oil tank farms. Bemis drove up to the front of the building, where Bobby placed a device with a tire against the exterior gas shingles. They then crossed into East Boston, where they parked along the river to survey the early progress of the fire. Although the fire was reported quickly, it went to five alarms. This time, they sparked the fire before splitting up for the night.

Early on Halloween morning, a Sunday, Stackpole, Grobo, and Bemis set the last fire for the month at a vacant two-story wood warehouse on Congress Street in Boston. The rear of the structure had a damaged overhead door with a loading dock facing the Fort Point Channel. After waiting for over an hour for people to clear the local drinking establishments, the arsonists planted a device within trash against the overhead door. Within 10 minutes, the fire was reported, but it still progressed to four alarms. Those responsible for the fire watched from a vantage point across the channel behind the Federal Reserve Building.

The month of October 1982 was over. The arson ring was guilty of setting 35 more arsons, many of them devastating in terms of firefighter injuries and real property damages. Several nights during this 31-day period were spree nights.

This was also a month that saw the arsonists step up their taunting of the Boston Arson Squad and other towns like Canton with telephone calls to the fire department. This was the first month in which they called in a phony bomb scare and a false alarm for a fire. Although they professed to adhere to greater safety measures, their sociopathic tendencies flourished. The conspiracy had nourished their careless behavior. October emphasized their callousness. Their reckless conduct showed that these guys had gone off the rails. The complete train wreck was just a matter of flipping the page on the calendar.

CHAPTER NINE

NOVEMBER 1982

This month proved to be a milestone for both the arsonists and the investigators.

The group added to their "list of accomplishments" starting on November 2, 1982, when Donny traveled to Gregg's house in Maynard. Donny enlisted Gregg for another job (*enlist* may be too strong a word; Gregg didn't need to be won over to set another fire). Donny proposed, "I figured I'd take a ride out to Hicksville to see what's happening."

Gregg asked, "O.K. Skinny, what's on the agenda for the night?"

"Well, I figured that since there hasn't been any fires out in this area lately, maybe we can stir up some excitement to draw the Feds away from Boston," Donny reasoned. The group obviously knew that we Federal investigators were conducting surveillances in Boston. They were trying to keep from being too predictable by breaking their pattern. This period also proved that the conspirators could no longer claim altruistic motives, as many of the police and firefighters who had been laid off had, by now, been rehired.

They headed for the City of Marlborough (sometimes spelled Marlboro by the less refined), an old industrial city some 30 miles west of Boston that was only a couple towns away from Gregg's house. They had their pick of rundown, abandoned buildings in Marlborough; two buildings made their list for the night.

The first target was an abandoned apartment house with a first-floor storefront directly in the center of town on Main Street, less than a block from the Marlborough Fire Headquarters. However, it was too early in the evening, so after grabbing a bite to eat, they headed for the more rural setting of their other choice, an abandoned farmhouse on Boston Post Road.

The road was established as part of the first postal route system between New York City and Boston in the 1600s. Post riders rode horses on this upper section over narrow paths through the woods. In 1982 this piece of the "Post Road" system was Route 20.[19]

The rickety house sat in a field far back from the road. Although it wasn't even 9:00 p.m., they parked at a nearby bar. After making the device, Donny and Gregg weaved through the tall grass to the farmhouse. The building had an attached porch with wide-open narrow-profile windows. It took quite an effort to crawl through those windows, especially for Stackpole. Inside, they found nothing but smashed debris, which they piled in a corner with the device. "Hey Donny, make sure you set it to give us a couple of extra minutes to climb through that damn window," directed Bemis.

By the time they returned to the car, the building was smoking. From the parking lot, the duo watched the smoke become thicker. However, due to the way it was dispersing, layering over the area, nobody driving by realized that the building was on fire. A half-hour later, the radio announced from Marlborough FD, "KCD-619 dispatching Engine 5 to the area of Post Road Auto Parts for a smoke investigation. Time out 21:15." It was 9:15 p.m. By then, the entire road was enveloped by smoke. Traffic came to a standstill, partly because drivers had a difficult time seeing and partly because they were curious as to the source of the smoke. Still, it was challenging to find that source.

---

19 The Boston Post Road, The Federal Highway Administration Fact Sheet

It took Engine 5 several minutes to locate the burning building. Apparatus and spectators swarmed the area. Now parked across the street from the scene, Bemis spotted a Marlborough Firefighter friend of his arriving to fight the fire. When he eyed Gregg, he walked over to him and queried, "How'd you get here so quick?"

"Oh, we were shopping up the street and smelled the smoke," Gregg explained. The firefighter just smiled as he walked toward the fire.

Twenty minutes later, they headed downtown to get the other building. After finding a suitable place to park, they walked a couple blocks to the rear of the target. The rear door was boarded up solid. The device was set outside among combustible debris and asphalt siding. Back at the car, Gregg said excitedly, "Hey, Skinny, I'll bet this one goes like hell!"

Donny added, "Boy, I'd love to see the look on their faces when they pull out of the firehouse. I'll bet they've never seen two fires in one night." The arsonists couldn't bear to miss the confusion that they figured was about to take place. When the call had not come in after a few minutes, the duo rode past the fire building; flames were blowing out of the entire structure. Again, traffic blocked the street as drivers gawked at the blaze. The radio announced the fire as they passed the location. It was 10:22 p.m. The boys maneuvered up a side street to avoid oncoming apparatus.

"Alright Donny, let's get the hell out of town. They'll know now that somebody is lighting up the town."

Donny concurred while laughing about the havoc transmitting over the radio. "Is there anything else around we can get?" Donny wanted more.

Bemis knew of some good places in neighboring Hudson, so they headed there. Looking for a safe spot to park, they pulled into a church parking lot that was packed with vehicles. An election campaign function was being held in the church. Hesitating at first to park there, they decided that the large number of cars provided great cover. They made the device right there in the car in the church parking lot.

Gregg and Donny sneaked into the woods behind the parking lot. After walking for a bit, they came to an old railroad track. Gregg knew that it ran behind a warehouse a few hundred yards away.

Once at the structure, Gregg found the place was now covered with tin siding. There were no open windows or doors. About ready to give up on the building, Donny suggested finding a tire and placing it under the tin where there was a wood base foundation.

During their trip down the tracks, the boys had passed a construction company. They went there to look for a tire. There was not a single tire to be found until Stackpole said, "Hey, look at that tire," referring to a huge tire for a front end loader.

"Are you shitting me, Skinny? That tire must be six feet tall and weigh 400 pounds!"

"What are you laughing for? Just think how it will burn."

"Yeah, that's what I'm laughing about. If we got the tire to ignite, it would be a second alarm by itself," Gregg chuckled. They tried to turn the tire on its tread, but they couldn't budge it, in part because the tire well was full of water, adding another hundred pounds or so to its weight. After bailing out most of the water, they got it upright. It still weighed almost as much as Gregg and Donny combined, but they got it rolling and skipping over the track. It was a struggle, but finally, with sweat starting to roll down their faces, they got it to lean against the building. After a short rest, they placed the device within the open tire. The device timer was set a little longer than usual. It was lit, and they left for the car.

Donny convinced Gregg to walk straight through the woods instead of taking the longer route by the tracks. Once they had traveled a few hundred feet, Bemis knew that they had made a drastic error as the thick brush in the dark was slowing them considerably. "Come on Donny, we have to move faster; the device is going to go off any minute," Gregg said urgently.

Gregg approached the parking lot ahead of Donny. He noticed that the church was emptying. People were filing toward their cars. Bemis motioned for Donny to be quieter, but Donny couldn't hear Gregg.

Somebody who heard breaking branches as they trampled through the woods called the police. Donny finally caught up with Gregg, who said, "Hey, dummy, you made so much noise; they heard you."

"Oh, don't worry about it. Let's just get out of here." Easier said than done. They couldn't just walk out of the woods now because there were too many people milling about in the lot. Compounding the bad situation, the device had already ignited the tire, which was generating loud popping noises similar to firecrackers.

"Oh, pissa, that's all we need, more noise for the people to hear," Gregg moaned. They crept to the end of the parking lot. Gregg had secreted himself behind a large pine tree when he spotted a police cruiser enter the parking lot. "Donny, get down, the cops are coming!" Donny jumped behind a small building at the rear of the parking lot.

The cruiser drove slowly with the car's alley lights trained toward the woods. Panicking, Bemis wanted to jump out from behind the tree, but that would have put him in plain view of the oncoming lights. The cruiser inched up right next to the tree where Gregg was hiding. The cop stopped there. Gregg held his breath, his heart pounding, beating out of his chest, sure he had been seen. After a few interminably long seconds, the cruiser moved slowly away, checking the remainder of the parking lot perimeter. Gregg started breathing again. With relief, he crawled over to Donny. They still had to wait before leaving their concealed position as people continued to stream out of the church. At least the police had left the lot. It was after midnight by the time they got to their car. Since they were about the last ones to exit the parking lot, they were wary that the cruiser might return.

The guys were thinking that the fire department must have been called for the fire by now, but not a word came over the radio. "Shall we take a ride past the building?" Donny asked.

"What, are you crazy? Too many people around here know my car!" With that said, they traveled several back roads out of town toward Gregg's house. He turned to Stackpole: "Well, Skinny, it wasn't too bad of a night considering."

Donny shook his head and replied, "I think I'll stick to Boston from now on. There's too many nosy people out this way." He blamed the local citizens for almost getting them caught committing a major felony.

The fire was finally reported at 1:26 a.m., but the fire was small due to an active sprinkler system inside the building that contained the fire. This fire would be listed on the Federal indictment as fire number 200.

On Tuesday, November 4, 1982, Gregg turned 22 years old. Of course, he wanted to celebrate. He hit a few bars with friends, then headed to Boston, where he met Donny at one of his South Boston security jobs.

Abruptly, out of nowhere, Donny said, "Hey, I meant to have you ride past the State Fire Academy in Stow the other night."

"Why, what do you want from there?"

"Well, that place must be loaded with fire equipment. Maybe we can get a couple of 4.5 Air-Paks for my truck," referring to his personal fire truck. He wanted some Scott Air-Paks from the Fire Academy for free; these self-contained breathing apparatus, the most common model used by firefighters, cost over $3,000 fully equipped. The 4.5 refers to the 4,500 pounds per square inch of working air pressure within the cylinder.

Bemis had never considered what equipment might be stored in the complex, but there surely would be some Air-Paks in a facility where fire training was taught daily. Gregg responded, "That's not a bad idea, but if we take them from there, we won't be able to use them without someone knowing where they came from."

"Not if we burn the building down to conceal the theft," Donny reasoned. Gregg immediately agreed with the proposition, reasoning that a different motive for the fire would be suspected; that is, someone who stole from the Academy would burn it to hide evidence of the theft. After all, a fire to conceal another crime is one of the top eight motivations. It would also deflect heat from the arson ring members. Bemis had another reason for wanting the Academy torched. He was still angry that the Boston Fire Academy had been closed due to the cutbacks. There were rumors that it may never reopen. Getting rid of the State Fire Academy, Gregg rationalized, could force the reopening of the Boston Fire Academy. It was too late to act that night, however, so they waited for a better night. The audacity of these guys never failed to amaze.

According to former Massachusetts State Fire Marshal Stephen Coan, who spent 20 years at that position, the Academy buildings had been built in the 1930s during the Great Depression by the Works Progress Administration. Later, the property was taken over by the Massachusetts State Forest Fire Control Bureau before finally becoming the State Fire Academy.

Bemis had the day off from work on Friday, November 5, 1982. He planned to head into the City, but got sidetracked when he stopped at a local watering hole in Maynard. When he walked out the door, Gregg had a pretty good buzz on. Like many people after drinking, he grew a bigger pair of balls than when he was sober. He decided to burn the State Fire Academy by himself.

Mr. Flare, himself, drove past the Academy complex several times to make sure all was clear. He parked across the street from the complex on a dirt drive. Gregg was quite familiar with the site; he had gone parking there with a girlfriend for several nocturnal trysts.

After opening his trunk, he assembled a device. With brown paper lunch bag in hand, Gregg quickly crossed State Road and disappeared into the darkness of the complex. One thing was nagging at Gregg. In recent months there had been several fires at the Academy. One unsolved fire was only a couple weeks old. He was concerned that the police would swing through the complex to check it out.

Bemis crept to the rear of the main building, where he squeezed through a small window opening to gain access to the building. The rear of the structure was used to store the equipment, whereas the front held classrooms and offices. The Air-Paks were stored in the middle section. An entire shelf of 4.5 Air-Paks presented itself to Gregg. Grabbing two, he carried them to an overhead door on the side of the building. The device was put aside until he completed his other task. After making sure the coast was clear, Gregg opened the overhead slightly and then crawled out with the Air-Paks, lowering the door behind him.

Each Air-Pak weighed about 30 pounds, so Gregg puffed all the way back to his car. He was out of breath by the time he loaded them into his trunk, but he was determined to continue. The Air-Paks were far too valuable to let them go up in smoke. By the time he lugged two more Air-Paks to his car, Bemis was exhausted. He decided to only snatch one more so that he could run faster to his car after he set the device.

After placing the fifth 4.5 by the overhead door, he grabbed some tar paper and a tire that he found, then set the device against an interior wood wall near an open stairway to the loft area. He figured that the fire would readily spread up the stairs, taking the roof off the place before the first fire company would have a chance to arrive. The theft should be well covered.

Bemis lamented leaving so much good stuff behind. The device was lit and placed into the tire. He lifted the door again slightly, picked up the Air-Pak, and ran through the darkness to his car. Gregg drove home, arriving just as Hudson FD struck the box for the Academy fire. Stow FD followed shortly thereafter. He unloaded the Air-Paks into his garage before racing back to the fire. The first arriving Hudson company reported fire already through the roof. When Bemis arrived at the scene, Stow had not yet arrived.

By the time the fire was brought under control, the entire front half of the structure had been destroyed, but not before most of the equipment had been saved. Bemis now worried that the missing Air-Paks would be noticed. Other than that issue, he was more than satisfied with his accomplishment. As a matter of fact, when I interviewed Bemis some 18 months later, after his arrest, he was very proud of this fire. If not for him, the state would not have the nice modern facility that is in Stow today.

▲

What a huge and potentially dangerous night November 9 into Wednesday, November 10, 1982, was to become. Gregg met Bobby and Wayne at Norton's house. He could see by the look in their eyes that they were planning a busy evening.

The schemers decided to throw the investigators off the track again by targeting someplace new outside Boston. "Hey, Gregg, how about Fitchburg?" Sanden suggested.

"I'm sure we can find a few places up there . . . as a matter of fact, I spotted a building up there a few weeks ago when I was riding around," Gregg quipped. The new target location was the hilly City of Fitchburg, another somewhat rundown, old industrial city about 50 miles northwest of Boston with an abundance of old mills, warehouses, and abandoned multi-family dwellings.

Ray agreed with the plan but stayed behind, giving the other three the head start they needed to choose their targets and set the first fires. They headed to Fitchburg in Gregg's black "nerf cruiser" Chevy Impala.

The night owls arrived in Fitchburg about 1:30 a.m. Cruising one section of town where there were several old factories, they spotted a vacant two-and-a-half-story wood-frame apartment building on Water Street. It had their favorite exterior siding, gas shingles, those tar shingles that burn like crazy. They put the building on their list but continued to look for their first target of the night.

The building that Gregg had previously spotted was a two-story wood warehouse at the dead-end of Cleghorn Street. The guys agreed it was another suitable target, but they intended to set several fires so that the Fitchburg Fire Department would be overwhelmed.

So they continued their hunt for another mark. On the opposite side of town from the previous building, they located a four-story vacant brick apartment building on Summer Street that was under renovation. Bobby got excited by that one: "Boy, that place will go!" Having selected three very good targets, it was time to get started.

Finding a few tires in an empty lot, they parked near the Oak Hill firehouse and made several incendiary devices. The crew returned to the Cleghorn Street warehouse area, but they didn't want to drive down the dead-end street where they risked getting trapped. Gregg parked on a street parallel to Cleghorn. They had to maneuver down a precipitous embankment a few hundred feet to their destination. They clambered down the steep, overgrown hill with a tire and a device, made even more difficult in the near total darkness and cold. After placing the device within the tire and leaning it against an old wooden loading dock, the trio scrambled back up the slope. Bemis felt like he was going to die of exertion as they reached his car.

Getting into the car, they saw a flicker of flame down at the building, just visible through the brush. Satisfied that the fire was underway, they headed for the Summer Street apartment building. Gregg dropped Bobby and Wayne off with another device and tire. He drove around the block while they placed the device. As he came around the corner, the other two just exited the building. "Okay, let's get the fuck out of here," Wayne shrieked.

Bobby was excited: "The whole fuckin' place is covered with open wooden lath." Gregg immediately sensed that this building was going to be the biggest fire of the night.

They headed directly for the third target on Water Street. Easily pulling next to an enclosed wooden stairwell on the side of the building, Bobby placed a tire with device there, and off they went to an empty parking lot to await the fireworks.

Bobby asked, "Are you sure you have Fitchburg Police and Fire plugged into the scanner?" They checked and double-checked with the frequency directory, and just then, the police channel broke the radio silence when a cruiser reported fire on Summer Street. The dispatcher responded that there were several phone calls reporting a fire in the Cleghorn section of the city. A couple minutes later, the third fire on Water Street was reported. Immediately, the police dispatcher reported that he was calling in the Massachusetts State Police to assist with the situation.

Bobby, never one to waste an opportunity, said, "Hey, you know a fourth fire right now would really put the icing on the cake!" Wayne and Gregg looked at him wide-eyed. Instantly, Bemis headed toward Falulah Road, where there were several more old factories and warehouses. They found a huge mill complex housing American Can Company and many other buildings. He stopped there to prepare another device. Gregg dropped Wayne and Bobby off near a railroad track that ran alongside the old complex.

While he waited for their return, Gregg noticed with exhilaration that the Fitchburg sky was all aglow, with three separate and distinct columns of smoke and fire visible in the distance. A multitude of sirens filled the city, coming from all directions.

Two minutes later, an announcement on his radio reported a fire at the American Can Company building. Gregg said aloud, "Shit, that's all we need!" He knew that was directly across the street from where he left his friends. Moments later, as Gregg was turning around to head back to the pick-up spot, several State Police cruisers screamed past him. He could not believe how fast the area heated up, so to speak.

Gregg realized that he had to do something quickly to alert Bobby and Wayne. He went into response mode. He drove to the other side of the complex, sounding his car horn with the prearranged signal; the same all-out signal used by fire departments everywhere to let inside firefighters know to evacuate immediately. He hoped that they could hear him amid the chaos and that they had not set the device yet, because another fire would only bring more units into the area, possibly trapping them.

While Gregg attempted to notify them, Bobby and Wayne had already set the device in a suitable spot, but as they started toward the pick-up spot, State Police and Fitchburg Police swarmed the area, like a riled-up hornet's nest. Racing through the woods, the two arsonists became separated.

Groblewski was some 20 to 30 feet into the woods off the road when a couple of cops pulled their cruiser to the side of the road. They started aiming their flashlights in his direction. Immediately, Bobby dropped flat onto the ground. His heart was hammering; he prayed he wouldn't be detected. Without thinking of the consequences, feeling the threat from the officers, Bobby instinctively pulled out his semi-automatic 9 mm pistol. He had it at the ready, depending on the officers' next actions, preparing himself for a him-or-them situation if they came any closer. He didn't know for sure that he would have taken them out, shooting them dead. That would raise the stakes of their game to a whole new level. He couldn't even breathe for fear of making noise. Every muscle was tense in these fight-or-flight moments.

Lucky and fortuitous for all parties involved, the cops didn't see him or suspect anything further. They went about their business, looking elsewhere for any sign of the perpetrators responsible for the three rapid-succession fires. Nobody had time yet to investigate the cause of the three separate fires. However, with all of the arsons in Boston and elsewhere over the past few months, the authorities were betting that these fires were all intentionally set and that maybe they could catch the offenders before they escaped the area.

Grobo breathed again. He righted himself and made his way to the rendezvous point. After Gregg sounded the signal, he drove cautiously into the complex. Fire trucks and police cruisers had flooded the area, but then he heard the radio dispatch alert all units that the call for American Can had been a false alarm. Gregg sighed with relief, knowing that with the other three fires blazing away, every unit would quickly leave this area. As soon as it quieted down, he headed to the pick-up spot, where both Bobby and Wayne showed up, running and jumping into the car.

Groblewski shouted, "What the fuck was going on out here?"

Gregg replied, "Oh, some fuckin' asshole thought they were being cute calling in a false alarm for the joint across the street."

Wayne couldn't believe it: "Tell me that wasn't a coincidence." It really was hard to believe that a false alarm had been called in for a place they were at that instant setting fire to. Cops have a hard time with coincidences, but no other information ever came to light about that false alarm phone call.

Wayne and Bobby told Gregg that they had planted the device. Bobby also related his personal close call. Gregg shook his head in amazement as he headed for the Summer Street fire since, on the radio, it sounded like it was the largest fire of the night so far. Upon arrival, they got a rush when they saw that the front wall of the four-story building had already collapsed and that the fire had spread to three adjacent structures.

Apparatus was still coming in from surrounding communities, including close-by New Hampshire towns. The crowds were growing by the minute, drawn to the area by the biggest series of major fires that most would witness in a lifetime. The arsonists were amazed by the destruction that their fire had wreaked in such a short period of time. They were basking in their achievement; everything seemed perfect. They had set an amazing fire that had grown to breathtaking proportions. Their fellow sparks had also excitedly responded to the area in large numbers. They had hoped for crowds, as well as the confusion of fire personnel and apparatus, but this was beyond their wildest imagination.

Just then, this night became even better. The Falulah Road fire came in over the buffs' pocket scanners. They raced to the scene, instantly observing heavy fire coming from the complex. Although they hadn't recognized any sparks as being from Boston, as they walked on the railroad tracks near the building, Gregg noticed a familiar figure, Nat Whittemore from WBZ Channel 4 out of Boston.

Nat had been in the business of chasing stories professionally for over 20 years at the time of these fires, with another 30 to follow before he retired. Beyond the duties relating to his job, Nat loved this aspect of his job more than most because he, himself, was also a card-carrying fire buff. His interest in fires went back to when he was a kid.

As you will recall from the earlier discussion of Gamewell fire alarm boxes, Nat's great-uncle Roger W. Babson, an entrepreneur, had purchased Gamewell in the early twentieth century. In 1919, Mr. Babson founded Babson College, a prestigious private business school in Wellesley, Massachusetts.

Nat's father had taught him to count the blasts of the town's fire horn as he learned the box locations from the cards that had the box locations printed on them. Wellesley fire signal notification 4444, as Nat recalled, was like today's robo-call from your local school department signaling a snow day; that signal meant "No school, all schools, all day."

One of the early fires that his father brought Nat to helped to hook him on the fire business. His father drove Nat in their brand new Mercury convertible to a major fire on the Wellesley side of the Charles River. They parked some distance from the fire due to hectic activity around a mill complex fire. A large wooden water tower had caught fire and completely collapsed, sending embers, ash, and smoke everywhere. When they hiked back to their car, they found that embers had landed on the convertible top, burning most of the rag-top.

When Nat became an adult, he wanted to become a firefighter. As most new hires were war vets, and he wasn't, he became a Wellesley Call Firefighter and went into photojournalism. Later he became a member of the Boston Sparks Association.

In Fitchburg, as Whittemore drew closer to the three torches, they quickly ducked into the bushes beside the tracks and hid there until he passed them. They left this fire before Nat could film them at the scene and headed to the Water Street fire.

Wayne came up with another idea: "Hey Gregg, why don't we give the Fitchburg Fire Department an anonymous telephone call so they'll know we were in town?" Gregg liked the idea and pulled over at the first payphone that he spotted. Gregg dialed 411, asked for the Fitchburg Fire Department business line, and then dialed the number. The dispatcher answered, but since the night was so busy, he placed Gregg on hold. Several seconds later, the dispatcher returned to the call and said, "Fitchburg Fire Department."

In a disguised voice, Gregg taunted, "Aren't you just thrilled that the Boston Arsonist came to town?" He hung up. The crew headed for home, completely satisfied with themselves.

Nothing seemed to perturb or stop these guys up to this point; not with so many firefighters getting hurt at fires like last month's E Street Military Barracks or nearly getting caught in Fitchburg. They were now pure adrenaline junkies, addicted to the game. Score another win for the serial arsonists and another defeat for the investigators. But some of that would soon change.

The four Fitchburg Fires in Worcester County were eventually listed on the 1984 Federal Indictment as:

Fire 118	290 Water Street	2:15 AM
Fire 119	73 Summer Street	2:20 AM
Fire 120	Falulah Road	2:54 AM
Fire 121	Cleghorn Street	2:55 AM

If you haven't yet read enough to form an opinion as to the mental state of these guys, I'll describe another fire set on November 13, 1982. Gregg and Wayne checked with Ray to see whether he made any of the Fitchburg fires. Ray said that he had tried to spark the fires, but he was stopped for speeding on the way, so he headed home before the cops could connect him with the fires. Ray asked them what they intended to target that night. Neither Gregg nor Wayne had intended to set any fires that night, but his query was all they needed to get their juices flowing. They told him to hang around the Roxbury neighborhood.

They decided on a large, vacant four-story brick building on Bartlett Street, the same structure that they had burned in August. They were thinking that there was plenty of building left to go to several alarms if it got a chance to get going.

Gregg and Wayne saw a slightly open door with some wood debris inside. With a newly made device and a tire ready, they drove right up to the doorway and placed the device. They found a good vantage point nearby on a hilltop looking down onto the building. A cold rain was falling. At first, they saw the fire progress rapidly, but then it seemed to slow or possibly go out.

Just then, the radio sounded. Box 2246 was struck. Radio transmissions reported which District Chief and what apparatus were responding to the scene. First due piece, Engine 14, upon arrival requested that Fire Alarm strike a second alarm for Box 2246, meaning that more manpower and equipment was needed for the fire. However, Gregg and Wayne were perplexed, because from their vantage point, the fire had not advanced at all. What they couldn't see was that the fire had progressed through the building's interior to the side opposite from their position. It had also extended to another building across the street. In short order, a third and fourth alarm were struck. Gregg and Wayne decided that enough time had elapsed for them to safely spark the fire.

The fire grew so rapidly that a fifth, a sixth, and a seventh alarm was struck in equally rapid succession. Fire was blowing out of all four floors of the original building. The top two floors of the building across the street were blazing. The roof of another exposure building across Elliot Square had ignited, causing an eighth and ninth alarm to be transmitted. Gregg took some photos for his collection.

Ray arrived, congratulating the boys for their successful fire. The fire devoured the structures as the walls of the original building deteriorated and swayed, and then, with a thunderous cracking sound, the four-story wall collapsed directly onto an abandoned Volkswagen Bug, completely crushing and covering it. A short time later, four small fires ignited in a rectangular pattern—the tires of the VW were burning. With the wall down, the firefighters could more easily attack the fire, bringing the fire under control.

Again, you can see just how cold-hearted these players were, and how ingenious. They knew how easy it was going to be for a second fire in this building to develop into multiple alarms. They were ecstatic that they totally destroyed this structure and caused the City to expend thousands of dollars to fight this fire. I don't know how many firefighters were injured at this fire, but my lack of that information is not the point (please pardon me; every civilian or firefighter injury is important, and these guys should not be forgiven for that). They had caused a situation, like so many of their arsons that had the potential to result in injuries or death. These guys had a date night, a good cheap date night. They had fun. That was all that now seemed to matter to these guys.

The very next night, the boys were at it again. After he finished his shift in Stow, Bemis, with Stackpole and Groblewski, chose two objectives in Jamaica Plain. The first place was a wood-and-brick warehouse complex formerly owned by the Haffenreffer Brewery.

The brewery was established in 1870 by German immigrant Rudolph Frederick Haffenreffer, who came to the United States after the Civil War. In1965 the brewery was closed after having been in business for nearly 100 years, even surviving Prohibition. By 1982 the complex was in a sorry state of neglect.

The three torches entered an open doorway. They placed a lit device within a conveniently located pile of wood stacked in a corner. Within a minute, they were back at the car.

From a nearby payphone, Bobby called Norton at home, waking him up and alerting him to the newest fire. When Bemis et al. returned toward the brewery, the fire was already visible in the sky, but not yet reported. Seconds later, the box was transmitted for the fire.

It was still too soon to spark the fire, so they drove to a vacant three-decker on Chestnut Street with a tire and device ready to go. The building stood out on the block ever since someone spray-painted the gas shingles fluorescent green. The neighbors probably wished the eyesore would burn.

Driving up to the front door, Donny then stepped out of the car, leaning the device with a tire on the front doorstep. Since they had now killed enough time, they went to the first fire scene. When Engine 42 arrived at the fire, they ordered a second alarm right away. Bemis and company pulled up near the fire. Norton pulled in behind them. They watched the blaze grow to five alarms.

Meanwhile, Chestnut Street had been reported. The torches drove there and saw that, although the bulk of the flames were knocked down, smoke was pushing from the interior of the structure. A second alarm was ordered. The boys left to set one last fire for the night.

Thinking really big, they set a seven-story vacant brick apartment building near Fenway Park on fire by setting a device with tire against a rear doorway. The opposite side of the Mass Turnpike provided a good place to watch the development of the fire. Within minutes, flames lapped up the side of the building. Unfortunately, from the arsonist's perspective, someone else saw the fire before it had a chance to get going. That was enough for one night.

▲

On Friday night, Bemis pulled up at the Metro Security trailer. Stackpole and Groblewski were there. Ray Norton soon joined them.

Donny suggested a nearby vacant two-story brick warehouse. Donny and Gregg merely walked from the trailer through the yard of a Metro account to the target to avoid any vehicular traffic. They took a device and grabbed a tire along the way. The enhanced device was placed against a wood overhead door. They ran back through the client's lot to the trailer, where they hopped into Donny's car. Driving a circuitous route to avoid being too close to the fire, they saw down the street that a BPD van, its blue lights on, had stopped at the building where flames were visible.

The arsonists were unhappy that the cops had discovered the fire too quickly for it to become a multiple alarm. The boys also spotted the Arson Squad and several fire buffs prowling the area.

They all cleared the area immediately and headed to Chelsea, where Gregg drove up to a five-story wood warehouse clad with gas shingles. Donny set the fire with the aid of a device and tire that he placed against the shingles. The guys drove up and down Route 1, which cuts through Chelsea, to view the progress of the fire. This fire, too, was also reported too quickly and held to a working fire. As the arsonists split up for the night, Stackpole directed Bemis to come back into the City the next night. It was to be a fateful night.

Again on a Sunday morning, November 21, 1982, I was notified of the Gerrity II fire. As we had done for the Gerrity I fire a month before, Group Supervisor Dowd and I responded to the site. Smoke was still spewing from the charred remains of the large lumberyard building, but no flames were visible. Dozens of firefighters were still on the scene watering down the hot spots.

We conducted some initial interviews; we already knew the management from Gerrity I. We also learned from Dedham Deputy Chief Dave Chisholm the general area of the fire's origin, showing us some remaining fire patterns. The origin area was at least 30 feet by 30 feet, in this case rather recognizable by a big empty area void of virtually any combustible material. The wood in this one area had been consumed to the point of leaving behind a foot-high pile of charcoal ash.

Once the origin of the fire was narrowed, we again learned and observed that there were no potential inherent ignition sources within that area. Based on that scene information, coupled with the determination that the first fire a month earlier was arson, we concluded that the cause of this fire too was incendiary.

None of the arsonists realized that early morning, as the sun was rising, that they had just been part of the beginning of the end of their conspiracy. Bobby's little foolish display with his handgun on the lumber pile had drawn attention that they would all live to regret. When recorded by TV Cameraman Nat Whittemore, Grobo and his fellow arsonists had placed a target on their backs.

Unaware of the impending troubles that were lurking in their future, they had all headed home satisfied with their massive fire. Only Ray

Norton didn't exactly head straight home. He was still fuming and out of control from his perceptions of Whittemore and Cambridge Investigator Ed Fowler. From a pay-phone, he made a couple of prank calls to the Cambridge Fire Department. His first call consisted of Ray saying in a disguised voice, "Eddie Fowler didn't catch me," and hanging up. His second call, a few minutes later, consisted of Ray saying only, "It's Cambridge tonight boys!"

Norton didn't know that he had just made a big mistake: He had called a CFD recorded phone line.

▲

Nat Whittemore wasn't about to sit on what he felt could be a goldmine. The video of Groblewski waving his gun while sparking the fire with a gang of rogue sparks could be key to solving the arson spree in the Boston area. Nat contacted Boston Police and Boston Fire, who in turn contacted ATF with news of the video bombshell. We were invited to the WBZ studios on Soldiers Field Road in Brighton. WBZ News Director/Producer Peter Brown ushered us into a small room, where a portion of the raw tape was shown to us.

We were excited when Stackpole, Norton, and Bemis were identified with Groblewski, a full-time Boston Police Officer. Nobody recognized or knew Joe Gorman. They had all been seen at far too many fires, more than the average spark. And they were often observed at the fire scenes earlier than other fire buffs. Because of their rude, abnormally rowdy, and sometimes suspicious behavior at fires, they now became subjects of focused interest. It was time to take some action, but not much could be done since they could not yet be connected to any crime.

Special Agent Bill Murphy and I conferred with Supervisor Dowd and with Lt. Steve McLaughlin. We planned to interview Groblewski first because he was a cop. We were hoping that our shared law enforcement careers would help convince Grobo to assist us with our investigation.

None of us knew for sure who exactly was setting the fires, but we were anticipating that Grobo had some knowledge of the arsons. A strategy for the interview was discussed to increase the chance that our one shot would succeed.

Billy and I further planned the interview, thinking that the results could be a huge break in the investigation if conducted right. I was only too glad and too lucky to be teamed up with Murph. You couldn't help being a better Agent by working with him. His work ethic and intelligent insights into an investigation often led to successful conclusions. Billy was quirky, funny, yet serious; working with him was never dull.

William "Billy" Murphy came on the job the same month I did, June 1976. An Irish kid through and through, he was one of the toughest, smartest tried-and-true investigators ever to wear a Federal badge. Billy grew up in Weymouth, a suburb just south of Boston, after his family left the City. He was always (and is to this day) a thin, wiry guy with simply cut straight blond hair. An American University alum, Billy joined the Army in 1970 and was sent to Vietnam after graduating from the Army's advanced Vietnamese language training.

Billy and I had something very much in common before we ever met. In 1970, after graduating from college and again after his military service, Billy had worked as a summer beat cop for then Lt. John Sullivan at Dennis Police Department on Cape Cod. In 1975, after graduating from college, I also worked for Dennis PD and now Captain Sullivan during the 1975 summer as an undercover cop. Dennis must have been a good stepping-stone to the major leagues, in a way like the famous Cape Cod Baseball League ballplayers who often end up in the big leagues.

This is how you should imagine Billy in your mind's eye. Picture a baseball player, like Trot Nixon or Dustin Pedroia for you Red Sox fans, or any of your favorite "Dirt Dogs," those players who always have a dirty uniform, the ones who dive for every ball, the ones who never quit.

Murph was the investigator whom other agencies always reached out to for assistance. If a truck passed by with a suspect in it on the highway, Billy would spot it. If he saw organized crime guys on the street, he would often follow them by himself, even when officially he was off duty; Billy was never off duty. One day, Murph even followed a bad guy to the airport. When the guy arrived at his destination, it ended up being his final destination. He was found dead shortly thereafter. You would not want Billy to sink his teeth into you as a subject of an investigation.

In the early evening of Monday, November 29, 1982, eight days after Gerrity II, Murph and I drove to Mediterranean Woods Apartments in Weymouth, where Grobo resided. Bobby answered the door moments after we knocked. After we identified ourselves, he genially allowed us in. He didn't appear flustered. He never flinched.

We asked about his sparking hobby, about his associates, and about his gun-slinging behavior. Groblewski gave us nothing of substance. He lied with the best of the best. His only admission was that he had always wanted to be a firefighter, but he couldn't get on the job before he was hired as a cop. Bobby stuck with his story that his lone connection to the fires was that he was a spark who liked to watch fires and firefighting operations as well as photograph them. We were getting nowhere fast.

Agent Murphy was unusually quiet, mainly letting me handle the interview. But he later told me that he couldn't concentrate on Grobo's B.S. once he spotted an item of interest. Sitting in plain view on the floor near the TV, only feet from where we sat, was a red and yellow Gamewell Boston fire voice box. As we were preparing to leave, Billy pulled on his usual tan trench coat, stood up, and casually mentioned something about the cool fire box, adding that his father-in-law liked to make lamps or birdhouses out of them. Grobo said something about getting the box at a flea market. Murph took a few steps, approaching the box to get a better look. He probably didn't need to get that close. The box number was plainly visible on the front in white paint. It was Box 1712. I handed Groblewski a business card, saying, "If you hear anything, give us a call." Yeah, right.

Billy was pretty excited as we left. His exhilaration had nothing to do with the words spoken by Groblewski. He wanted to check the list of missing and stolen fire boxes that he had back at the office. With more than a little bit of speed, we headed back into Boston, someplace we didn't need to be at this hour of the evening. But this possible juicy discovery recharged our internal batteries.

Up to the eleventh floor of the Batterymarch Building we went. Once through the locked door, Billy went straight to his desk, lifted his desk blotter, and retrieved the single-page list of boxes. There it was, right at the top of the page. Box 1712 was the first box to "go missing" on May 29, 1982, having been discovered missing at 0430 hours. It was the same night that the serial arsonists set fire to 77–83 Thetford Avenue, Dorchester, a vacant six-family duplex.

Normally, in any given year, on average one or two fire boxes vanish from their assigned perches. No matter how they disappear, they are the property of the City of Boston. A person in possession of a fire box is considered in receipt of stolen property, technically, even if the person allegedly purchased the box at a flea market. Agent Murphy and I knew what we had, but we had to confer with Supervisor Jack Dowd as to how we should proceed.

The next day, after speaking with Jack, we referred the information to the Boston PD Internal Affairs Division because Groblewski was already being investigated for the gun-waving incident. Billy's father-in-law ran the IAD. Sometimes it really is such a small world. Billy and I ended up supplying the information for the affidavit in support of a state search warrant through Suffolk County for Groblewski's apartment and for seizing Fire Box 1712.

With warrant in hand, Murphy and I, together with three or four uncomfortable and unhappy Boston PD Detectives, drove back to

Groblewski's apartment. The cops didn't want to be involved with an investigation into one of their own. They weren't disappointed when we found that Grobo was not home. The apartment management let us into the unit. The firebox was still sitting in the same spot. Any fear that Billy and I had was quickly assuaged when we saw the box. We were surprised that it had not disappeared in the 24 hours since our visit; yet more evidence of the cockiness of Bobby and his criminal associates. He apparently was not concerned after we interviewed him and noted that he had the fire box. He didn't give us any respect.

Murphy and I continued to search for other fire boxes and any other evidence that could connect him to other thefts and the arsons. Our search included looking in closets and drawers. Within a minute after seeing the fire box, one of the Boston cops grabbed Billy's arm and said that we were done, let's get out of here. We were taken aback. He persisted. We continued to search, more or less ignoring him. We also explained to him that the warrant allowed us to continue. We were there legally searching for some other incriminating evidence, maybe something better than the fire box that would really put Groblewski in the trick bag. Under protest, a few minutes later we completed the search. Now there were two steaming ATF agents and three pissed-off Boston cops. At least we had the stolen box. Groblewski's world as he knew it was about to change.

Billy ran into one of his close BPD contacts a short time later. Murph was advised that he was persona non grata as far as the Boston cops were concerned. Grobo had told them that he had gotten the box at the Neponset Flea Market. They wanted to believe in one of their own.

CHAPTER TEN

DECEMBER 1982

About a week later, Groblewski came into our JFK Building office to submit to a polygraph examination. He arrived with his attorney. We were all surprised—and even a bit skeptical—that he was going to take the poly. Agents learned not to count on a subject's taking the exam until he's hooked up in the chair, and even then, some subjects get up and leave the room. We also wondered what his appearance meant to the investigation. Was he really innocent of being part of the arson ring? Was he arrogant enough to think he could fool the test? Was he foolish enough to think he could screw with us with no repercussions?

In most jurisdictions, barring special circumstances, the results of a polygraph exam are not admissible in court. We knew that, but a polygraph exam is nevertheless a useful tool for investigators. Sometimes a subject who successfully passes the poly can be eliminated as a suspect: Passing the polygraph is a good indication to investigators that the person is being truthful about his knowledge of or involvement in the case. If the results indicate otherwise, whether the results are inconclusive or the results indicate that the person failed the exam, investigators have another reason to interview the subject, to inquire why the results indicate deception. Some examinees will then confess their sins; others will swear to their innocence.

Still, others will believe that the test was rigged, tell us to go to hell, and walk out. This is often a defensive move by a guilty person.

Our polygrapher, Gerry O'Reilly, had set up his little exam room. He needed peace and quiet in order to conduct a test. Gerry O. was a kindly, soft-spoken, grandfatherly man who could make almost any nervous examinee a little more comfortable. As a standard part of the pre-exam process, the questions are presented to the subject. There are no surprises. The polygraph is not trickery. Grobo's attorney was okay with everything. The exam was conducted.

Among the significant questions were, "Do you know who has been setting fires in Boston over the past few months?" "Have you planned with anyone to intentionally set fires in Boston?" and "Have you participated in the intentional setting of fires in Boston?"

Groblewski's answer to these questions was no, no, and no. He failed the polygraph miserably. To this day I don't know what he expected.

I spoke to Bobby's attorney about interviewing Grobo further as to his apparent deception. After a little side conference with Bobby, his attorney came back to me and plainly stated, "He can't talk."

My instant reaction caused me to blurt out, "What does that mean, he can't talk?"

Counsel merely repeated, "He can't talk, that's all I can tell you." Meeting over. Hope for some decisive information that would enable us to solve the arsons was dashed. What the heck did that mean, "He can't talk?" Did the cat get his tongue? Was he afraid of losing his job? Did he fear someone would harm or even kill him if he told us what he knew? Well, as of the first week in December 1982, we were not going to get the answers to any of these questions. I was perplexed and disappointed.

It was time to regroup. ATF ceased any direct investigation of Groblewski while the Boston Police IAD conducted their investigation. Dowd, Murphy, and I tossed around some thoughts as to what happened and how we could capitalize on the setback. We planned to interview some other members of Groblewski's club.

My first choice to be interviewed was Wayne Sanden, since he too was a full-time police officer. We thought that we could work the kinship law enforcement angle again. Sanden and I were close in age, and we both had a wife and kids. Maybe we could play on that and his life responsibilities to get him to talk. We also knew that Sanden's real career goal was to be a Boston firefighter. Sanden hadn't been known to be an arrogant, loudmouth asshole like Norton or Stackpole. Our initial research on him suggested that he may not be as involved as some of the others in Groblewski's inner circle.

The next week, Billy Murphy and I waited outside the BHA Police Headquarters in Jamaica Plain when we knew Sanden was working. We didn't want to go inside and tip our interest in Sanden to some inquisitive party, or go to his house and upset his family, so we chose the parking lot of the BHA Police.

Just as Groblewski had done, Sanden greeted us cordially. He was much quieter than Grobo, not as dynamic, but he, like Bobby, seemed unshaken by our appearance. I guess you can't be a co-conspirator involved in a couple hundred arsons without some nerve.

After our interview of Groblewski and the seizure of his fire alarm box, the arsonists had all discussed keeping a low profile with the new focus on them. Interestingly, Grobo never mentioned taking the polygraph exam to his pals. From this point forward, Sanden would play his part within the conspiracy in a strange way.

During this first meeting, Wayne never admitted that he or his friends were setting building fires. He gave small tidbits of information. For example, Sanden said that Stackpole and others had told him that they had set abandoned stripped cars on fire in Southie. That elicited a big yawn from me. My heart didn't even skip a beat, but at least it was something. It was worth pursuing Sanden further. Unlike Groblewski, Sanden agreed to assist us. We set up further lines of communication.

Since Sanden was a full-fledged police officer, he could only become a source of information for me and ATF. There was a prohibition against having a cop as a formal confidential informant (CI). Normally, someone who provided information to us was documented with a CI number, and all of their personal data was locked in a safe in the District Office.

During this period, regarding the string of fires, hindsight is always 20-20. There had not been one fire that fit the pattern of the past several weeks since Gerrity II. Also, there had not been one night with multiple fires. It was now some 15 days since the execution of the search warrant at Grobo's apartment. It would be another 15 days before another fire occurred. We had to consider any number of possibilities. This gap could logically suggest that we were on target with Groblewski and his team of militant sparks. Maybe the pressure was getting to the group and they were lying low. Maybe the arsonists had gone on vacation. Or possibly the arsonists had been arrested for some other crime.

Nothing was as simple as it seemed at first glance. Even if we concentrated our attention on members of the Groblewski-Sanden inner circle of sparks, what exactly could we do? These guys were fairly law enforcement savvy. A surveillance of any one of these guys in the middle of the night would have been blown within the first hour. We didn't have enough information for any kind of warrant for a wiretap or a bird-dog device on a vehicle that assisted in tracking a car.

Possibly, this case was going to come down to a lucky break, something like catching the arsonist lighting a fire. Maybe the good old police technique of talking to people, knocking on doors, and interviewing as many people as possible until one cracks would make it happen. That's possibly where Wayne Sanden could help.

The fall of 1982 was certainly momentous for the Mr. Flare arsonists. They had graduated to bigger, nastier fires that caused more firefighter injuries, many of them serious and life changing. They had called in bomb scares and false alarms. Their targets were spread out far and wide to screw with any investigative surveillance. And they had become irrationally reckless. Calling to taunt fire departments and waving a firearm in the air in front of people with cameras would certainly epitomize their increasingly brazen if not psycho behavior.

If you believe that at first they genuinely acted in the cause of protesting the effects of Proposition $2^1/_2$, you must now believe that these guys had become serial arsonists who were merely enjoying their fires and relishing beating the investigators day in and day out. Would they have stopped the fire spree on their own? Or had they become so addicted to their cat-and-mouse game that, like other serial criminals, they would not stop until they were nabbed?

Well, it was high time for us to start building that better mousetrap. But, like Rome, it was not going to be built in a day. We continued to plod along. Patience was certainly a virtue during this investigation; this case was important work that had to be handled carefully and by the book to get the job done. And get it done right.

CHAPTER ELEVEN

WINTER 1982–1983

By the winter solstice, Tuesday, December 21, 1982, Bemis and company had not set a fire for a full month. The Groblewski fiasco did have some effect on the frequency of their criminal activities, albeit a temporary one. This was about to change.

Bemis pulled into South Boston about 8:00 p.m. He found Stackpole sitting in the security trailer, "Hey, Skinny, what's going on?"

"Oh, I was just out chasing some project rats out of the yard that were trying to steal some copper."

The two discussed what they felt was a catch-22 predicament. They realized that setting fires increased their risk of getting caught. But they agreed that stopping now would look like an admission of guilt for their past arsons. The two decided they had to set a few fires, and they sought their next target.

They chose a block-long vacant five-story brick warehouse on Pittsburgh Street. Using an overgrown alley that ran behind the building, they climbed into an open basement window with a device and tire. The massive basement was littered with wood pallets. Donny and Gregg stacked about 30 pallets until they touched the ceiling, which was actually the underside of the flooring on the level above. It was constructed with heavy planking supported by large wooden beams. Bemis figured that the large stack of pallets would impart sufficient energy to ensure ignition of the floor assembly. After placing the device at the base of the pallet mountain, the boys exited through the window and returned to their car.

As they drove away, smoke was already pumping out of the building. Bemis stayed at Stackpole's place for the night. Upon arriving at Donny's, the box transmitted for the fire. Surprisingly to the arsonists, the fire was held to two alarms.

▲

On January 7, 1983, Groblewski moved into a new house in Weymouth. Because he needed some financial assistance to pay the monthly expenses associated with his new place, Gregg moved in with Grobo on the same day. It was a marriage made in hell.

▲

The conspiracy was in full swing just after midnight on Monday, January 17, 1983. It had been almost three weeks since their last fire. Maybe they had been busy celebrating the holidays. Or maybe the weather had been just too snowy and cold to be out setting fires.

When Bemis arrived in Southie at the security trailer, Donny was inside waiting for him. "Hey, Skinny, are we going to get the Sparks Club tonight?"

With a smile on his face, Donny replied, "We sure are!"

The Sparks Club, or Boston Sparks Association, is a venerable organization that provides a great outlet for fire buffs to keep traditions alive. Located in a four-story brick building on West Fourth Street in Southie, besides being a place to gather where buffs can exchange fire stories, photos, and memorabilia, the Sparks Club provided canteen service to firefighters at active incidents and joined with other organizations to preserve fire history.

Groblewski had suggested to his pals that they burn the Club because some of the Club members were allegedly spreading rumors about him and he didn't like it. A week earlier, a meeting had been held at Norton's house to discuss just how they would go about getting the Club. Present at the gathering were Ray, Bobby, Donny, Joe, and, of course, Gregg, who had been present at every fire to date. Grobo didn't have to convince any of the others to hit the Sparks Club. A simple suggestion was enough. Ray and Donny hated many members of the Club, and the entity itself, because they refused to allow them to join the Club due to their behavior at fire scenes, among other reasons. Gregg thought that it would be a "statement" fire that would get everybody's attention.

The plan was discussed in detail. They needed strong alibis since they would most likely be blamed for the fire if it was determined to be an incendiary fire. Ray told the others to let him know exactly what night and time the fire was to be set so he could arrange a false burglary report at the liquor distributor where he worked. This would give him a verifiable alibi for the time leading up to the fire. The fire was to be set on a night when Bobby was working in the turret at BPD and Wayne was working at the BHA so that neither of them could be blamed for the fire. Joe planned to stay home on the night of the fire.

Donny and Gregg were the chosen arsonists for the night. Once the fire was lit, they would disappear to avoid being seen by other fire buffs or by the Arson Squad.

With all the plans in place, the night for the fire had arrived. Gregg asked, "Hey, Donny, did you get the key for the Sparks Club from Bobby yet?"

"Yeah, he dropped it off earlier and told us to put it back in the ash-tray of his car after we lit the fire."

As planned, Grobo's car was parked near the front door of Boston Police Headquarters on Berkeley Street. Ray had already been notified what time the fire was to be lit.

The plan was put into action. Donny and Gregg drove to the Neponset neighborhood to drop Donny's car. In Gregg's car, a device was assembled. Then, they drove back into Southie. Gregg parked in an empty spot near a busy nightclub. From there, the duo walked to the West Fourth Street target.

After making sure nobody was watching them, Donny pulled the key from his pocket. He inserted the key into the lock. Just then, Donny spotted an old tire that had been discarded in the grass near the doorway. "Do you think somebody is trying to give us some help?" Donny couldn't help smiling. Gregg chuckled a bit but reminded Stackpole that, if possible, they shouldn't make the fire look deliberate. There would be no way to hide the steel belt remnants unless the building completely collapsed.

Inside the door was a stairway that led to the rented third-floor premises of the Sparks Club. A plumbing supply business occupied the first floor. The second floor, now vacant, had been another fire enthusiast club, the Tapper Club. The fourth floor was also vacant.

As they climbed the stairs, Bemis noticed the door to the second floor was open. "Hey, Skinny, let's check this out first." Donny agreed and they entered. The interior rooms were a mess. In an old office, Gregg suggested placing the device in a corner where a cluster of exposed wires would make it appear to be an electrical fire. They stacked some desk drawers and papers on top of a desk right in the corner under the exposed wires. Donny opened a couple of windows to provide plenty of air to the fire. Gregg lit the device and they exited the building.

After reaching Gregg's car, they drove straight to BPD Headquarters to drop off Bobby's key. Gregg pulled up next to Grobo's car. Donny climbed out. He opened the door to Bobby's car with his own car key, as his happened to be cut the same as Bobby's key. He placed the Sparks Club key in the ashtray and relocked the car.

The duo proceeded to a vantage point from which they could watch the fire's progress. The box for the fire was transmitted within a few minutes. Flames were lapping out of the second-floor windows. A second alarm was struck for the fire. Both Gregg and Donny mused that the fire should have gone to a fourth alarm due to its size and the tight congestion of the neighborhood. Donny quipped, "Well, it looks like the Fire Department hates the Club as much as we do."

"Yeah, this ought to go down as the biggest second alarm in Boston Fire Department history," laughed Gregg. He drove Donny to his car and followed him to his house, where he stayed overnight.

The following day, Stackpole and Bemis placed calls to Groblewski and Norton to see if everything was all right. Ray was happier than a pig in shit. Bobby was in high spirits as well. He had watched the entire fire from a window of the turret.

However, the members of the Sparks Club were devastated. Several of them stood outside the building, huddled in the cold but heated inside by anger and despair. Once allowed inside, they were able to save some priceless memorabilia. The items that were lost crushed some of the guys' spirits.

Photos above and below: Boston Sparks Club location

A couple days after the Sparks Club fire, Sanden met Bemis at the security trailer. Gregg outlined for Wayne how he and Donny had set the Club fire. After reliving their "trophy" fire, the two traveled to Chelsea to set a five-story wood warehouse on fire, a target they had tried but failed to get before.

Driving up next to the building, Wayne, my new source of information, alighted from Gregg's car to place the tire and device against the gas shingle siding. Shortly after they departed from the area, the fire was reported. This fire, too, failed. With that outcome, the arsonists retired for the night.

Several times during the early part of 1983 I had conversations with Wayne Sanden, mostly by phone. At times, I felt that he was just jerking me around, stalling giving me any information that I could use. But I didn't have anything on him to put pressure on him to do the right thing. He was balls deep, not only in the conspiracy, but in actual fire-setting. He was another terrific liar who had no qualms about the consequences of his actions.

Another month passed before these guys set another fire. They had certainly been lying low during the frigid midwinter period. But on Friday, February 25, 1983, after completing his shift, Bemis met with Sanden again. The two drove around to see what was going on. As they passed over the Southeast Expressway, Gregg pointed to a large column of black smoke rising ahead of them. Wayne said, "It must be a car fire."

"Are you kidding? I never saw a car fire with that much smoke," Gregg rebuffed him. Sanden sped up, steering his car toward the smoke. Approaching the area, they could now tell that it was a building fire, but they couldn't understand why the radio had been mute to this point. Just as they were in front of the firehouse for Engine 14 and Ladder 4, the box struck for the fire with the overhead doors opening to the firehouse.

"Come on Wayne, if they see us, we'll get blamed for sure." A wood building was fully involved directly in front of them. Sanden took a series of turns to avoid detection. He said, "Boy, that doesn't happen too often," referring to discovering a roaring structure fire before it had been reported.

As they headed up Blue Hill Avenue, Gregg spotted another plume of smoke, this time rising above the Codman Square neighborhood. When Wayne saw it, he exclaimed, "This can't be another one!" But sure enough, there was a row of taxpayers blowing smoke out of every pore.

Bemis was incredulous as they drove by the fire: "I don't fuckin' believe this shit!" The box came in for the fire. Once again, they sped out of the area before anyone could see them. Bemis felt that it was some sort of omen to find two fires in one night that had not yet been reported. And he and his pals had nothing to do with these fires.

Wayne suggested that since there were already two good fires in the City, why not make it three. Bemis was all in, but he didn't have any Coleman fuel, since they hadn't done any buildings in a while, and he didn't want the device components in his trunk anymore in case he got stopped by investigators.

After pondering the situation, they stopped at Store 24 near Fields Corner to see what they could find there to improvise. They purchased a can of Ronsonol Lighter Fluid and some zip lock bags. With that task completed, they needed to find a suitable place to burn.

They parked near a vacant, wood three-decker and walked up the dark, desolate street to the front door. "I hope this thing works," Bemis said as they entered the vandalized building. The interior was torn up and the plaster was missing, leaving the exposed wood lath. Wayne handed Gregg the device, then lit a cigarette. Gregg placed that in the matchbook. They waited for the first signs of smoke before leaving the area.

After an hour went by with no report of the fire, the guys decided to call it a night, but not before riding by the target. Gregg followed behind Wayne. As they passed through Edward Everett Square, Bemis spotted Eddie Fowler, the Cambridge Arson Investigator, sitting in his car parked side-by-side with another car talking to another buff. Gregg thought it was just their luck. To himself, he muttered, "What fuckin' kind of jinx is this to find Fowler prowling around at 4:30 a.m. and sticking his nose where it doesn't belong?"

Sanden obviously hadn't seen Fowler in the parking lot. He turned down the street toward the fire building. Bemis could only hope that the fire had gone out on its own. But, as he glanced down the street, he saw that the building was fully involved. Gregg didn't hesitate to get out of the area. Minutes later, the box was transmitted for the fire. It went to three alarms. Bemis knew that the mere fact that there were three fires in one night in Boston was sufficient for Fowler to blame Bemis and his crew for the fires.

That was all for the fires set by Mr. Flare and company for the winter of 1983. It was a pattern that was to play out during the remainder of the year, except for a slight uptick during the warmer months. By early 1983, the vast majority of the firefighters and police officers had been rehired and many closed firehouses had been reopened. So their alleged main objective in setting the rash of fires had been met. Perhaps they slowed for fear of getting caught. But they still had to feed their addiction, have fun with their hobby, and screw with the fire investigators.

CHAPTER TWELVE

SPRING 1983

Like everything else that spring brings, our ATF team would soon experience a renewal of effort to solve the arsons that had plagued the City and surrounding communities. And the arsonists were also feeling a sense of rejuvenation since there had been no further repercussions or pressure on them by the investigation.

There was not much to report from the investigative standpoint. I had a few contacts with Sanden, but not much else was happening. In hindsight, it was definitely the proverbial calm before the storm.

On the last Monday of March, Bemis met with Sanden and Stackpole at the South Boston trailer. They decided to target a building since it had been four weeks since their last fire.

They set fire to trash in a closet within a large, vacant three-story stucco apartment building in the Mattapan neighborhood. The trio parked at a shopping plaza to watch the fire develop. Smoke and a glow were soon visible in the sky, but it took about 30 minutes for the box to be transmitted. The fire failed to amount to much. Still leery of being seen at fires, they went home instead of sparking the fire.

Another gap of three weeks transpired before another fire was set. About this time, the case took another twist that would become important to the investigation several months later. During the period when I was utilizing Sanden as a source, he became more active both in actually setting fires and in being present at fires as they were being set. I'm no psychologist, but there seemed to be some connection between his increased participation in criminal activities and his cryptic pseudo cooperation. It was as if he wanted to get caught.

Meeting at the BHA Police Station in Jamaica Plain, Bemis and Sanden got down to business, that is, finding a good target to burn. Right behind the firehouse for Engine 17 and Ladder 7 in Dorchester, while still riding around in the BHA police cruiser, they targeted an empty wood triple-decker. Wayne ditched his cruiser temporarily at a BHA elderly housing project. In Gregg's car, they made a Coleman Fuel device, parked directly behind the firehouse, and walked to the rear of the target. Sanden placed the device against the exterior gas shingles. Once the device ignited, they went back to the project to retrieve Wayne's car. The box was transmitted within minutes. As Engine 17 pulled out of quarters, they ordered a second alarm. Once again the arsonists chose not to spark the fire. Since sparking the fires was one of the joys that they got out of setting the fires, it seems their caution stole some of their fun.

On the following Tuesday, Bemis again teamed up with his new best friend. He and Wayne discussed how Donny wanted them to divert the Federal agents' attention away from them by lighting a fire in Concord, Massachusetts. Another spark lived in Concord, and Donny reasoned that a fire there might throw investigators off their trail by focusing on that spark. Wayne wondered what made Donny think about this move. Gregg explained that when he had spoken to that spark a couple weeks earlier, the spark had complained that he was being harassed by State Police arson investigators. Gregg added that Donny, with his derisive attitude, figured that a fire near the buff's house could throw suspicion onto the innocent spark.

Sanden thought that the idea was worth a try. "The place we are going to get is a complex of several attached three-story warehouses with gas shingles right near the spark's house. The place is a furniture factory," Bemis told Wayne. He had it all planned out.

They headed straight to Concord. After inspecting the target, they parked a half-mile away in a condominium complex parking lot because there weren't many places in Concord to surreptitiously park when you're planning to set a building on fire. After Wayne parked his car, they made a device and climbed onto railroad tracks that led behind the warehouse. As they walked, Wayne began to wonder if he wanted to walk all that way to set a fire and then have to trek back to the car afterward, but once he saw the complex, his attitude changed: "Boy, this place looks like it's just waiting for someone to burn it."

They planted the device in a rear corner section where a wood passageway connected to the next section. As they ran back toward the car, they turned to view the fire develop. By the time the two arsonists reached Sanden's car, flames were soaring above the roof of the building. Driving some distance to a vantage point, they only managed a fair view of the fire. Wayne didn't have a fire radio in his car, so they couldn't monitor the fire. With that, they called it a night. The next day they learned that the fire had gone to three alarms, but the interior fire had been thwarted due to a working sprinkler system.

Thus far, the 1983 fires set by the arson ring were sporadic. Since November, only one fire was set on any single night and fire nights had occurred at intervals of one to four weeks.

Then, in mid-May, Bemis picked Sanden up at the Metro Security trailer in his new car so they could ride around Boston. Gregg had just gotten the car painted black, and the radios had been installed. He no longer had the antique car of the group. Instead, he now had the newest car in the crowd. There was no doubt that it looked just like a new unmarked police car. Wayne commented on how nice and smooth the new mock cruiser rode. Bemis beamed with pride. But as you all know by now, rides around the City usually led to fire-setting. For the first time in 1983, the Mr. Flare arsonists were going to burn two buildings in Boston. It was early Tuesday morning, May 17.

The first was in Dorchester. Wayne and Gregg entered an open wood duplex three-decker. When Sanden turned on his flashlight, the light saved Gregg from falling through a hole in the floor on his next step. The interior wall surfaces had been stripped to the bare wood lath. The device was placed against the open wall that separated the two halves of the duplex. It was quite breezy out that night, which they expected would help rapidly spread the fire.

Finding a place to park on the opposite side of Columbia Road, they sparked the blaze as it erupted into the black sky. A few minutes later the box came in for the fire. It quickly went to a second alarm.

Immediately, they traveled about three miles south, where Dorchester meets Mattapan. Bemis parked his "cruiser" directly at concrete steps to the front door of a vacant house. They were now front door guests. Wayne placed the device in a set of built-in bookshelves in a rear room. The device was lit and they departed quickly.

Bemis drove Wayne back to his car and they both headed home. Gregg detoured slightly to drive past the second fire. He saw heavy smoke and fire blowing out of the backside of the structure. He continued home to his room at Groblewski's house in Weymouth. When he arrived, Bobby was already asleep. The next morning Grobo walked into his room telling Gregg that he had gone to a good flick (slang for fire) in Dorchester that had come in as he got off work at the turret. Gregg just smiled and said, "Yeah, I know all about it." Bobby returned the smile, knowing exactly what Gregg meant.

On Saturday, May 22, 1983, Wayne Sanden was again the driving force behind the night's fire, with Gregg Bemis, of course. Wayne recommended hitting a partially vacant brick factory in Norwood. There's that term that Bemis used again, "partially vacant" building. That means that the structure was also "partially occupied." They hadn't set any fires in Norwood before; it was another densely populated, nice suburb south of Boston, just west of Canton across Interstate Route 95.

When they arrived at the Norwood factory complex, they placed a lit device within a tire against an overhead wood door and departed the area. The fire was soon reported, and the Norwood firefighters quickly quelled the fire before it had a chance to cause much damage. With that mediocre effort, they quit for the night.

June 9, 1983, clearly illustrates a couple of points that I've noted about the arsonists' activities over the past several months. Bemis met Sanden at the trailer about 7:00 p.m. while it was still light out. In the greater Boston area on that date, the sun doesn't set until almost 8:30.

Neither guy had any intention to target any buildings that night. They were just cruising around to kill some time. However, as life presents itself in mysterious ways, as they crossed Dresser Street in South Boston, Gregg spotted what appeared to be a car parked in the middle of the narrow street. "Hey, Wayne, make the block. I think there's a hot box sitting on Dresser Street."

Wayne took a right, then another and another, turning up Dresser. Sure enough, just as Gregg surmised, there was a late model Cadillac stripped of all of its tires and its radio. Whoever stripped it must have been in a real hurry because the engine was still running. Pretty weird; it was running, but with nowhere to go.

Coincidentally, the Caddy was also parked next to the very first building that Bobby and Donny had set afire way back in February 1982. Wayne looked at Gregg and asked, "Why don't we do the owner a favor and torch it so he'll collect and get a new car rather than have to piece it back together?" There's that Robin Hood theme again; let's help out the small guy while messing with the large insurance company. And they get to spark a fire at the same time.

Gregg readily agreed. They checked the Caddy to ensure that no valuables had been left behind. Following the search, Bemis placed a piece of newspaper under the front seat with a lit cigarette and matchbook device. They then parked up the street to be sure that the device ignited.

Just after they parked, loud noises were heard emanating from a storage building next to their position. They saw some kids stealing stuff from the building, passing the items over the roof onto the street below. About to yell at the thieves, the arsonists decided to watch the progress of the fire instead. By then, the car was fully involved, igniting the adjacent building. Within seconds, the rear of the structure was fully involved. The kids on the roof finally spotted the fire and made a quick getaway.

Gregg and Wayne left the area themselves with no further action that night. The fire was held to a working fire.

On June 14 and again on June 19, 1983, Bemis and Sanden set one fire. Those two fires brought their total number set during spring 1983 to 11. In 1982 they had set that many arsons within two or three nights. And Sanden had participated in nearly all of the 1983 fires. I don't know if he was having marital problems or what, but he certainly ramped up his activities outside his home.

The June 14 fire was set in a vacant three-story brick apartment building next to the construction for the MBTA Southwest Corridor Project. After climbing over a fence, Gregg and Wayne waltzed through another open basement door on the rear of the structure, where Gregg spotted a small closet filled with trash and an old tire. The tire seemed like some kind of sign to the arsonists. They wasted no time in placing a device within the tire. Sparking from up the street, they heard the fire called in immediately, but it went to three alarms.

The June 19 fire was the fire that I mentioned in Chapter Seven that was connected to a September 11, 1982, fire on the Chelsea/Everett line. These were the two buildings that, totally by chance, were set by the arsonists, but were owned by the same individual. Remember my description of the little old man who was verbally abused during an interrogation by a State Trooper? That was the only fire set by Gregg and Wayne that night because they had almost been caught in the act by a security guard cruising the area. Being caught by a security guard would have been ironic.

There were no other fires set in June 1983. There was no information at all that any other fires were set for the next five months.

CHAPTER THIRTEEN

SUMMER 1983

By the summer of 1983, my relationship with Sanden was still distant. He was a strange character, very hard to get close to. He always kept me at arm's length. We never did become friendly. His reasons for providing me with little tidbits of information to keep me interested in him and his comrades were elusive. He kept giving me just enough to keep me on the hook. If he had just told me to take a hike, this case could well have gone on even longer. Or if he had ever fully come clean and told me about his real involvement with the arson ring, then he most likely could have saved himself some jail time and helped prevent lots of damage, injuries, and heartache. As it was, I had to keep pursuing him and plugging along because we had nothing better going for us.

During July, Sanden started giving me some juicier snippets of information, things that started to tickle my interest. Wayne told me that Groblewski and Stackpole had been involved in insurance fraud relating to stolen vehicles. He listed several other crimes that he said the two had committed, including stealing at least one car and stealing parts off of several other vehicles. He also told me they had stolen numerous fire alarm boxes. Finally, Wayne said that the boys had burned multiple cars and that at least one building burned as a result of one of the vehicle fires. Sanden never, not once, told me that he was involved with this particular fire or any other fire. He only casually told me about the burning car catching onto the building in generalities. Sanden never said that the fire was the June 9 fire on Dresser Street that he and Bemis set. Why was he feeding me half-truths?

Those alleged crimes were somewhat interesting, but we would only go after those offenses with our local partners because there were no Federal violations that were provable. Nothing that Sanden had given me to date was verifiable as probable cause for a warrant we could use to find some of the stolen items. In the words of the famous Wendy's commercial, "Where's the beef?"

We were toying with the possibility of getting Wayne to wear a wire while performing in an undercover capacity to elicit incriminating evidence from his pals. To this point, Sanden had balked at wearing a wire. He claimed he was too uncomfortable to do that and that he was fearful of retaliation. We needed to find something that we could corroborate; it was still possible that he was just playing us. I had to deal with my supervisor over this issue. After all, about seven months had passed since Sanden and I had started to converse. And what did I have to show for it?

The arson crew had been on hiatus for several weeks at this point. It seemed to the co-conspirators that the conspiracy itself had pretty much fallen apart as far as the members were concerned. The heat from the Arson Task Force also seemed to have cooled off.

One night Grobo was off duty. He took a ride into the City. He pulled into the Merit gas station on Old Colony Avenue in Southie. Not thinking there would be any problems, he left his keys in the ignition while he paid the cashier for his gas purchase. Just as he turned toward his mock cruiser, he saw his car racing out of the station with two skinny teenagers in the front seat.

Groblewski was fit to be tied. From a payphone, he immediately called the turret and directed them to put an all-points bulletin (APB) out for his car. He then ran up D Street toward the Metro trailer, hoping that he would find his friends there. However, they were still out on patrol. Grobo had no way to get hold of them.

About 20 minutes later, when Donny, with Gregg as a ride-along, finally pulled up to the trailer, they found Bobby frantically waving his arms like a madman. He yelled, "Where the fuck have you guys been? I just had my fuckin' car stolen!" He climbed into the back seat of the Metro cruiser and they set out in search of his car.

Donny suggested, "Well, we should check all of the housing projects since that is where they'll probably dump it or torch it." Southie had three or four housing projects. After checking two projects, they saw Mark Svendbye speeding out of one of the side streets. Svendbye was another Metro Security guard who was on the periphery of the arson conspiracy. Bemis had introduced Svendbye to Stackpole, who then hired him.

Mark Ekland Svendbye, born in December 1962, had become the youngest member of the conspiracy and the last person to join the conspiracy who was involved with setting fires. Svendbye stood about 5 feet 11 inches tall, with a medium build. He had brown hair, brown eyes, and a mustache. He also had a cop wannabe swagger and a little cockiness.

Svendbye was similar to most of the other conspirators in that he drove a 1981 black Ford four-door sedan with a radio scanner, a whip antenna, and a siren. He also regularly carried at least a handgun. At some point, Svendbye had been arrested for impersonating a police officer after he flashed his "cruiser" lights to pull over a vehicle.

When Mark saw his friends, he stopped and asked them what was going on. After they filled him in, they also advised him to be extra cautious, since he was driving around in a car that was identical to Grobo's stolen vehicle.

They then continued down Columbia Road, where Gregg noticed a Ford LTD with darkened tail lights turning into the McCormack Projects. Bobby exclaimed, "That's it!" Gregg put his foot down on the pedal and sped after the car. Unfortunately for the culprits, the narrow streets were even tighter, with parked cars on both sides and a taxi in the middle of the road blocking their path. The hoodlums started to back up when they realized that they were being hunted. The two teens jumped out of the car, which was still in reverse. It slowly backed into the Metro cruiser, colliding with a metallic thud.

The thieves ran in opposite directions, with Bobby and the others in pursuit on foot. Bobby yelled for one of them to stop. Grobo then fired two warning shots, most likely another violation of Boston PD rules. One suspect stopped in his tracks. He was summarily tackled on the front doorway of one of the buildings. The other suspect escaped capture. Bobby walked over to the young thief, who was pinned to the ground by Gregg. Grobo placed his gun right up against the scoundrel's head and threatened to blow his head off unless he identified his partner. As is customary for young men from the area, he didn't talk. And Bobby didn't blow his head off.

The warning shots brought instant attention from a large gathering crowd. Sirens could be heard approaching from all directions. When the first BPD cruiser pulled up, Bobby threw the suspect in the rear seat. Grobo advised the officer that he would meet him back at the station to fill out the paperwork.

Bobby checked his car for any damage. He then headed toward the station, with Donny and Bemis following him. Just as they passed the intersection of Columbia Road and Dorchester Avenue, another BPD cruiser noticed Bobby's car. Apparently, the APB on the stolen car had not yet been canceled. The cruiser quickly pursued, pulling Bobby over. Two cops alighted from the cruiser and approached Grobo's car with their guns drawn. After Bobby safely explained to them what had transpired, they all laughed and continued on their way.

August would prove to be more than just a calendar page-turner. What the Nat Whittemore video of Groblewski at Gerrity II did to focus our efforts on Grobo and his associates, a comparable event would do this month. In spite of the significance of what was to occur, it would still be another five months before we began to put down the hammer on these guys and put cuffs on any wrists.

Sanden delivered more information about Grobo and others stealing a car. He told us how they had stolen a brand-new unmarked police cruiser right off the parking lot of Natick Ford in the middle of the night. It was a black Ford LTD that was to be delivered to the Randolph PD just south of Boston.

Bobby had wanted to update his personal "nerf" cruiser with some new parts, including the taillights, headlights, and grill. After the stolen vehicle was used for his purposes, the car had been driven off the edge of a parking lot on Atlantic Avenue in Boston right into the Fort Point Channel. Even after all that we had experienced up to this point, it was still hard to believe the balls of these guys. What a waste of a couple thousand pounds of metal! They could have at least recycled the car remains.

This was something that we could work. It was easy to substantiate the theft of the vehicle from Natick Ford. And we didn't need probable cause for a search warrant to search for the car. All we needed was a dive team. That was easy to get.

August 24, 1982, was a warm, cloudy, and humid day. Members of the Boston Police and Fire Department Dive Teams met several of us in the parking lot off Atlantic Avenue. They all suited up and dipped into the dark water armed with the knowledge of our objective. We had arranged for a large crane to set up in the parking lot. We all were dripping with anticipation.

Within minutes, the Dive Team supervisor popped his head up to advise us that they had located a couple of cars, including one that looked like our target. Our excitement level was buoyed by that bit of good news. The divers took the crane straps and hook, dove down, and hitched up the first car. Minutes later, a drenched black Ford LTD broke the water's surface. By the time the cruiser not-to-be was lowered onto the parking lot surface, it was easy to see that it had no tail lights, no headlights, and no front grill assembly. Without even having to check the Vehicle Identification Number (VIN), we knew that we had the right vehicle.

Our state case against Groblewski had just gotten a little stronger. Whether we would be able to charge him with theft of the vehicle depended on whether or not Sanden decided to cooperate further. A case for receiving stolen car parts would be stronger since Grobo had the stolen parts on his personal car. It certainly wasn't an arson case, but it was a felony charge against Bobby to make him realize that his life was about to get worse.

However, we decided not to act on charging Groblewski right away. We even had the Dive Team bring up the other car, just so that the press or any onlookers wouldn't be able to figure out exactly what we were up to. The arsons had slowed down dramatically, but we wanted to try to catch them in the act of setting a fire. Sanden had just told me that Stackpole was planning to burn a security company car sometime in the near future. It was not a building fire, but it could draw a Federal charge because insurance/mail fraud fell under certain Federal laws. Onward we marched.

▲

In August, Bemis made what could have been a momentous move for his career and life. But, because life has a way of catching up to you, his move turned out to be short-lived.

Gregg quit his dispatcher position with the Stow Police. With some assistance from his pal Wayne Sanden, he took a police officer position with the Boston Housing Authority. It appears that a thorough background check didn't turn up anything disqualifying about Bemis.

Within months, he worked his way up to the rank of sergeant within the unit. He was responsible for answering calls in all of the elderly housing projects and, if needed, he would also respond to calls within the family projects, which were normally patrolled by a different division within the BHA Police.

Before winter, Gregg was again promoted, this time to Acting Tour Supervisor of the midnight-to-eight shift. That promotion gave him the temporary rank of Lieutenant and, as such, he was the supervisor of the midnight shift. This rapid advancement shows that Bemis had a lot on the ball when it came to being a good civil servant. It's too bad that he also had a lot on the ball when it came to being an accomplished criminal. These guys were all enigmas, an unfathomable mix of good versus evil.

CHAPTER FOURTEEN

FALL 1983

On September 19, 1983 (technically not yet fall, but, as they say, close enough for government work), I wrote the first of tens of dozens of 3270.2 reports, similar to the FBI 302's, initiating a new investigation of the alleged arson activities of Robert F. Groblewski and his associates within Boston and the surrounding area. Before this date, we had several active investigations open that involved the fires set by these characters, but they had various case numbers.

Some readers might ask why it took so long. I think that same question was asked by several people over the years, including those at ATF HQ. Even I pondered that same question.

Let me try to briefly explain. First, life happens; life gets in the way. Some things have to be dealt with every day. There are normal family issues with a wife and two very young daughters. I have always been torn when I didn't give them the attention that they deserved. ATF also got in the way. I understand certain protocols have to be followed, but the bureaucracy can really screw up some efforts. Mandatory training and firearms proficiency four times per year all took time away from investigative efforts.

Vacation and 10 Federal holidays per year also bit into investigative time, but I wasn't about to give up the time off. We worked a lot of long nights and weekends as it was. An ATF investigator also had other cases that needed to be worked. Other cases did come to an end for me when this case finally resulted in an arrest. Maybe I could have been more aggressive and pursued leads faster and harder. The information that I was receiving from co-conspirator Sanden was given begrudgingly, with many diversions and lies. And delays; I was always waiting for more. Perhaps more direction and leadership could have been provided, but an agent's work requires a certain amount of self-motivation. Many issues contributed to the lengthy time it took for the investigation to become sufficiently focused to obtain significant results.

Oh, that's right; we'd also had roughly 250 fires to contend with during the past 18 months. Of course, ATF did not investigate every one of those fires, but even if we became involved in only one fire per week, that is a lot of investigative time spent at the fire scene and in contact with firefighters and investigators. Interviews of owners had to be conducted as well as interviews of any witnesses. There is much more to it than this brief description, all of which takes time. And every little bit takes time away from the big picture that was slowly evolving.

That first report, with the Unique Identifier for the investigation number 63210 83 1002D 01, was to be my life for the following 18 months. Even more time, work, and energy would be expended than was expended during the previous 18 months. As you will recall, I began with the fledgling ATF Arson Task Force group in March 1982 and the arsons began in the same time period.

In report 01, I detailed that we first became aware of Groblewski at the November 1982 Gerrity Lumber Company fire, that we had later interviewed him, and that we had recovered the stolen fire alarm box. I also reported that Groblewski had failed the polygraph relative to his involvement in the fires. Importantly, and another reason for the delay in the investigative progress, I reported that ATF ceased any investigation of Groblewski for the time being while the Boston Police Internal Affairs Division conducted their own investigation, which was in its ninth month.

I further reported that during July and August 1983 I had become privy to new information from a source close to Groblewski and his associates. That source was Wayne Sanden. The information received was relative to the stolen Ford, stolen car parts, vehicle fires, at least one building fire, several stolen fire alarm boxes, and the recovery of the stolen vehicle from the Fort Point Channel.

The report stated that this investigation was being termed sensitive because if Groblewski, as a Boston Police Officer, was involved with ***several*** (remember this word later) building fires, the national media would focus on him for causing many of the Boston arson fires that drew national attention during the summer of 1982. Every one of the reports, until the final report, finished the same way: "Further information will be reported at a later date."

▲

On September 28, 1983, after several conversations with me during the preceding weeks, Sanden finally agreed to wear a wire. He wore a Nagra recording device and a transmitter at our direction. Special Agent David Watts, our technical wizard, and a longtime friend since he came on the job the same day as I did, taped the wire to Sanden's body in one of our vehicles that night. The Nagra at the time was a fairly sophisticated Swiss-made reel-to-reel recorder that measured about four inches by three inches by one inch thick. It had its own pouch with elasticized girdle-style wrap. By today's standards, it was ridiculously large. On several occasions, while performing undercover work, I wore the device. I always sensed there was a big bulls-eye painted on me when I wore it; I felt uncomfortable and vulnerable.

The plan was for Sanden to meet with Groblewski and Stackpole at the Metro Security trailer in South Boston. A loose script was laid out for

Sanden so that he could try to elicit incriminating evidence directly from the mouths of the suspects. The equipment was tested before Wayne got underway. Everything seemed to be working fine. The anticipation among the Agents was high as we sent Sanden on his way.

Several ATF surveillance teams blanketed the area. I was parked nearby with Dave Watts because the transmitter range was very limited, especially amid so many city buildings. We could hear Sanden walk into the security trailer. Stackpole's voice was unmistakable.

But that's about when the rest of the night went downhill. First of all, Groblewski was a no show. Next, we heard only sporadic transmissions of the conversations between Sanden and Stackpole. The device was cutting in and out intermittently. Damn equipment, I was thinking. We sat there disgusted and miserable. Well, at least the recorder would catch what was said.

When Sanden departed from the trailer an hour or so later, we met him at a prearranged location. We debriefed Wayne before he left for the night. He told us that the only somewhat significant statements made by Stackpole were comments that only implied that he had set the Sparks Club fire. Only innuendo. Sanden added that Stackpole implied that the new club looked ripe for a fire. Years later, after reading Gregg's diary, I realized that that last statement by Stackpole was probably given to us verbatim by Sanden because he used the word "ripe," a word often used by the arsonists, according to Bemis.

Much to my disappointment, Dave Watts informed me that nothing was on the tape recording because Sanden never operated it properly. In light of no recording, and the faulty functioning of the transmitter, Watts was convinced that Sanden intentionally screwed with the equipment. Dave could find nothing wrong with the equipment. Of course, since Sanden was my source of information, and we had a whole team of Agents tied up for the operation, I didn't want to believe that Sanden was being a super double agent. Only time would tell. I was pissed. And I felt like crap, as my alleged source was seemingly a damned liar.

On Monday, November 28, 1983, the latest person to become a full-fledged member joined the conspiracy to set fires. He also became an arsonist officially, if he hadn't been one before this. The newest co-conspirator was Mark Svendbye, the Metro Security guard. You may recall that I met Svendbye in June 1982 in the parking lot of Boston Plate Glass, one of the major South Boston arsons, where he approached me and started asking questions.

On that foggy, raw November night, Bemis met with Svendbye at the security trailer. Mark had been bugging Gregg for a while, urging Gregg to tell him about the rash of fires in Boston. Stackpole had told Mark about some of their activities. Gregg was reluctant to tell anyone else outside of their tight little group about their criminal acts. After additional prodding from Mark, though, Gregg told him a little of what they had done.

Once he learned about the incendiary device that the arson ring had been using, Svendbye was keenly interested in trying it out. Bemis advised him that the group had been keeping a low profile for the past several months since the Arson Squad had been keying on them. Mark relentlessly urged Gregg to set something on fire. He even told Gregg that he knew there was a vacant building near his father's house in Dorchester that would be an easy target.

Bemis couldn't resist and he couldn't dissuade Mark, so he agreed to take a look at the building. He justified to himself that since it was foggy, it was a good night for a fire anyway. It didn't take a lot to make an addict backslide into his old ways.

The building was a large three-story vacant apartment house. At the time, a tractor-trailer was parked in front of the place; directly behind the building ran the MBTA train tracks.

Bemis still balked when faced with any obstacle in the way of setting this fire. This was in stark contrast to their fire-setting in 1982 when they seemed blithely confident of overcoming any complication. Fear of getting caught caused him great anxiety and made him very cautious. "Okay, how are we supposed to get over that chain link fence without waking up the entire neighborhood?"

Mark answered, "I know where there is a hole in the fence where we can crawl through." After more arguing, Gregg agreed to show Mark how to target a building.

Their next task was to obtain some flammable liquid to use in the device. Gregg no longer carried any Coleman Fuel. Mark suggested using gasoline since it was easy to get at that time of night, but Gregg argued that that was too dangerous, especially when making the device in a car. He further explained that gasoline melts through the plastic zip-lock bags much faster than Coleman Fuel does.

They tried and failed to find a substitute fuel, and Mark finally persuaded Gregg to use gasoline after all. Bemis then suggested that they use unleaded gas, which allegedly doesn't eat through the plastic as easily as leaded gas would. They bought a gallon of gas, returned to the trailer, and manufactured an incendiary device in violation of Federal law. Gregg nested several zip lock bags one inside another to minimize the chance that the gasoline would leak all over the place.

After completing the device, they drove to a parking lot near the target. Grabbing a tire iron, they headed for the hole in the fence that Mark had mentioned. Halfway to the hole, the duo stumbled through a large pile of trash and branches that made a loud racket. It's very true how deafening sounds like snapping branches can be when you're trying to sneak about in the still of the night. Suddenly, a dog started barking loudly. "Well, that's that," Gregg fumed as he turned to trek back to the car.

Back at the car, Mark asked, "What's the matter?" Bemis advised him that if the neighbors didn't hear them tramping over the brush, they sure as hell heard that mongrel howling away. Once again they argued and once again Gregg acquiesced to take a second shot at the place. Instead of heading the same way for the hole in the fence, they walked over an overhead footbridge that ran over the tracks toward the structure.

Once at the rear of the building, they found a loose board on one of the basement windows. Here, the tire iron came in handy to pry off the board. They both crawled into the basement. Gregg explained to Mark why a particular spot was the best place for the device. The incendiary device was planted and ignited. After returning to the car, they drove past the fire building. The smell of smoke was evident, but it took 45 minutes for the fire to be reported. The arsonists observed the building from a short distance. Since Mark's car did not have a scanner, they listened for approaching sirens. After a few minutes, they climbed atop the footbridge to spark their achievement; the fire went to six alarms.

CHAPTER FIFTEEN

WINTER 1983–1984

'Twas the night of Christmas when Bemis finished his BHA shift at midnight, and in the City a few creatures were stirring— arsonists who wanted to burn a house. Sanden just started his shift at midnight. He asked Gregg to ride around with him in the cruiser for a while. About 2:00 a.m., Wayne suggested that they target a couple of buildings since the arson squad would be running a skeleton crew and there hadn't been any fires lately. Bemis instantly agreed. So there went two Boston Housing Police Officers, one on duty, in a City-owned vehicle cruising around choosing buildings to burn.

The first building was a vacant three-story brick row house on Blue Hill Avenue; the second target was a large vacant two-and-a-half-story wood-frame building. They drove back to the BHA on Amory Street in Jamaica Plain to exchange vehicles. After making a couple of devices, they returned to the Blue Hill Avenue target. Entering the basement from the rear of the structure, they placed the device in some trash. Despite being reported within minutes, it quickly grew to three alarms.

They went straightaway to their second objective. Walking through bushes to an open side window, they entered and placed a device against an open lath wall. Neither guy stayed around to watch the fire. Gregg left for home. Around 5:00 a.m. the fire was reported. It went to four alarms. The arsonists left two multiple alarm fire presents for the Boston Fire Department. Then, they bedded down for a long winter's nap; well, for a few days, anyway.

Happy New Year 1984! The New Year brought us a new supervisor, Philip J. Tortorella, for the Arson Group. Phil had just returned from a stint in ATF Headquarters in DC. He had a couple of jobs there, but he was well aware that Boston was in the midst of an arson wave, and the problem had not been resolved by us back in Boston. It seemed to HQ that we were floundering and that perhaps a new supervisor for the Arson Group could provide a new direction that could culminate in arrests. One of the main objectives for HQ was making "blue jackets," as our formal case reports in their light blue cardboard covers were nicknamed. Cases were important to the Bureau; besides the obvious benefits of solving crime, it looked good when ATF could go to Congress for funding with some good numbers to show the effect that ATF had on crime.

Philip Tortorella had been sworn in as a United States Customs Security Officer "Sky Marshal" on December 24, 1970, the same day as another arson group member, Terry Barry. The program had been ramped up by President Richard Nixon in response to increased air hijackings. The two new Sky Marshals only flew with that program for a short time. They both became ATF agents by February 1971.

Born in Boston, Phil grew up in the suburb of Avon, about 20 miles to the south. As a mathematics graduate of Bridgewater State, part of the UMass system, Phil's first postgraduate job was as a laborer unloading freight cars. He soon realized that type of work was not his forte. That's when he pursued a law enforcement career.

When I was a rookie agent, Phil was one of my On the Job Training Agents (OJTs). Each new agent went through his first year assigned to two or more experienced agents to learn the ropes. I soon realized that Phil emphasized the analytical by-the-book approach to successfully get the job done. He was a physically fit, no-nonsense, very straight agent. You could almost tell from a look from Phil how he felt about you. If you weren't a hard worker with some semblance of intelligence, he didn't have much tolerance for you.

His altar boy, strait-laced looks were complemented by his pseudo preppie wardrobe. Years before working together in the Arson Group, we were in Supervisor Jack Dowd's group trying to make gun cases. Once Phil and I drove a 1967 Corvette as part of an undercover effort in Brockton, Massachusetts, an old major shoe and textile manufacturing city about 25 miles south of Boston that was famous for its native sons, boxers Rocky Marciano and "Marvelous" Marvin Hagler. By that time, the city, like many other mill towns, had become rundown, with severe drug, gun and crime issues. Our goal was to infiltrate some of the groups that would sell us some illegal guns, usually stolen from some house break-in.

On at least one occasion while we worked the investigation, Phil looked like an all-American boy, complete with his neat short blond hair, clean-cut looks, and inability to grow facial hair. As it was wintertime, he also wore nicely pressed clean corduroys with a turtleneck sweater and an expensive-looking leather jacket. He just looked too neat and clean-cut to pull off working in working-class, drug-infested bars. I wasn't quite comfortable with his appearance whereas I looked like a regular shithead, unkempt and slovenly. Although we didn't make any good cases together, Phil said one thing to me that I learned to appreciate more as my experience grew. He advised me that getting results wasn't all about how one looked; it was more about how and what you said and how you handled yourself. Those results came when you knocked on doors and properly interviewed your targets with a solid plan in place.

Phil's first supervisory position was as the Resident Agent in Charge (RAC) in Portland, Maine. From there, he had various positions at

Headquarters in Washington, DC and as the Chief of Training of the ATF Academy at the Federal Law Enforcement Training Center in Georgia. By late 1983 Tortorella wanted to head back to Boston as a Group Supervisor rather than move further up the management ladder. At the time, ATF Deputy Director Phil McGuire made a deal with Phil; you get to go back to Boston as the Arson Group Supervisor, but you must solve the arson problem.

Phil often polarized people in the office. He was very focused and he played hardball, pushing agendas that some agents never understood and didn't like. When he took over as the Arson Group Supervisor, he knew that he was not going to be very popular. But then again, Phil never tried to win a popularity contest; he just did what he felt was right to get the job done.

During the transition, Group Supervisor Jack Dowd and incoming Group Supervisor Phil Tortorella discussed the two major investigations going on in the group at that time. Besides the arson ring investigation, Billy Murphy had an investigation going on with some East Boston wise guys who had been robbing banks and armored cars, with at least one shooting murder under their belt. His case was completely different from mine, but it, too, was sensitive, time-consuming, and deadly serious. Murph had gotten to one of the hoodlums, who started providing information, but a lot of work needed to be done. This is what we always wanted, to work on big cases. Now, our office had two incredibly important, complex cases at the same time.

Regarding the fires, Jack tried to impress on Phil that the Boston FD Arson Squad had been bending over backward to keep us abreast of new developments on the street level. Jack advised Phil that Chief White was a stand-up guy and that his crew had been working with us seamlessly. Above all, Dowd warned Phil that we had to keep them in the loop and not to screw them over. Jack felt dejected and a little miffed that he wasn't given the opportunity to see these cases through to fruition.

During his first days as our supervisor, Phil reviewed each Agent's cases. He sat me down, emphasizing that we needed to make something happen on my investigation. We had fiddled around with it for too long. With input from the group members, Phil presented our new strategy. Our focused attention now had a singular goal in mind: put pressure on the targets, the persons of interests, as we now call potential suspects.

Senior Special Agent James Karolides was added to the Arson Group. He was the oldest guy in our group, about 20 years older than me. He was experienced in many ways, formerly a street cop in Danvers, Massachusetts, a working-class town north of Boston. He knew his job, and he had a special talent for talking and interviewing people, witnesses and suspects included. Not only did he have street cop smarts, but Jimmy was also a thespian, a card-carrying actor with a special knack for drama. And he took no crap from anyone.

Jimmy was somewhat portly with that barrel-chested look. Sometimes he came across as arrogant and verbose. He knew a lot about a lot of different topics and it seemed that he wanted you to know that. The way he carried himself, always dressed well and well-coiffed, his thinning black-gray hair neat and slicked back, he could have been any businessman you see walking on city streets. You should have seen him acting as an undercover agent; he couldn't have played his part any better. He became an important component of the group.

▲

The arsonists had a strange, but not unexpected, way of celebrating the New Year. Gregg Bemis and Mark Svendbye were riding around looking for targets when Mark said, "Hey, turn onto Blue Hill Ave. I want to show you a building I torched the other night." When they passed the building, Mark proudly pointed, "That's the one."

Bemis immediately told him that he was full of crap; Gregg and Wayne had actually burned it a week earlier. Mark was taken aback since he didn't think that he would be caught in a lie so easily. Gregg admonished him, "I hope you haven't been running your mouth off about it."

They settled on an abandoned six-story brick building on Mass Ave. next to the MBTA Southwest Corridor construction. Once they found a suitable place to park, they climbed over the fence to gain access to the newly constructed tunnel. They climbed down a ladder into the tunnel and walked toward Mass Ave. The tunnel was well lit, but since it was near midnight on New Year's night, nobody was working. Once Gregg estimated that they had reached Mass Ave., they found one of the tunnel emergency fire escapes that brought them back up to the road level. Luck was on their side; they came out right next to the target.

Checking the plywood on one of the basement windows, they were amazed to find that only a couple of loose nails held it in place. Just then a car parked nearby. Gregg and Mark dropped to the ground until the people from the car entered another building.

Once it was safe, Gregg noisily pulled the sheet of plywood free. They hadn't taken a device with them, so they figured that they would wait a while to make sure nobody had seen or heard them.

Back at the car, a device was made. The arsonists retraced their steps through the tunnel again. At the building basement window, Mark climbed inside. Gregg handed him the device and then clambered in. The incendiary was planted in scrap wood near the basement front wall. With the long distance back out of the building and through the tunnel, the two hurried back to the car. From there, they watched the progress of the fire, which was held to a working fire. This fire ended up being the same morning as the ATF Arson Task Force began its new phase of the investigation of the nearly two-year arson epidemic in and around Boston.

Saturday, January 7, 1984, brought more changes in the lives of Groblewski and Bemis. Bobby asked Gregg to move out of his house in

Weymouth so that his girlfriend could move in. Gregg had only moved in one year before. Gregg certainly did not want to intrude on their privacy. He moved into Lenny Kendall's house in Acton until he could locate an apartment to rent. Actually, it was the home of Kendall's parents, who treated Gregg like another son while their son was away in the Air Force. These life changes for Bemis and Groblewski would normally be momentous for most people, but they would prove to be minuscule compared with the life changes that would soon occur.

▲

All day Thursday, January 12, 1984, was spent at the ATF Arson Group planning and organizing, scheduling, making arrangements, and preparing for what was to become an extremely long night. And it was to be an even longer, tougher upcoming 15 months due to bombshell revelations about to be disclosed that nobody had yet foreseen.

That day, meetings were held with Suffolk County Assistant District Attorney James Hamrock, Boston Police, and Boston Fire officials at our ATF offices. The plan was for Boston Police Deputy Superintendent Jack Gifford, Detective Billy Kelley, and his partner, Detective Donovan, along with Senior Special Agent Jim Karolides and me, to meet at Boston PD Headquarters to interview Bobby Groblewski. We were going to let him know that he was now to be charged with a major felony, to wit, the theft of the vehicle and receiving more stolen property. The object was to seek a confession about his criminal activities and/or solicit his assistance with his crew of arsonists. The best outcome would be that he confess and "flip" on his accomplices.

Flipping is a key law enforcement tool that has been used next to forever. Of course, the "flipper" witness often has a dirty background. For that reason, good law enforcement work strives to obtain additional evidence that corroborates the information garnered from the witness. A person who flips is only a "rat" in the eyes of other criminals. One familiar aspect of numerous TV cop shows that reflect real life is when a suspect is told that the first one in the door could get the best deal. Flipping is a totally legal instrument, in spite of what the President of the United States thinks.

At about 8:00 p.m., in typical Boston January temperatures but no snow, the five of us assembled at a large office at BPD HQ, a 100-year-old multi-story gray granite structure that covered the entire block. The office was old, but kept up. The walls, which were painted that industrial drab beige, rose 10 or 12 feet. Numerous incandescent and florescent lights lit the room. Several desks and chairs filled the space.

Grobo was working at his administrative position in the "turret," on an upper floor of the building, where the police dispatch was located. He would have no choice but to meet with us, but he didn't have to talk to us. We didn't concern ourselves with legal representation for Bobby at this point. We were not going to interrogate him about the pending stolen property charge on the firebox. We were going to question him about the stolen vehicle and about fires. He was not under arrest at this point. He was free to go at any time, although at his own peril. He certainly would know that he would be facing termination, no matter what.

Grobo was summoned from the turret. The excited anticipation in the room was palpable. We each had a different horse in this race.

Deputy Gifford, being one of the highest-ranking officers in the department, had one of his men possibly involved in one of the largest crime rings ever by a Boston cop. Gifford was stuck betwixt and between; trying to maintain the integrity of the department, but on the verge of being hated by the rank and file officers for cooperating with the Feds and sinking one of their own—the typical "Blue wall" mentality.

I happened to know Jack Gifford when he was the commander of Area E, which covered the Roslindale, Hyde Park, Jamaica Plain, and West Roxbury neighborhoods of Boston. We always got along extremely well. I used to ride along with his Area E anticrime units in 1980 and 1981 to build relationships with the cops and to, hopefully, gather information that would lead to gun cases.

But this ride-along served another purpose. Due to cutbacks by the Federal administration, we were only allowed to purchase $25 worth of gasoline weekly with the Government credit card for the G-ride. We all had Government vehicles (for official use only) that we took home and used daily. We were available 24/7/365 to respond to any urgent situation. Gifford allowed me to fill up once a week at his Boston PD gas pump outside his building. It was a lifesaver. Virtually nothing could be done on the tight gas rationing. I really appreciated Jack's contribution. Plus I learned a lot about the area and policing efforts in Boston.

Auto Squad Detective Kelly was a solid investigator who possibly went over the line on occasion when he felt that the ends justified the means. He seemed like one tough bastard. He had no love lost for Groblewski or his band of criminals. His partner, Detective Donovan, felt the same.

Agent Karolides was wearing a dark gray pinstripe three-piece suit. He dressed impeccably for a "fuckin' Danvers cop," as Stackpole and Sanden referred to him. His gray hair was slicked back from his high receding hairline. Complete with his dark-rimmed eyeglasses, Jimmy put on his serious game face, gearing up for the confrontation to come. He was in his no-nonsense, take-no-prisoners mood. Being a senior, more experienced guy, he was to lead the questioning of Groblewski. The thespian that he was had prepared him for this leading role, one of his most significant parts ever.

Me, I was about to turn 31 years old. I did not know that I was on the verge of the biggest case of my career, only four years after being the case agent on a 46 machine gun case that also featured 17 other stolen firearms and a million dollars' worth of stolen goods. In ATF, and maybe elsewhere in similar agencies, the machine gun case made me a rising star. Not my words; that's just the way it was and probably is today. Those types of cases don't come every day. They don't even come in every career for those who don't work hard or have some luck. My rising star was about to jump to a new galaxy. I was nervous, to say the least, beyond excited. Where was this to go? Thinking about my part—the good cop, as usual.

The stakes were rather high. This was somewhat of a make-or-break approach. Grobo could decide to send us on our way, or say arrest me if you have the evidence; we could be screwed for now. This was our best shot at this point.

Bobby walked into the room, still looking and acting cocky, full head of dark hair neatly parted and combed to the side, mustachioed, with a sense of bravado. That was about to change.

Deputy Gifford spoke first. "Bobby, take a seat over here," he said, pointing to a seat centered at the far end of the room away from the door. Was there a little psychology in play, in case Bobby's fight-or-flight instinct kicked in? Gifford reintroduced each of us, but Bobby already knew us all by name, face, and reputation.

"Bobby, you know you have a right to a union rep or an attorney. You're not under arrest at the moment, but we have some things that we need to discuss with you."

Bobby did not seem surprised at all. He just said matter-of-factly, his expression stoic, "Okay, let's hear it."

Detective Sergeant Kelly spoke next, "Bobby, we executed a search warrant on your car. We recovered that new unmarked black Ford LTD from the Fort Point Channel that you guys stole a few months ago from Natick Ford," letting Grobo know that we had substantial information and evidence. "Your car has several stolen parts on it from that stolen car. We are going to charge you with the theft of the vehicle and with receiving the stolen parts, felonies. Your career is over." He let this statement dangle in the room. The tension was building.

What we didn't know at the time was whether Groblewski was aware, although he had the new grill and headlights on his "Smurf-mobile" or "nerf-mobile," that none of those parts had any serial numbers on them that could positively identify them as being from the stolen car. It was a strong but risky bluff. We couldn't actually prove where these parts originated from, except through the information from Sanden that they stole the car and the recovered vehicle from the water had those parts missing. A good attorney could have gotten Bobby off on this one. But Bobby didn't know this.

Karolides took over. He should have been nominated for an Oscar for his performance. The actor took the stage. He was standing, pacing the floor in his conservative business suit, then standing over Bobby. His gruff demeanor likened him to one of those famous courtroom attorneys from the movies. Jimmy K leveled both barrels on Bobby: "You gave an oath to protect the people of Boston and the Commonwealth of Massachusetts. Who is going to protect them from the likes of you? You're a failure. You need to tell us everything. We want to know about the fires. You hang out with a crew that we know are setting fire after fire, and you are in the middle of it. We're getting close and the first one in the door can get the best deal."

On and on he went. I was staring at Bobby from my seat several feet away. We all were staring at him. You could see his bravado fading; any cockiness that he came in with was all but shriveling. His body was starting to crumple. Then, Karolides let the hammer drop. I'll never forget his next statement, or the rest of the night for that matter.

He bellowed, "There are six guys in this room with badges and only five of us deserve to have them!" The coup de grace, the finishing or decisive blow or shot given to kill a wounded person or animal, was just delivered. Karolides was mercilessly putting Bobby out of his misery.

Long, pregnant pause. Bobby's head dropped to his chest. This was a classic sign taught to us way back in New Agent Training. Don't anyone say a word. Wait for it . . . wait for it. Then, Bobby, defeated, uttered, "What do you want to know?" The confession was underway. For the next 30 minutes, my head was spinning. I felt nauseous. The culmination of nearly two years' work was just beginning to spill from Bobby's mouth.

Groblewski could not get the words out fast enough. His confession was a regurgitation of words, flooding from his mouth, relieving the stress from his body of the secrets and pressures that he had held for the past 250 fires. While still at Boston PD that night, he had spilled information relating to his involvement in a conspiracy with several other men wherein they had set at least 29 fires. He said that he had more information, but before he could supply any more about one of the most amazing stories any of us had ever witnessed, we had some decisions to make, and we had to make them soon.

First, it was discussed among the non-felon law enforcement officers in the room that we had to get Boston Police Officer Robert Groblewski, now a confessed arsonist, away from our present location to the more protected confines of our ATF office at the Batterymarch building. Who knows what could have occurred if we stayed at BPD Headquarters?

We placed a call to the home of Group Supervisor Philip Tortorella, who had left the office late after waiting for word from us for hours. He headed back to the office.

We all traveled to our ATF office. We sat Groblewski in our eleventh-floor conference room so that we could continue our interview with him. We had good information from him on the 29 fires plus other information on another couple dozen fires that he could recall as we sat in utter astonishment to what was unfolding right in front of us.

Supervisor Tortorella advised me that we needed to get an Assistant United States Attorney on board immediately so that everything was done by the book. We didn't want to let some technicality cause our case to be thrown out of court.

Phil had worked with Assistant United States Attorney James Dineen before. We all had a lot of experience with AUSA Dineen, who was intelligent and who had put a lot of effort into ATF cases. But when we placed a call to the AUSA 24 hour line, we were routed to another AUSA who also had a lot of experience. He was also a man who had gained a lot of respect from us. His name was Robert S. Mueller III. (Yes, that same Robert Mueller that is now a household name, the former Director of the FBI and the famous Special Counsel who headed the investigation into Russian meddling with the 2016 elections and other matters.)

I found AUSA Mueller to be an extremely bright, fairly quiet, unassuming attorney. He listened intently as we briefed him on the arson investigation, including the activities of the night thus far. After some discussion and legal direction, it was decided to place Groblewski under arrest. Legally, Grobo would have been free to leave at any time up to that point had he so desired. However, he never asked to leave and he never requested to have a lawyer present before he kept speaking to us. If he had gotten up to walk out the door, I probably would have choked. The decision to place him under arrest for Federal violations was justified by his confession in conjunction with other corroborating information and evidence that we already had uncovered. We also had to consider that he could be a risk to himself. Might he try to commit suicide once on his own, thinking about his dismal prospects? Other reasons to place him under arrest included that he may make a run for it, that he may commit another arson or some other crime, and that if he walked out he could alert his co-conspirators.

So, on January 13, 1984 (Friday the 13th, somewhat unlucky for Bobby, but rather lucky for us) at 3:20 a.m., I had the pleasure and official duty of placing Robert F. Groblewski under arrest. He seemed okay with that. He was wiped out from his confession and the late hour, although he was used to staying up late lots of nights. However, I think he usually had more fun during those other nocturnal escapades.

We lodged Grobo at the Holiday Inn at Government Center, where we babysat him the remainder of the night. I spoke with Bobby, saying, "You did what you did. That is all over now, it's the past. Now you know that you have to answer for your actions. What you just did is the beginning of your atonement; you're doing the right thing." Then, I told Bobby that line that you have probably heard before, "Today is the first day of the rest of your life." He had no visible anger, but he no longer had that swagger that he had when we first saw him hours before at Boston Police Headquarters. Vanquished, he readily fell asleep in the hotel bed.

Earlier in the evening of January 12, 1984, Special Agent John D'Angelo and Boston Fire Lt. Steve McLaughlin knocked on the front door of Lenny Kendall's parents' house in Acton. Bemis was in Lenny's basement bedroom. Mr. Kendall, who had answered the door, let Gregg know that somebody was at the door looking for him.

As soon as Gregg saw McLaughlin's face, he knew what they wanted. He spoke with them for a few minutes, but it was obvious that the investigators wanted to speak to him in private. Gregg suggested that they talk at the Auxiliary firehouse.

They all sat at a table on the second floor. Immediately the Task Force guys asked Bemis what he knew about arsons in Boston. Gregg just lied, saying that he knew nothing about the fires. The agents were not satisfied with that; they hadn't come all this way just to be blown off.

Agent D'Angelo stated, "You know, we were sitting outside your house for two hours waiting until the rest of your friends could be questioned simultaneously." Johnny D. was an old-style quiet and unassuming local Italian guy who had almost 20 years on the job. He knew how to interview a hostile witness.

"Well, I don't know anything about who is lighting fires in Boston."

The trio went back and forth about different fires. After about a half-hour, John D'Angelo said, "We've got a witness who saw a person fitting your description on the roof of a building on Midway Street in South Boston just 10 minutes before it was set on fire."

"Well, I don't know what to tell you, but it wasn't me," said Gregg. "What was the date this supposedly happened anyway?"

Lt. McLaughlin answered, “It was Saturday, April 30, 1983, in the late afternoon.”

Bemis searched his mind to see if he was even in the City on that date. “No, I wasn’t there and I didn’t have anything to do with it.”

“Are you willing to take a polygraph test about it?” D’Angelo asked.

Without hesitation, Gregg replied, “Sure, I’ll take one.” The investigators appeared stunned that he was willing to take the polygraph on a fire that they felt sure he set.

“Okay, come into the JFK Building tomorrow afternoon at 4:00,” Agent D’Angelo countered.

About 10:00 p.m. Bemis called Stackpole at the security trailer. “Donny, have the Feds been to talk to you tonight?”

“No, but something is going on at the turret. Bobby seems to have disappeared.”

“I’ll be right in. Stay there until I get there,” Gregg replied as he hung up the phone. He immediately jumped into his car and raced toward Boston. When he arrived at the trailer, Donny was waiting for him.

“Donny, Steve McLaughlin and a guy from the ATF came out to Acton asking me about fires,” Gregg uneasily said.

“You didn’t say anything to them, did you?”

“No, I didn’t say a word, but they told me that they were talking to all of us tonight to see if our stories matched and they want me to take a polygraph tomorrow.”

Donny replied, “Nobody has talked to me, but that may explain what is going on at the turret. Wayne was here a while ago. He said that Bobby called him on the radio earlier and wanted Wayne to bring him a sandwich up at the turret. When Wayne arrived, they said Bobby wasn’t around, but his car was parked in front of Headquarters.”

“Did you try calling Bobby at the turret?” quizzed Bemis.

"Yes, but they keep on saying he's not available and they ask who's calling," answered Donny. Something was obviously fishy. They decided to check out BPD Headquarters to see if Bobby's car was still there; they looked all around the building, but they couldn't locate his car. Donny and Gregg spent half the night trying to figure out where Bobby was, but it was no use; he was nowhere to be found.

"You aren't going to take the polygraph, are you?" Donny asked nervously.

"Yes, I am. I know I didn't do the fire they want to question me about so I figure it will get them off our backs."

"Well, I still don't like the idea. They are known to fix those tests so it looks like you're lying even if you're not," the annoyed and suspicious Stackpole countered. I don't know who Stackpole meant when he referred to "they." Over the years, I have had dozens of test subjects; ones I suspected were guilty of wrongdoing and ones for whom I had no information linking them to any transgressions, but not once did either the polygrapher or I ever lie or fix any test results. Sometimes I was surprised when someone I felt was dirty passed the polygraph, but that never swayed us from keeping on the up and up.

"Don't worry, Skinny. I have an airtight alibi if they try anything smart. I was working on the desk at the Stow Police Station that whole afternoon and evening."

Donny reacted, "That's great. Maybe it's not a bad idea to take the test after all."

The two confused and nervous arsonists called it a night since there was nothing else they could do until they could get in touch with Grobo. Gregg headed for home in Acton with a frightening thought he couldn't shake: The Feds had gotten Bobby to talk. He didn't sleep at all that night.

At approximately 8:00 a.m. Groblewski telephoned his lawyer, who would represent him in this matter. Shortly after the call, Special Agents Terry Barry and Dennis Leahy transported their prisoner to the ATF JFK office, where he was processed. He was fingerprinted and photographed and his rights were again formally read to him. At this time, Grobo stated that he understood his rights and that he wanted to waive his rights in order to cooperate with ATF. He said that he felt relieved to have gotten this off his chest. To the agents, he then admitted to being a sparkie, that if he had the choice, he would much rather be a Boston Firefighter than a Police Officer, and that he was responsible for the Canton barn fire.

The Agents then drove Groblewski to the Post Office Square location of the Federal Courthouse and deposited their detainee at the U.S. Marshal's Office. The Marshals took custody of him. Later in the day, they brought Groblewski to the courtroom, where he faced a U.S. Magistrate for his initial appearance. Bobby met with his attorney at the courthouse. He was released on $15,000 bail with surety, pending his next appearance.

This was the last day that we were able to speak with Bobby until May. Supervisor Phil Tortorella and I filled in newly appointed Special Agent in Charge Terrence McArdle and Assistant Special Agent in Charge Alan Cole with details of Groblewski's confession and our immediate plans for the investigation. Paperwork was promptly prepared and forwarded to ATF Headquarters to update the HQ bosses on the status of this sensitive investigation.

▲

Late in the morning, Bemis called Stackpole to see if he had heard anything from Groblewski. He hadn't. This made Gregg even more uptight. As he drove into the City that he had tried to burn down, he was hoping that the polygraph worked as he planned.

Bemis parked his car in the North End, about a mile from the JFK Building where the polygraph test was to be administered. Paranoid and afraid, Gregg thought parking so far away from the JFK would prevent us Feds from messing with his car or following him after the test. As he walked through Quincy Market to the JFK, the cold wind was biting.

On the nineteenth floor, Gregg was met by Agent John D'Angelo. After being asked a few questions, Gregg was introduced to the polygraph examiner, Special Agent Gerry O'Reilly, who gave Bemis the standard explanation of the exam process. He told Gregg what questions would be asked on the test, calibrated the machine, and then ran a sample test before running two sets of the real subject questions. Since Gregg had never taken a polygraph before, he, like most others who take the test for the first time, was a little apprehensive.

By the time he finished the test, he thought there was nothing to it. That is, until Agent O'Reilly advised Bemis, "You're in this conspiracy up to your neck, son. You're as guilty as sin." Now Gregg got pissed. He thought that Donny was right; he had been set up.

Gregg was truthful regarding the one fire that he didn't set. He didn't realize that when he was questioned about fires in general and his knowledge of those responsible for setting the fires, he couldn't hide the truth.

Gregg was escorted to an interview room, where Agent D'Angelo and Lt. McLaughlin were waiting with several reports. For an hour, Bemis was asked question after question, but he stood his ground, denying any involvement with setting any fires, although by then, he had personally been directly involved with setting over 250 arson fires.

Bemis was suspicious when he was asked about several fires he had actually lit. However, he was not about to trust the investigators since he already felt that he had been lied to about the polygraph results. Lt. McLaughlin left the room and was replaced by Special Agent James Karolides. Jimmy K. advised Gregg that if he didn't cooperate he would be buried when an indictment came down. This wasn't meant as a threat; it was merely a statement of fact. Gregg's immediate reactions to the pressure were anger and determined resistance.

Karolides showed Bemis a mug shot of Groblewski taken that very morning. Gregg was told that Bobby had been arrested and that he was cooperating. Bemis agreed that it certainly was a shot of Bobby, but he was not convinced that Bobby had been arrested. He definitely wasn't ready to believe that Bobby was cooperating. At that moment, Gregg would have given anything for an opportunity to speak with Grobo.

It was one of those times as a law enforcement agent when you wonder why the person who sits across the table continues to sit across the table. At this point, he could have gotten up and left at any time. He didn't have to stay and be subjected to an interrogation, as the interview had long ago moved past that stage. He had more options than we had, but Gregg, who didn't look like he had a strong personality, was strong under duress. He stood steadfast.

Bemis didn't let Karolides know that he had an established alibi for the Midway Street fire because he feared that we would destroy the Stow Police records before he could make a copy. I don't know what TV shows he must have watched or where he learned that these devious acts were common. We never once gave him a reason to believe that we were corrupt, and we never even thought of something like that.

After another hour, Bemis left the ATF office. Around 6:45 p.m. he met with Stackpole at the security trailer. He explained how the afternoon unfolded in great detail. Donny's response to the failed polygraph results was, as expected, "See, I told you they were a bunch of stinking liars."

"Yeah, I know, but there is one thing that's bothering me. They showed me a mug shot of Bobby and said that they had arrested him."

"I think that they're bluffing. Bobby wouldn't say anything even if they did arrest him," Donny declared.

"I hope so," a sullen Gregg replied; he did not feel reassured.

They still didn't know Grobo's whereabouts. Gregg even called Bobby's parents in south central Massachusetts. After speaking to his mother for a few minutes, Gregg could tell that she was very nervous, but she had not heard from Bobby in days. This only made Bemis more panicky himself.

The two wracked their brains to think where Grobo could be. They tried another Boston cop friend of Bobby's. The call aggravated Donny's paranoia. When they hung up, Donny said he felt that Bobby was there, but the friend just wouldn't admit it.

Several days of extreme uneasiness followed before Stackpole finally got in touch with Groblewski. Immediately after hanging up with Grobo, Donny called Gregg and told him that they were all going to meet in Quincy that night. Once they located Bobby parked on a side street, they pulled up to him. Impatiently, Gregg fired, "Hey stranger, where the hell have you been?"

"Oh, I've had a lot on my mind with those fuckin' Feds busting my balls all the time," Bobby replied. He explained the predicament that he was now in with the Federal arrest and all. 'I haven't said anything to the Feds," he lied, "and I won't. But somebody is talking. They have too much information to just be a coincidence."

Stackpole played a tape for Bobby that he had surreptitiously (and illegally) recorded when ATF agents visited Donny at his house after Grobo's arrest. On the tape, agents could be heard playing part of the January 13 confession recording of Bobby. Donny said that the voice on the tape sounded like Bobby, but he was skeptical since he could not believe in his heart that Grobo would give them up. Bobby shook it off by saying that the sneaky Feds with their unlimited budget could have edited his hours of being on the air as a police dispatcher fabricating a phony tape. (Wow!)

Donny seemed to accept the explanation. "Who do you think is talking?"

"Your pal, Wayne, is a perfect candidate," barked Bobby as he glared at both Gregg and Donny because they were both close to Sanden.

"Well, let's make sure we don't say anything incriminating to him just in case," proposed Stackpole. After they both reassured Bobby that they would help him in any way they could, they all left.

Now that we finally had a criminal case and one defendant, we quickly realized that, if we thought we had been busy before the arrest of Groblewski, the amount of work that we had to put in after January 13 would tax the entire office for the foreseeable future. We had to scratch and claw to perfect a criminal case against other members of the arson ring. Sure, we had Grobo's confession, but that alone, even with the information that we had independently developed from Sanden and other evidence, would not hold water if we prematurely arrested the co-conspirators. Bobby, although he was ready to cooperate, was abiding by his attorney's directions to stay quiet at this time.

We also had to firm up the elements of the crimes that Groblewski had been charged with to this point. The paper chase was just beginning. This is where the quality of the Agents in the Arson Group started to shine. They did everything that they were asked to do, and they did it well. Every day, members of the group collected evidence from numerous sources, including interviewing those responsible for keeping records needed to prove the case. Over the next several weeks, I had constant meetings with AUSA Mark Robinson, who now led the prosecution. I was usually accompanied by Supervisor Tortorella, Agent Terry Barry, and/or Agent Jim Karolides. I also had contact with many other investigators, witnesses, and people who were involved with the case in one way or another.

Agent Barry and I worked hard and long assisting AUSA Robinson with the preparation of the indictment in Grobo's case. Special Agent Terrence "Terry" Barry, T. Barry or T.B. (Long before TB12 Tom Brady was around) as we often referred to him, was one of the craziest sons of bitches you ever met. A Hudson, Massachusetts, kid, he was a hockey stand-out there. Terry was extremely smart, well-spoken as well as outspoken. His words and actions were often unconventional. I can still visualize the day that he jumped up onto his desk in the Group office ranting and raving like a madman. T.B. had a charismatic personality, but it was sometimes polarizing.

Terry was also an excellent Agent, who worked this arson case as hard as anyone. He and I later spent hundreds of hours together debriefing Robert Groblewski, hanging out with him at the U.S. Attorney's Office, prepping for trial, and working with the two assigned AUSAs Mark Robinson and Ralph Gants. Terry and I were later photographed with the two AUSAs (although Ralph was misidentified as William Weld, the U.S. Attorney at the time and later Governor of Massachusetts) for the April 1985 issue of *Life Magazine*.

The two Assistant United States Attorneys assigned to prosecute this high-profile case may have been young, but they both were sharp as tacks and smarter than the average attorney.

AUSA Mark E. Robinson received his undergraduate degree from Duke University and earned his law degree from Boston University. Tall and lean, with good looks, Mark had a full head of dark hair that reminds one of the Kennedy men. His thick mane earned Mark the nickname of "Buffalo head" from Agent Barry.

Robinson had been working as an attorney in the private sector when he opposed future United States Attorney Weld in a court case. Weld liked the work done by Mark during the case. When Weld became U.S. Attorney, he invited Robinson to work in the Civil Division within the Boston office. With his aggressive style, Mark clawed his way into the Criminal Division. He had a hankering for prosecuting criminal cases. AUSA Robinson sparred on even footing with prominent trial attorneys who had decades more experience.

Each Assistant U.S. Attorney is assigned several categories of crimes to prosecute. Among AUSA Robinson's areas were crimes on Federal reservations, counterfeiting, pornography, and postal violations. Mark also handled ATF crimes, including firearms violations and arson.

On the morning of January 13, 1984, Chief of the Criminal Division Robert Mueller asked AUSA Robinson to come to his office. Thirty-year-old Mark Robinson initially had a bad feeling about the request because of Mueller's previous strict handling of the young assistant. Mueller advised Robinson that he was being assigned to prosecute a case involving a Boston Police Officer who had been arrested in connection with the series of arsons that had plagued the Boston area in 1982 and 1983. Further, he was told that the case could lead to a much larger conspiracy. As Mark stood up to leave Mueller's office, he was instructed to make sure that he caught everyone involved in this case. The prospects presented by this case excited Mark.

This case was in general unlike any he ever had in terms of the number of potential conspirators and the potential charges. It was also his first arson case. Most cases prosecuted by the U.S. Attorney's Office are usually developed over weeks and months in a cooperative effort between the AUSA's and the criminal investigators. Mark was thrown into this case hours before Robert Groblewski walked into the courtroom for his initial appearance. However, Mark immediately jumped into the fray without hesitation.

Over the next 13 months, Mark and second chair, AUSA Ralph Gants, became extremely tight with several of us agents from the ATF Arson Task Force Group. We worked tirelessly together for over a couple of thousand hours during that period. Besides the work, we ate together, drank together, and had family gatherings together. It's one of those relationships that develop that you hate to see fade away when the case is over and all parties go on to other ventures.

Assistant United States Attorney Ralph D. Gants received his B.A. from Harvard University in 1976, graduating summa cum laude as a Phi Beta Kappa. The following year Ralph received a degree in criminology from

Cambridge University in England. Returning to Cambridge, Massachusetts, Ralph earned a J.D., graduating magna cum laude in 1980 from Harvard Law School, where he was the notes editor of the *Harvard Law Review*.

After law school, Gants served as a law clerk for a U.S. District Court judge. From 1981 to 1983, he worked as a Special Assistant to Judge William H. Webster, the Director of the FBI. In 1983, Weld appointed Ralph as AUSA for Massachusetts, where he worked gun cases with ATF. Later he served as the Chief of Public Corruption Division.

For the entire duration of the arson case litigation, Ralph Gants played the straight man in the duo of government attorneys. His even keel and dry sense of humor kept Mark in line despite the heavy workload and constant stress of the case. Ralph excelled in his knowledge of the law and legal issues, while Mark constantly pressed us for the evidence necessary to perfect the case for trial. As is often the situation with good, aggres-sive attorneys, Mark usually wanted the information yesterday. He was demanding, sometimes irritating, but we all managed to get the work done and remained close friends. The respect flowed both ways.

The value of both attorneys would be proven during the next year through numerous plea deals and two trials.

During this period, I also had to assist Billy Murphy with the writing of the ATF case report in a timely manner since Groblewski had been arrested. In most other instances, the case report is written first and then the arrest of an individual is made. But on this occasion, since the arrest was made on the spot, it was ATF policy that the case report be completed expeditiously.

In order to complete the case report, as part of the work that needed to be done, Special Agent John Spooner obtained copies of the Boston Arson Squad reports of fires that Grobo had confessed to. These reports, with their origin and cause investigations, were necessary to provide corroborating evidence of where and how the fires occurred. Spooner also collected police reports that mentioned seeing the arson crew on the streets.

Some of the dates coincided with the fires set by the arson ring members. Therefore, we had further corroboration substantiating their whereabouts at certain times.

If these fires were occurring in the present day, investigators would have the benefits of technology that did not exist, or that was much less sophisticated, in the 1980s. Today, investigators can use cell phone information, exercise trackers, and vehicle GPS data that can all be obtained by authorities that place the location of a suspect at a specific time. Also, in the present day, there are security cameras, either at public locations, such as at intersection signal lights, or at businesses and private residences, that can capture all sorts of nefarious transgressions. Sometimes I wish I were still working with all of those newer technical resources and social media.

Special Agent Richard Cain interviewed the owner of Morrell Lumber, who stated that they buy and sell cedar from the states of Washington and Oregon and that they also stock spruce from Maine. This proved the interstate nexus that was one of the elements of the Federal crime of arson. This had to be done for many of the burned properties.

We also had to determine ownership and insurance information for every building that Grobo and company had allegedly burned. Again, please remember that this was 1982; there were no computers with Internet access yet in our Federal offices. The various county Registry of Deeds had to be visited; the records had to be hand researched. Then, the agents had to seek out the owners of the various properties to include the Federal government, the City of Boston, and numerous private individuals to interview them.

People often feel that arson is a victimless crime if nobody is killed or injured during the fire. For those of you who have never experienced a fire, whether accidental or intentional, yes, your house or business and the contents can be replaced, those whose photos and other personal memorabilia have been destroyed and lost forever would argue that there certainly were victims in this crime. Countless people think that if the insurance company pays, then nobody gets hurt. However, untold numbers of victims of fires do not have insurance coverage or, for various reasons, have insufficient coverage, and they get hurt financially, the effects of which last for years.

As a poignant example of this, Tobe Deutchmann, the owner of that barn in Canton that the group burned, the one where the fire truck was parked that Stackpole was interested in, was interviewed to solidify the ownership issue. Mr. Deutchmann, 87 years old at the time, said that he lost not only the barn but all of its contents, including costly farm equipment, antiques, rugs, furniture, and other household items that had been stored in the barn. He had also just completed replacing the roof at a cost of $10,000. He added that he had been in the process of obtaining insurance for the barn and its contents, but that at the time of the fire he had no coverage. Thus, he suffered a blow he may not have been able to recover from. To my knowledge, the barn had not been rebuilt when he died a few years later.

This intense period of work in early 1984 highlighted Supervisor Phil Tortorella's leadership abilities. He thought of the many duties and aspects of the investigation yet to be accomplished. He organized his group members, stirred them to action, and doled out the assignments. He held the front office at bay. I never felt any heat from the top bosses; Phil handled and deflected all of it. He even dealt with Headquarters and outside agencies, such as BFD and the State Fire Marshal's Office. The work for all of us became a daily grind.

Further, we investigators interviewed the various suspects. On January 23, 1984, Special Agent James Karolides and I visited the Roslindale home of my primary pseudo-source of information, Wayne Sanden. Why did I choose to use such a term for the information provided by Sanden? For months, Sanden had misled me with partial truths and flat-out lies, all the while doling out tidbits to keep us going with our investigation into his crew. For all intents and purposes, his spurious conduct caused so much more damage with so much more physical and financial pain. For these reasons, Sanden should have received the longest prison sentence no matter how many fires he was personally responsible for. Did he think we were so stupid and inept, or did he just think he was so smart?

He could have short-circuited the arson wave and protected himself from a long prison sentence, but instead, for reasons that he never made clear to me, Sanden chose to screw with the authorities, including me. I took it personally because I couldn't understand what his end game was. Now, armed with Groblewski's admissions, we were on a well-defined path that would, in all likelihood, eventually lead us to Sanden's front door with an arrest warrant.

In the meantime, we interviewed Sanden to see whether he would finally roll, and add to our mounting evidence, or bury himself in new lies that we could use against him when the time came. Sanden told us that both Stackpole and Bemis had called him to discuss Grobo's arrest. Stackpole had told him that if ATF came to question him he should break their balls by getting an attorney, also advising Wayne that the entire group was to be arrested.

Sanden told us that he was not present for the Gerrity Lumber fire, as he was working at BHA and had the work logs to prove it. With bravado, Sanden volunteered to take a polygraph exam relative to his lack of involvement with the Gerrity fire. On the spot, we arranged for him to take the poly on January 25.

Sanden admitted that he was a sparkie, often going out with Bemis, Groblewski, Stackpole, and Norton, but he still evaded the truth by only describing how Stackpole and Groblewski had used the device to set cars on fire. He said that Stackpole, in his opinion, was the leader of the group and that on one occasion he had been shown how to make the incendiary device. Sanden demonstrated to us how the device was made.

Surprising us, Sanden provided information about Mark Svendbye, the security guard for ETR Security Company. This is the first we had heard anything about Svendbye. He added that Svendbye had told him that if ATF came to get him, he would get a hand grenade and blow up the ATF office. At the time we did not know that Svendbye just might be capable of such a crazy deed.

Sanden stated that he would not testify against this group in fear for his life and the safety of his family. He reiterated his willingness to submit to a polygraph exam about the Gerrity fire and, astonishingly, he added that we could ask about any other fire in Boston.

January 25, 1984, was busy for me. Early in the day, I was with AUSA Mark Robinson. I prepared to testify before a Federal Grand Jury as to facts in the Groblewski matter. Back at our JFK office in the afternoon, I prepared for the Wayne Sanden polygraph, but he was a no-show. I ended up speaking with him later that evening and convinced him to come in a couple of days later.

On January 26, 1984, our office learned from the Office of Special Investigations, U.S.A.F., that Lenny Kendall, the short-time arsonist, was currently stationed at Upper Heyford Royal Air Force Base in the United Kingdom.

On February 3, 1984, the City of Boston made a token gesture of good faith by reopening Engine 54 on Long Island. Bemis was incensed by this action. He felt that, of the 22 fire companies that had been shut down, Engine 54 least deserved to be reopened. Virtually all the runs by Engine 54 are on Long Island itself, with most of those responses to the Long Island Hospital, a nearly 100-year-old facility for the chronically ill. The firehouse averaged about 100 runs per year, compared with busy companies' 3,000 runs per year. Bemis considered the opening of Engine 54's house a waste of tight money that could have been better utilized. Boston actually had renamed Engine 54 as the Fire Brigade since it was not fully manned. Gregg felt that it was reopened for the specific purpose of catering to old cronies who should have retired.

On February 6, 1984, I testified before the Grand Jury. An indictment was returned shortly thereafter formally charging Robert F. Groblewski with numerous counts relating to the conspiracy and arsons.

On February 9, 1984, shortly before the midnight hour, Gregg's night took an ugly turn for the worse. As he climbed out of his personal car in the parking lot of the BHA Police Station in JP, two plainclothes men walked toward him. He instantly knew they were some sort of detectives. One of them asked, "Are you Gregg Bemis?" Gregg answered in the affirmative. The same guy replied, "I'm Detective Sergeant Kelley and this is Detective Donovan from the Boston Police Auto Squad. We have a search and seizure warrant for your car."

"Oh, pissa," Gregg let slip.

Kelley continued, "We want you to come down to Headquarters with us so we can ask you some questions."

"I'm supposed to be on duty in about 10 minutes," Bemis implored them.

"Well, you will have to tell them that you have to go to Headquarters to work on an investigation. Make up a story and we'll back you," Kelley improvised. Gregg agreed, telling his supervisor he had to head over to BPD about Bemis's being shot at a couple of days earlier.

A tow truck drove off with Gregg's car. Bemis rode to BPD HQ with the detectives. Kelley had a few words for Gregg: "Now, I want to get one thing straight with you right now. If you tell me what I want, you will get your car back and you will not be arrested. If you bullshit me, I'll make you wish that you were never born."

Gregg immediately reared up mentally, thinking that Kelley was nothing but a fuckin' asshole trying to intimidate him. At Kelley's office, the Detective fired off question after question about stolen cars, burned cars, and insurance fraud. His aggressive manner provoked Bemis into holding to his denials. When Detective Kelley ran out of questions, he stepped out of the office and ushered in Special Agent Karolides and me. Gregg already knew Karolides, but Gregg and I were about to get acquainted.

We asked Gregg more questions about stolen cars and arsons, but got nowhere. We finished with Bemis around 3:00 a.m. Sergeant Kelley told Bemis again that if he didn't answer some questions, he would be arrested. Gregg challenged him to arrest him then.

We all left the room, but Detective Donovan returned to reason with Bemis: "Gregg, you're in this thing too deep to deny it. I didn't believe Bobby was involved in it until I heard him admit it right in front of me." For a minute, Bemis sensed that Donovan was telling him the truth, but his mind quickly went back to Donny's statement about not trusting anyone because they were only trying to break the guys down, turning friends into enemies.

Gregg simply responded, "I'm sorry, but I can't help you." With that, Sergeant Kelley returned to the room and typed up an arrest sheet. Gregg was fingerprinted and taken to the Area E station, where he spent the remainder of the night in a locked cell. Several Boston cops acquainted with Gregg saw him there and wondered what was going on.

Due to the circumstances and the noise around the cells, Bemis hardly slept. In the morning he was arraigned in West Roxbury District Court, scheduled for March 12, 1984, trial, and released on personal recognizance. His boss let him borrow his pickup truck to get around while Gregg's car was impounded. However, his boss had no choice but to suspend Bemis, as the charge was a felony. Gregg understood that he had to be suspended and thanked his boss for the use of his truck.

February 17, 1984, provided a bright spot for Gregg. Mark Svendbye and his girlfriend introduced Gregg to a young lady. The four of them went out for drinks. Gregg hit it off with Madeline. They started to date regularly, growing close within a short time.

However, Gregg had this gnawing, guilty feeling about not warning her to get too attached to him because he "didn't know what was going to happen in the future with all the shit the Feds were saying." I had to put the quotation marks in that last sentence because of the peculiar wording used by Bemis in his treatise. How about the fact that his future was in jeopardy because of all the crimes that *he* had committed? We were only doing our job, that is, perfecting a criminal case against guys who had burned over 250 buildings.

Speaking of doing our job, on this same date we executed search warrants for Bemis's and Groblewski's vehicles, both of which were being stored at Auto Service & Tire in Mattapan. We recovered some incendiary device components that Bemis had kept in his car.

The court day for Bemis on the stolen auto parts case had arrived. Madeline was in the courtroom for support, and Gregg's attorney intended to call Wayne Sanden, the lying, scheming source, as a witness on his behalf. But the charges were summarily dismissed because the Boston Detectives failed to show for court. Bemis attempted to retrieve his car from Auto Service & Tire, but he had no luck getting the car released for several weeks.

A short time later, Gregg's boss told him that Gregg had to return his truck because there was a notice on a Boston PD bulletin board alerting all units to keep an eye out for a black GMC pickup (including the boss's truck's license plate) because the occupants may try to steal two black Ford

LTDs from the Auto Service & Tire tow lot. Bemis figured Detective Kelley was behind the notice, probably helping to supplement his income by splitting storage fees with Auto Service. Donny lent him a Metro Security cruiser in the meantime.

On March 19, 1984, Agent Karolides and I served a subpoena on Ray J. Norton, Jr., at his residence. Norton, in his usual abrasive way, instantly lit into us, yelling a stream of defensive and offensive invective. "Why are you persecuting me? You've got it all wrong. I haven't done anything wrong. You've got nothing on me. Get out of here and leave me alone!"

We immediately left to avoid any further confrontation. That evening I received a message from my ATF Office. The duty agent, who manned the phones and radios from 4:00 p.m. to midnight, relayed that Norton had telephoned our office requesting to speak with me. He left a number for me to return his call.

With some reluctance, I dialed the number. I was completely taken aback when Ray apologized profusely. He said that after we had left his house, he spoke to his more level-headed brother about the subpoena. Norton stated that he had acted foolishly by becoming so upset when we served him. I told Norton that Groblewski had recently confessed to setting fires and that he, Norton, may have some information about the criminal activities of Groblewski and others, including the setting of fires. We set up a future meeting.

A week later Norton presented himself to our Batterymarch office with his attorney. I am not sure why he bothered to pay for an attorney, because all he did was deny any participation or knowledge of any criminal activities. Period. End of meeting.

On March 30, 1984, I was once again surprised by Norton. He called our office requesting that I meet with him at Boston Fire Headquarters. Later that morning, I met him at the maintenance worker's room, where we could speak alone. His attitude was vastly different from the pissed-off guy we served two weeks earlier.

Norton told me that he had informed Stackpole and the others who were under investigation to stay away from him and not contact him anymore. He added that they had caused him nothing but trouble. Norton echoed his denials of any knowledge of anyone setting fires or of any wrongdoing on his part. He criticized himself, assailing his own big mouth and his pleasure in harassing those people he dislikes. Ray provided vague information about seeing someone at the American Legion Post fire who he thought had set the fire, but he had no solid information as to why he thought this person had set the fire. He didn't even know the guy's name!

Norton alleged, "If I could give you any information about the activities of the arson ring, I would." I just nodded at the bullshit he was slinging.

"Ray, would you be willing to speak to members of the group while wearing a transmitter?" I threw this out to him, baiting him.

Norton hesitated, and then replied, "I would consider it, but I'm not having any further contact with any of those guys." I told him that I would get back to him in a few days. Fat chance. For a moment I thought Ray was about to take some affirmative action to withdraw from the conspiracy. But he was just trying to protect himself while continuing to lie to us.

Since our investigation had already produced a confession from Groblewski on the American Legion Post fire, and Norton's information was so blatantly vague, I didn't pursue Norton's story. Norton was feeling the pressure from our investigation. His reaching out to me was his way of trying to develop a rapport with me for his own purposes. After meeting with Norton, I conferred with Supervisor Tortorella and AUSA Mark Robinson about the conversation with Ray. We decided that we had no desire to have Norton wear a wire.

On April 1, 1984, Ray Norton testified before the Federal Grand Jury. The most important question posed to Norton by Assistant U.S. Attorney Robinson was, "Have you heard anything, sir, or seen anything that would give you any reason to believe that they, Groblewski, Sanden, Stackpole, and Bemis, might have been involved in setting those fires?"

Norton's response was a blatant lie, "No, sir, nothing. I don't know of anybody, of any involvement, and if I did, I'd have turned them in, friend or no friend, because I don't like arsonists and I don't like fires." He had his big chance to do the right, moral thing, unless you believe that standing by your arsonist friends who destroyed so much property and hurt so many people was the right and moral thing.

CHAPTER SIXTEEN

SPRING 1984

During the first week of April, I spent days preparing for a suppression hearing in the Groblewski case. Grobo's attorney had to go through this process. He did not have much to work with since his client had confessed and we had solidified the case with an abundance of corroborating evidence. A suppression hearing is a legal maneuver often used by defense attorneys in an effort to exclude evidence that may be legally inadmissible. Both sides, the prosecution and the defense, present testimony and evidence before a judge, trying to support their positions and make their arguments as persuasively as possible.

In this case, the defense attempted to get Groblewski's confession thrown out, claiming that it was coerced. Part of their argument was that Grobo was interviewed at Boston PD in front of Deputy Superintendent Jack Gifford, obviously one of Bobby's superiors. This was alleged to be a form of coercion.

Besides testimony by Gifford, myself, and others, we had a tape recording of Bobby's confession from the early morning interview of January 13. It was recorded with his awareness and his permission. This tape was the critical piece of evidence. As the judge listened to the recording, it was obvious how low key the interview and confession had played out. All of our mannerisms were professional and cordial. Grobo's responses to our questions were cool, calm, and collected, stated matter-of-factly. Nothing on the tape alluded to any form of intimidation or pressure.

On April 19, 1984, the Federal judge ruled that the confession was admissible; the motion to suppress the confession was denied. This finding put extraordinary pressure on Groblewski to seek a favorable plea agreement or face an extremely lengthy prison sentence.

During April and May, Billy Murphy and I spent dozens of hours each completing the criminal case report. You know the saying about making a Federal case out of something. Well, the final product was exhaustive. It consisted of several hundred pages, slightly over three inches thick and weighing in at six and a half pounds of paper. For comparison, most other case reports prepared by ATF ranged from a mere one-quarter inch for a run-of-the-mill firearms case to one inch for more complicated cases. The Boston arson case report was a record in terms of weight alone.

▲

On April 26, 1984, as their conspiracy was crumbling, Bemis and Svendbye burned a vacant three-decker near Codman Square in Dorchester. Near the target, they made a device in the ETR Security car while under cover of darkness. Just as they had done at over a hundred other fires, they crept inside a poorly secured building, placed a lit device against the exposed wood lath of an interior rear wall, and left, awaiting report of the fire.

On the first pass near the structure, the entire rear of the place was fully involved. They heard three distinct waves of sirens, indicating that the blaze had gone to three alarms. Choosing not to spark the fire so that their faces weren't associated with the fire, they returned to work in Southie. Even with the threat of arrest looming, these guys were willing to risk setting more fires. Maybe they were being fatalistic; if they were arrested for all those fires, one more was not going to make a difference.

A week later, the same two arsonists struck again. Bemis and Svendbye traveled to Mark's house in Malden. On the Charlestown/Somerville line near Assembly Square Mall, eagle-eye Mark suggested hitting a large warehouse covered with gas shingles.

Gregg readily agreed, but they had no supplies for a device. The two of them went shopping and returned to the scene of the soon-to-be crime. They set the device against the exterior siding and returned to Assembly Square Mall to watch the fire's progression from a safe distance, far from the heat of the flames.

The fire was reported quickly. It went to a working fire, but because the MBTA owned the building, an interior sprinkler system controlled the fire until the firefighters knocked down the remainder of the flames.

As April gave way to May, the other members of the conspiracy were all being a little smarter about committing more crimes.

Groblewski already had his hands full with the arson case pending. Under the Federal judicial system, the proceedings move along rather quickly; trial is often only months after the arrest. And he had been working behind the scenes to help himself.

Stackpole, although completely obnoxious and unlikable to many people who knew him, was one of the shrewdest guys in the group. When the shit was hitting the fan, he not only lay low, he tried not to say anything incriminating.

Wayne Sanden, who for a while in the recent past had been Gregg's fire-setting buddy, now tried to stay out of sight and out of mind. He and I were no longer in contact. Now that Groblewski, in his partial confession in January, had implicated Wayne in numerous arsons, we weren't willing to rely on him as a source or utilize him for any law enforcement purpose.

Boston Firefighter Ray J. Norton also had no further contacts with his fire ring associates. He kept his distance in an attempt to save himself.

Joe Gorman was just being Joe, mostly aloof and distant from the embattled conspiracy. Nobody had seen or heard from him in months.

And then there was U.S. Air Force member Leonard Kendall, whose timing in joining the Air Force was fortunate. Unfortunately, he had the wrong friend in Gregg Bemis, and he had become involved at the beginning of the conspiracy. Because he was out of the area for most of the past 20-plus months, he had had minimal contact with the group, and during the spring of 1984, he was not involved at all.

That brings us to Bemis and Svendbye. Gregg was not being smart; on the contrary, he was both naïve and incredibly foolish. His words and actions were all based on an unrealistic belief that we investigators were all a bunch of liars, faking everything and staging Hollywood-style scenarios. Meanwhile, his pal Mark was just a liar, a thief, an arsonist, and a poor excuse for a wannabe cop.

On May 21, 1984, early Monday morning, Bemis and Svendbye set another fire, this time in Roxbury. The duo found an open doorway on the side of an abandoned three-story apartment building. On the second floor, the device was placed amid lightweight combustible fuels near open windows. This time Mark lit the cigarette and placed it within the matchbook, which Gregg placed in the brown paper bag before they departed from the site.

Cruising the street, the pair smelled smoke, but nothing was visible. An hour later, flames vented from the second-floor windows. They sparked this working fire from nearby.

That was the last known fire set by any member of the arson ring.

Nevertheless, Svendbye remained an active participant within the conspiracy. During this period, he accompanied Stackpole to coach Gorman before his Grand Jury appearance. Mark took the Scott Air-Paks that had been hidden at Stackpole's mother's house to Gregg's house, where he hid them in the attic. These were the units that Bemis had stolen from the State Fire Academy just before he torched it. Svendbye also accompanied Bemis to dump the stolen fire boxes in the Fort Point Channel. These actions would come back to haunt Mark Svendbye over a year later.

CHAPTER SEVENTEEN

THE NOOSE TIGHTENS AROUND THE RING: MAY–JULY 1984

Two days after the last fire set by the serial arsonists, on May 23, 1984, a momentous occasion occurred. Robert F. Groblewski, the only member of the arson ring conspiracy arrested so far, pled guilty to arson and conspiracy to commit arson in both Suffolk County Superior Court and U.S. District Court in Boston. It was one very busy, emotionally draining day for Grobo. He had done this without the knowledge of his co-conspirators, although they had to suspect the day was coming.

Gregg and the others read about it in the newspapers. When they contacted Bobby by phone, he denied that he had even been in court that day. Bemis was more than a little confused: Who was shitting whom?

He met with Stackpole and Bobby. Bobby told them to their faces that he had not been in court, which fed Donny's fantasy that the Feds were playing games and this was all an elaborate hoax. "That's right, Bobby, you wouldn't plead guilty to something that we have an airtight alibi worked out for," Donny said.

Bobby replied, "Of course not." He was a first-class undercover agent with an uncanny ability to lie to his longtime friends. His sociopathic tendencies were showing.

Bemis could not believe that the Feds would go so far as to stage a phony court appearance, but he told himself that that wasn't entirely impossible either. This is a prime example of Gregg's paranoia, his naïveté, and his foolishness.

After Groblewski lost that suppression hearing, he fired his attorney and indicated that he wanted to cooperate with us in exchange for some sort of deal. Grobo hired Rikki Klieman, a criminal defense attorney based in Boston at the time. Attorney Klieman has gone on to a remarkable career as an attorney, a lecturer, a teacher of law, and a legal analyst for numerous TV networks and shows. Bobby and his new attorney worked with AUSA Robinson to hammer out the plea agreement. In exchange for his full, complete, and truthful cooperation, a 12-year prison sentence was recommended by the U.S. Attorney's Office.

The following week, we began debriefing Groblewski. The first day, AUSA Robinson, Agent Karolides, Boston Police Detective Chip Fleming, and I met with Bobby for some nine hours. Over the following weeks, we rode around with Grobo to well over 100 addresses where the arson ring had set fires. Many of the scenes were now vacant lots, as the burned structures had been subsequently demolished. Nonetheless, at each site, Bobby recited who was present and how and where the fire was set. On the spot, I dictated nearly word for word everything Grobo said.

On June 6, 1984, based on new information, for the second time, we utilized the Boston Police and Fire Dive Team. They were back in the Fort Point Channel, but under a bridge this time. Six fire alarm boxes were recovered. The evidence kept piling up. The dominoes kept falling.

Friday, June 15, 1984, was another interesting, busy day. The first half of the day was spent conducting a fire scene examination of Groblewski's Ford LTD. It was still impounded and stored in the tow lot. But now somebody had torched it.

Back at the office, a new investigative step was taken. An undercover, tape-recorded telephone call was made by Groblewski to Stackpole. We had worked with Bobby to script what he should cover during the call and the intended goal of the call. The initial results of the call were minimal, but the call seemed to break the ice with Stackpole. A face-to-face meeting was planned.

The main purpose of undercover contacts was to obtain incriminating admissions. Since the target of the call or meeting is not under arrest or represented by an attorney for the matter at hand, there is no right or guarantee against self-incrimination. An individual always has the right to keep his or her mouth shut, but if the target wants to talk, investigators merely provide the opportunity.

Some may think wiretapping or secretly recording a conversation is trickery, but it has been a necessary tool used by law enforcement since we were able to make recordings. Criminals use all sorts of nasty little tricks without regard for you or the law. Undercover recordings have been court-approved for decades as long as certain caveats are followed.

Also, for those readers thinking of the word *entrapment*, don't get confused. These recorded conversations were largely about crimes that had already occurred. Entrapment involves a law enforcement agent's or government agent's coercing, pressuring, or enticing someone to commit a crime that the person otherwise would be unwilling or unlikely to commit. It is entrapment, for example, if the government agent introduces the idea of the crime into the head of the subject for the first time or offers the subject an excessive amount of money to commit the crime. Entrapment most often occurs before or during the commission of the crime. This was not the case here. The only future crime that was discussed on tape was related to Groblewski's flight from justice. However, there was never an offer of money to anyone to do this, plus it was suggested by Stackpole and the others to help protect themselves.

The disclosures resulting from covert recordings provide investigators and prosecutors with material that can dramatically bolster a case against a future defendant. The information gathered can lead to probable cause for search warrants that result in physical evidence of the crime being investigated. Often, the unwitting subject says things that he or she wouldn't want to get out in a courtroom full of the general public, reporters, or a spouse or other family member. The ultimate objective is to secure a guilty plea or cooperation to roll or flip on others involved.

The next Monday, we investigators had a plan with the blessing of the attorneys. Remember all those photos of the fires in progress taken by Bemis and Groblewski throughout the fire rampage? Well, Bobby made slides of all of his photographs.

On this day, we visited the home of Grobo's adoptive parents about 50 miles west of Boston, where Bobby had stored his slides. We retrieved an olive-drab canvas Army duffel bag full of slides on carousels, a treasure trove of pictures placing the arsonists at the scene of fires while they were burning. Not that there's anything wrong with that, in and of itself—just placing a guy at a fire scene doesn't prove he's an arsonist—but it can discredit an alibi such as a claim that the guy was at work at the time and not at the fire scene.

More significantly, these slides were about to become props in real-life theater. The plan was for Bobby to tell Bemis and Stackpole that since he was going to keep his mouth shut and go to prison soon, he wanted to view the slides one more time, then give the slides to the guys so that they could enjoy them while he was away. We hoped that the slides would solicit conversation and admissions about the fires set by his co-conspirators. We even bought one of those handheld slide viewers so that they could sit anywhere to view the slides.

That afternoon Bobby tried to reach Stackpole on the phone. Back in 1982, there were only two places to call with hopes of catching up with Donny—his home and the security trailer. But Donny was nowhere to be found that afternoon. This allowed us to view the slides ourselves so that we could find a few gems to get the conversation started. Administratively, we had to update the electronic surveillance request. The paperwork was a necessary evil to keep everything on the up and up. It seemed like paperwork was never done.

Supervisor Phil Tortorella, our tech guy, Special Agent Dave Watts, and I walked the short distance from our office to that of the U.S. Attorney. We met with AUSA Robinson and the Chief of the Criminal Division Robert S. Mueller. We had a lively discussion as to how we were going to utilize the electronic surveillance equipment within legal guidelines. Everybody except tech man Watts was for the proposed plan. He was skeptical about how well the devices would work with our plan. Mueller won this discussion; our undercover mission was a go.

The following day we briefed Groblewski further. Then, several of us traveled to Scituate, a small South Shore coastal town about 30 miles from Boston, to scout the meeting location. Stackpole lived in a small house on a corner lot among a neighborhood of modest homes. Donny had a nice built-in pool in the backyard. The location was going to be difficult for a mobile surveillance, except that Stackpole wasn't going anyplace so he wouldn't spot a stakeout as long as the vehicle stayed a block or two away from his house. The vehicle itself would be a nondescript van. The team would be fine as long as a homeowner didn't call the cops because a suspicious vehicle was parked by their property.

The next day, June 20, 1984, was a top ten weather day, sunny and 76°, perfect for sitting out by the pool. We outfitted Grobo with a recording device hidden in the duffel bag plus a transmitter/recorder within my personal Wilson red-and-white gym bag. We did not risk putting a wire on Bobby in case he tried to get a suntan or take a dip in the pool. Who would blame him—his sentencing day, and the end of his freedom, was less than three weeks away.

Bemis also planned to be present during this get-together. We had the ATF airplane ready to assist with the surveillance. All teams took up positions. The plane maintained an altitude between 5,000 and 8,000 feet in a wide circle from Boston to Scituate.

The surveillance began in Boston around noontime because we had Groblewski take a bus from Framingham to South Station, where Donny picked him up for the ride to Scituate. It was all part of the plan; Grobo had no car, as it had been impounded (and burned), and he had stayed at his parents' house.

As soon as Bobby got in Donny's car, they started talking business. Immediately, Stackpole begged Bobby not to take the plea agreement, saying that the government had nothing on him. They talked about Grobo's car being burned, but they didn't have any clue as to who torched it. Donny told Bobby that he was lining up a place in the States for Grobo to run to, someplace where he could hide. Bobby tried to get more information from Stackpole about where, but Donny changed the subject. Then, they just talked about NASCAR and other BS.

As they arrived at Stackpole's house, Bemis showed up. The three friends headed out to the pool area. Bemis and Stackpole tried using the Air-Paks in the pool, but they had very little success. Meanwhile, Groblewski was unloading some of the slides from the carousels. He was sticking to the script.

Just then, Stackpole looked up, pointing toward the sky, and said, "ATF."

Bobby went along with the thought, "Is that them? No, that's not one of their small planes, right?" Stackpole replied that maybe it wasn't them because they (ATF) had a nice Cessna, not a shit Cessna, one probably seized from some drug dealer. They dropped the subject as the plane moved higher in the sky and farther from the area. Little did he or Bemis know that it was indeed the ATF plane, but a really sharp Brazilian-made Embraer, not a Cessna.

Finally, they looked at the slides. The memories started flowing. Their conversations proved it. Gregg was laughing away while enjoying the slide show. Stackpole was playing coy, too shrewd to implicate himself via his own words. For instance, when Bemis joked that Donny just wanted to see the Sparks Club fire slides, Donny retorted that he didn't want to see them, adding that he didn't know what happened to the Club. Stackpole said very little, and much of what he did say was some sort of denial. When one slide showed the first fire at a Thetford Street fire, Grobo said aloud to Donny, "You were there."

Stackpole's response: "I went nowhere. I was nowhere and I didn't do that crap."

Multiple times, Bemis oohed and aahed when he saw a good photo of a fire scene. It was amazing that almost instantly, he knew the street where the fire building had been located. Bobby and Gregg reminisced when they saw the fire where they joked in front of the Arson Squad about anybody having a spare tire and about the Three Torches matchbook.

Groblewski asked Donny if he was going to call the guy for him, referring to Bobby's becoming a fugitive. Stackpole replied that he would make the call that night. With that, Donny lent Bobby one of his cars to drive himself back home.

The next day, we tried another undercover telephone call to Stackpole. Again, we had rehearsed Bobby with a script. He actually was pretty good at this type of business. The call was placed at 4:20 p.m. Donny answered the phone. Grobo explained to Donny that he had spoken to his attorney and that every legal angle looked bleak. Bobby asked if there was any news on the flight issue, but everything was spoken in code over the phone. Stackpole replied that the guy had not been home the night before, but he would try again and take care of everything. After Bobby again asked where he would be heading, Donny replied it was on this side of the Mississippi.

Stackpole had been in contact with longtime friend Christopher R. Damon of Ohio. Damon was born in 1956 in Hingham, Massachusetts. Several years prior to the origins of the arson conspiracy, Damon had lived across the street from Stackpole in Scituate. They had become friends sparking together in the late 1970s. Now living in Ohio, Damon had a civilian job as an equipment maintenance person. He was not involved in setting any fires. However, when old friend Stackpole contacted Damon for assistance with a problem, he was willing to help, even if that aid amounted to a criminal act.

Once again, since time was getting short, Groblewski placed another call to Stackpole the next afternoon. Stackpole advised him that the move might be made within the next couple days, depending on the guy's schedule at the other end of the line. He would let Grobo know soon.

On the tape, Stackpole liked to call us investigators "nitwits." I'll let you decide who the nitwits were in this story.

▲

Joe Gorman, one of the lesser players involved in this scheme, had been subpoenaed to testify before the Federal Grand Jury. When Joe presented himself to the Federal Courthouse, he waited outside the courtroom for his turn. His nervousness showed as he paced the floor. And waited, and waited. At the end of the day, AUSA Robinson advised Joe that the Grand Jury was retiring for the day. Joe was told that he was still under subpoena and had to appear in the near future.

When Joe finally appeared before the Grand Jury, he didn't invoke his Fifth Amendment against self-incrimination—that is, to remain silent under questioning. He didn't stonewall any longer. He answered the questions honestly, cooperating with the government.

A day after his Grand Jury testimony, Special Agents Terry Barry and Jimmy Karolides debriefed Gorman in a recorded interview. They had additional questions for Joe that were not thoroughly vetted in the Grand Jury so that the case against his co-conspirators could be strengthened. The words that follow are excerpts from that interview. Although these excerpts can't convey the nervousness in Joe's voice and responses, his candid and open exchange with the Agents provides insight into how callous he and the others were while they plotted their terroristic acts.

Barry: Was there any conversation previous to your trip to the Grand Jury about what should we say in the Grand Jury?

Gorman: Nothing to any extent of stories, but they more or less just told me to tell them that I knew nothing.

Barry: And Bemis and Stackpole previous to your appearance told you to tell the Grand Jury what?

Gorman: They said just keep quiet, tell them you don't know anything, we have told them nothing, we don't plan on telling them nothing. Bobby has told them nothing. They said they don't have anything, so shut up about it.

Karolides: At what point in this conspiracy to start lighting fires, did you join in and who was involved in this group effort?

Gorman: Well, I've known these guys for a long time. I've known them before this all started.

Barry: Tell us who Joe, who you knew?

Gorman: Stackpole, Groblewski, Bemis, Sanden, Norton. I knew those people before 1982.

Barry: Ok. What was the common interest between all of you? How did you meet?

Gorman: Sparking.

Barry: Could you explain to us for the record what you mean by "Sparking"?

Gorman: It's an interest in firefighting and Prop 2½ started the whole thing. They said 2½ is gonna start taking away fire engines from different companies. Bemis was the most upset about it. Their idea behind this with Prop 2½, the more fires that they set, they believe they would get busier that year and that would require more manpower and more equipment. This is what their thinking was and they said if that's gonna happen they can't lay off guys, they're gonna bring guys back.

Barry: Joe, can you remember at any one point in time that they said, let's start setting fires? Do you remember the first fire?

Gorman: First fire I remember that they set, I wasn't present, but they told me about it the next night. I would say it probably would have been Bemis and Groblewski or Bemis and Stackpole or Bemis and Sanden. A lot of times Bemis went out by himself.

Karolides: And how did he set these fires?

Gorman: He used the device that was described yesterday.

Karolides: Did you ever see it assembled? What was in the device?

Gorman: I saw it assembled. There was a brown lunch bag; it had a bag, a plastic bag on the bottom with fluid in it, like white kerosene, lantern fluid, Coleman fluid. That was on the bottom, and on top of that was tissue paper and on top of that was a cigarette and matches. And that's all it was.

Barry: Where did he get the components to make this thing?

Gorman: Various stores.

Barry: What type of car was it?

Gorman: It was a '78 Chevrolet black.

Barry: Can you describe it further? Was it . . . ah. It was . . . was it vinyl top, whitewalls and [unintelligible]?

Gorman: Ha, ha, ha it was solid black, blackwall tires, little hub caps, it had two antennas on it, one on each rear fender and one on the left front center.

Barry: What did it look like to you?

Gorman: Oh, an old police car.

Barry: How did Bemis dress? Could you describe specifically?

Gorman: Like a fireman. Dark blue pants, dark blue shirt. Always some kind of a fire department shirt with some kind of a logo on it. Black work boot, just like he would at the firehouse.

Karolides: Do you recall any conversation about the conspiracy where people were told that they should keep their mouth shut?

Gorman: Probably within the last half of last year to early this year. I remember distinctly, one night Svendbye, I'll say Mark 'cause I can't keep saying his last name, Mark and Bemis or Mark told me that if they catch us they'll never get us because Bemis and him had made a pact, that they'd shoot each other before they went in jail. Mark is a little loose anyway as far as I'm concerned and he's an asshole in my book. Yeah, they had signed a contract, he said that if they got caught that they were gonna blow each other's brains out before they went to jail, they weren't gonna go to jail for it.

Karolides: Whose idea was it to take the fire alarm boxes?

Gorman: Bemis thought that by taking them out, they would disable them so that would be a longer period of time in between the scene of the fire down the street. They would disable this box and this box that would give it a longer span of time before it was reported in various neighborhoods. I asked them one day what do you want with fuckin' fire alarm boxes. He says you take them out, the city's not gonna replace them, they haven't got any money.

Karolides: Who told you this?

Gorman: I think Bobby had one. I don't know if that was one of the stolen ones or not. Ah, Bemis had a bunch of them.

Karolides: Do you have any knowledge of what happened to the fire boxes?

Gorman: They got dumped in the harbor.

Barry: Who told you that?

Gorman: Bemis.

Karolides: Have you ever heard of the name of Mr. Flare, the Boston Arsonist, or the Friday Firebug?

Gorman: Mr. Flare yeah. That was Gregg's nickname. I don't know where the name came from, but that's what a lot of the guys called him. That's what the general name for the firebug was.

Karolides: Did you know about any letters that were mailed?

Gorman: Gregg Bemis, that's another one of his things. His name comes up more often ha, ha, ha. He's the one that wanted to send the letter to the Fire Commissioner. He wanted to type it and he wanted to say something about the fires, ah, how do you like this now or something like that, a letter to the Fire Commissioner in other word busting his balls saying ha, ha, ha, you know, here I am I'm burning the City. I think he sent another one like you see in the movies, cut the letters out of the magazines.

Karolides: Do you know anything about phone calls that were made?

Gorman: They told me that there was an out of town fire. Bemis and Stackpole mentioned it. The city was getting too hot. They went out of town, they set the fire, Bemis called the fire department and he said get ready or something like that. Here it comes. Mr. Flare is in town or something like that and then two seconds later they got the call for the fire.

Karolides: What do you know about stolen automobiles related to this group and who knew or participated in the stolen car business?

Gorman: They bought the Fords. The Fords, 80 or 81, had single headlights and they were unhappy with that and one day, but they said, did you hear about Natick Ford? One of their cars was stolen last night. I said is that right? I said well who stole it? Bemis said we don't know, but the car is in the harbor now. So evidently they took off with it. I guess they took the car, it was running when they drove it in. And off the front of the car, they took the headlights, took the taillights, the front seat and some other small stuff. And the front doors. Bemis drove the car from Natick Ford to wherever they stripped it. He said he was doing a hundred miles an hour in a brand new fuckin' police car so, that after they stripped it, it was still running; and they brought it down right along Atlantic Avenue.

Karolides: Ok, now fires come in and you go there. Who tells you that they did it?

Gorman: They didn't have to tell me. You just knew. They didn't have to come right out and tell me that they did it.

Karolides: Ok, do you remember a big fire in a barn in Canton?

Gorman: They said that there was a fire truck parked out in front of the barn. An old ladder truck. Groblewski, Bemis, and Stackpole were involved in that one, because Stackpole wanted to buy that fire truck, but I don't know if the guy wouldn't let him buy it or he couldn't get it.

There were two fires in Canton. There's one in the center of town. Ok, they did that one too. It's right off the center of town, there's a main drag that goes through the center of Canton. They said when they got there, the building was hidden off the street and was one of the real old type buildings and level to the ground.

Karolides: What kind of coverings would these buildings have that they'd look to burn?

Gorman: The one that was in Canton, not the barn, the other one had like tar shingles. Shingles, they call them gas shingles.

Karolides: Do you know if they ever used automobile tires in setting fires?

Gorman: I guess they were having problems, the device kept going out; it wasn't enough to get it going so they needed the tire that would help other things get going. They leaned the tire against a wall, or building or whatever standing up and they put the bag on top of the tire. It was either on top or it was inside.

Karolides: Why have you decided to confess and tell us what you know and your involvement? Fair to say Joe that your conscience was getting to you?

Gorman: Yeah. I won't be ashamed to say that since yesterday I feel better, I'm nervous, I'm nervous about it. Okay, I'm nervous about what's gonna happen to me and what the other guys are gonna do, but I feel much better about it.

Although we did not learn anything new from Joe, his frank responses provided more independent corroboration of numerous aspects of his crew's actions. It helped to solidify our case in the event he was needed to testify in any upcoming trials.

At the time that Gorman came in from the cold, we only had Groblewski aligned with us as a government witness. And who knew how Grobo would hold up under the pressure of cross-examination? And how would the jurors react to his testimony, this cop who was sworn to serve and protect but who now was trying to protect himself by making a deal with the government? What if the defense attorney for one of his co-conspirators could convince the jury that Groblewski was lying about his involvement to help his own cause? You can never have too much evidence to assist in perfecting a criminal case, and this inconceivable case needed a lot to make it credible to a jury. Thus, Gorman's admissions provided us with a little more cushion.

Joe Gorman may not have been the worst of the criminals involved with this group. He never actually set a fire himself. I am not forgiving him for his actions and inactions, not in the least. I am just stating the facts. Not once did Gorman express remorse for his or the group's egregious transgressions. During the interview, he casually answered the questions posed to him as if he were going to a job interview. He also never came forward on his own to report the actions of this group before they created so much havoc. Gorman seemed to just be a follower; he went along with these guys because they were his friends.

I never got the feeling from Gorman that he was in fear of bodily harm from the group; that only developed as the conspiracy started to collapse. I don't know whether Joe was just weak or somewhat of a coward. You can form your own opinions as to Joe's motivations and his strengths and weaknesses. In the end, he confessed out of fear that his co-conspirators would drag him deeper into their criminal acts than his actual involvement and save his ass from a long stretch in Federal prison. Being the second man in the door without actually having been arrested, Gorman hoped that his cooperation would land him a better sentence.

▲

On June 26, 1984, the day after Groblewski's twenty-eighth birthday, he met his good friend Gregg Bemis while acting in an undercover capacity. This was our seventh UC recording to date. We wanted this one-on-one meeting because we knew, based on Gregg's enthusiasm while looking at the photos at the previous meeting, that he would most likely make more incriminating remarks.

At Gregg's apartment, Bobby played his part superbly. He asked a series of questions like, "Who made the phone call that night? Remember, when we called the fire department?"

Bemis also played his part splendidly by replying, "Yeah, I did, using a disguised voice, though."

To every question Grobo asked about a fire, Gregg responded in detail. There was lots of conversation about who was talking and where the Feds were getting all of their information. Groblewski repeated that he would never say anything, and Gregg believed him. Bemis said so much that he would have no defense whatsoever.

During this entire period, everyone in our Arson Task Force Group was putting in lots of hours. As an example of a typical day, my ATF diary for Thursday, June 28, 1984, read "63210 83 1002D [the Unique Identifier for the Groblewski case], from 0730 to 0800 Travel to Boston." From 0800 to 2030 hours, the diary read, "Pick up R. Groblewski, review, transcribe u/c tapes, property forms, review slides, debrief RG re: 6/20 u/c operation; u/c call to D. Stackpole; confer w/ AUSA Robinson, group re: u/c call, plan of action." Near the bottom of the page, I wrote another note, "Stackpole telephoned R. Klieman's office at 1708." I finished the day about 8:30 p.m., just another typical 12- to 13-hour day.

On June 29, 1984, we had Bobby make an undercover phone call to Chris Damon to discuss Grobo's alleged plan to go on the lam. The call was made to the place where Damon worked.

Again, with the good work by undercover Groblewski, rather simply he got Damon to admit that Stackpole told him everything and that Bobby would be living with him for a while, and to describe plans for food, expenses, and a phony license. After Chris asked whether the phone line might be bugged, and Bobby replied that the Feds wouldn't bother because they had him by the balls, Damon gave Bobby his home telephone number. That was good for us since we couldn't just Google his name back then. We wanted his home number so that we could do a reverse directory check and get his home address. During the UC call, Damon expressed that he knew how serious Grobo's problem was and that he would do anything to help. The dumb son-of-a-bitch didn't know what he was getting himself into. Traditionally, the long arm of the law catches the guys who think they are smarter than the investigators, yet the bad guys that we catch are usually not the sharpest tools in the box.

On July 3, 1984, we conducted a surveillance of the undercover meeting of Grobo with BHA Lieutenant Wayne Sanden at the Jamaica Plain office of the BHA Police. Bobby walked right into Wayne's office. He sat down and the two men talked for the next half hour.

Again, there was a great deal of discussion as to who was talking and where did the Feds get so much information. Wayne told Grobo that the Feds had shown him portions of transcripts of Bobby's confession on the night he was arrested. Some of the recording had even been played for

Wayne. He told Bobby that he and his wife were very upset about Bobby's guilty plea. His wife could not believe that Groblewski was involved with setting fires.

Wayne said that the Feds had excellent information on the workings of the arson ring, but they also had numerous mistakes within their evidence. Sanden said that he had been struggling with the possibility that the information had come from Grobo, but he still did not want to believe it. His belief and trust in Bobby showed during this encounter; it led Wayne to jeopardize his own future by speaking so freely.

At one point, Sanden tried convincing Groblewski not to run to Ohio, but to go to someplace like Canada. Sanden added that he would take off to Canada or Australia. He would leave behind his wife, but he felt that he had to support his kids.

Sanden told Bobby that AUSA Robinson and ATF told him of Bobby's several days of debriefing. Regarding this, the following exchange occurred between the duo:

Sanden: Those guys, they would fuckin' hang their own fuckin' mother if they had a chance. They're liars. They are liars. They're bullshit artists. They'd do anything. They'd promise you the fuckin' world. And then they shove it right up your ass. Cause they did it with me up at the Grand Jury. That fuckin' motherfucker, what's his name? Tortorella. Did you meet him?

Grobo: Yeah, the night I was arrested.

Sanden: Tortorella, I'll tell you. If I had the fuckin' money, I'd go see Diane's Uncle Tony. I'd have that guy eliminated.

Grobo: [laugh]

Sanden: You think that's . . . you fuckin' laugh. That guy, he was the worst of them all.

Grobo: Really?

Sanden: And Miller and Karolides, fuckin' Karolides. He's a fuckin' asshole. He's nothing but a fuckin', local fuckin' Danvers cop.

Grobo: Oh, he's a Danvers cop?

Sanden: No, he's with the ATF now. That's all, that's all he was, he's a nothing for Christ's sake.

Isn't it amazing how some people think? I had spoken to Sanden on dozens of occasions with never a nasty word between us. He never said a bad word about me that I know of, but I had given him every opportunity to cooperate, with not the least hint from him as to his depth of involvement with the conspiracy. He was his own worst enemy.

Those words about Phil Tortorella were considered by ATF and the U.S. Attorney's Office as a threat against a Federal Agent. We took his words seriously. For the foreseeable future, while Sanden was a free man, he was kept under constant surveillance.

We also learned that Sanden planned to use his BHA Police Department logs to substantiate when he was working, which would have alibied him for being at any fires on those days. However, Wayne didn't know that we had recently received significant news that would derail his plan. She was known to Sanden and his friends, and subsequently to us, as "the Tarantula."

Wayne, the married father of one young child and an infant, had kept a secret from his wife. He had a young mistress on the side. Not that this makes him an arsonist. The Tarantula was interviewed by Special Agent Dick "Father" Cain, who admitted to us that the moniker appropriately fit her. Dick was one of the nicest guys. He never swore and often gave fatherly advice. He easily could have been a preacher. Agent Cain described the Tarantula to us. He told us to picture that Goth look: dyed black hair, black lipstick, and long fingernails painted pure black, all topped off with black clothing.

The Tarantula was a pretty good kid overall, except for being involved with a slime ball. She didn't want to get mixed up in any of his extra pursuits. She readily told Agent Cain that old Wayney boy would come over several times a week, most often in uniform while he was working. Bingo! Eventually, a check of the subpoenaed BHA work records for Sanden revealed no time off for visits to the Tarantula. Oh, well, that just blew his alibi.

Thursday, July 5, 1984, took another page out of "Bizzaro world" for the conspirators. Donny was in the last planning stages with Christopher Damon to temporarily house would-be fugitive Robert Groblewski.

Donny called Gregg, asking to meet him at his mother's house. He didn't want to talk about the purpose of the meeting on the phone. When Gregg arrived, he said, "We have to reserve a seat for Bobby on an airplane to Cincinnati."

"So what do you need me for?" responded Bemis.

"Because he's going to need a ride to New York City so that there won't be any record of him leaving Logan Airport." Now, Gregg understood what his job was to be, although he wasn't so sure that the beat-up ETR Security car he was using would successfully make the trip. He suggested that they check Hartford's airport for flights. Hartford was about 100 miles from Boston versus about 200 miles to New York City.

Donny grabbed the Yellow Pages phone book and looked up airlines. He tore out the necessary pages. Both guys headed to a mall, where they made the calls from a payphone to several airlines. They booked a flight from Hartford to Cincinnati using the false name of Robert Jackson to reserve the seat. In those days, you did not have to show any identification to get your ticket or get on the flight.

"Okay, the flight is 6:30 p.m., so once you pick up Bobby, you'll have to book it to get to Hartford on time," advised Stackpole.

"Okay, where do I pick up Bobby?"

"He'll be waiting for you in front of 28 State Street," right in the middle of downtown Boston, "at about 3 p.m."

"If I have any problems, where can I get in touch with you?" asked Gregg. Stackpole wrote a number down on a piece of paper, adding that he would be there or at home.

Bemis departed for the City. Traffic was extremely heavy, and Gregg arrived at the location a few minutes late. Bobby was standing on the sidewalk. Gregg blew his horn. Bobby looked toward him with a quizzical look, asking, "What are you doing?"

Bemis waved, "Come here." Bobby walked over and leaned into the passenger side window.

"Where the fuck is Donny?"

"He's at home," replied Gregg. He could tell that Bobby was pissed.

Bemis later learned that his pal Bobby was wired, recording the conversation. The aim was to record Stackpole with Grobo during the meeting because thus far, he had not said anything on tape that was incriminating, in contrast to the reams of recorded statements from the loose-lipped Bemis. We figured that when Bobby told Donny that he was pleading guilty instead of fleeing, the change of plans would probably elicit statements that would implicate Stackpole.

Later, when Gregg learned of the undercover recordings, he was aggrieved that the electronic monitoring had been done without his knowledge. As a brief explanation, Massachusetts is a two-party state when it comes to recording conversations. That means that if someone wants to record a telephone call or any other conversation, both parties have to have knowledge that the conversation is being recorded. For instance, when you are on the phone with your credit card company, and the automated voice says that this call may be recorded for purposes of quality assurance, you tacitly consent to the recording by staying on that call. In Massachusetts, a person could go to jail for surreptitiously recording a conversation.

There are a couple of notable exceptions to this law. In Massachusetts, state and local law enforcement must obtain a warrant in order to record conversations. But the Federal agencies do not have to seek a warrant because Federal rules allow one-party consent. Thus, the ability to secretly record a conversation can more easily be accomplished. Of course, there are other situations and complications that sometimes need to be addressed.

The bottom line was Bobby was not going to run and evade justice. Naturally, when Stackpole heard about this change of plans, he was not pleased. He was already suspicious about Grobo's final plans. Why do you, the reader, think that, unannounced Stackpole had Bemis drive Bobby to the airport? He didn't seem to ask Gregg, he told him to, and he didn't explain why. Maybe he had a premonition that Bobby was cooperating with us and planned to record their discussions.

The day after the canceled escapade, July 6, 1984, was Groblewski's sentencing day. In Suffolk Superior Court, Bobby received a six-to-ten-year sentence. In the U.S. District Court, Judge Rya Zobel followed the ATF recommendation, imposing the twelve-year sentence. Specifically, Groblewski received five years for the conspiracy charge and seven years to be served on and after the five-year sentence for his part in setting the E Street Military Barracks fire where 22 firefighters were hurt. Several other charges were all rolled into the sentence.

Gregg watched the TV news of the sentencing. Every local station covered this story. A Boston Police Officer pleading guilty to being an arsonist who had set a couple dozen buildings on fire was sensational news. Bemis was thinking that, from the sounds of the statements that were made about the sentencing, the rest of the group members were in for a real treat shortly. Right after the sentencing, the co-conspirators met several times to iron out their alibis in the event they were indicted. There was nothing else they could do at that point. It became a nerve-wracking game of wondering and waiting for what would come next.

From Groblewski's sentencing date until the indictments of the remaining members, I expended countless hours transcribing the undercover tapes. At the behest of Group Supervisor Phil Tortorella and AUSA Robinson, I reviewed the tapes and reviewed them again, checking and rechecking the transcripts. For court purposes, the transcripts had to be as perfect as possible. There were numerous unintelligible segments where words were difficult to distinguish.

On July 24, 1984, the 83-count Federal Indictment was issued by the U.S. District Court, District of Massachusetts. It was entitled United States of America v. GREGG M. BEMIS, WAYNE S. SANDEN, DONALD F. STACKPOLE, LEONARD A. KENDALL JR., RAY J. NORTON JR., JOSEPH M. GORMAN and CHRISTOPHER R. DAMON.

The Grand Jury charged Gregg M. Bemis with over 70 counts of violating Federal laws, including two counts of Conspiracy (18 U.S.C. § 371), 18 counts of Malicious Destruction of Interstate Facility by Explosives (18 U.S.C. § 844(i)), one count of Malicious Destruction of Federal Building (18 U.S.C. § 844(f)), 48 counts of Manufacture and Possession of Unregistered Incendiary Device (26 U.S.C. §§ 5861(d),(f); 5871), plus one count each of Obstruction of Justice (18 U.S.C. § 1503) and Mailing Threatening Communication (18 U.S.C. § 876).

Donald Francis Stackpole was indicted on two counts of Conspiracy, six counts of Malicious Destruction of Interstate Facility by Explosives, one count of Malicious Destruction of Federal Building, 17 counts of Manufacture and Possession of Unregistered Incendiary Device, plus one count of Obstruction of Justice.

Sanden was charged with similar charges including Conspiracy, 15 counts of Manufacture and Possession of Unregistered Incendiary Device, three counts of Malicious Destruction of Interstate Facility by Explosives (one with personal injury), and one count of Malicious Destruction of Federal Building. He faced the potential maximum penalty of 215 years in prison and $220,000 in fines.

Raymond J. Norton, Jr., was charged with one count of Conspiracy, two counts of Malicious Destruction of Interstate Facility by Explosives, one count of Manufacture and Possession of Unregistered Incendiary Device, and one count of Perjury.

Leonard A. Kendall, Jr., was charged with one count of Conspiracy, one count of Manufacture and Possession of Unregistered Incendiary Device, and one count of Perjury.

Gorman and Damon were charged with a couple of counts each.

▲

On July 24, 1984, Bemis picked up his new BHP uniform, then returned to the Dorchester apartment where he was staying with Madeline. After months on suspension from the job due to the stolen vehicle parts charges, Gregg had been reinstated. Despite the potential arrests for his part in the arson ring looming in the hot humid air, Gregg was happy to be back to work.

Mark Svendbye, waiting for Bemis when he arrived at the apartment, advised Gregg that BPD Sergeant Billy Kelley had been in Southie looking for Bemis. Gregg became extremely agitated and initially couldn't care less why Kelley was looking for him. A half-hour later, Wayne Sanden showed up at the apartment.

"I just came from Amory Street [the BHA Police HQ]. Sergeant Kelley called there looking for you," stated Wayne.

"Something is definitely rotten in Denmark," Gregg snapped.

Wayne replied, "Oh, you're too suspicious all the time. Why don't you just call him and find out what he wants." Gregg let a bunch of expletives fly as he had had more than his fair share of ball busting from Billy Kelley. After the guys argued back and forth, Bemis relented and called Kelley's office.

A female voice answered the phone. When Bemis identified himself, she said, "Sergeant Kelley is out on the road right now, but he told me to get your number and he will call you back." Gregg instantly felt that he was being set up, so he gave the woman a phony number. After a while, he called Kelley's office again. The same female repeated the same message. Bemis again gave her a bogus phone number, sensing that Kelley had more than a phone call on his mind. As far as he knew, the authorities did not know his current address. Investigators routinely conducted a simple reverse directory search from a telephone number to identify that number's location.

Gregg never did get in touch with Kelley that night, so he and Madeline called it a night and went to bed in their first-floor apartment.

CHAPTER EIGHTEEN

THE ARRESTS AND DETENTION: JULY 25, 1984–NOVEMBER 1984

Early in the morning of July 25, 1984, while most people were still asleep, dozens of ATF Agents, Boston Arson Squad members, and Boston Police organized for the arrests of Bemis, Stackpole, Sanden, Norton, and Joe Gorman. Federal Agents were teamed with several Boston Arson Squad members and with Boston Police Officers, both uniformed officers and detectives. The two remaining defendants, Kendall and Damon, were to be arrested elsewhere. We had sizable teams because we were not taking these arrests for granted.

My assignment was to arrest Gregg Bemis. We arrived at his apartment in Dorchester at approximately 7:00 a.m. I walked along the right side of the building, which ironically was a triple-decker, but without gas shingles. I peered into each window as I walked. About halfway toward the rear, I pressed my nose against a screen at an open window. I could see Gregg asleep in bed. I tapped on the frame of the window.

Bemis awoke to the noise at his window, rolled over, and found himself face to face with me. As he sat up, I commanded, "Gregg, don't move. It's Wayne Miller from ATF. Keep your hands in view. I have my gun pointed right at you." We had to be extra cautious about these arrests. Most of the suspects carried guns, and with the world about to tumble down on them, who knows how they might react.

Just then, Gregg's girlfriend, Madeline, popped up in bed. I was momentarily surprised; she had been sleeping against the wall side of the bed out of my view. I told Gregg, "Just have Madeline open the front door for us." She got up confused and visibly upset, but she complied. Gregg tried to calm her.

When the door opened, several law enforcement officers entered, including me. "Well, Gregg, we finally got you after all this time. You're under arrest," I said with some satisfaction. He was in his underwear. I told him to put some clothes on, which he did as several pairs of eyes watched. He chose a pair of dirty white painter's pants. After Bemis tried to reassure Madeline that everything would be all right, he was loaded into an ATF car and whisked away.

Since I had other duties to take care of at the time, Special Agents John D'Angelo and Dick Cain transported Bemis to the JFK Federal Building for processing. Gregg's favorite Boston cop, Sergeant Billy Kelley, sat right beside him in the back seat.

Johnny D. squirmed with enthusiasm in the front seat, knowing that we finally had Bemis and his partners in crime. He started in on Gregg, with a smile on his face: "We've got you on tape admitting to Groblewski that you were with him lighting fires. Yeah, we've got you by the balls now."

Agent D'Angelo was trying to scare Bemis into submission. Intentionally letting Gregg know about the recordings showed him that our case was solid, with Grobo as a cooperating witness.

The vehicle turned onto Congress Street to access the underground garage below the JFK building. Several TV camera crews were waiting. The vehicle with the prisoner entering the building all became part of the TV news later that day. What Bemis didn't realize was that six of his co-conspirators were also being arrested nearly simultaneously.

Special Agent Henry "Hank" Foderaro placed Joseph M. Gorman under arrest. Hank looked more like a Corleone family member in The Godfather rather than one of the good guys. He was one tough-looking bastard, but an absolutely great guy. Gorman just went along with the arrest, which he knew was inevitable.

Stackpole's arrest occurred at his house without incident. He mumbled to himself. Donny, downtrodden and disheveled, shuffled along to the awaiting Federal car to transport him to Boston. In spite of this, he remained defiant; Donny would fight the government to the end.

Billy Murphy had the pleasure of arresting Wayne Sanden. Sanden's wife was not a happy camper. Later, when Sanden was being escorted from the court, his sister spat on one of our agents because we were persecuting her innocent brother.

Ray Norton was shocked and pissed when he was picked up. Belligerent and sullen, Ray was suddenly in a bad place emotionally, screwed by his friends, screwed by his own dumb self.

Christopher R. Damon was arrested in Hamilton, Ohio, charged with one count of Conspiracy and one count of Obstruction of Justice. Damon was brought before the Federal Magistrate there for his initial hearing.

Leonard A. Kendall, Jr., was arrested in Valdosta, Georgia, after being flown back from England to Moody Air Force Base. The long arm of the law was in use here.

As often occurs when someone is arrested for some bizarre crime or series of crimes, the family and friends of the defendant tend to express their shock in terms of astonishment that so-and-so could ever be involved with such a severe transgression. We heard it all the time: "Not my son," "not my neighbor," "he was such a nice guy," and on and on.

A moving illustration of this revolved around Wayne Sanden. A couple weeks after his arrest, Special Agent Terry Barry and I interviewed a Boston Fire District Chief regarding his nephew, Wayne. The Chief voiced his amazement that Sanden had been arrested for these arsons. He found it difficult to believe that Wayne, whom he had known since he was a young boy, could commit an arson, let alone an arson in which he had hurt so many firefighters. The Chief was crushed; he knew Wayne was a spark and had wanted to be a full-time firefighter. He shook his head resolutely in pain and disbelief; the Sanden facts shook him to his core. His reactions were typical of most people who knew these guys before their arrests.

At noon on the day of the arrests, a press conference was held at the ATF Office in the JFK Building. BFD Chief John White was not timely invited. He missed the entire show. He understandably was completely and utterly rip-shit. When he showed up at our office, he ranted and raved to the first people he saw, Billy Murphy and Jack Dowd. Both profusely apologized to him, but the damage was done. He had to answer to the Commissioner and Mayor White, but he had been left hanging in the breeze. This was one of those inexcusable total screw-ups by the ATF brass that, for whatever small benefit that the front office got out of it, cost the street agents dearly in relationships with the Boston Arson Squad members.

Bemis and the others were processed, including mug shot photos and fingerprints, on the nineteenth floor, the same place Bemis had been months earlier for his polygraph exam. Once done at ATF, Gregg was moved several blocks south to the John W. McCormack Post Office and Federal Courthouse. There, as is customary, he went through another processing procedure at the U.S. Marshal's Office. Then he sat in a cell awaiting his appearance before a U.S. Magistrate. While he sat there, Gregg's co-conspirators streamed in for their turns at processing and were placed in the same cell.

Bemis thought that Norton was in the worst shape of all the guys. He looked shell-shocked. He was still wearing his Boston Fire Department uniform. They were all looking at each other, but everybody was hesitant to say anything for fear that they would be overheard. Also, they were even more hesitant to trust any of the others, since they all suspected each other of rolling over.

Each prisoner was handed a copy of the Federal indictment, which looked more like a Sears catalog. The tension was high in that warm cell block, but a look from face to face gave them some assurance to remain cool. The fact that the indictment was loaded with errors made them all feel a little better about what lay ahead of them.

At 2:00 p.m., Bemis, Norton, Stackpole, Sanden, and Gorman were escorted to an arraignment hearing before U.S. Magistrate Joyce London Alexander. The courtroom was packed, standing room only, crowded with other prosecutors and media from all over the place. This was one of the premier cases at the U.S. Attorney's Office at the time. Numerous other AUSAs were present to support Mark Robinson and Ralph Gants.

To Bemis and his crew, it seemed obvious that Assistant U.S. Attorney Mark Robinson had rehearsed his spiel as he smoothly portrayed the arsonists as the worst criminals to come along since Al Capone. AUSA Robinson was a strong speaker. He never minced his words. The suspects were accused of an unusual number of serious crimes. The conspiracy and the arsons that caused so many injuries deserved a strong argument by the Federal prosecutor to ensure for no bail for the alleged offenders. Between the rampant publicity and the well-presented argument by AUSA Robinson, it seemed certain that bail would be out of the question for most of them.

Bemis, Stackpole, and Sanden were held without bail. Besides the number of arsons and the severity of the crimes, the recorded conversations about running from justice and putting a hit out on ATF Supervisor Phil Tortorella insured that no bail would be granted for those three. Norton and Gorman were released on bail. Chris Damon and Lenny Kendall were being held in other states awaiting extradition back to Massachusetts.

At 5:00 p.m. the U.S. Marshals transported the three detainees to the Essex County House of Correction in Salem. They were in for a rude awakening. The Salem jail was over a hundred years old at the time. It was in such extremely rough condition that inmates sued the County for unsafe conditions, and the jail was eventually closed in 1991. The trio changed into prison garb and were led to the Protective Custody tier, where cops and snitches were housed. All three men were placed in the same five-foot by eight-foot cell with one bed and no toilet, only shit buckets. The jail provided two more mattresses.

The entire jail became aware of the identity of the new inmates and what they were locked up for. Considering that they were cops, they were treated as well as could be expected. Some said that they were lucky to be in Salem and not Lawrence, which was in even worse condition.

Their first night was a nightmare. The noise was incessant. The summer heat was intolerable; there was only natural air conditioning in the building, that is, any air that infiltrated to the interior. There were two trash fires set on a lower tier that night. A couple of shit buckets were thrown on people. Bemis learned that the inmates would light paper airplanes afire and sail them into trash cans outside their cells. These were common occurrences having nothing to do with new guest inmates.

Breakfast lasted five to 10 minutes. Inmates were indoctrinated to eat like animals, something that affected Bemis for years to come.

The inmates were locked in their cells for 23 hours a day. In their one "free" hour, they took showers and were allowed to make phone calls, but they seldom could do both with so many inmates versus the number of phones and showers.

The lawyers for the three inmates visited a couple times. Bemis was not satisfied with his high priced attorney; he always seemed to be a step behind the others' attorneys.

By the end of the first week in August, after two weeks of hell in jail, Stackpole, Sanden, and Bemis were back in Federal Court for a bail hearing. Each was granted bail in the amount of $250,000 surety. There was no way that any of the three could get the required amount. Even if they did, they figured that Suffolk County would soon indict them, holding them on high bail again.

Based on information received from Groblewski about the Mr. Flare letter that was sent to WBZ-TV back in 1982, Arson Group Supervisor Tortorella assigned Special Agent Terry Barry to find the letter. On July 17, 1984, Agent Barry interviewed Boston Arson Squad Inspector Michael King about the letter. Inspector King stated that on July 27, 1982, he was instructed by Arson Squad Chief McCarthy to retrieve a threat letter that had been mailed to the television station. An Assistant Assignment Editor gave Inspector King the Mr. Flare letter with the original envelope that it had been delivered in. He, in turn, gave the newly acquired evidence to Lt. Louis Scapicchio of the Boston PD, who was assigned to the Boston Arson Squad.

On the same date, Agent Barry interviewed Lt. Scapicchio, who stated that he had received the original Mr. Flare letter made of cut-out lettering with the envelope addressed to WBZ-TV, Soldiers Field Road, Boston. He then delivered the evidence to the BPD Identification Section for fingerprint analysis.

The following day, Agent Barry interviewed Detective William Powers, BPD Identification Section. Powers advised that a Fingerprint Examiner had tested the Mr. Flare letter for latent (hidden) fingerprints. A portion of a print was raised, but there were too few points to identify the print when compared to known prints of the subjects involved with this case. He added that he also raised two prints from the original envelope, but they didn't match any of the subjects. Powers retrieved the evidence from a file drawer and released it to Agent Barry.

From there, Terry forwarded the evidence to the ATF Laboratory in Rockville, Maryland. Laser illumination was used on the two items, but no new identifiable latent prints were raised. However, a closer analysis of the partial latent print that had been developed by the Boston Police revealed sufficient points to identify the impression as the right index finger of Gregg

M. Bemis. This finding added another felony against Bemis because the letter threatened further destruction of buildings if the firefighters weren't rehired, a threat as serious as that of someone who calls in a bomb scare.

▲

On August 14, 1984, our case against the main cast of characters became even a little stronger. Late that morning, Mark Svendbye presented himself at our office to be interviewed and provide his cooperation. I had the opportunity to conduct this interview with BFD Chief John White of the Arson Squad and ATF Agent John Spooner.

Svendbye confessed to his late involvement with the criminal activities of the arson ring and about his knowledge of the fires committed by other co-conspirators. Mark also provided good information about the location of the stolen fireboxes. Based on his information, we retrieved several of the Scott Air-Paks that had been stolen from the Massachusetts State Fire Academy. I told Svendbye that we would be seeking an indictment for his crimes, for which he would be arrested, but at the moment, he was free to go.

▲

Life was about to change again for the three cellmates on Friday, August 17, 1984. Wayne was out of the cell visiting with his attorney. Out of nowhere, Donny blurted out, "Hey, I'm not going down for this shit. I'm not going to spend the rest of my life in jail."

"What have you got in mind, Skinny?" asked Gregg.

"Well, it's obvious that Bobby was the one that was shooting his mouth off and now Joe and possibly Mark, too," an enraged Donny ranted.

"Yeah, here we were listening to Bobby say it was Wayne that was talking and instead it was him all the time," Gregg added.

"Yeah, and now he's trying to unload some fires on us that we never even did. Well, I've got it all figured out."

Gregg was wondering where this was going. "I'm listening."

Stackpole continued, "I've got it all set to have Bobby and Joe knocked off."

"You mean killed?" Gregg asked in disbelief.

"Yes. I know I can get Joe's roommate to put cyanide in his cocaine and then . . . " Donny made a sniffing noise.

"Are you crazy?" Bemis, asked, dumbstruck.

"Well, we've done everything else. It had to come to this sooner or later."

Gregg's brain was churning. "Well, don't make any drastic moves just yet," he said while thinking how he could stall the plot. He knew at that moment that it was all over. He could not keep his mouth shut any longer.

Fortunately for Bemis, shortly after that murder discussion, his brother and sister came to visit him. He directed them to get hold of his attorney as fast as possible. They could not believe what was happening. Gregg told them that he thought he had stalled Stackpole for the time being, but he did not know for how long. After he implored them not to tell anyone but his attorney, his siblings departed from the lock-up.

Later that weekend night, Gregg's attorney arrived. Bemis was taken from his cell to confer with his counsel. After filling in the details for his attorney, he left to get an emergency message to the U.S. Attorney's Office. The situation was critical. Stackpole's plan could result in a dangerous, tragic outcome that would raise the stakes exponentially. Returning to his cell, Gregg didn't tell Donny or Wayne what had occurred with his attorney.

The next day, Gregg's attorney returned with AUSA Robinson and ATF Agent Terry Barry to hear what Gregg had to say. AUSA Robinson had been at the annual U.S. Attorney's Office summer outing when he received the emergency call. Bemis immediately laid his cards on the table.

He didn't want anything to do with a murder plot so he was willing to cooperate fully.

Gregg saw Robinson trying to hide his absolute elation to have Gregg's cooperation. The defense attorney advised Robinson that Gregg was not going to incriminate himself until he had an immunity agreement. When AUSA Robinson was advised that the indictment was full of errors and missing a lot of information, he offered Gregg immunity in exchange for a plea deal.

Gregg was handed a plea agreement handwritten on a napkin that was being offered by the U.S. Attorney's Office. Bemis nearly dropped dead when he read that in return for his cooperation, the U.S. Attorney would recommend a 30-year prison sentence.

Gregg couldn't believe it. He looked at Robinson and shrieked, "What, are you crazy? How much time were you going to recommend if I had gone to trial?"

Robinson seemed taken aback by Gregg's outburst, but replied calmly, "We were going to recommend 50 years if you had gone to trial."

Bemis asked to speak to his attorney alone. When AUSA Robinson and Agent Barry left, Gregg turned to his attorney and vehemently claimed, "I'm not signing an agreement for 30 years!"

"I know it sounds bad, but 30 years is better than 50 and besides, we will get it down after they find out all you have to give them," counseled his attorney.

With great hesitation, Bemis signed the agreement, making the second biggest mistake of his young life. (Gregg thinks it was *the* biggest mistake. I beg to differ; the second mistake would never have occurred if he hadn't become the most prolific arsonist in Boston history.)

Robinson and Barry reentered the room. Over the next half hour, Bemis briefly outlined what he had to offer the Government. When the others left, Gregg was placed in a different cell. Stackpole and Sanden were moved to different tiers within the jail. Although they were physically separated, the three were still able to converse by yelling to each other. The other two conspirators were very curious about what had just happened. Donny yelled up to Bemis, "What's going on, Gregg?"

Bemis quickly thought up a story. "That was Robinson that just left. He was trying to get me to roll over," Gregg lied. First, Wayne Sanden lied to everyone. Then, Robert Groblewski lied to his criminal cohorts. Now, it was Gregg's turn.

"You didn't tell him anything, did you?"

"No, I didn't say a fuckin' thing, but he had a fit when he found out that we were in the same cell," answered Gregg with a plausible explanation.

Stackpole responded, "Well, that explains why we all got split up." Wayne had nothing to say, but he seemed to be buying what Gregg was selling.

The next afternoon, the U.S. Marshals swept Bemis up from the jail. Gregg thought that he was on his way to the U.S. Attorney's Office, but once the Marshal's vehicle started heading in the wrong direction, he asked where they were going. One of the Marshals advised, "You're going to Lawrence." Bemis sank back into his seat, shivering while recalling all of the horror stories he had heard about the Lawrence House of Corrections. As they pulled into the parking lot, Gregg got his first look at the old, scary granite stone building that was to be his new temporary home.

The jail was far worse on the inside than its exterior suggested. He was housed in a granite-floored cell with a blanket that looked like it had belonged to a dog, but no pillow or anything else. He was never given a towel, so he never showered. The line for the phone was 20 deep, so he never had time to make a phone call.

Eventually, Gregg's attorney came with AUSA Robinson and ATF Agents to further debrief Bemis. Gregg supplied a smorgasbord of information, including Stackpole's plans to murder Groblewski, Gorman, and Svendbye, numerous fires that had not been included in the initial indictment, errors in the indictment, and the location of hidden photos and stolen fire alarm boxes. He also told them that Mark Svendbye was another co-conspirator.

Regarding the murder plot, Bemis related that Stackpole had said the hit on Joe Gorman was planned to occur before Donny was released on bail so he could use his incarceration as an alibi. His bail was anticipated soon, as Stackpole was putting up his house and other property as collateral. Stackpole said that he didn't care if he and other family members lost their properties that had been used for his bail, as long as he could get away. Bemis added that Stackpole would only use the payphone on the lower tier to make the hit arrangements for fear that the payphone that he would normally use was tapped.

Bemis recounted that Stackpole had a wealthy friend with a large boat who planned to help Stackpole jump bail to the Cape Verde Islands off the coast of Africa. This same friend had also allegedly been solicited in a plan to murder Robert Groblewski. Bemis stated that Stackpole was capable of having someone murdered, as, in Gregg's view, Donny would do anything to beat the charges against him.

When the Feds left, Bemis confided in his attorney that he had some psychological and emotional problems relating to his mother's death when he was a teenager. The attorney advised Gregg he would secure a psychiatrist for him and that possibly would carry some weight in Gregg's defense. Bemis was then placed in a protective custody cell by himself because everybody knew by then that he was a cooperating witness.

At one point, when Bemis was being transported to the Federal courthouse, he saw Lenny Kendall. They spoke briefly, nothing of importance. That was the last time Gregg saw Lenny throughout Gregg's prison years.

Later, Bemis was transferred to Plymouth County, which was one of the nicer facilities in the State, while he awaited his day to plead guilty and be sent to his Federal home away from home.

The ATF Arson Group agents, plus Task Force member Lt. Steve McLaughlin and other Boston Arson Squad investigators, still kept busy shoring up the cases against all of the defendants. In spite of confessions and expected guilty pleas, more evidence was needed in case any of the deals fell apart. Additionally, confessions can't stand alone to convict a person; there must be corroborating evidence that substantiates the confession. There was a tremendous amount of work necessary to prepare for the potential trials of one or more of the defendants. Some of what we learned after the arrests is outlined below.

After the arrest of Lenny Kendall, I interviewed the Air Force recruiter who signed Kendall in 1982 to join the U.S. Air Force. The recruiter stated that the main reason Kendall joined the Air Force was to become a firefighter, his dream job, as there were no local firefighter positions available and no prospect for years before a position would become available.

Federal Grand Jury subpoenas were issued for all kinds of records all over the place including for Keeper of the Records for the BFD, as well as employment, attendance and telephone records for each of the suspects.

Lt. McLaughlin and Special Agent Bill Murphy interviewed a 15-year-old male in the presence of his mother because he was a juvenile. "David" had been a very close friend of Firefighter Ray Norton for the past couple of years. He often slept overnight at Norton's house and went on vacations with him.

David provided information that corroborated some Bemis information. David told us about a winter trip to the White Mountains of New Hampshire. Ray was particularly interested in a monstrous white hotel with a red roof right below Mt. Washington, the largest mountain in New England. It was the Mt. Washington Hotel, which in those days was closed during winters due to heating deficiencies. Bemis had earlier relayed to us how Norton suggested burning the hotel because it would make a spectacular fire.

The Mt. Washington is one of the last "grand" hotels left in the country. It was completed in 1902, built mostly of wood. With the location of the hotel being rather isolated in the woodlands (especially in the early 1980s), and the town having only a small underequipped volunteer fire department at the time, a fire in that building would have been a rip-roaring conflagration. It would have broken the hearts of so many as it is such a beautiful place.

David also related how he often accompanied Norton to the scene of fires. He said that Norton would even get him out of bed after receiving a telephone call so they could go to fires.

Lt. McLaughlin and Agent Murphy also interviewed Elliot Belin, that friend of the arsonists, super spark, and the civilian with access to Boston Fire Headquarters. There was never any information that Elliot did anything illegal to assist the arsonists in any way, but they may have tried to unwittingly solicit information from him.

We had information from Bemis that Stackpole had been calling Belin from prison because Elliot had three-way calling. Stackpole's goal was to arrange the murders of Groblewski, Gorman, and Svendbye without leaving a phone record that could be traced back to the murderers-to-be. Belin confirmed that Stackpole had used his three-way, calling several times.

Belin related that Mark Svendbye had come to him after the arrests of the arsonists. Mark told Elliot about the criminal activities of the arson ring, including his own criminal activities. Svendbye also expressed his fear that Stackpole would try to have him killed. Belin advised Svendbye to go to the authorities with his information, which he soon did. When Belin learned the incriminating information from Svendbye about Stackpole, he refused any further calls from Donny.

In September 1984 an employee of ETR Security provided some valuable information. We had learned that Stackpole planned to use Detex tapes as an alibi for the nights that he was accused of setting fires.

Detex was the brand name of the most popular watch clocks used by watchmen. As their rounds are made within a building or at properties, a watchman would take a key from the location and put in into the clock. The key was numbered for the specific location. It would be recorded on a paper within the watch clock for location, date, and time. When out on bail, Stackpole planned to meticulously fake Detex tapes to cover his crimes. It sounds like a lot of work, both time consuming and tedious. There was one main problem with the plan. The employee and others said Stackpole never used a Detex clock to do his rounds. He also told his employees not to worry about using one; if anything ever happened, he would make a tape up after the fact. His plan was now thwarted.

This same employee explained that Stackpole planned to use him as an alibi for the June 3, 1982, Spero Toy fire. That morning, the employee had spoken to Donny on the phone at his house. However, that was hours after the fire had been set. One other anecdotal story was related by the employee. Stackpole often complained about the building in front of the security trailer that blocked his view to a client's property. And mysteriously, it had burned to the ground.

▲

During the first three weeks of September 1984 Agent Terry Barry, Lt. Steve McLaughlin, and I interviewed Gregg Bemis at length. We viewed all of the sites that he listed as places that the arson ring had set on fire. None were actually fire scenes any longer.

Gregg's memory was incredibly sharp when it came to the fires. He could look at a list of runs in Boston and recount immediately who, what, where, when, and why. As we sat in front of a property, Gregg told us where they parked that night, the weather conditions, and who did what, supplying details of the structure and how the fire progressed. He would make a superb witness when it came time for trial.

During this period, T. Barry and I spent many, many hours with Bemis. Our relationship could be described as weird. When you spend days together, eat together, and talk about life outside of fires, bonds do form. Bemis thought of Terry and me as his friends, but we really couldn't be his friend, although we did develop some affection for the kid. We had a job to do, and we had to keep Gregg talking and cooperative, so we kept it amicable, but professional. In a sense, he became a member of our prosecution team. It was a shared effort by all of us. With his uncanny memory of the fires, Gregg acted as if he was an investigator at times, weirdly trying to supply the corroborating evidence to his own testimony.

Of course, during this period of debriefing and prepping Gregg for trial, he had a couple of requests. He had a couple of small ones, like a certain sandwich. He also had a couple of not so small ones. We brought his girlfriend into the Federal courthouse and escorted her up to the U.S Attorney's Office. Gregg was in one of the AUSA's offices. His girl joined him. We left the two alone inside the office for about an hour, while we waited outside the door in the hallway. There was no other way out of the office, except via the nineteenth-floor window. Afterward, and it's only a guess on my part, but the Cheshire cat smile on Gregg's face alluded to the satisfaction that only a conjugal visit could have provided.

On September 6, 1984, Bemis pled guilty to nearly all of the 83 counts. He was eventually housed in the Federal Correctional Institution in Sandstone, Minnesota. His sentence was subsequently revised to a 138-month sentence on one count, with all other counts to be served concurrently. So, in essence, Gregg ended up serving about 12 years, far less time than that original 30-year plea agreement.

The dominoes continued to fall on September 18, 1984. Our finding out about the Tarantula had another major effect on our case against Wayne Sanden. Rather than face a trial where we would parade *all* of our evidence before the world, including his extracurricular activities, he decided to plead guilty.

Wayne was the strangest guy in the group. After stringing me along for months and keeping me interested in the arson ring's activities, he never, ever admitted his role in setting about 50 of the fires. Remember, he was the one who supplied the information about the stolen vehicle that had been dumped in the Fort Point Channel. Eventually, that car helped make Groblewski decide to cooperate. Even at his change of plea proceeding in front of the Honorable Rya Zobel, where an allocution, or formal statement of a guilty defendant, is often required of the defendant, Sanden failed to explain his involvement. The defendant in a Federal case usually admits in detail his actions and his reasons for his crimes in exchange for a reduced sentence. Sanden barely uttered a word, but Judge Zobel accepted Sanden's guilty plea on 20 counts.

On September 19, 1984, a Federal Grand Jury returned a superseding indictment now charging Stackpole with a total of 19 counts in the new 25-count indictment. The remaining six counts were for Ray J. Norton, Jr., and Leonard A. Kendall, Jr. The reason a superseding indictment was sought was to add new charges based on additional information that was learned through interviews with cooperating co-conspirators Bemis, Gorman, and Svendbye. Stackpole continued to refuse to cooperate or plead guilty. We didn't want or need his cooperation anyway, but a guilty plea would have saved a lot of time, effort, and headaches. His trial was scheduled for November 1984.

Also, in September, AUSA Mark Robinson, Special Agent Terry Barry and I traveled to the Federal Correctional Facility in Otisville, in upstate New York. As we drove through the tiny town of a thousand residents, we noted the older New York-style houses. There were no traffic lights. Some people were hanging out mid-day on the front door stoops and porches. We all had the same thought: the town reminded us of the movie Deliverance. Terry jokingly started singing the "Dueling Banjos" melody. Knowing that we would soon be inside the prison in this town gave us a freaky feeling. Mark asked us to stop at a general store so he could pick up a couple items requested by inmate Robert Groblewski.

After Mark completed his errand, we wound through the outskirts of town, where FCI Otisville sat on a bare hill since all of the trees had been removed. The prison looked new and imposing. All three of us had been on the inside of quite a few prisons over the years; interviewing inmates was just part of the job.

During processing to visit an inmate, we had to secure our weapons and be screened. There was a problem with the screening of AUSA Robinson. Unbeknownst to either of us Federal agents, Mark tried bringing two cans of beer into the prison for Grobo. Somehow, he didn't think beer would qualify as contraband, or maybe he just thought that an AUSA could take in anything he so desired as long as it wasn't drugs or weapons. The guards confiscated the beer and that was that, or so we thought.

Bobby was so happy to see us; he really was. It may seem strange, but he also considered us as his friends. After hours of prepping our witness for the upcoming trials, a correctional officer came to get us. He escorted us to the principal's—oops, I mean warden's—office. The stern, non-smiling warden certainly expressed his displeasure with the attempted smuggling of the beer. Terry and I shrank behind Mark. We let him deservedly take the brunt of the scolding. I am not kidding when I say that it was just like getting in trouble in high school. It's a wonder that we didn't get detention, locked in a cell for a few hours with some of the convicts. This was one of those little anecdotes of the case that still makes us laugh.

During the week of September 24, 1984, I took the full week of annual leave, the term used on our time sheets for vacation time. The following two weeks I also stayed home, but that was due to sick leave. I had pneumonia.

On October 5, 1984, Joseph M. Gorman pled guilty to one count of conspiracy and one count of making and possession of an incendiary device. He was sentenced to a five-year prison sentence. On October 29, 1984, Gorman found no-cost housing at Danbury FCI, Federal Correctional Institute. Lenny Kendall pled guilty to his charges. He was the only member of the group to escape jail time; he was given probation.

The remainder of October, members of the ATF Arson Group and I spent 10 to 16 hours a day preparing for the Stackpole trial. The threat assessments relative to Stackpole were completed. There were daily conferences with AUSA's Gants and Robinson. Witnesses were re-interviewed and prepped. The tapes and transcripts from the undercover contacts again had to be checked. And the paperwork, always so much paperwork, had to be done. And it was always done.

Groblewski and Bemis needed to be coddled; their testimony was critical to the upcoming trial. The U.S. Marshals transported both witnesses from their prison cells to the U.S. Attorney's Office several times per week, making sure the two former criminal associates were never in the same area on the same day.

We ATF agents became friendly with several of the Marshals during this period because they sat in the hallway for hours while we prepped Gregg and Bobby. The Marshals also sat in the courtroom daily throughout the two trials. Two of the Marshals are worthy of note. Nancy McGillivray went on to be appointed by President Bill Clinton as the first woman who came up through the ranks to be the United States Marshal for the District of Massachusetts, where she served for eight years with distinction. Deputy U.S. Marshal William F. Degan was an affable, hardworking, and dedicated Marshal who became a leader of numerous high-profile operations. Seven years after these trials, Bill was mortally wounded in a firefight while serving a warrant during the 11-day Ruby Ridge standoff in northern Idaho. Deputy United States Marshal Degan was buried in his hometown of Quincy, Massachusetts. Both Bill and Nancy were the ultimate professionals, and we were proud to work alongside them.

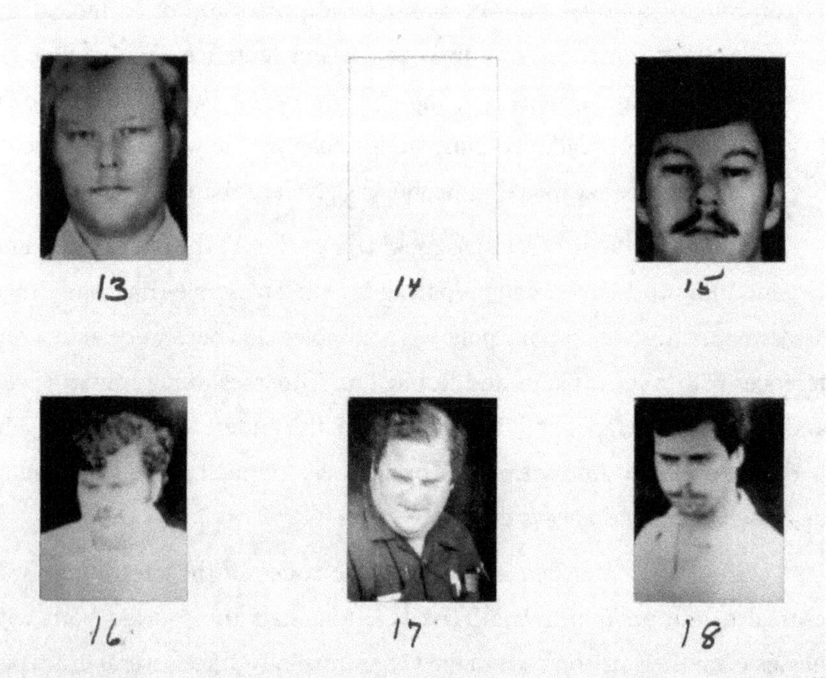

Clockwise from top left: Wayne Sanden, Robert Groblewski, Mark Svendbye, Ray Norton Jr., Donald Stackpole

CHAPTER NINETEEN

TRIALS: LATE 1984–EARLY 1985

The Federal trial of Donald F. Stackpole began on Tuesday, November 6, 1984, in Courtroom Three, assigned to Judge Rya Zobel. Stackpole faced 19 counts of violation of Federal laws. The counts included:

Count 1: Conspiracy to set fire to 220 buildings in the Boston area between February 1982 and April 1984;

Counts 3–17: The following relates to the manufacture and possession of an unregistered destructive device used to set a fire on:

April 3, 1982, to a building at 70 Midway Street, South Boston, MA;

June 3, 1982, to a building at 410 E Street, South Boston, MA (Spero Toy), plus the arson of that interstate facility by means of an explosive;

June 11, 1982, to the American Cellophane building at 165–195 Brookside Avenue in Jamaica Plain, MA;

September 15, 1982, to Patriot Tire Company, at 20 Glenwood Avenue, Hyde Park, MA, plus the arson of that interstate facility by means of an explosive;

September 15, 1982, to a building at 2016 Washington Street in Canton, MA;

October 11, 1982, to a building at 232–234 Roxbury and 13–19 Centre Street, Roxbury, MA;

November 20, 1982, to a building at 154 Rear West Second Street, South Boston, MA, plus the arson of that interstate facility by means of an explosive;

November 21, 1982, to the Gerrity Lumber Company, 8 Whiting Avenue Extension, Boston, MA, plus the arson of that interstate facility by means of fire and explosive;

January 17, 1983, to a building the Boston Sparks Club, 99–101 West Fourth Street, South Boston, MA, plus the arson of that interstate facility by means of fire and explosive;

Count 22: The attempt to obstruct justice by counseling co-conspirator Joseph Gorman to testify falsely before the grand jury;

Counts 23 and 24: Conspiracy to obstruct justice by attempting to cause co-conspirator Robert Groblewski to flee and hide prior to his sentencing, as well as the actual attempt to obstruct justice; and

Count 25: The submission of phony Detex time clock tape records before the grand jury in an effort to support a false alibi.[20]

Most of the following information relating to the Federal trial of Donald Stackpole was derived from the trial transcript of *United States of America v. Donald Francis Stackpole,* CR-84-0242-Z, as transcribed by Official Court Reporter James E. McLaughlin. The remainder of the recounting of the trials comes from my recollections and from the various interviews that I conducted for purposes of this book.

Day One started with motions being heard by the judge from both attorneys, John F. Herlihy, Jr., for the defense and Mark E. Robinson and Ralph D. Gants for the prosecution. Some motions were the usual and customary ones, such as asking for the defendant to be able to sit at the defense

---

20 Appeal of Donald Francis Stackpole v. US of America, pp. 2–4, by AUSA Ralph D. Gants

table during the trial. The motion was granted with no discussion from the prosecution.

The defense wanted all witnesses to be sequestered, including all of the Federal agents that worked on this case. That would have meant that Phil Tortorella, Terry Barry, Jimmy Karolides, and I, who all spent many hundreds of hours of our lives working on this investigation, would not be able to sit in the courtroom until after we testified as a witness, if we were indeed even called to testify. Witnesses are often excluded from sitting in the courtroom from the beginning of the trial to prevent them from being influenced by other witnesses or evidence, to stop a witness from learning new information, or to keep the witness from altering his/her testimony to correspond to the stories of others. It was argued that we already knew all of the witness testimony and the evidence plus our testimony was rather predictable, such as introducing a piece of evidence. After much discussion, the ruling to sequester all witnesses, except us Agents, was made by Judge Zobel.

The remainder of Days One and Two were spent seating a jury. Since there had been so much media coverage of this case during the epidemic of arsons in 1982 and 1983, including the arrests and motivations of the high-profile arson ring conspirators, both the prosecution and defense wanted to choose jurors that they felt would suit their purposes best. It was a fairly lengthy process.

Mr. Herlihy asked for an extraordinary 100 peremptory challenges. Both parties to a trial get to challenge potential jurors for basically two types of challenges, one for cause (such as the impartiality of the juror), and the other peremptory, wherein no reason has to be given for the challenge. There is usually no limit to cause challenges, but peremptory challenges in Federal Court are often limited to three unless the judge allows more. Judge Zobel granted 10 peremptory challenges in this trial. Attorney Herlihy said that he would settle for 50, but the Judge quelled any further discussion saying that he may get a few more than 10, end of discussion.

Next came individual voir dire of the prospective jurors. Voir dire, from the French meaning "to speak the truth," is a preliminary oral questioning of potential jurors to test their qualifications and fitness to serve on the jury in an attempt to seat a fair and impartial jury. Judge Zobel had a long list of questions that she planned to ask the prospective jurors. The following are the types of questions that were posed to the candidates:

Have you read or heard anything about this case?

Do you know anybody that has been affected by an arson fire?

Have you worked for a fire department or law enforcement agency?

Do you know what a sparkie is? (One person answered a dog.)

Do you know what a fire buff is? (One answered a fire bug.)

Do you have strong feelings about Proposition $2^1/_2$?

Do you have any feelings relative to the truthfulness of a witness who has been convicted of a felony?

Do you have any feelings relative to the truthfulness of a witness who has been granted immunity before they testify?

Do you have strong feelings about gun control laws?

Can you accept that the defendant is innocent until proven guilty?

Of course, there would be variations on these questions and follow-up questions depending upon certain answers. Once the jurors and alternates were tentatively selected at the end of Day 2, the judge asked one final question: "Would you please look over the list of names that you have just found on your seat and tell me whether you know any of these people after you have looked at the list?" Nobody responded in the affirmative. The jury was then sworn in, and the remaining prospective jurors were dismissed. The jury of 12 had been impaneled, and four alternates were also chosen in case any of the 12 had to be excused once the trial was underway. The stage was set, the actors were all rehearsed and prepared, the director was on the bench, and the curtain was raised.

To end Day 2, AUSA Robinson gave his opening statement. He eloquently laid out the conspiracy, the fires, and the crimes for which Stackpole had been indicted. AUSA Robinson also explained about the investigation and the co-conspirators who would be witnesses for the government, Gregg Bemis and Robert Groblewski. As I read the trial transcripts, I could actually hear the voices of AUSA's Mark Robinson and Ralph Gants with their inflections and accents. Although the transcripts are fairly long, I recommend reading at least parts of them if you get the chance.

Courtroom Three was packed; every seat was taken. There was no standing room allowed. Tickets could have been sold for this show. Besides other attorneys, both Federal and local, and lots of press, there were family members and Boston Firefighters, some of whom had been seriously injured while fighting fires set by the arsonists. There were even several retirees in the crowd who figured the trial would be unlike any they would see again.

To begin Day 3, Attorney Herlihy presented his opening statement. He succinctly portrayed his client as the good guy who had been wronged by an overreaching government. And as for those friends who became government witnesses, according to Herlihy, they would say anything to protect themselves.

Finally, the government called its first witness, the youthful, but already well-experienced in life 24-year-old Gregg M. Bemis. The first questioning covered Gregg's prison sentences of 30 years on the Federal charges that ran concurrently with his 15-to-20-year sentence on state charges. The government's attorney, Mark Robinson, continued with a well-choreographed questioning of his star witness. The testimony worked its way from Gregg's upbringing, to his love of all things relating to fires and firefighting and on to his becoming friends with the defendant and the other co-conspirators.

Bemis was a natural on the witness stand. If he was nervous in front of the crowd or in his role as a witness for the prosecution, he didn't show it. His responses were clear and concise during the direct examination portion of his testimony. He never hesitated or stumbled. There was not even a hint of embarrassment from the former law enforcement officer. When the questions came about his agreement with the government, Gregg nonchalantly stated that he received a 30-year sentence in exchange for his full cooperation, including testimony. He testified that he knew he could be eligible for parole in 10 years, but he had no agreement or promises for a reduced sentence based on his cooperation.

AUSA Robinson asked about fire after fire, never leading the witness. He repeatedly asked, "What details do you remember about that fire?"

Gregg's responses were intimately detailed. He explained who made the device and who went into each building. He described most of the structures, down to the holes in the walls and the floors. Bemis painted the picture with sharp strokes for the jury. He explained where the device was placed, how long it took for the building to emit fire, and whether they sparked the blaze. Gregg's testimony served as the building blocks for the evidence, except these blocks were being constructed with heavy equipment, not hands. From my point of view, his testimony was a thing of beauty.

All in all, Bemis testified that he, himself, was present at most of the fires, while Stackpole participated in almost half of the arsons. Using large charts with each fire listed in chronological order, Bemis was allowed to come off the stand to explain his testimony.

Gregg was asked to explain why he and his friends would set several fires in one night. As an example, Bemis listed fires for the night of June 24 into early June 25, 1982, the day my second daughter was born. It was also the night that they burned six buildings.

Bemis told the jury that their plan was to set one fire in one part of the City, with maybe a second in the same area to force several apparatus to respond to that neighborhood, and, then set another fire in a different fire district to stress the Fire Department and cause increased response times to the additional fires. The delayed response with limited numbers of pieces and firefighters resulted in the fires growing larger in size. The out-come of the larger blazes and the multiple fires meant more media cover-age. The increased attention from the press was their ultimate goal because the news coverage usually highlighted the plight of the drastically under-manned and underequipped Fire Department.

Bemis described the incendiary device with the addition of the tires. Court adjourned for the day at 12:56 p.m. Trial was scheduled for 9:00 a.m. to 1:00 p.m. each day because Judge Zobel had other duties to attend to during the afternoon. This allowed both sides an opportunity to prepare for the next day.

Usually, after grabbing lunch at one of the local restaurants, AUSA's Mark Robinson and Ralph Gants worked with Terry Barry and me for several hours. We all spent hours prepping Bemis for the next day's work and his eventual cross-examination. Routinely we completed our work between 6 and 9 p.m. Somehow, I rarely felt tired most of the time. And I hadn't started drinking coffee until years later, plus I rarely drank soda. We didn't have Red Bull or 5-Hour ENERGY drinks back then.

Day 4 of the trial, Friday, November 9, began with a demonstration video of the making and lighting of the incendiary device. ATF Agent Jimmy Karolides and Boston Fire Lt. Steve McLaughlin had created the demonstration at the Boston Fire Academy on Moon Island. On the day of the demonstration, I witnessed the display. As the Coleman fuel within the incendiary ignited, flames swirled robustly around the tire well. Plumes of acrid black smoke from the burning tire billowed into the sky carried by the breeze. This was quite impressive to the jury. The video demonstration highlighted the immense destructive potential of the device.

Tires can be difficult to ignite unless there is a competent first fuel that comes in contact with the tire with sufficient heat energy to volatize the petroleum products that compose the tire. Once the tire ignites, it contributes a fierce flame to the fire dynamics scenario. In our test, with the tire leaning against a concrete wall (which is noncombustible unless a nuclear device detonates), the heat generated by the combination of the Coleman Fuel and the burning tire caused rapid expansion of encapsulated water that is always present in concrete. The water started to boil inside the concrete causing it to spall or explode in bits and pieces, suddenly shooting shards of concrete outward in a shotgun bird-shot pattern directly toward our viewing position. We all scurried backward to escape being hit by the shrapnel. No injuries were reported. Pain and embarrassment were avoided.

Those photos that had been taken during many of the fires when the arsonists had returned to the fire scenes to spark the fires now were being used by AUSA Robinson during the questioning of Bemis. Gregg pointed out Stackpole in many of the photos, some with the fire building blazing in the background. Sure, the photos were taken during the sparking phase of the night, not while the fire was set. However, when Stackpole tried to use witnesses, like his wife, as an alibi witness saying he was home all night, the photos presented irrefutable evidence that Donny was at the scene at some point during the night, not at home.

Gregg's testimony was a reiteration of fire after fire connecting Stackpole to each arson and their conspiratorial ways. Using maps, charts, and photos in conjunction with Gregg's words, the story was being laid bare before the judge and jury.

When the fifth day of the trial convened on the following Tuesday, November 13, the first order of business was the admissibility of the WBZ-TV film shot by Nat Whittemore at the Gerrity II fire in November 1982. There was a lively discussion between AUSA Robinson and Defense Attorney Herlihy before Judge Zobel. Herlihy argued that the video was inflammatory (his actual word) and should not be admissible. AUSA Robinson argued that the video showed the co-conspirators in their natural setting with words and actions that help to establish the conspiracy when used in conjunction with the testimony of Bemis. Herlihy also argued that no sounds heard on the video should be allowed into the record, but the judge ruled against him on both points because it was relevant that Stackpole had said something on the video to Robert Groblewski as he waved his pistol in the air that Bemis had heard at the time and could now testify to as to what he heard.

The morning brought more testimony of fires, including some of those set outside Boston. Bemis laid out in detail the actions of the conspirators on the night of Gerrity II inferno with the playing of the video with the lumpkins on the woodpile. I could see that the jurors' interest had been piqued as they gazed at the movie screen while AUSA Robinson asking Gregg about the particulars. The Bemis narration completed the scene with him on the lumber pile with Donald Stackpole, as Robert Groblewski waved his personal sidearm and Joe Gorman used his jacket to partially cover his face. Ray Norton, who arrived late after the others beckoned him via phone to the fire, was sitting on a nearby lumber pile just outside of the frame of the video.

Bemis testified that he had had several friends in the Boston Sparks Club, but after they started bad-mouthing Groblewski about being involved with the fires, even before he had been arrested, his feelings toward the Club changed. Gregg testified that Grobo had gotten upset because he couldn't believe that the people whom he considered good friends from the Sparks Club were now turning against him. Bemis further attested that Stackpole never liked the Club, but now he and the rest of the arsonists felt that it was time to take action against the Club by burning it.

It seemed strange to me that Bemis and his cohorts were angry that Club members had turned against Groblewski because he may have been involved with the Boston arson spree. Here were the criminals, setting fire after fire, who felt so strongly for their cause and felt that they had a right to get upset about the snub by the Club. That warped and upside-down thinking certainly took a tremendous amount of gall.

Bemis answered questions relating to the nicknames used by the group. Of course, Bemis was "Mr. Flare." AUSA Robinson asked Bemis, "Did Mr. Stackpole have any names that he used to call the investigators, the Arson Squad, or the ATF?"

The witness answered, "Yes. He used to refer to them as nitwits." We investigators had become aware of our moniker, deserved to some degree because it took us so long to solve this case, but what I was thinking as I watched the trial unfold was, who is the nitwit now?

Next, testimony concentrated on the agreement among the group to lie to investigators and the Federal Grand Jury and on the schemes that were discussed for alibis. Bemis detailed the plans to move Groblewski plus the plans to eliminate him and others as necessary to escape from the justice system.

Just before the scheduled end of Trial Day 5, Robinson completed the government's questioning of Bemis. The judge instructed Attorney Herlihy to start his cross-examination of the witness.

Immediately, the attorney asked Bemis questions that emphasized how Gregg appeared to have skewed portions of his testimony. Herlihy had to make Bemis appear to be a liar for the government who was just trying to save his ass from many years of incarceration. Bemis admitted that he had worked with investigators for several hundred hours after he became a government witness preparing for the legal proceedings. We always hoped that a jury could see through that tactic; the preparation of witnesses was key to putting on a good, competent presentation.

Further, Attorney Herlihy highlighted the potential maximum sentence and fines that Gregg could have faced, that is, 735 years in prison and $735,000 in fines, had he not cooperated with the government: "...with no prospect whatsoever on this green earth of ever making bail. And you were one scared kid, weren't you?" I have to admit that I would have crapped my pants if facing that daunting dilemma.

For some reason, AUSA Robinson chose not to introduce the Mr. Flare letter during the direct examination of Bemis. Well, Mr. Herlihy decided to try to make hay with it.

Day 6 of the trial began with Gregg Bemis on the stand for his fourth day of testimony. Herlihy whacked away at Gregg for leading the band of arsonists at every turn. And he wasn't way off base with that line of questioning!

Bemis had been the one who griped the most about the Prop 2½ cutbacks, although Stackpole was the one who suggested that the only way to make the people listen was to set a lot of fires. Bemis had been the one who came up with the incendiary device. He had been the one who chose more target buildings than all other group members combined. It was his car that had been used the most while traveling to set the fires, partly because he knew the streets. He was the one who bought the supplies for the incendiary device and stored them in his mock cruiser. Gregg had also been the person who took the most photos of the fires; that was mainly because he was the only member of the group to be present at over 250 of the 264 arson fires. No wonder the U.S. Attorney's Office offered Bemis 30 years for his full and complete cooperation and testimony.

Attorney Herlihy picked at Bemis, hammering home the fact that he liked to set fires, not just for the motive related to Prop $2^1/_2$, but because he liked fires, the flames, and the destruction, and he liked having the power with "the City in the grips of his hands." When Herlihy pressed Bemis about the group's objective, which was to have an impact on the law of the land, and insisted that after months of setting fires they had, in fact, failed to influence the law, Gregg fired back. Here, during his trial in late 1984, more than 30 months after the arson conspiracy was formed, Bemis stated with authority that he believed that the group's setting of fire after fire was solely responsible for the passage of the so-called Tregor Bill, which eased some of the tax shortfalls.

Herlihy pounced on that response, "So you think you did a good public service? You're proud of yourself?"

"No, I'm not proud of myself."

"But you think you did a good—you're the sole reason for—one of the major reasons for the Tregor Bill passing?"

"Yes," responded Gregg.

Herlihy wanted to drive his point home, "What a price to pay. How many firemen were injured?"

Bemis stated with no hesitation, "Several hundred."

As he shook his head in wonderment, Herlihy repeated for weighted effect, "Several hundred firemen injured." Shortly thereafter, Attorney Herlihy stated that he had no further questions.

AUSA Robinson cleaned up a few points with Bemis on redirect examination. For instance, he asked Bemis about his expectations regarding any reduction in sentence because he was cooperating (no expectation). When asked about framing Stackpole, Bemis explained that when he agreed to cooperate, neither he nor the government knew who would eventually plead guilty or go to trial, so his initial information was not aimed directly at Stackpole. Gregg cleared the air relative to any lies or false testimony; he stated that if he lied at all since the agreement was made, the deal would be off and he could incur additional jail time. After a short re-cross-examination from Attorney Herlihy, Bemis was excused after nearly four days on the witness stand.

As a critique of his testimony, overall he did extremely well. He never got flustered. He barely hesitated. Under the cross-examination barrage, he kept his anger under wraps, but he stood his ground and didn't falter under the onslaught. Only time would tell how well his testimony played with the jury. The proof would be in the verdict.

But there was far more to this trial to come. Mr. Bemis was a fact witness; the next witness to be called was as an expert witness. A witness who is called as an expert has to have special training, education, and experience to qualify as a witness.

ATF Explosives Enforcement Officer Tom Cousins testified that the incendiary device used by the conspirators fit the criteria of a destructive device or explosive as defined by Federal law. Under the Gun Control Act of 1968 (GCA), and the National Firearms Act (NFA), registration is required to possess certain firearms and explosive or incendiary devices, and a license is required to manufacture them. This means anyone, barring some disqualifying factor, could possess certain weapons or explosive devices if one would only choose to register them. As an example, one can own a fully automatic machine gun, as long as it is registered (and state law is also followed).

In an effort to provide effective counsel, Mr. Herlihy had some obligatory questions to challenge the expertise of the witness and other inquiries to contest whether the Mr. Flare device met the legal definition of an unregistered incendiary device. Although Attorney Herlihy tried to muddy the water, the evidence was fairly straightforward that these guys had manufactured an incendiary device, in violation of Federal laws, approximately 250 times during their arson spree.

On the same day, Boston Fire Deputy Fire Chief John "Jack" White testified that he was also the Fire Marshal for the City in charge of the Fire Prevention Division, including the Arson Squad. Chief White spoke of policy and procedures of the Department, particularly regarding hiring. The Chief clarified that there were physical requirements that possibly could have excluded Stackpole from being hired and that a felony conviction barred someone from being considered for the position.

Chief White recollected that by 1982 some 600 firefighter positions out of about 1900 were lost due to the Proposition 2½ cutbacks, about 275 through layoffs and the rest through an incentive retirement offering. There was no hiring of recruits for at least a couple of years. Also, he said, 22 out of 75 fire companies were disbanded until funds were restored.

Chief White provided a BFD viewpoint of the extraordinary number of dumpster fires in 1981 and 1982—2,600 and 2,500, respectively—and compared that with the number in 1983, which dropped to about 1,600. Besides the high numbers of these fires, an unusual pattern had formed wherein the fires were in the high-rent district of places like the Back Bay, where many dumpsters in a row burned nearly simultaneously. The Chief recounted the sharp uptick in multiple alarm fires that occurred in vacant buildings mainly after midnight, under the cover of darkness on certain days of the week. He provided the opinion that most of these fires were intentionally set because there were no inherent ignition sources within these abandoned buildings and the fires were often heavily involved upon arrival by the FD.

Chief White testified that a pattern was noticed wherein many of the fires were set around closed fire stations, plus fires pulled apparatus to one area of the City with additional fires set elsewhere so that the first response would be delayed. This indicated that the perpetrators had knowledge of fire department procedures and likely monitored the FD radios. The Chief also described finding tire remains at the fire scenes and the abnormally high number of voice call fire boxes that disappeared in 1982 (15) compared with one in 1980 and one in 1981.

Chief White was above all else a Boston firefighter, one with many years' experience. Jack described for the court how the smoke inhalation that he suffered from the Spero Toy fire affected him. The Chief was one of 33 jakes injured during that fire. A fire officer in a Boston Fire Department uniform of Chief White's stature and demeanor made an impressive witness. Attorney Herlihy asked a few superfluous questions of the Chief; he knew it was not a good idea to screw with this witness.

Next up on Day 6, the government called as a witness a good friend, WBZ-TV videographer Nat Whittemore. Nat testified about his job shooting video of numerous fires during 1982 and 1983. A good deal of time was expended on his knowledge of the subjects of the arson ring. Nat explained how he noticed the uptick in fires in towns that were adjacent to Boston that required mutual aid from Boston. He detailed the way the order in which the fires were set tied up the short-handed Boston units, resulting in delayed responses to the fires. Nat also shot video of the devastating E Street Military Barracks fire and rescue of the injured firefighters.

A highlight of his testimony was his observations of Stackpole and the others on the woodpile at Gerrity Lumber. Nat told the court that he had been in fear of his life when Groblewski momentarily pointed his handgun in his direction. The video was then introduced, with Nat as narrator. The visual left a lasting impression on the jury, although without the testimony of the co-conspirators the video evidence proved nothing. Nat described how he notified the authorities about the video, which he authenticated for the Court.

The following day the next witness was the always interesting Elliot Belin, one of the most well-known sparks at the time. He had no official paid position at the BFD for the longest time; he just worked there. It was a unique situation. He knew so much about the Boston fires, an expertise that some of the BFD brass took advantage of. Eventually, he did get a paid position.

Elliot always had an unusual relationship with Stackpole and the arson ring. They would bust his chops to his face and behind his back. They liked him, but also made fun of him. They confided in him, but not to the point of admitting they were setting fires, because they all knew he would strongly oppose taking their protest to that level.

Belin also had a way with words along with a gift of gab. On several occasions in the 1980s and 1990s, I spoke with Elliott. Each visit was entertaining because he never ceased to amaze me with his knowledge and word usage.

A minor issue arose with his personality on full display during the trial. Initially, the questioning of Elliot centered upon his knowledge of people who had problems with Stackpole and issues with the official Sparks

Clubs. Elliot didn't have a lot of specific information, but his responses to the questions posed by AUSA Robinson often went beyond the scope of the inquiry. Rightly so, Attorney Herlihy objected to several responses and the line of questioning by Robinson, which seemed to stretch legal limits on relevance. Numerous objections by Herlihy during Belin's testimony were sustained. I felt that Judge Zobel performed her job better than I had seen any other trial; she was extremely fair and judicious to both sides throughout the proceedings.

Elliot spoke of his sightings of Stackpole at fires and conversations with Stackpole after the arrest of Groblewski and before his appearance before the Grand Jury. Also, Donny used Elliot when he asked Elliot to provide details of the dates and times for several fires. Stackpole needed that information so that he could make up his phony alibis with the Detex tapes.

Elliot offered an especially interesting explanation to the question from Robinson, "Was there anything unusual about their [Stackpole's and his arson pals'] conduct at fire scenes?"

"There's sort of an unwritten rule of conduct on the fire ground" he answered. After an objection from Herlihy, which the judge overruled, Elliot continued, "There's a certain decorum that if you're going to go to a fire regularly, you just stand back and you don't really get too abhorious [sic] about it. It's not a spectator-type of sport thing. But Bobby and Donny acted more like this was a spectator sport, like they were a cheering section at some sort of a game. The problem was that they sort of cheered for the visiting team."

AUSA Robinson asked, "What do you mean by 'the visiting team'?"

"Well, they actually cheered for the fire."

"As opposed to the firefighters?"

Elliot responded emphatically, "Exactly."

Attorney Herlihy took a great deal of time during his cross-examination of Belin trying to show the jury that the way Elliot acted, dressed, and drove around in a mock cruiser was essentially no different than the same mannerisms exhibited by Donald Stackpole. His actions didn't equate to being an arsonist, but that was the point of the questioning.

Cambridge Fire Investigator Ed Fowler testified to his sightings of Stackpole and his friends at various fires. Besides being a spark himself and a professional photographer, Fowler's expertise as a fire investigator also allowed him to testify about observing some of the fires during their incipient stage, where he made observations of the fire's point of origin. Eddie was even able to see a couple of tires burning at the base of the fires.

On cross-examination, Attorney Herlihy tested Fowler's memory about seeing Stackpole at certain fire scenes. He also wanted to know which if any of Stackpole's actions at any of these fires made him a suspect in Eddie's mind. Except for his seeing Stackpole and the others fairly early at many of the fires combined with the odd behavior by the group members, Fowler admitted that he had nothing but a hunch. And what a hunch it was!

At this point, on Day 8, the government made a pitching change. AUSA Ralph Gants had been tasked with questioning businesspeople who owned buildings that had been affected by the arsons set by Stackpole and others of the arson ring conspiracy. The purpose of this testimony was to provide evidence that the burned businesses affected interstate commerce. This was done to satisfy that element of the Federal law.

For instance, Signal Industries, which operated at 154 West Second Street in South Boston, purchased urethane foam from Baltimore to manufacture foam coverings for clothes hangers and foam padding for clothing. They sold these items to a distributor in New York and elsewhere. Thus, the business within the building that was damaged by the fire affected interstate commerce. The questioning was brief, clear, and concise, with very little cross-examination as this was merely a formality of the law that was either a fact or not a fact.

Another business, Patriot Tire Company, which burned in Hyde Park in September 1982, was represented. Some 2,000 to 4,000 tires were damaged in that fire. The witness testified that the losses incurred in that fire forced the business to close 13 months after the fire. After this somewhat sorrowful direct testimony, Attorney Herlihy had no questions for the witness. The wanton destruction of the arsons had just been humanized for the jurors.

The next witness added another face that was directly affected by the June 1982, Spero Toy Company fire in South Boston. That face belonged to Richard Sparrow, a firefighter who had been assigned to Ladder Company 29. Mr. Sparrow testified that he had been on a two-story section of the building cutting a hole in the roof, attempting to ventilate smoke and toxic gases from the building. He testified that suddenly, without warning, his entire right leg and his right side up to his back fell through a collapsed section of roofing. After being pulled from the hole by other firefighters, Firefighter Sparrow continued his duties, completing his shift.

After going home to get some sleep, Mr. Sparrow awoke in terrible pain, hardly able to move his right leg or lower back. Those injuries caused him to miss work for two months with physical therapy and associated treatments. Firefighter Sparrow explained that the pain continues as of the day of his testimony, although he was able to return to full duty. There was no cross-examination of this witness.

The last witness of the day to be questioned by AUSA Robinson was sure to keep the attention of the jury; it was one of the prosecution's star witnesses, convicted felon, arsonist, former Boston cop, 27-year-old Robert F. Groblewski. However, after Groblewski had been on the stand for only a few minutes, the Court was adjourned for the day, scheduled to reconvene on Monday morning. In that short time, he was asked about his arrest, his indictment, his decision to plead guilty (with particulars about his plea agreement with the government), and his prison sentences.

Monday, November 19, 1984, was Day 9 of the trial. Grobo began that day's testimony by stating that he was in the Federal Witness Protection Program while serving his 12-year prison sentence. His testimony was similar to that of Bemis, but Bobby was not as crisp as Gregg was in the details. He added a few tidbits, though, that Bemis never mentioned about Stackpole. Donny allegedly was the one who provided Mr. Flare with a Hispanic flair, nicknaming Gregg "Gasoline Gomez." Groblewski also testified that Stackpole would refer to one of their busy nights of setting several fires by quipping, "Pyros was out tonight," jokingly referring to a made-up Greek god of fire or implying that a person with a compulsion to set fires was busy.

Multiple times, AUSA Robinson was forced to rehabilitate Bobby, meaning that he had to clarify previous misstatements and erroneous testimony because Grobo had made quite a few mistakes concerning who was with him at certain fires. Some of the errors came well after midnight on the night of his arrest, when we recorded his first confession while he was in a state of shock. Whatever the reason, his testimony certainly was not as clean and self-assured as that of Gregg Bemis.

At this point in the trial, Groblewski answered one of the questions that had perplexed everyone who had seen the Whittemore video of Grobo waving his gun in the air at the Gerrity II fire. When asked by AUSA Robinson what prompted him to take his gun out, Bobby responded, "I don't know. All the yelling and screaming. We were just acting crazy." He was just caught up in the exuberance and being an idiot. It was a very regrettable act, but he didn't know that he had been captured on film until it was too late.

Groblewski continued to testify on direct examination about various fires, about being caught with the stolen firebox in his apartment after the Gerrity fire, and about the group's reactions after Grobo failed the polygraph exam.

On Tuesday, November 20, 1984, AUSA Robinson asked Bobby numerous questions concerning his involvement with the undercover recordings that he made at our direction. They went over the 12 phone calls and five face-to-face meetings with the various characters.

When Attorney Herlihy cross-examined Groblewski, he instantly attacked Bobby about wearing a wire and recording the phone calls without anyone's consent or knowledge at the other end of the line. Grobo countered that, of course, he wouldn't advise anyone that they were being recorded because it would ruin the investigation.

Herlihy asked Bobby whether he had fun doing the undercover work, to which he replied that it was no fun at all and that he was scared by the whole process. To make his point, Attorney Herlihy read the final words from Groblewski on one of the undercover recordings, "That's a wrap, boys. Well, I hope you like what I done." He asked Grobo about how these words sounded like he had been enjoying his role.

Bobby defended his choice of wording: "Instead of saying that's all right, that's all over, I said, 'Okay, that's a wrap.' Just a statement, that's all."

Herlihy retorted, "It's a bum wrap [sic], isn't it."

"*Objection!*" AUSA Robinson jumped to his feet. Herlihy was trying his best theatrics to paint Groblewski as a rat who was just trying to save his own ass at the expense of his innocent friend.

Attorney Herlihy spent the remainder of the day beating Groblewski up about the head and ears with inconsistent statements that were made during his January 13 confession, the undercover recordings, his Grand Jury testimony, and his trial testimony. To be fair, there was a tremendous amount of information to organize concerning 264 fires that occurred over two years. Plus, Grobo answered the questions that were asked of him during the Grand Jury and his first confession to the best of his ability. A lot of the details of the fires were unknown to both the investigators and the AUSA's until after Bemis cooperated. Then, there were the debriefings, the trips to the fire scenes, and the undercover recordings. Thus, it was completely understandable that a witness in this situation would not be perfect.

During the afternoon, AUSA Robinson did his best with a litany of redirect questions for Bobby to clarify the confusion sown by Attorney Herlihy. Defense counsel was only trying his best to do his job with the mess in front of him. The day ended during the redirect questioning, which meant Groblewski should have been back on the stand in the morning.

Day 11 arrived with Grobo done. The attorneys and Judge Zobel conferred and agreed that there was nothing further needed from Groblewski. This day saw a parade of witnesses who held the jurors' attention.

The spark friend who had received a voice fire alarm as a present from Grobo was also the one that Stackpole had urged to get rid of the fire box so that the Feds wouldn't find it during the execution of a search warrant at his house. This action by Stackpole amounted to the charge of obstruction of justice. The witness was on the stand for 10 minutes with no cross-examination.

Several more witnesses were called to provide evidence that their burned business had been involved in interstate commerce. Mr. Herlihy stipulated easily provable facts, such as that the Spero Toy Company was a subsidiary of Unicare Services of Wisconsin. Job Lot Wholesale, another subsidiary of Unicare, had also been in the E Street building when it burned. They bought products from Asia, from Mattel, and Ideal Toy, among others, and sold them elsewhere, all of which established the interstate nexus.

AUSA Gants inquired of James Gerrity of Gerrity Lumber Company about the plastic strips that hung over the large door opening to the warehouse that kept pigeons from entering the building and soiling the contents. The importance of getting this testimony before the jury was that it corroborated the testimony of Bemis and Groblewski, who had earlier testified that they entered the warehouse through these hanging strips.

Boston Firefighter Alfred E. Smith of Engine 17 testified about his experience at the same Gerrity fire. Firefighter Smith stated that he was operating the deck gun, which is a heavy stream appliance that sits atop the fire truck and spews water at pressures exceeding 150 pounds per square inch. He related that the nozzle blew off the tip, knocking him off the top of the Engine to the ground some 10-plus feet below. Smith was transported via ambulance to the hospital, where he was treated for back and hip injuries that kept him out of work for over two months.

The importance of this testimonial evidence is that the injury enhances the penalty by double for that particular fire. The testimony of all of the day's witnesses was short and succinct. Plus, Attorney Herlihy did not challenge any of them; he asked no questions whatsoever.

Mr. Zeolla, who along with his brother, owned the building and plumbing business that operated out of 99–101 West Fourth Street, South Boston. They leased space to the Boston Sparks Club in that building, which burned in January 1983. Besides establishing the interstate nexus, Mr. Zeolla testified that as of the date of the trial, nearly two years after the fire, they still had not recovered and rebuilt the structure.

Boston Fire Investigator Leo Marino of the Arson Squad testified that, based on fire patterns and other information, he determined that the fire at the Zeolla building originated on the second floor, which used to be the Tapper Club. He also concluded that the fire cause was incendiary, based upon the locked doors to the building and the fact that there were no potential ignition sources in the area where the fire started.

As an interesting example of the varied work that we investigators performed in order to perfect the criminal cases against these arsonists, Special Agent Richard Cain testified that he executed a search warrant at the home of Donald Stackpole's mother. The object of the search was one New England Telephone Yellow Pages Directory dated 1983. Agent Cain testified he located the phone book in her kitchen. The importance of the book was that it was missing pages 40–46, those sections that included the airlines and airline reservations. Those were the same pages that Stackpole had torn from the phone book when he and Bemis used a payphone at a mall to make plane reservations for Groblewski so he could flee justice by flying out to meet Chris Damon in Ohio. The phone book with the missing pages became evidence of an act in furtherance of the conspiracy and the crime of obstruction of justice. The old expression "The devil is in the details" is apt here; like the related expression "God is in the details," it makes the point that minute details matter.[21] This phone book, although it seems like a small aspect of this massive conspiracy, was at the crux of the work necessary to get this job done right.

The next witness, Boston Police Officer Randall Lamattina, was assigned to the Boston PD Bomb Squad office on D Street in Southie. He was first to discover the November 1982 fire at 154 Rear West Second Street. He testified that he could see piles of trash and tires placed against large loading dock doors that appeared to be the origin of the fire. He also testified that, as he was blocking off the street, a cruiser-like vehicle sped right past his outstretched arms. The vehicle had several antennas on it and the license plate read LAD-5. When he saw that the passenger, who was known to him, was Robert Groblewski, he assumed that they were part of the roving arson investigators who were flooding the streets due to the ongoing arson rampage. Lamattina was upset that they raced past him, and he stated that the vehicle's lights were then suddenly turned off and that the car never stopped at the fire.

I had another connection with Randy Lamattina several months later, in August 1985. Officer Lamattina was attempting to render safe a pipe bomb. In the process, the incendiary explosive device detonated, and Randy's face and hands were caught in the blast with flash fire. Although Randy survived, he suffered the loss of several teeth, three fingers, and second-degree burns, plus multiple medical procedures. I was part of the ATF and Boston Police team that conducted the subsequent investigation.

Canton Fire Lieutenant Anthony Franco testified about several aspects of the night of the barn fire. He testified that Canton Fire Station 2

---

21 Titelman, Gregory, Random House Dictionary of Popular Proverbs and Sayings, Random House Reference, March 5, 1996

is located across the street from a golf course with a loud horn that can be heard up to five miles away when it sounds to call firefighters. Lt. Franco admitted that he was the one who made that famous statement when he first observed the fire, “It’s going to the moon!” He also stated that about 150 homes had to be evacuated because of the PCB air contamination from old transformers stored in the barn. His information again confirmed the testimony of Groblewski and Bemis.

I took the stand for a few minutes to close out the day. My testimony was not all that exciting, except for one semi-famous line. AUSA Robinson asked me what was so special about a Special Agent. I was taken aback by his question. I had just taken the witness stand in this implausibly large conspiracy case termed by then United States Attorney William Weld as “the largest arson case in the history of the country,” in terms of the number of fires set by the conspirators. Here I was, a fairly young Special Agent, only 32 years old, some nine years on the job. How do you respond to a rare moment of levity in the normally serious decorum of a Federal courtroom?

Well, several thoughts raced through my head in the seconds I spent fumbling for an answer. As a Federal ATF criminal investigator, I was well trained in my job with some good instincts; did that make a Special Agent special? From the viewpoint of those alleged criminals that we set our sights on, does that make a Special Agent special? To my two daughters at the time, they thought of me as A Terrific Father, their hero, a very special Agent. So, my answer was, “It all depends who you ask,” which drew a snicker from the jury, the gallery, and even Federal Judge Rya Zobel.

I answered questions about interviewing Stackpole when we played a snippet of Grobo’s confession to him about his involvement in the arson ring. The interview tape was played for the jury, wherein there was some discussion with Stackpole relative to Gerrity II and about the Sparks Club fire. Court ended for the day to be resumed the following Monday after the Thanksgiving holiday weekend.

On Day 12, November 26, I retook the stand after the administrative matters were handled. In response to a series of questions, I explained to the jury about the investigation into the June 1982 Spero Toy Company fire and how we didn't start focusing on various subjects as being involved with the arsons until the filming of the group at the Gerrity II fire.

I described the 17 undercover recordings that we had Groblewski make. We played portions of the recordings for the jurors, which should have been somewhat exciting for them. Their attention to the content of the recordings was evident; nobody fell asleep. However, in practice, the process of coordinating the correct spot on the tapes to play for the jurors in conjunction with the proper place for them to read transcripts was tedious. The choreography between the director, AUSA Robinson, and the witness actor, me, broke down a bit at this juncture. It was a little sloppy, but we slogged through it. The evidence came out in the end.

The cross-examination tactic by Attorney Herlihy was interesting, to say the least. When running for president in 1980, Ronald Reagan promised some constituents that he would abolish ATF. Once in office, President Reagan found it difficult to get rid of the Bureau or merge it with other agencies because of the unique niche that ATF occupied. However, as part of his overall strategy, President Reagan did cut budgets across the board.

This is the angle that Herlihy tried to take advantage of by attacking our ATF investigation of this arson ring. He tried to get the jury to question our motivation for making this case at any cost to give ATF a strong foothold in the arson investigation field in order to save the Bureau. I'm a much simpler person. I never thought of the case that way. Rather, I was thinking that there was a major arson problem in Boston that needed to be resolved. That was my focus. Only on the night that Groblewski confessed did I know that this case was huge. It was the biggest case of my career thus far, quite possibly the most important case that I would ever work. If that was good for the Bureau in the long run, then so be it.

Next, Attorney Herlihy attacked the number of investigators, Federal and locals, who worked on this investigation plus the number of hours and dollars that were expended over the course of two and a half years. Again, I just did my job, kept my nose to the grindstone, so to speak, without a thought as to those types of issues. If someone is committing major crimes within ATF's jurisdiction, then time and money have to be expended to solve the crimes. It is the criminal who is causing the government to make those expenditures. Herlihy's strategy on this point yielded little in his client's favor.

As I retired, I finally looked back at the cases that I worked on and marveled about how few significant cases one gets to investigate during a career. But some of them were big cases that needed to be made. And I was glad to have been part of them.

Herlihy tried to make Groblewski and us look like the bad guys when we used the undercover tool to further the investigation. Actually, it was a good, legitimate move, not entrapment, as Herlihy tried to portray it in front of the jury. In his final jab at the investigation, Herlihy questioned why other so-called sparkies (his word, not mine) were not investigated further and eventually arrested, but no evidence led us in that direction. Again, with what he had to work with, Attorney Herlihy did his best using several approaches to sway the jury in his client's favor. After a short redirect by AUSA Robinson and a couple of re-cross questions, I was excused from the witness stand.

Co-conspirator to obstruction of justice, 28 year-old Ohioan Christopher Damon, was called to the stand. Damon testified that, as of the time he was testifying, he intended to plead guilty to the charges. He stated that he had no agreement as of that date and he was told that jail time would be recommended with no term specified. Damon further testified that he had been friends with Stackpole for seven years and that Donald had introduced him to sparking fires around 1976. He said that he had also lived with Groblewski for a short time in the late 1970s. Damon had only moved to Ohio in the spring of 1982, but he had come back to the Boston occasionally later that year, at which time he had gone sparking with Stackpole a few times to some large fires.

AUSA Robinson asked Chris about conversations with Stackpole about Grobo's arrest and the first talk of helping Grobo to flee to Ohio. Damon recounted how in June 1984 Donny had called him in Ohio asking him to help get Bobby out of Massachusetts. Damon initially balked at the request, telling Donny that life was good for him now with an important job, but he would think it over. When Stackpole called him back a week later, Damon said that Donny was noticeably more uneasy, with Bobby's sentencing date about 10 days away, telling him that Bobby had the goods on him that could implicate him. Donny was quite nervous that Bobby might talk to the authorities unless they got him out of town. Chris also explained his remaining calls with both Groblewski and Stackpole, including the final call from Grobo advising him that he was not going to flee; he was going to take his prison sentence. That was welcome news to Damon.

Over the next couple of days, there was a parade of lesser witnesses who supplied testimony and evidence to fill in any gaps and to provide corroboration to previous testimony.

But notably on Day 13, the fourth co-conspirator to become a witness in this trial, Joe Gorman, was called to the stand. Gorman admitted to the jury that he had been involved with about 10 percent of the fires set by the arson ring. Joe testified that when he rode around with his pals at the onset of the conspiracy when they were using the pellet gun to shatter car windows in their early protest effort to affect Proposition 2½ cutbacks, he didn't really care about the law. He said that from his viewpoint he was vandalizing the cars just for kicks.

Gorman also stated that when the first building fires had been set by other members of the group, Donny told him that he might as well join them setting structure fires because if the others ever got caught, he would also go down with them for his involvement in the dumpster fires. Donny tried to convince him by adding that arson was the hardest crime to prove, that investigators would virtually have to catch a person with a match in their hands. At that point, Gorman acquiesced to Stackpole's arguments and joined in the fire-setting.

The remainder of Gorman's direct testimony, on Day 14, mirrored Groblewski's and Bemis's in miniature, as Gorman's involvement was vastly less than the other two. The importance of Gorman's testimony was that the jurors got to hear from another past friend of Stackpole who provided an additional viewpoint by a co-conspirator.

Attorney Herlihy, during his cross-examination, exhorted Joe about his inconsistencies in his testimony and how his cooperation agreement protected him from the potential of being behind bars for up to 50 years. Gorman had received a 10-year sentence for the conspiracy charge and one fire, but he never actually set a single fire. Herlihy unleashed a furious fusillade on the witness for most of the morning. Joe, in his laid-back style, held steadfast under the browbeating by defense counsel. Herlihy worked extremely hard to make Gorman, as well as Groblewski and Bemis, look like the lowest worms that crawled this earth for cooperating with the government to save themselves from longer prison sentences.

Gorman was the last government witness. After a few stipulations by both sides, the government rested. The Court recessed.

After the recess, it was the defense's turn. Herlihy's first witness was a relative of Stackpole's who testified that Donny had used the Detex clock during his security rounds. This witness, who worked for Metro Security for a short time, also testified as an alibi witness for the Gerrity II fire, saying that he was with Donny until 4:00 a.m., well after the lumberyard was set afire. This testimony was designed to show that the quartet of co-conspirator witnesses either were all wrong or all lied during their testimony. We were all a little surprised when the witness testified that he saw Groblewski with an Uzi machine gun, "It's the type I've seen the CIA carry." I found that statement interesting since it was unclear when he saw the CIA with an Uzi. Never once did we ever have any information from any other source that Grobo had a machine gun of any type.

The second defense witness was a character witness who was the Program Manager and Director of Human Resources, who had placed a severely emotionally and mentally handicapped woman within the home of Stackpole and his wife. The witness testified that, after rigorous interviews and investigation of the Stackpoles, the woman was placed in their home in August 1983. The testimony painted Donald as a caring, consistent, kind, and patient person even after the client had been in their home for over a year. The witness also stated that Donald was home most of the time when visits were made to their residence.

I couldn't help to wonder how this witness's testimony would play with the jury. Keep in mind that we investigators had conversed with dozens of people who had nothing good to say about Donald Stackpole. Even his so-called friends, his closest co-conspirators, had few positive comments about Donny's character. Maybe the thousand dollars a month that the state paid to the Stackpoles for their services made Donny a kinder, gentler person. On cross-examination, the witness stated that their investigation into Donald Stackpole never revealed that he was a convicted felon. It seemed that this single revelation brought out by AUSA Robinson in just a couple of questions may have tarnished the reputation of Donny all over again and diminished the quality of that "rigorous investigation."

Mrs. Donald Stackpole, Melody, was the next person to testify. She and Donald had met about 11 years before the trial when she was 16 years old. When they were dating, Donny would take Melody to the HoJo's parking lot to go sparking. They would wait for a fire to come in, but if one didn't, the two would grab a hot dog and head home. I guess, in addition to all the nice things we had just heard about Donny, he could also be a suave and debonair fellow, although not a big spender. But in his defense, many of us know how we had to scrimp during our young dating years.

As a dutiful wife, Melody testified that she specifically recalled that her husband was home on the nights of the Spero Toy fire, the Canton barn fire, and the Boston Sparks Club fire. She also admitted that she had no recollection about the nights of the other fires that Donald had been charged with. She stuck by her story in spite of the contradictory testimony of several other witnesses. Upon completion of her testimony, the defense rested.

The night of April 3, 1982, with the two Midway Street fires, one at #70 and the other one next door at #72, became an interesting point of contention to end the evidentiary portion of the Stackpole trial. Attorney Herlihy introduced a certified copy of the National Weather Service report indicating that sunrise on the morning of the fires was at 5:24 a.m. There had been a discussion as to whether Stackpole was at one of these fires, with one of these fires taking place in the middle of the night and the other one occurring near dawn.

So AUSA Robinson called Boston Fire Lieutenant Paul Hurley as a rebuttal witness to solidify the issues surrounding those two fires. Lt. Hurley was assigned to Engine 39 on the night of those fires. His company fought both fires, but after fighting the first blaze at #70, they returned to quarters. The fire at #72 came in a short time later at 4:51 AM. A photograph was in evidence that portrayed, in part, Lt. Hurley at one of the fires. He testified that based upon the darkness and the flames coming out of the front windows of the building, that this was the first fire of the night.

On cross-examination, Attorney Herlihy pushed Lt. Hurley to the point of absurdity. He asked Hurley how he could distinguish which fire was shown in the photo. Was it the difference in how the buildings looked before the fire? No, the lieutenant responded, it was just the darkness and the fire extending from the windows.

Herlihy persisted, "So darkness is an important factor, correct, in your judgment that it's 70 rather than 72?" Lt. Hurley replied that it was a factor because it was getting light out when they responded to the fire at #72. He further testified that the call for the fire came in at 4:51 a.m. So

Attorney Herlihy tried to pull a Perry Mason moment when he produced the U.S. Weather Service report that showed that sunrise on that day was at 5:24 a.m. "So, the fire started in darkness, you'll agree to that?"

Lt. Hurley refused to agree to that. I guess Herlihy never really got up before dawn because if he had he would have known that the breaking dawn sky lightens up considerably before the actual sunrise. I think every juror who ever woke up before sunrise recognized the folly of his ploy.

But wait, Herlihy wasn't done. He inquired of Lt. Hurley that fire venting from the windows means that there was a fire load burning, correct? Well, of course, there was some fuel, be it contents or combustible parts of the structure itself, was the firefighter's rejoinder.

Perry Mason moment number two was about to be sprung. Lt. Hurley knew that something was burning in the building; he just didn't know what that something was. It was at this time that Attorney Herlihy pulled out the official BFD Field Incident Report for the fire at 70 Midway. It is the same form used by fire departments across the country. Most of the report consists of numbered blocks to be filled in by selecting one or more given choices. Herlihy asked Lt. Hurley to read what was typed under the heading Occupants. There was one word: "Vacant." Counsel then asked if the Deputy Chief who issued the report indicating that the building was vacant was correct in that assessment. Lt. Hurley said it was most likely correct. Herlihy then asked, since the report for 72 Midway said that the occupant was a pallet company warehouse, how fire could be blowing out the windows from a vacant, unoccupied building. Herlihy was trying to create reasonable doubt in the minds of the jurors over this count of the indictment that Stackpole wasn't present for the fire at 70 Midway. Lt. Hurley just shook his head and replied that there could still be plenty of fuel in a so-called vacant building.

Now for the aha moment. AUSA Robinson, on redirect, asked Lt. Hurley about that the term "vacant" as used in the report. It doesn't mean that the building had nothing in it. Rather, it refers to the building not being occupied by an ongoing business or by one or more people living there. Vacant does not mean the building was empty. There could be furniture or other items left behind when the structure was vacated. Think back to all of the vacant building fires set by Bemis and his pals; there often was plenty of wood, trash, and debris inside that made up the fuel load. So a supposedly "vacant" building could burn like hell. I don't know whether Attorney Herlihy had a clue when he pushed this point, or he was smarter than we gave him credit for. How did Herlihy's gambit play with the jury?

This was where the work of AUSA's Robinson and Gants, and the work from our investigators, all came together. We had built a case based on the testimony of four co-conspirators, which was supported by the testimony of innocent witnesses, those not involved with the crimes in any way. We had worked so hard for so long. The case was strong, but would the hard work be properly rewarded?

Attorney Herlihy then asked the Court for a ruling on what amounted to a directed verdict of acquittal. However, Judge Zobel explained that she found all of the government's witnesses credible and that there was sufficient evidence for the case to go to the jury. Further, Judge Zobel ruled that the statements of the co-conspirators would be allowed into evidence as well as the hearsay testimony because of the special hearsay exemption of statements made by co-conspirators. Closing arguments were scheduled for the next day.

First things first, though. The afternoon of Day 14, Judge Zobel listened to Attorney Herlihy's pleas to throw out nearly every count based on innumerable legal arguments, but she denied each contention. She explained in detail to the attorneys what her instructions to the jury would entail. The Judge specified the elements for each count in the indictment. This portion of the trial required the first full hour of the day. Finally, the closing arguments were about to be presented.

Judge Zobel explained this phase to the jury, including that summations are for each side to sum up the evidence that has been presented over the past two weeks. The Judge stated, "... the Government will try to persuade you that it has proven beyond a reasonable doubt each of the elements of each of the offenses that it has charged Mr. Stackpole committed. The Defendant will attempt to persuade you that the Government has failed in its burden of proof."

Both of the attorneys were masterful during their respective summations. AUSA Mark Robinson pounded home the 25 counts against defendant Donald Francis Stackpole. Robinson stressed that the government team, including the ATF Agents, Boston Police and Fire investigators, and the Federal prosecutors, used a two-plus-one rule. In putting the criminal case together, we decided that in order to charge a certain fire, we had to have two witnesses and at least one item of corroborating evidence, such as a Boston Fire Report that pinpointed the origin of a fire.

Robinson emphasized that the inconsistencies in the testimony of the main witnesses shouldn't be viewed as a fault; instead, it is positive proof of the witnesses experiencing the different fires from various viewpoints rather than a well-rehearsed coordination of lies. There were also discrepancies in testimony due to the passage of time, the exceptionally high total number of fires, and the several different lines of questioning over a considerable period.

Defense Attorney John Herlihy reamed the overreaching government with their lying and confused witnesses. Herlihy attacked every aspect of the government's case. He accused us of manufacturing evidence where there was none. Attorney Herlihy made the undercover contacts by Groblewski with Stackpole and others sound like a sin had been committed rather than being a good useful investigative tool. He also asked the jury to consider why we only chose half a dozen or so fires in which to charge Stackpole, when there were hundreds. Why did the evidence seem so weak on these charges? The defense didn't have a lot to work with, but Herlihy worked wonders with the cards he was dealt. Kudos to him for his efforts.

Now, it was time for Judge Zobel to charge the jury. This is the term used when the judge reads and explains instructions to the jury about the law that applies to the facts of the case. This meticulous process took over an hour to detail each count and the elements for the individual law. Upon completion, Judge Zobel sent the jurors to the deliberation room. The jurors spent the remainder of the afternoon deliberating; that is, discussing the evidence and voting on the fate of Stackpole. Late in the afternoon, after a few hours of deliberation, the jurors were dismissed for the evening.

The next morning, Day 15, Friday, November 30, 1984, the jurors continued their deliberations. Just after lunch (who would want to miss a free lunch on the government?), at 2:35 p.m., the jurors came back with the verdict. Donald Stackpole was found guilty of 17 of the 19 counts against him. The man who had often arrived at fires in a red station wagon and dressed as a fire chief was convicted on five arson counts and 12 other charges in connection with the fires for his part of the largest arson ring in the nation's history. He was found not guilty of Count 6, relating to the fire at American Cellophane, and Count 25, presenting the phony Detex tapes to the grand jury. Well, you can't win them all, but we could not understand the verdict on the American Cellophane fire. The photo from that fire was the one I mentioned earlier that served as inspiration every time I looked at it. It even inspired me to write this story, serving as the cover of this book.

The New Year was not looking up for Donald Stackpole. His sentencing date was January 3, 1985. What could he possibly be looking forward to in his life? In the morning, Stackpole pleaded guilty in Suffolk Superior Court to six additional state counts of arson and was sentenced to a term of 19 to 20 years at the Walpole state prison.

In the afternoon, Stackpole, looking like a plump-alump, stood before Federal District Judge Rya Zobel. During sentencing, the judge said, "'These were either acts of terrorism or sheer malice, I don't know which,'" as she sentenced Stackpole to 40 years in Federal prison. All told, he faced about 60 years behind bars. The Federal sentences in 1985 were imposed prior to the establishment of enhanced sentencing guidelines. Stackpole would have been in prison forever under the new system, but under the 1985 rules, he was actually eligible for parole in 10 years. Ironically, Gregg Bemis, the star witness who was sentenced to 30 years, was also eligible for parole in 10 years.

The next stage of the case, the Federal trial of former Boston Firefighter Ray Joseph Norton, Jr., started on January 21, 1985. There were a lot of similarities between his trial and that of Stackpole. And there were also a lot of differences. Norton was only being tried for three counts, not the 19 that Stackpole faced. He was charged with the general conspiracy charge relating to setting the fires. He also faced a perjury charge for his false testimony before the Grand Jury and an aiding-and-abetting charge relating to the fire at the gravel yard across the street from his house. The witness list was similar for both trials. The amount of time in terms of trial days was virtually identical, about 15 days from seating a jury to the completion of presenting the evidence.

AUSA Mark Robinson was the sole prosecutor for the government, as AUSA Ralph Gants had other matters to handle. Special Agent Terry Barry and I were allowed to participate and assist Robinson during the trial.

Norton's attorney, Jack I. Zalkind, now deceased, had a wild knack for theatrics. He would shout, laugh, cry, and wave his arms in gyrations all within a five-minute span. As flamboyant as Attorney Zalkind was, he was a highly intelligent and respected criminal trial lawyer whose career spanned over 40 years.

As in the first trial, sitting in the courtroom gallery each and every day were Manny Gregorio and Ray Martin, two of the jakes who were seriously injured at the E Street Military Barracks back on October 2, 1982. Both men, and rightly so, harbored a great deal of animosity toward the defendants in both trials. Their feelings were a little mixed when it came to listening to the testimony of the co-conspirators turned witnesses, Groblewski and Bemis. As much as Manny and Ray wanted to see the solid testimony from the two witnesses that would help to convict the other defendants, they still despised Gregg and Grobo for what they did to cause such destruction and harm.

Rather than belabor the points covered at the Norton trial, I'll present only the highlights of that trial. Attorney Zalkind was very colorful during his opening, painting Groblewski and Bemis as the most prolific arsonists and liars and arguing that no reasonable person could possibly believe their testimony. Due to Ray Norton's physical and psychological deficiencies, Zalkind explained to the jury, these confessed criminals duped Norton into becoming involved in their dastardly deeds.

Again, as during the first trial, those of us involved in the daily prosecution efforts often left our houses in the dark, about 6:00 a.m., and returned to our abodes in the dark, usually between 7:00 and 8:00 at night. At the end of one of those long days, as I was packing up and preparing to leave the Federal Building, I could not find my car keys anywhere. Befuddled and confused, I headed to my vehicle, parked on the main street just on the other side of Post Office Square, thinking that maybe I had locked my keys in the car.

Light snow had fallen the entire day, coating cold surfaces such as on a car that had been parked all day with about an inch of snow. But, lo and behold, my car was the only one parked on the road that had no snow on it. In fact, my car was toasty warm, as it had been running for the past 10-plus hours, unlocked and untouched! Aah, I may have been losing my mind, but at least I had found my keys! And I didn't even have to clear the windows before I drove off toward home. But I did have to stop for gas on the way home.

AUSA Mark Robinson told the jurors that the evidence would show that Norton didn't join in the conspiracy until after several building fires had already been set by other members of the group. Throughout the testimony of many of the government witnesses on direct examination, Attorney Zalkind must have energetically raised objections about 500 times. Of course, he had the right to object, but his actions seemed designed to disrupt the testimony so that jurors couldn't digest the evidence without interruption. I know his objections irritated me as I observed the trial, and the jurors didn't look particularly enamored with Attorney Zalkind's antics.

During Groblewski's direct testimony, Attorney Zalkind's crush of objections relative to Grobo's conversations in terms of where, when, and what was specifically said were so numerous that Bobby got frustrated. This then exasperated AUSA Robinson, because the plan for well-choreographed testimony from Groblewski was getting sliced and diced by Zalkind's tactics. Attorney Zalkind did have a good argument, though, because if you get a chance to read the transcript, you will see that AUSA Robinson continually asked Groblewski leading questions. On direct examination of a witness, asking leading questions is a no-no. For instance, instead of asking, "What did you do next?" Robinson would ask something like, "Did you drive to the building and set the fire by the front door?"

On cross-examination, as had been done by defense attorney John Herlihy during the Stackpole trial, Attorney Zalkind worked hard to destroy any semblance of the integrity of government witnesses Bemis and, more particularly, Groblewski. Zalkind had an additional tactic of questioning that had not been available to Herlihy. Grobo had written a letter to famous Boston crime author, and former Assistant United States Attorney, George V. Higgins to inquire whether he would be interested in collaborating on a book about this arson case. Zalkind tried to show the jurors that Groblewski was attempting to profit and become famous by writing a book about his crimes. Zalkind also portrayed Bobby as willing to embellish his testimony to enhance the marketability of his intended book.

Attorney Zalkind got Groblewski to admit in open court that, besides being a major arsonist, he was also a thief. Grobo divulged that, although he was a sworn police officer, he assisted Gregg Bemis while stealing copper from the South Boston junkyard that Stackpole's security outfit was hired to protect. He further confessed that he had profited from the sales of the copper by Bemis.

Attorney Zalkind relentlessly sparred with Groblewski over his ill-advised use of firearms at various times during his part of the crime spree. Zalkind skewered Bobby while questioning him about the night in Fitchburg when Grobo pulled his gun when he was nearly caught near the scene of one of the arsons. The two also fenced over the gun-waving incident at Gerrity II and about the use of the pellet gun to shatter a couple hundred car windows during the initial phase of the conspiracy. The jousting was painful to watch and listen to. It was hard to gauge the jurors' reactions to Grobo's testimony. The more Zalkind hammered at Groblewski, the more Bobby looked shifty and evasive. At times, Zalkind had Grobo tied up in knots.

Throughout his cross-examination, Zalkind was letting the jury know that Groblewski had been a police officer who acted more like a criminal. Also, Groblewski had only been charged with a mere fraction of the total crimes that he had perpetrated.

The cross-examination of Grobo brought out a couple of interesting tidbits that provided more fodder for the jury to consider. During his testimony, Bobby confessed that he participated in every aspect of the arson conspiracy concerning setting the fires with the incendiary device except one particular and a rather peculiar facet of the crime. He stated that he never actually placed the incendiary device in any of the targeted buildings, contrary to the information in the Bemis diary. He was psychologically and morally willing to help make the device, carry the device, and light the cigarette that was then laced into the matchbook, but he could not bring himself to actually lay the device next to combustibles within a building. He couldn't quite define this quirk except to say his conscience would bother him. He even had no problem placing the tire at the point of origin, but he could not place the device itself. It sounded like a bunch of bull crap, like he was trying to protect himself from some infamy associated with burning so many buildings. If Attorney Zalkind had only gotten Bemis to testify that Groblewski had, in fact, placed numerous devices, maybe the tide would have turned. Zalkind failed to solicit this specific testimony from Bemis.

At the behest of his attorney, Bobby also had several visits with a psychiatrist between his arrest and sentencing. Attorney Zalkind queried Bobby as to what was wrong with him: "Were you having some sort of trouble with your mind?"

Groblewski responded, "Well, obviously, there was something wrong with me, and I wanted to know what it was.

"Obviously there was something wrong with you?" retorted Zalkind.

"Certainly."

Zalkind persisted, not knowing what response he would receive, a cardinal sin for attorneys. "Why do you think there was anything wrong with you?

Groblewski replied with the most profound statement imaginable, "No one in their right mind would light 200 some-odd fires." That might have been the understatement of this entire case.

Closing arguments were made by the attorneys, AUSA Mark Robinson and defense attorney Jack Zalkind. According to the casting and script, Robinson meticulously enumerated the evidence against Norton with no games, no frills, and no drama. On the other hand, Zalkind was often overly dramatic. His sarcastic remarks filled the courtroom. He bashed both the government's case and the already convicted witnesses. He very nearly came to tears during his emotional explanation of alleged physical and mental challenges that Norton had experienced throughout his life.

After the closing arguments and judge's instructions, the jury began deliberations early in the afternoon on February 11. The jury was adjourned for the day at approximately 5:30 p.m. The next day deliberations began just before 9:30 a.m. At about 4:00, the jury sent questions to the judge, which often signifies that the jurors were still contemplating some issues. However, to our surprise, the jury came in with a verdict at 5:30 p.m. They found Norton guilty on Counts 1, 7, and 21. Sentencing was scheduled for March 29, 1985.

At the sentencing hearing, the government, in one long compound sentence, recommended that Norton be sentenced to 10 years in prison. Conversely, during his turn, Attorney Zalkind worked Judge Zobel over during an extended appeal. He pushed for probation because Lenny Kendall had previously gotten probation after he pled guilty. After all, Kendall had participated in setting a couple of early fires, whereas Norton had not actually participated in setting any fires. Zalkind further argued that Norton should not be penalized by exercising his right to go to trial.

Attorney Zalkind also referred to the April 1985 *Life Magazine* article (which had hit the newsstand in mid-March) about this arson ring. Mr. Zalkind was concerned that Judge Zobel would be influenced by the article, in which the "prosecution's staff" as he referred to AUSA's Gants and Robinson, along with Special Agent Terry Barry and I, were photographed in front of a wall of blazing building fire photos that had been used as evidence in the two trials. However, the Judge admitted that she was unaware of the article.

Again, the theatrical Zalkind was on the verge of tears as he tried to justify the actions of a bumbling Norton, who was never able to overcome numerous psychiatric issues. He brought the Judge all the way back to Ray's childhood. Zalkind detailed Norton's neurological problems that were never treated properly. He said that Ray was always a lost soul who sought recognition. Attorney Zalkind implored the Judge, "I beg of this Court to sentence this man, not the crime."

After listening (and listening some more) to the sentencing recommendations, Judge Zobel, in a brief explanation, stated that she had to balance Norton's many problems with the severity of the overall case and his minimal participation, but that participation occurred while he was a firefighter. Norton was sentenced to concurrent four-year terms for Counts 1 and 7, and he was given two years on and after for Count 21, for a total of six years.

After the final sentencing came in, AUSA's Robinson and Gants, Special Agent Terry Barry, and I went a block over from the courthouse for lunch and a celebratory drink or two. Then, I headed over to the JFK Federal Building, to our main ATF Office. It was my scheduled turn to be the Duty Agent to sit on the radio and phones from 4:00 p.m. to midnight. I arrived at the office just before 4:30. SAC Terence McArdle wanted to speak to me when I showed up. McArdle reamed me out for being late. He told me that he didn't care who I was or what I had just accomplished, I was to be on time for Duty Agent no matter what, even though the office was staffed until 5:00. That response was so typical of a bureaucracy and a bureaucrat.

***LIFE* Magazine photo by Enrico Ferorelli (deceased) for April 1985 *"We Are the World"* Issue**

The federal prosecution team (from left to right) backed by some of the photos of the Boston fires: ATF Special Agent Wayne Miller, Assistant U.S. Attorneys Ralph Gants and Mark Robinson, and Special Agent Terry Barry (In the magazine, AUSA Gants was misidentified as U.S. Attorney Bill Weld)

EPILOGUE

In July 1985, though the trials of Stackpole and Norton were complete, there were still several technical issues to contend with, includ-ing authorizing the release of some evidence and deciding what evidence might still be needed for the potential trial of Mark Svendbye.

On Thursday, November 21, 1985, Svendbye was finally arraigned after being indicted on 14 counts, including conspiracy and his part in setting five fires. These fires caused 13 injuries and approximately $94,000 in damage. Svendbye pled guilty later in 1985. He received a short prison sentence. In one way or another, all evidence had to be disposed of, except anything that had to be held in the event of appeals by Norton and Stackpole.

In a quote to the *Boston Globe*'s Philip Bennett, former Boston Fire Commissioner George Paul stated, "These convictions are probably to a very great extent going to resolve the arson problem as it has existed in this city for a long time."[22] He was right on the money.

22 *Boston Globe,* Philip Bennett, December 1, 1984, p. 1.

By the time the Groblewski file, originally 2403 0883 0002V, then changed to 63210 0883 1002D due to administrative modifications, was closed, the last report was numbered 200. The file was one of the most extensive and voluminous ever in the Boston ATF Office. Altogether, the case covered over two and a half years, with nine defendants who were responsible for 264 building arsons that resulted in over 200 firefighter injuries and $22 million in property damage (early 1980s values).

For a few years after his sentencing, Gregg Bemis used to send Christmas cards to our office, always as a friendly gesture. He kept in touch with Special Agent Terry Barry for years, as they had formed an unusual connection. He never asked anything of us while he was incarcerated. Another unusual connection that Gregg maintained was with reporter Kevin Cullen, then of the *Boston Herald* (now of the *Boston Globe*), who had covered both the Stackpole and Norton trials. For years, Bemis called Kevin so often that the always busy Cullen began to think of him as a nuisance.

Twice in the early 2000s, I ran into Gregg Bemis. Once, in a town west of Boston, we were setting multiple training fires in a building. Gregg was parked in a driveway across the street. He still had friendly contacts in the fire community and had gotten a head's up about the training exercise. When I was made aware that Gregg was there, I walked over to his vehicle. We had an amicable conversation for a few minutes. He was working at the time for a small fire equipment company. Apparently, he still couldn't resist a good fire.

A couple years later, I was with a fire investigator friend of mine at a restaurant north of Boston. As I returned from the men's room to my seat at the bar, a guy playfully stepped in front of me, impeding my path. It was Gregg. He had recognized me as I passed by him. Again, we had a friendly conversation.

Gregg never blamed us for his situation. Once he matured and saw things from a different viewpoint, he knew that we were just doing our job. He had one major objection though; he and his attorney should never have agreed with the U.S. Attorney's Office to take a 30-year prison sentence. The amount of information that he provided, including testimony in two trials, proved vital to obtaining convictions, so the 30-year sentence seemed out of line compared with all other conspirators' sentences. On the other hand, he was the only member of the arson ring that devised the incendiary device that was used at over 250 fires. He was the only one who made the Mr. Flare letter. And he was the only one who was present at nearly every one of the 264 fires. I can tell you for a fact that several firefighters who were seriously injured fighting those fires think Bemis got exactly what he deserved. Eventually, Gregg's sentence was reduced based on his cooperation, and he was released from prison after 11-plus years.

One other point: I think Gregg still takes credit for and thinks of himself as the sole reason that Massachusetts firefighters have the benefits of a new, modern fire academy.

On February 12, 1987, the United States Court of Appeals for the First District, which includes Boston, affirmed the convictions of both Ray J. Norton, Jr. and Donald F. Stackpole. The appeals were not pursued further.

Thus, with the appeals quashed, the case that stunned the citizens of Boston and surrounding towns for the two years spanning 1982 and 1983 was complete. The City of Boston had finally escaped from the extortion plot that held the City hostage for that period. The streets of Boston were certainly quieter. The numbers of multiple alarm fires within Boston have become a mere shadow of the former quantities of the '70s and early 1980s. The number of arsons is dramatically down. There have been a handful of small organized cases involving only a couple of fires. Bostonians' nerves slowly calmed; they no longer were awakened nightly by wailing sirens. Both the Boston Fire and Police Departments have healed from their wounds caused by the defection of members of their ranks who became major felons.

The Boston Sparks Association and other fire buffs have rehabilitated their image after being dragged into the spotlight by the eight local arsonists who had counted themselves as sparks. The hobby of being a spark is no longer confused with being an arsonist. The new club location is a perfect complement to the Boston Fire Museum, both located in the historic Congress Street Firehouse. One day when I visited the club, visitors from all over the country were streaming into the building.

Over the next three decades, the Bureau of Alcohol, Tobacco and Firearms (now the Bureau of Alcohol, Tobacco, Firearms and Explosives) did take on a premier role in the Federal fight against arson. Although the Arson Program has been somewhat downgraded, with the Boston ATF Arson Task Force Group and others having been disbanded, the National Response Team members and other Agents continue to assist state and local agencies with arson and explosion investigations.

I feel that with all of the technology that has been developed in the past 30 years, including social media and so many security cameras that blanket the streets, we will never see such a prolonged, "successful" arson ring operate like the Mr. Flare crew in this country again. Cell phones and vehicles can be too easily tracked today to allow such persistent offenders to commit so many arsons for so long.

Also, the real estate scene in Boston, and Massachusetts overall, as in other major metropolitan areas, is vastly different. There are far fewer vacant structures to tempt would-be arsonists; most are torn down or rehabbed and repurposed. And the empty structures are usually secured with better methods than were employed in the early 1980s. Others were torn down or rehabbed into expensive real estate. The political environment created by Proposition $2^1/_2$, combined with a militant group of sparks who were willing to become criminals, created a perfect storm scenario that hopefully will never be re-created.

Retired Boston Fire Lt. Stephen McLaughlin still resides in an ocean town south of Boston enjoying total retirement. He carries his one-of-a-kind ATF/Boston Fire Department business card in his wallet. He continues to walk several miles every day.

Retired Boston Fire Photographer Bill Noonan also lives south of Boston with his wife. His legendary collection of fire photos that cover almost four decades is unmatched in the Boston area. Nearly every photo in this book was contributed by Bill.

Nat Whittemore has been a lifelong resident of a town west of Boston. He was inducted into the Massachusetts Broadcasters Hall of Fame after 50-plus years as a videographer. Nat has been my biggest supporter in this project. He will be my close friend always.

Retired Special Agent Bill Murphy still resides south of Boston with his wife, spending time with his brood of grandchildren, writing his own book, and bartending as a hobby. We keep in touch regularly.

Retired Group Supervisor Jack Dowd also lives with his wife in an ocean town south of Boston. He is one of those dads who dutifully does special jobs for his adult kids and cares for the grandchildren.

Retired Special Agent Terrence Barry, and old friend, has lived on Cape Cod and other parts unknown, as he wishes to remain incommunicado.

Former Assistant United States Attorney Mark E. Robinson still has a full head of hair, albeit it is now silvery gray. His smile and enthusiasm continue to shine as he remains politically active in Massachusetts while also working in the private sector as an attorney for Mintz Levin. Mark works on high-priority state and international cases.

In 1991, former AUSA Ralph Gants joined the Boston law firm of Palmer & Dodge LLP, becoming a partner in 1994. He has taught at Harvard Law School, the New England School of Law, and the Northeastern University School of Law. Governor William Weld appointed him a Judge of the Massachusetts Superior Court, and Governor Deval Patrick appointed Justice Gants to the Massachusetts Supreme Judicial Court in December 2008. Governor Patrick then appointed Ralph as Chief Justice; upon confirmation, he was sworn in on July 28, 2014. As of 2019, Chief Justice Gants remained the top judge in the state.

I got to spend an additional 16 years in the Boston ATF office as a street agent. I chose not to move up into management. There were lots of good cases that I had an opportunity to work on during those years. None of those investigations matched the intensity or high profile of the Mr. Flare arson ring case. I chose an addition to my career track when I volunteered to become a Certified Fire Investigator, graduating from the ATF two-year program in 1988. Since 1980, I have been part of over 2,300 fire and explosion origin and cause scene investigations in 43 states, combining my public career and 18 years in the private sector.

After his release from Federal prison, Donald F. Stackpole died in 2012 at the age of 56. He is buried in Braintree, Massachusetts.

Robert F. Groblewski resides in Massachusetts under a changed name.

Gregg M. Bemis also resides in Massachusetts. Never once in all the contacts with Bemis from 1985 to the present has Gregg ever shown anger toward me or my associates. In writing this book, I have had recent contacts with Gregg, who has supported this project.

Ray J. Norton, Jr., resides in Massachusetts as a registered sex offender for several 2009 convictions. During the peak of our investigation of the arson ring, we often had questions about Norton's inclinations to young males. Although we found no information about his proclivities back then, he did surround himself with teen boys. It eventually was his second downfall. He is nearly 80 years old as of this writing.

I have no information about the other conspirators who were involved in this case. Intentionally, I did not seek any information about them. I figured that I would let them be.

The remainder of the arsonists have all served their sentences. They are out and about. To my knowledge, they have not committed any more arsons. *Or have they?*

ACKNOWLEDGMENTS

Thanks to ATF for providing me with a career in Federal law enforcement that I thoroughly enjoyed for 25 years and a week.

Thanks to author George Hall, may he rest in peace. I met him in or around 1993 when he came to the Boston area to research his book *Ring of Fire.* His book alone refreshed so many memories that are woven into this book.

Thanks also to retired Boston Fire Lt. Stephen McLaughlin for his insights into the BFD during the early 1980s. Thanks also to remembrances from retired BFD Lt. Rick Splaine and the remainder of the Boston Arson Squad who have always been by my side.

Boston Fire Photographer Billy Noonan was one of the prolific photo takers and collectors who arguably documented more Boston fires than any other person in history. His recounting of his contacts with the members of this arson ring supplied another significant angle to those sparks who went rogue. I am grateful to him for permission to use his photos, which add great visuals to my story.

Nat Whittemore, retired WBZ-TV cameraman, provided the most support and friendship of all. I will be forever indebted to him. He became my "business manager/adviser." Besides his recollections, Nat made available numerous people who have all contributed in some way to this project. He provided a path toward the successful completion of this book.

John "Jack" Dowd, as the first Boston Arson Task Force Group Supervisor, provided me with guidance and support on the job and valuable insights that are laced throughout this book.

Phil Tortorella helped me to initiate the writing of this book. A meeting at his house inspired me to start typing. His perception of this case from a Group Supervisor's perspective provided me with a different viewpoint that I, as a street Agent, was never aware of.

Bill Murphy, my longtime friend, and colleague, also motivated me to write the story of this arson investigation. His intelligence and enthusiasm inspired me to write every day for over a year while I was still working full-time.

Attorney Mark Robinson and Chief Justice Ralph Gants each provided me their invaluable time, remembrances, and wisdom. It was great fun to discuss and rehash parts of this case with them 30-plus years after the fact.

Early in 2018, Alex Kingsbury, formerly of the *Boston Globe*, now with the *New York Times*, started to explore writing an article on this case for the *Boston Globe Magazine*. It was his interest that pushed my long desire to write this book into action.

Former Boston Sparks Association President Robert Bowers provided insight into the Club and its history before and after the 1983 Sparks Club fire. Dick Bangs is another past member who provided good information on the period. The BSA and its members have been one of my biggest supporters throughout this project. Thanks to you all.

I am proud to have had Retired Boston Fire Commissioner Paul Christian, artist and author, write the Foreword to this book.

Authors Raymond K. Anderson, Andrew Watts, Daniel Zimmerman, Ed Nordskog, and Mike Foley provided great advice on getting my first effort at a book published.

I also wish to thank *Boston Globe* reporter, columnist, and author *(Whitey Bulger)* Kevin Cullen; *Boston Globe* Editor Mike Bello; Former WBZ News Director and Producer Peter Brown and Audio Technical Adviser Art Donahue; and the Wright Group, Inc. staff for all their support.

I consider each and every one of the above-listed persons as lifelong friends. Any and all information that was provided by all of these individuals will always be greatly appreciated. The story would have been incomplete without their input.

The BookBaby editor, as well as my assigned specialist, Damon Glatz, did a fantastic job with insights I never would have expected.

Lots of love and undying thanks to my wife, Joyce, my family and my friends for constant support and encouragement to begin and complete this project.

CPSIA information can be obtained
at www.ICGtesting.com
Printed in the USA
LVHW082136101220
673885LV00010B/38